BERKSHIRE

BERKSHIRE

IAN YARROW

Illustrated and with a Map

Robert Hale & Company
London

© *Ian Yarrow 1952 and 1974*
First published in Great Britain 1952
Second Edition 1974

ISBN 0 7091 4172 6

Robert Hale & Company
63 Old Brompton Road
London SW7

(e

Printed in Great Britain by
Redwood Press Limited
Trowbridge, Wiltshire.

PREFACE TO THE SECOND EDITION

Time marches on relentlessly and Berkshire has seen many innovations during the quarter century which has elapsed since I started to write this book. Most major changes have come through extensive urbanization and new road systems, especially where concerned with the 45 miles of Motorway 4 across the County from east to west. Inevitably some sections of my book have become out of date and readers of Part V – Open Road – are cautioned to check with a decent modern map before setting forth, for some of the old roads do not cross but end abruptly against the M4. I am grateful to the publishers for being able to include the route of this motorway on the map at the beginning of this book. Some towns, most notably Bracknell, have changed out of all recognition, and even Reading itself, now with skyscraper office blocks, multi-storey car parks, flyover and underpass, one way traffic and miles of double yellow lines has lost most of its former charm though its historic kernel remains intact. Indeed few places do not show signs of what may be progress.

Not only places but also people have changed for improved road and railway services have allowed a widening of the 'commuter belt' and with it a 'best kept village' approach to rural life not always welcomed by the older inhabitants.

As the countryside diminishes it becomes as important to preserve its wild-life as it has been to preserve ancient and historic buildings when towns and villages expand and to this end in 1959 a Berkshire, Buckinghamshire and Oxfordshire Naturalists Trust was formed which by now safeguards a variety of our plants, birds, animals and insects in some eight reserves within the County. Even in a heavily wooded county such as ours, tree preservation has an important part to play if we are to carry our heritage into the future though one might wish that its more vociferous dilettante protagonists would realise that each tree, however beautiful, has a life span and should not be expected to stand at attention until the final crash. Dutch elm disease, alas, has become rife in the southern part of the County and everywhere grey squirrels have become a major source of injury to our trees, both these plagues seemingly unconquerable. Myxomatosis has replaced the rabbits of our lanes, field corners and downlands with thorn scrub and rank vegetation to the detriment of many attractive flowers we were accustomed to see. On the other side of the coin feral Canada Geese have greatly increased in numbers and with various kinds of wild duck enjoy the flooded gravel pits which urbanization has left behind. A noisy but attractive recent immigrant from the Continent is the Collared Dove whose carefree trusting nature and complete lack of road sense may yet prove its own undoing in this country.

Finally, a glance into the future – by recent Act of Parliament new county boundaries have been fixed by which Berkshire north of the Ridgeway, that is to say from Streatley to a few miles north of Lambourn, will become a part of Oxfordshire. In exchange for rolling downland with our prehistoric White Horse, Uffington Castle, Dragon Hill, Wayland Smith's Cave and a host of other places including such major towns as Wallingford, Didcot, Abingdon and Wantage, all intimately involved in the history of our County, we will receive the very different 'countryside' of Slough and neighbourhood – a pretty left-handed deal by all standards.

I. H. H. Y.

Whitchurch,
near Pangbourne.

Berkshire

1973

FOREWORD

SINCE childhood days Berkshire has been my happy hunting-ground, though little did I know then that it was to become my home. First, then, my hobbies and later both work and hobbies have taken me to the innermost recesses, to the topmost pinnacles of this county, and rarely have I found it anything but good. But like rolling stones, our English counties are fast losing their moss and, whether we like it or not, the leafy lanes are changing into broad highways and the babbling brooks are one by one disappearing down concrete drainpipes. But it is not for us to exalt the Past any more than we should decry it, for we, like the Bibroci and the Segontiaci before us, are nothing more than a stage in evolution, a phenomenon of time in a universe that is constantly changing.

Nevertheless, it is inevitable when writing about a county to stress the Past, for the Future we cannot safely predict, and the Present is too short to be more than a link between the two. So I have endeavoured to take you, page by page, through the snapshot album that is Berkshire, explaining the fading prints one by one before the yellowing of time removes all semblance of reality from them.

From the start it was obviously out of the question for me to write everything about everything, even if it were possible for any one person to accumulate such a wealth of facts and figures, and I have therefore chosen to describe the odds and ends, which, though not to be found in the usual sort of guide-book, are every bit as important if one is to appreciate the County as a whole. It is my hope that reading about them will prove as pleasant a pastime as hunting them through the hills and vales, through the dust of venerable tomes and through the smoke of innumerable country pubs.

I. H. H. Y.

DEDICATED

TO THE TINKERS AND TAILORS, NO LESS THAN
THE RICH MEN AND POOR MEN OF BERKSHIRE
WHO HAVE HELPED ME, OFTEN UNWITTINGLY,
TO FIND THE THINGS I WANTED TO KNOW

CONTENTS

PART V
Open Road

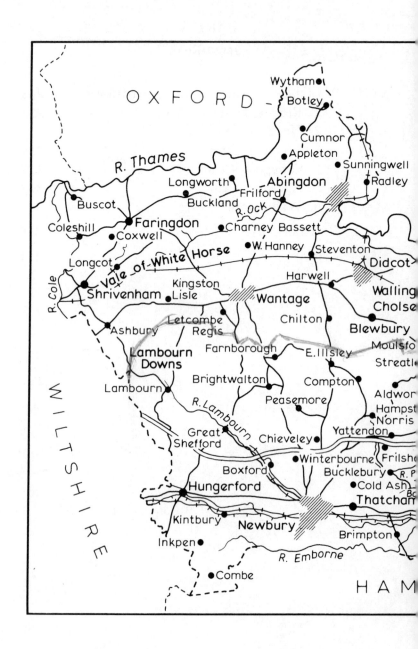

Motorway
Roads
Railways
Canal

0   Miles   10

BUCKINGHAMSHIRE

R. Thames

Cookham
Dean
Bisham
Hurley
Cookham
Maidenhead
Bray
Wargrave
Ruscombe
Twyford
White
Waltham
Windsor
ngbourne
Reading
Winkfield
ilehurst
eale
nnet
Wokingham
Bracknell
Sunninghill
Shinfield
Ascot
Burghfield
R. Loddon
Swallowfield
Finchampstead
maston
atfield
ortimer
Blackwater
Sandhurst
SURREY
R.
HIRE

ILLUSTRATIONS

xv

ACKNOWLEDGEMENT

All the above illustrations are reproduced from photographs supplied by de Normanville Studios, Berkhamsted.

PART I
Dim and Dusty Past

CHAPTER I

GEOLOGY AND SCENERY

I DO not wish to go into great scientific detail, to scare you with stratigraphy and tire you with palæontology, but simply to show, in as brief and perhaps unscientific a way as possible, what Berkshire is made of and what it looks like, and the more exacting reader who wants to know more than I propose to tell him would do well to consult the various scientific journals and textbooks, paying particular attention to Mr. N. H. Pizer's *Survey of the Soils of Berkshire.*

I think it is generally understood nowadays that it is what is beneath the soil—the rocks, the clays, the sands and pebbles —that have made our scenery what it is, so that one may guess, with some accuracy, the type of landscape from a knowledge of the geology, and *vice versa.* For instance, rolling downland, bare except for clumps of elms, indicates chalk with pockets of clay, for though the elm is not a deep-rooted tree, it does not grow on the chalk itself. Again, heather, bracken and pine trees suggest the sands and gravels of Bagshot beds, while the oaks, deep-rooted trees, tell of clay seams running through them.

The County may be considered as consisting of three ridges running from west to east (or east to west if you like), but the dip (a geological term indicating the slope of the beds, irrespective of the contours of the land they form) being north-west to south-east (not south-east to north-west, however). These ridges are separated by two great flats or valleys, through which rivers run—mere trickles compared with their former size, as shown by the gravel deposits within their valleys. The northernmost ridge can be called the Faringdon ridge, and it runs along the upper reaches of the Thames, between Lechlade, which is just outside the County, and Oxford, which is also just outside the County. These hills are not particularly high, rising above 500 feet only at Boar's Hill, below Oxford, and at Badbury Hill (530 feet), near Faringdon. Below this lies the great lowland valley of the

White Horse, stretching right across the County from west to east and drained by the river Ock and its tributaries, running into the Thames below Abingdon. Clays are predominant in the valley, forming good arable farming land, where wheat and roots are grown extensively, while on the valley gravels and heavier gault soils barley is grown. Cherry and apple orchards there are in plenty on the greensand strip which runs below the Downs across the County from Oxfordshire to the Wiltshire border. The whole vale has the appearance of typical English farming land, the corallian Faringdon ridge, full of ammonites and corals and with road-stone quarries, enclosing it to the north, the mighty chalk hills of the Berkshire Downs coming from the Chiltern country, and passing into Wiltshire, bounding it to the south.

We now come to the Downs, those great rolling hills that are perhaps more typical of Berkshire than any other geological formation. They have not the white cliffs and blue sea of the South Downs, no sickening sudden drop to rocks below, nor salty wind, yet they are every bit as pleasant to walk, just as lovely to watch, rolling away into the distance with the Ridgeway like a backbone passing from ancient camp to ancient camp, the barrows, the clumps of elms sheltering lonely farmsteads.

H. J. Massingham, writing in the way that he alone can, says of our Berkshire Downs : "Continuity of line and surface is thus the signature of these Downs, the long level line which seems to me the quintessence of downland, and by its suggestion of infinity, the most austerely beautiful of all its forms. Even a dramatic hill like Uffington, well over 800 feet and distinguished by its fluted buttresses and giddy combes hollowed out with masterful audacity, does not disturb the equanimity of that perfect line." How perfectly these words describe our Downs; his *English Downland* is a joy to read and should certainly not be missed by those who love this type of scenery. Chalk, in places more than 700 feet thick, is composed of the fossil bodies of tiny creatures which once lived in a sea covering much of England and Europe. Dudley Stamp in his *Britain's Structure and Scenery* gives maps showing just how much of England was under water when the chalk was being formed, and mentions the theory held by many geologists that not all the chalk was formed from shells of foraminifera, but may have been precipitated by chemical action. But however it may have been formed, chalk, where it is not covered by more recent deposits, produces the same sort of scenery everywhere.

This great belt of chalk which runs across Berkshire is cut by the Thames from the Chilterns at Goring Gap, and long years ago stood up out of the swampy forest land which lay on either side, where ferocious animals, mercifully no longer living in this world of ours, made life too dangerous for the ancient men, forcing them to live and travel on the safer ridges. Chalk, upper, middle and lower, and clay-with-flints comprise the greatest part of the Downs and the slopes below them. These slopes have long been under cultivation, growing oats, barley and roots, and with the drive for an increased acreage under the plough during the recent war much land that had not been broken within living memory was persuaded into useful production.

In days gone by it would have been impossible to view the Downs and not see sheep. Many a Berkshire man sent himself to sleep counting "ship" pass through some well-known "ge-ut"; it required no great imagination, yet to-day there must be children born in this part to whom a sheep is about as strange as a kangaroo! Then, many a Berkshire shepherd counted sheep by day and night, helped his ewes at lambing, dug them out of winter drifts and took them, proud and happy, to the great sheep fairs at Ilsley. But this has all gone, the men, the sheep and the fairs. Agriculture, here at any rate, no longer wants sheep to tread the dung, and the fleecy by-product is no longer Berkshire's most important industry. With the passing of sheep we must not forget that at one time our Berkshire Downs supplied nearly the whole of England with wool for cloth-making, and many men made fortunes from their flocks and fulling mills.

Perhaps the chief scenic feature of downland is the gently rolling, wave-like movement of hill and vale, the "peace which passeth all understanding" of a summer day, the haze, the butterflies, the distance of vision, the proximity of the

2

blue sky. Even to-day, with all our modern helps to comfort, few people live in the downland villages, and the villages themselves are few and far between. At the Streatley end we find Aldworth, where the De la Beche family built a castle at the time of William the Conqueror; the castle is gone, but this family has remained unforgotten in Aldworth on account of their tombs, which suggest that, far from being stunted like the downland trees, the men of this family were giants, the tallest of whom was Sir Philip, 7 feet from head to toe. Aldworth, once a centre of sheep farming, is now a quiet and rather straggling little place, the old church and its ancient and famous yew carrying one back to long ago when the music of sheep bells would have wafted down the wind. The Comptons and the Ilsleys, once the very heart of the sheep trade, rarely see a flock now, unless it be from the Agricultural Research Council's experimental farm.

Lambourn, standing near the upper end of the valley, takes its name from the Lambourn stream beloved of fly-fishermen which flows to join the Kennet outside Newbury. The downland from Lambourn to Streatley is extensively used for training racehorses, and many a pound has been won by our Berkshire-trained horses, and many a plot has been hatched in the stables and pubs where at times the uncertainty of winning has been enhanced and at others certain money has failed to materialise. A string of racehorses, silhouetted against an early morning sky, a plethora of racing newspapers and racing talk, a population of little men whose match-thin legs are fitted into jodhpurs so tight that surely they can never come off—this is the Downland village of to-day. The Downs can offer many a pleasant walk, though some of them are longer than modern legs require, and in these days when time, like everything else, is worth its weight in dollars, these downland tracks are apt to be left unwalked. But the return of motoring has made it possible to tour the downland area, for, though there are not many roads, those which there are run through some lovely country.

Our next division, the Kennet valley, lies directly below the Downs and runs to the Hampshire border, embracing at the extreme south-west corner some of Hampshire's chalk; contrasting with the vale of the White Horse, the gravels and sandy formations of the Kennet valley are responsible for the heather- and bracken-covered commons and the mighty stands of pine. Drift gravel overlies lower Bagshot sands, with the inevitable result that there is no underground supply of water; soils dry out at a surprising rate and are extremely acid, and unless doctored with nearly all the patent medicines of our modern agriculture they defy cultivation; bracken, that persistent and dominating landlord, smothers large areas, defiant and proud, standing 6 feet high or more where clay seams hold some moisture, stunted and cringing where the peaty soil is dry as tinder. Beautiful though they are, these heatherland places are almost useless to us, for the cost of their conversion to anything like agricultural land is stupendous, and even then returns are doubtful. It has been done, I know, but the water table must be the deciding factor, for surplus water can be taken away, while nothing short of miracles can hold water where the sands and gravels lie deep above the clay. During the early years of the war a part of Burnt Common beside the "Welshman's Road," near Padworth, was transformed into something a great deal more useful than bracken and heather, but those who know the place will remember the way water stood forming lakes several inches deep, wherein winter snipe paddled among the grass tufts, and where in spring wild duck nested on the grassy islands. Considerable areas are given over to softwood production, and much is ruined every year by fire, for this whole land is hot in summer, just waiting for the careless match, the piece of glass or, even worse, the senseless deliberate firing by children from a certain village just over the Hampshire border. Berkshire does not own these people, better known for evil than for good. I was recently told how boys used to push a phosphorus match into one end of a bootlace and light the other end, the considerable time elapsing before the match set off the heather allowing the boys to be well away from the scene of the fire. Another tale tells how, on the day when all the keepers from a neighbouring park were attending the funeral of the head keeper's wife, a force set out from this village to raid the coverts. But they are bad poachers, entirely unversed in the niceties of this "art," relying on their numbers rather than their skill and using the threat of fire as an everlasting black-mail. But they don't belong to us, and no pure-bred gipsy would have them near his caravan, for honour among thieves means nothing here; and yet among them you can find people as kind and charming as you could wish. It takes all kinds to make a world.

By no means all the Kennet valley is useless heatherland, for along the riverside there are pleasant water-meadows, soft and lush in summer and often flooded badly throughout the winter. One must remember that at one time the Kennet was a much wider river than it is to-day, carrying much more water; times changed and the water supply decreased, the river shrinking and running slower, depositing the alluvium we know to-day. Along with other deposits, peat was formed, at times to a depth of 14 feet, and, apart from providing a local industry, has provided us with interesting fossils of several animals now extinct, or at any rate extinct in England. Remains of beaver, marten and wolf suggest that the climate was considerably colder than it is to-day, and plant remains substantiate this, while Neolithic implements and pile dwell-ings indicate that even in those far-off days man was on the move. On the north side of the river Kennet are Reading beds resting on the underlying chalk, and composed of the clays and sands laid down in the bed of a huge river. From a farming point of view the Reading beds are not ideal, for where they are sandy they dry out terribly in a hot summer, while in a wet winter the clay soils waterlog readily and are quickly damaged by heavy stock. Rising higher, towards the base of the chalk Downs, London clay, a marine formation, gives us considerable grassland, while the lower Bagshot sands and plateau gravel produce the bracken-covered common land between Bucklebury and Hermitage.

Passing now to the east of the County, we find three quite distinct kinds of scenery; to the north, in the loop formed by the Thames between Wargrave and Maidenhead, chalk pre-dominates and is in places overlaid by Reading beds, valley gravel and in a handful of isolated spots by alluvium; lovely scenery results, not only by the riverside, but on the thickly

wooded hills, where chalk workings give away the nature of
the land to eyes which cannot read the other clues of shape
and vegetation. South of this, between Reading and Windsor
and north of the Wokingham-Ascot road, but turning down
to the Hampshire border near Swallowfield, the land is
largely London clay, covered in scattered places by plateau
gravel, and alongside the river Loddon, by valley gravel.
Farms are largely concerned with wheat, oats and potatoes,
and dairy cattle and, until the war, permanent grass figured
largely in the landscape. The ease with which the Loddon
floods each winter has long provided excellent duck shooting and bird watching for those who are thus inclined. While
writing of the Loddon one cannot omit to mention that
beautiful flower, the Loddon Lily as it is often called, which
like the Fritillary grows in certain places near this river
(places which for obvious reasons are best not mentioned by
name). Places there are where one can pay to go and see the
fritillary growing, and how much nicer it looks there than
in a gipsy's basket in some Reading street.

The third area, which encloses Wokingham, Ascot, Sandhurst, Crowthorne and Finchampstead, is typified by tracts of
infertile wasteland covered with silver birch and bracken, and
capable of growing little else. It is reputed to be the poorest
land in the whole County and has largely been given over to
building. Like the heathland of the south Kennet valley, to
which it really belongs, the ground dries out and catches fire
in summer, the evenings vibrate to the rattle of the nightjar,
and the smell of pines fills the air. It is a land for naturalists,
not for farmers, and being not worth a "tinker's cuss" is
made hideous by little tin shack holdings, which not even the
stately residential houses can atone for. About 80 per cent.
of this area of some 33,000 acres is unsuitable for agricultural purposes, being composed of Bagshot, Bracklesham
and Barton sands and gravels capped by plateau gravel.

CHAPTER II

PREHISTORIC MEN

BEFORE delving into the mysteries of the very distant past it is helpful to recall the "shape of things that were," so vastly different were they from anything we have ever seen on maps of our country. The Pleistocene Age, to which we refer, began somewhere about one million years ago, and what we call Berkshire now was somewhat different from what it is to-day. So was the whole of England, which was no more than the north-western extremity of a vast continent drained by the Rhine and its tributaries, the Thames, Ouse, Trent and Forth. The Thames ran out into the Rhine on a level with the Wash, while the Ouse and Trent joined together somewhere between the present Wash and the mouth of the Humber. All the Berkshire rivers were much larger than they are to-day, as can be seen from the valleys they have carved out, and much of the land was covered with dense forest and marsh, the only open ground being on the chalk hills and near to the rivers. Animals, terrifying because of their size and noise, roared in search of food and shelter, while smaller animals, such as mosquitoes, must have made the damp forests unbearable.

Into such a place as this our earliest Berkshire ancestors wandered, eating leaves and berries and probably sleeping hidden in the tree-tops. Their implements were so crude that many experts refuse to believe they are more than naturally shaped flints with perhaps no other significance. But later we find stone implements showing very distinct signs of deliberate construction. The very earliest of these, made by what has been termed "Driftman" (because he lived on the gravel river-banks), are the "hand-axes," which have been found in numbers in the valleys of the Thames, Kennet and Loddon. How a man could set forth to slaughter large animals with such a weapon I cannot imagine. He must have been incredibly tough, this prehistoric fellow! He made other stone implements too—scrapers for getting the fat off skins, borers,

blades, chisels for carving bone and other less easily explained
tools. Many of these have been found near Thatcham and
Greenham in the Kennet valley, and are credited to Mesolithic man. Stone implements of this period are remarkable
for a great decrease in size, a greater skill in chipping sharp
edges removing the need for weight. Some of their tiny instruments, called microliths, are so neat and precise in shape that
one is forced to recognise their makers as skilled craftsmen
with delicate touch, quite unlike the ham-fisted bludgeoning
Palæolithic fellow.

It seems certain that during the Palæolithic period the
population of what was to become England was small and
confined to the southern half, conditions farther north being
too severe. From time to time, due to the arrival and depar-
ture of the several glacial periods, conditions altered enormously, man and beast advancing and retreating accordingly.
With the end of the Ice Age, however, climatic conditions
moderated and traces of Mesolithic man have been found in
Scotland (including the earliest known canoe) and in the
northern parts of England. It is odd to think that man's first
sight of fire was undoubtedly a lightning-struck tree—how
many of us to-day have seen a tree burning? Storms may well
have been fiercer then and the forests abounding in dead
trees. One can imagine this ancient man huddling in the
warmth on some dirty night, like a night-watchman asleep
beside his brazier. By Mesolithic times, of course, fire was
quite deliberately caused with flints and lumps of iron pyrites.
In fact, in the late Palæolithic times, when the true "Cave
Man" lived, there were fires in the home, produced in the
same manner. By the way, Cave Men, or, as archæologists
call them, Aurignacian, Solutrean and Magdalenian men,
really did live in caves when they could find them. They were
in no way connected with the film industry and they would not
have subscribed to the modern use of their name; some of
them had the artistic temperament, without a doubt, for their
wall-drawings of animals are really beautiful.

It was during the Mesolithic times that England became
an island. In the first place, the sea inundated the low-lying
land between England and France, leaving for a long time

connecting bridges, the Dogger and Dover-Calais bridge.
The Dogger went under first, and later, with the submersion
of the remaining link, England was an island. This was about
6,000 B.C., and we have remained an island ever since. We
may have remained an island, but we have to thank other
lands for much that has subsequently happened within our
island since that time. Domestication of animals, cultivation
of plants, the making of pottery and a variety of other things
we cannot claim, much as we might like to, for while men in
England were attacking wild animals with stone implements,
in Egypt men were planting and harvesting wheat and rearing
cattle. But this is no discredit to our land, for we did not get
to know these things for thousands of years, and when we did
we took full advantage of them.

We can picture Berkshire in the Mesolithic Age as consisting largely of forest and marsh, the chalk downs bare except
for clumps of trees growing on clay pockets, heathland with
gorse and heather covering the gravel soil much as it does
to-day. Large shallow lakes partly filled the Kennet valley,
and the origin of these lakes is usually ascribed to beavers
damming the stream; their bones have been found in the peat
beds laid down in these lakes and in the shell malm beneath
the peat. Beaver skulls and bones have been found at several
places along the Kennet valley in the peat beds, and a long
narrow bank at Marsh Benham, west of Newbury, is thought
to have been a beaver dam. Another dam running beneath
Newbury and another at Crookham are inferred from deposits
of shell malm supposed to have been deposited on such
obstructions by the river in flood.

The Neolithic Age, which lasted perhaps from 5,000 to
1,750 B.C., is the earliest of the prehistoric periods, relics of
which we can see without digging, for it was in the latter part
that such monuments as Stonehenge and Avebury were
erected. But we are running a little too fast. We must not
overlook certain developments which took place in the first
half of the Neolithic Age. Agriculture became really important. Cows, sheep, pigs, goats and possibly horses were
the farmer's animals, and he had dogs to control them and
to drive them straight into yards fortified with stockades

against wolves. Wheat was grown and ground into flour, pastureland was "ploughed up" by hand, using a stone hoe. Village life began, usually on hill-tops, and the houses stood in streets. Earthenware vessels of two distinct types were manufactured, and trading in goods of one kind and another required a system of roadways, leading from village to village. Thus the ancient roads were begun, perhaps some 3,000 years B.C. Berkshire was crossed by one of these, the Ridgeway, of which I have more to say later, while another road, running along the South Downs and on to Devon, passed our southern border near Inkpen.

It is evident that the country was developing swiftly, for houses, roads, streets, pots (there were no pans yet, of course), farms, farmers and domestic animals savour very much of the kind of life we know. Flint arrowheads and axes have been picked up along the Thames, Kennet, Pang, Loddon and Lambourn. A Neolithic village has been discovered at Abingdon, where in 1905 the excavating workmen turned up the skeleton of a girl, and pots, hearths, scrapers, borers, axeheads, arrowheads, flint knives, antler combs and a bone pin have been found in this village.

Archæologists are certain that these changes which took place in Neolithic times were not developments of something already here, but were due to an infiltration of people from north-west Europe; they themselves had benefited by a similar infiltration from Persia, Egypt and Mesopotamia, and they brought with them ideas entirely foreign to our land. The time had come to build the huge stone circles such as Avebury, Stonehenge, Woodhenge and, nearer home, Rollright. Berkshire has no such Megalithic monument, probably because at this time Berkshire was merely land supporting the Ridgeway—a portion of the railway line between two stations, as it were. But we have a specimen or two of the long barrow, the mausoleum of the Neolithic Age. (The Neoliths, if one may thus term them, had long heads and buried their important people in long barrows; the Bronze Age people had broad round heads and buried in round barrows.) Our most famous long barrow is Wayland's Smithy, on the Downs near the White Horse, and the legends attached to it I will describe elsewhere; for the moment it is sufficient to consider it only as a tomb.

Wayland's Smithy was investigated scientifically for the first time in 1919, when remains of eight skeletons were found in the chambers and a ninth was found just outside. Two iron currency bars of early Iron Age were found close to the stone upon which legend says money should be placed. There are three burial chambers arranged in the form of a cross, the entrance passage forming the long arm. There is another long barrow near Inkpen, in the south of the County, not far from the ancient road from Sussex to Devon. It has not been scientifically examined, and on it stands the famous Combe gibbet. A third long barrow has been discovered quite recently (1935) among the Lambourn Seven barrows, while two or three other supposed long barrows have been discarded. Axeheads of this period have been found close to the Thames below Oxford, from Hungerford and Denford, Newbury, Inkpen, Lambourn, Easton, Bagnor, Boxford, Eling, Thatcham, Burghfield, Bradfield, Pangbourne, Purley, Reading, Ruscombe, Twyford, Wokingham, Waltham St. Lawrence, Sunninghill, Sonning, Woodley, Bisham, Maidenhead, Bray and New Windsor; not all these are of flint, but all are polished or at least prepared for polishing. Dolerite, quartzite, shale, greensand and basalt were in use for the making of axeheads, but flint was still the material most commonly used.

The making and using of stone implements continued well into the Bronze Age—one can imagine some old fellow saying: "I don't 'old with these 'ere metal tools; give I stone."

The so-called "Beaker" people, who came to this country from the continent, got their name from hand-made (as opposed to wheel-turned) drinking vessels, which were placed alongside the dead in their round barrows. Only a very few beakers have been found in Berkshire, at Abingdon, Cholsey, Lambourn Downs, Padworth and Theale. Perforated stone hammers have been found at North Hinksey, Aston Tirrold, Peasemore, Cold Ash, Stancombe Down, Newbury, Cookham, Remenham, New Windsor and Sunninghill; these hammers are said to be miniature battle-axes and indicate a linkage with the Nordic Battle-axe people, who invaded and occupied England at the close of the Neolithic period. Bronze objects, such as daggers, axeheads, cups and spearheads, have been turned up in many parts of Berkshire and may be seen in the museums of Reading and Newbury. The places from which they have been found suggest that the distribution of population during, at any rate, the earlier Bronze Age was similar to that in Neolithic times. In later Bronze times things altered, for, judging by the numbers and places of finds relating to this period, there must have been a great influx of people to the open downland, a decrease or movement away from the vale of the White Horse, and an increase in the Thames and Kennet valleys. Socketed axeheads, leaf-shaped swords and riveted spearheads are typical of the late Bronze Age. Two bronze shields were brought up from the river bottom beneath Swinford Bridge at the beginning of the nineteenth century, one of which can be seen in the Ashmolean Museum in Oxford. Another shield was found about the same time in the river near Wittenham, and swords, scabbards, daggers, razors and knives have been dredged from the Thames at various other places. From Bronze Age round-barrows flint arrowheads, daggers and cinerary urns have been unearthed as well as the bones of the occupants.

Somewhere about 500 B.C. iron found its way into Berkshire, though there is little doubt that before this date iron, bronze and flint implements were all in use together in England. The Early Iron Age, as it is called, is the last of our prehistoric periods, for it ends with the Roman conquest in A.D. 43. Once again England was well behind the times, for the news of this novel material had to travel far—from Egypt, through the Mediterranean, across the continent and finally across the Channel and North Sea. Perhaps it was fortunate that it took about 3,000 years to get here, for when it did finally arrive the Iron Age culture was in an advanced form. On the continent two distinct periods of Iron Age are recognised, but in England only the later of the two is known for certain, though pottery of the earlier period has been found here and there. So far the earliest known Iron Age settlement in Berkshire is at Hinksey Hill, where some of the pottery found is of the Hallstatt type (the earlier of the two Iron Age periods). A fine collection of Iron Age bridles, terrets and pins was unearthed beside the Icknield Way on Hagbourne Hill. From Knighton Hill, above the Icknield Way, comes some more Hallstatt pottery. Fragments of pottery have been found near Theale, Thatcham, Boxford, Reading, Cookham Dean, Abingdon, Appleford and Radley. At Wormstall House, near Kintbury, a vase full of silver coins was found by men digging a pond; it is said that the coins were shared out later at the Five Bells Inn at Wickham and that, except for a single coin which the local schoolmaster presented to Newbury Museum, all have disappeared. The existing coin was struck between 290 and 240 B.C., and bore the head of Janus. Other Iron Age coins of both silver and gold have been found at West Hagbourne, Hampstead Norris, Letcombe Regis, Arborfield, Maidenhead, Ruscombe and Waltham St. Lawrence.

We have now reached an important time, for Julius Cæsar started paying visits. Parts of England had been occupied by Gauls for a considerable time, and Berkshire, or most of Berkshire, was occupied by the Atrebates, centred upon Calleva Atrebatum (Silchester), ruling the old Segontiaci, who lived along the Thames below Goring, and the Bibroci, who may have lived either in the Kennet or White Horse valley. It was a time of strange names such as Cassivellaunus, Commius, Vercingetorix, Tasciovanus, Tincommius, Eppillus, Epaticcus, Cunobelin, Caratacus, Antedrigus Boduoc and Verica (the last was a ruler of Berkshire and a man, not a girl with a pretty name!). Remains belonging to this period have been found up the Thames valley as far as Great Faringdon, in the form of spearheads, swords and horse-bits, and all the way down to Windsor iron weapons of one kind or another have been found. The iron currency bars (what a purse one would have needed to carry around a few of the 2-feet-long bars!) of this time have been found at the long barrow known as Wayland's Smithy (*q.v.*) and some have been dredged from the mud beneath Maidenhead Bridge. Many other of the ancient roads which traverse the country

Pangbourne's smithy

were formed during this time, for the need to move about was greater than ever before; hill-top camps, too, were built during the early Iron Age, whether by defender or invader; there are quite a number of them on the Downs, and I propose to refer to them in another chapter. Likewise the great White Horse, the purpose of which is still undecided, is generally agreed to belong to the last 100 years B.C. The shape of the horse closely resembles that on uninscribed British and Gaulish coins, and it has been suggested that invading Gauls carved this gigantic creature in the chalk. Some of the stories of the White Horse and its periodic scouring I will relate in some other place. So we reach the end of the prehistoric road; to a certain extent we have been able to brush aside the dust which envelops our past. Starting with a veritable ape-man creeping up the Thames valley, it has taken about half a million years to reach the first Roman invasion. Everything we know about those years has of necessity come out of the ground or the rivers, and, except for the planned excavation of a precisely known site, has come to light entirely by chance. Thus the whole picture of prehistoric life as present-day archæologists see it depends upon the correct interpretation of chance discoveries. It is a wonderful story of detection, one which is never-ending and one which is not only nation-wide but also world-wide; and we must remember that, although it is fashionable to think of ourselves as something quite distinct from and much superior to our continental neighbours, but for the whim of nature we might yet be a mere north-west corner of that continent.

The mighty yew in Aldworth churchyard

CHAPTER III

THE RIDGEWAY AND OTHER
ANCIENT ROADS

I T is odd to think that once there were no roads; it is likewise odd to think that once there were no potatoes, no baccy, no telephones, but while we can appreciate the absence of these things, it is as easy to visualise no sea and no sky as no roads. Somebody once wrote that travel in the days of our great-great-grandfathers was more akin to prehistoric conditions than to anything we know to-day. For roads are needed only for organised journeys from place to place, not for the wanderings of Stone Age men in search of food and shelter. And prehistoric man can have had little idea of where he was going and certainly nothing but his memory to act as a map.

To my mind, the ancient travelways as we know them to-day suggest a line of least resistance rather than an urge to go from A to B. Many generations of aimless wanderers all influenced by the same conditions would unintentionally mark out a track that could readily be followed—in fact, becoming easier to use with each succeeding generation. It is only then that places on that track assume importance and give the impression of being linked together. Rabbits move from field to field just the same, for once the pioneers have made the way the rest is merely a matter of time. First for pedestrians, then for flocks and herds, there was little need for metalled surface. Harnessing of animals was something new and first occurred in the late Bronze Age, at which time wheels first came into use. By late Iron Age times chariots were in use, and remains of these have been found buried with the warriors who owned them. Before this, no doubt, wooden agricultural vehicles were in use, but, being of wood, remains of these are rare and then fragmentary.

The use of wheeled vehicles must have altered the course of many ancient walking ways, and maybe the first attempts at deliberate road-making and bridging were made at this time. Yet the traveller, with his merchandise, did not use wheeled vehicles, but loaded up one or more pack-horses; the sign of the "Pack-horse" is often an indication that some-where close is an old trackway. There is such an inn at Steventon on what is probably the site of the track running from Newbury to Abingdon via Beedon.

Now what have we got in Berkshire? First and foremost we rejoice in the possession of what has been described as the oldest existing road in the world. This may be so, and the Ridgeway's great age has been taken by many writers to show that some form of civilisation existed, radiating from Avebury in Salisbury Plain, as long ago as Neolithic times, or at any rate in the Megalithic stage of the New Stone Age. The Ridgeway, though so typical of Berkshire, is no more Berk-shire than the County's share of the railway from Paddington to Bristol. It is, indeed, simply a section of a national road stretching across England from the Wash to Wiltshire and on into Devon. But originally it must have been padded down by the feet of the local inhabitants, who had no thoughts of walking to Avebury, only of keeping up out of the marshy valleys in their search for food. For topographical reasons Avebury became the focal point of these ancient roads; Avebury was not a place at all then, and the originators of these trackways knew not where they were going. It was those who followed in their footsteps, who have left their mark in the form of settlements, barrows and the like, who made the track a highway. This great road, starting near the Wash, runs to Thetford, past the old flint-mines called Grimes Graves, past Cambridge to Hitchin, and then as the Icknield Way to the Thames at Streatley.

Most writers prefer to describe the Ridgeway going east-wards from the Wiltshire border to Streatley, but if one is going to acknowledge the "pull" of Avebury one should surely travel towards the magnetic force ahead in the setting sun; one should not put the donkey ahead of the carrot. So let us start in Streatley and follow the Ridgeway to Lidding-ton Camp, where it enters Wiltshire. From the bridge, with Goring behind across the river, we go up to the Bull Hotel, crossing the main Reading-Oxford road and straight up Streatley Hill, with an occasional halt to puff, to Hungerford

Green. Here, instead of following the metalled road round
to the village of Aldworth, we turn off right, joining a section
of the Ridgeway, running down through Upper Basildon to
Pangbourne. Our road, now rough and stony, runs straight
for the Downs, past Streatley Warren and Starveall Farm.
The Warren long ago used to provide food for the shepherds,
who took their flocks in summer to Starveall : Starveall farms
are common in sheep-down country, suggesting that in these
high-up places there was little keep for man or beast. A mile
on from Starveall we are joined by a branch of the Ridgeway
running back to Streatley by a different route. Traversing the
slope of Thurle Down, past the great mass of Ham Wood
and Unhill Wood, past Warren Farm and the golf course, it
runs out below Lough Down on to the Streatley-Blewbury
road.

At Warren Farm, an old shepherd used to see the ghost
of his wife, tripping around the garden in her nightie; subsequent search discovered a blonde-haired lady discreetly but
unorthodoxly buried close at hand. But let us go back to the
Downs. From the point at which we left the Ridgeway to
follow back to Streatley we can see the Roden Downs ahead,
Lowbury Hill, with its early Iron Age camp away out on
the right, backed by the ridge of the Fairmile. A lovely view
down Dean's Bottom and Unhill Bottom on the right, and
over to Compton on the left, and we leave the Ridgeway for
a while to visit Lowbury Camp. The camp is so obviously
Roman with its oyster shells and rectangular shape that it is
easy to forget that Bronze and Iron Age things have been
unearthed here and that the Roman oyster shells should more
properly be grouped with the bottle tops and ice-cream papers
left behind by twentieth-century invaders. Lady readers may
be interested to know that here at Lowbury the skeleton of a
woman, her skull smashed in, was found buried in the foundations of a stone wall. She and the more modern lady down
at Warren Farm are unlikely to be related, but it all goes to
show that a girl cannot be too careful up on the "Downs so
free."

From Roden Down we walk on to Blewbury Down, over
the railway at Churn station, over Compton Down, Several

Down and Abingdon Lane Down, where we meet the New-bury-Abingdon road. Over the road by Gore Hill, up over Bury Down to East Hundred Down and on to Scutchamer Knob. There are various ways of spelling this name, of which Cwichelmeshlaew, the burial-place of Cwichelm, is the most difficult to spell and pronounce. Scutchamer is believed by some to be a corruption of Scotchman's Knob, while others see in it a reference to Captain Scutchamer, a gentleman killed in the Civil Wars. The "Knob" in its grove may have been a barrow, but nothing has been found inside it that will settle the matter, though some Iron Age pottery discovered in the surrounding ditch may indicate its age. Birinus, the mis-sionary, preached from here in the seventh century, and Shire Moots sat on it. But we have stayed here long enough and there is a lot of walking to be done yet.

From Scutchamer the Ridgeway turns to run between East and West Ginge Down and on to Ridgeway Down, past the monumental cross, erected upon an ancient barrow in memory of Lord Wantage, soldier, farmer and husband of the wealthy heiress of Lockinge, and over the Newbury-Wantage road to Lattin Down. A mile or two more and we are over the Hungerford road and close to Segsbury Castle; the track goes on with some lovely views of downland architecture to left and right, past Rats Hill and Round Hill till you look down into the Devil's Punchbowl below the lordly Hackpen Hill. Away to the south on the Lambourn Downs the tinkling of the long-gone sheep bells is surely no figment of the imagination here, where larks hang in the air like humming-birds and meadow pipits rise at every step. Strings of race-horses are a part of the scenery; on Beckhampton Down and Eastmanton Down you cannot fail to see them, and ahead the grand old Ridgeway, or the "Rudge" as the local people here call it, running straight ahead for White Horse Hill. Hidden behind Sparsholt Down are the famous Seven Barrows, and running away on the right towards Blowing Stone Hill and the Icknield Way are the great spaces called Childrey Field and Sparsholt Field, both traversed by the ancient trackways Icknield and Ridgeway.

It is not a long walk down the hill to see the Blowing Stone

standing in the front garden of a cottage, once the Blowing
Stone Inn. Alas! it lost its licence long ago for being a haunt
of poachers. What a lot of lost licences there might be nowadays! The correct thing to do here is to pay and have a blow.
The chances are that you'll do nothing more than spoil your
walk up the hill again. Legend says that King Alfred used to
call up his men by blowing into one of the many holes, and the
mighty sound thus produced could be heard seven miles away!
The chaffinches made more noise in the tree above than I got
from the Blowing Stone. In reality this stone is simply a
sarsen which at one time stood on White Horse Hill, before
Squire Atkins brought it down for reasons best known to
himself.

So back up the hill if we want to approach White Horse
Hill from the "Rudge," but personally I prefer the approach
from the twisting Icknield Way, over the brook and the
sunken track which goes to Fawler and up to the Uffington
turn and then the scramble up to Uffington Castle. Once I
spent a memorable night in the Castle, standing on the ramparts to revel in the sunset, to see the White Horse turning
pink, and later in the dark perhaps I heard the movements of
ancient men preparing their spears and piles of stones against
the rampart: perhaps I heard the happy crowds of men
scouring the Horse and getting ready for the "Pastime." I
may have done, for I slept restlessly, frightened to miss the
dawn. It was cold then and a mist lay down below; larks were
singing though it was scarcely light, and away below some
dogs were barking. As the sun rose the mist broke up and I
looked out over a silvery triangle or, more accurately perhaps, a silvery sector of England lying more or less between
Kingston Lisle, Frilford, Boars Hill and Oxford on the
northern side and Farnborough, the Ilsleys, Compton and
Reading on the south. I was the centre, the circumference was
the horizon, and as the sun rose higher the angle increased,
bringing in the Cotswolds and the ridge of the Hampshire
Downs: a semicircle and on behind to make the full circle, I
turned my back upon the green, then showing up in the silver
mist, and walked back to the gateway at the western end,
looking out over Swindon and Avebury towards the Bristol

Channel. I had been the Iron Age watchman, the sentry, scanning the hills and valleys, for in the half-light an army might move up under the hillsides, ready to attack with the dawn. Sunrise in a way is more impressive than sunset, but some days there is neither and a thick blanket of cloud hangs over the Castle, obscuring everything, and must have struck a chill in the hearts of its ancient defenders.

Leaving the Castle behind us, we follow the Ridgeway beside Woolstone Hill to the little grove of Wayland Smith's cave, crossing innumerable tracks which run up from Lambourn over Knighton Down and the Celtic fields of Odstone Down. Wheeling round by the roads and bracken of Ashdown Park, at Idstone we reach a track to Alfred's Castle, a miniature Iron Age camp, where pottery from Cunobelin's time has been found. In half a mile we reach the County boundary, with the tempting Bishopstone lynchets just out of reach; there is no frontier here for you, and if the lynchets and Liddington entice you on towards Marlborough Down and Avebury I must leave you, for mine is a prescribed area and nothing but my eyes may stray across the border. Before we part, for I well know the urge to follow the Ridgeway on and on, I would ask you to remember, as you gaze at the megaliths of Wiltshire and get lost among the camps and barrows of the Plain, that you have travelled England's oldest road, the patriarch of all roads, and that the twenty-three odd miles which run along our Berkshire hills are the best you'll find throughout its length.

Naturally the Ridgeway is not the only ancient road in Berkshire. Indeed no, for there are dozens more with an equal claim to similar antiquity and also called ridgeway roads. They run along all the crests in downland, skirting the valleys, bridging the gaps. A glance at the Ordnance Survey map will show what a multitude of tracks criss-cross the Downs.

Berkshire's second most important prehistoric road is the Icknield Way, running roughly parallel to the Ridgeway but below it; it was probably in use as a track in late Neolithic times, and certainly so in the Bronze Age, following the almost unbroken line of chalk from Hunstanton in Norfolk.

Running as it does just above the level of the springs, this road would be much more pleasant to use than the higher and more exposed Ridgeway. It has been thought by some to be an alternative to the Ridgeway, for use when occasion demanded. So far as we are concerned, it came out of the Chilterns to cross the Thames at Goring.

No two authors appear to agree upon the actual route of Berkshire's Icknield Way, and, what is more, maps, which we are all inclined to take as "gospel," differ too. Some, indeed, confuse the two or show no lower road, making our mighty Ridgeway Icknield. But from Streatley the Icknield Way follows the modern road, though probably not always exactly the same line, to Lollingdon Hill, where it is joined by a branch coming up from Moulsford; on past Aston Tirrold, Blewburton Hill and Blewbury; at Upton it crosses the present hard road and the railway and proceeds on south of Harwell's cherry orchards, over the Newbury road and over the airfield, which is to be England's atom research laboratory, on south of the Hendreds, past Roundabout Hill between Ardington and Lockinge to Wantage. Here it is joined by a major branch called the Port Way, which runs back to the Thames at Wallingford, following the Reading road to Harwell, thence south of Didcot's shocking sprawl, on beneath Sinodon Hills to Brightwell and Wallingford. These two great branches, joined at Wantage, follow the modern Swindon road right through the most exciting part of the White Horse vale to the County boundary at Ashbury. Although the views are not so extensive, there are sections of the Icknield Way which rival the Ridgeway, for the full majesty of the Downs is to be seen from below rather than above.

Another fascinating old road sweeps through the centre of the County at right angles to the Ridgeway. This is Old Street, which runs between Hermitage and the Ridgeway near Scutchamer Knob. Although its rather pompous name suggests something more than a trackway, it is in places less than that, where a ferret would stand a better chance of following it than a human being. From Newbury a great long road ran out past Grimsbury Castle to Hermitage, where Old Street

breaks off westwards past Langley Wood towards Peasemore, on past Catmore, famous in history for its Eyston
family, and over Old Down between Farnborough and West
Ilsley. At Land's End it crosses the hard road and then a fan
of tracks spread out towards the Ridgeway above, making it
impossible even if desirable to pick out the original. Back at
the Old Street fork at Hermitage the track from Newbury
runs by Eling to Hampstead Norris, past Perborough Castle
to Compton and then up on to the Downs. The Ridgeway and
Fairmile are crossed near Lowbury Hill and still the track
goes on, down to the main road and over behind Blewburton
Hill to Aston Upthorpe, crossing the Icknield Way. From
here its path is lost, but no doubt it went towards the Thames
near Wallingford. It is known as Long Lane, and rightly so.

Another track from Newbury runs northwards past Bus-
sock Wood Camp in the Winterbourne valley and on to
Beedon Common, and passing east of Peasemore joins Old
Street to reach the Ridgeway.

Of the truly Roman roads one would expect better things
with Silchester so close, but the Roman occupation has left
very little behind it in our County. The guide-book to Roman
roads is *Antonine Itineraries,* which, while satisfactory in
some respects, gives many a headache at times. I have referred
to these roads radiating from Silchester elsewhere, but I must
describe them in more detail here. Starting from Silchester,
you will find the road to Staines marked on the map. From
the east gate it runs out dead straight across the railway up
to Butler's Lands Farm, where beside a pond it crosses the
Mortimer-Bramley road. For the next two miles it follows
the County boundary as a muddy lane lost beneath huge
hedges straight for the edge of Stratfield Saye Park. Since
Butler's Lands Farm its name has been the Devil's Highway,
and crossing the river Loddon at Stanford End it proceeds
straight for the river Blackwater, which it crosses close to or
at the existing ford called Little Ford, where Blackwater and
Whitewater come together. On through West Court, which is
built right upon the old road, through the heather and pine
trees behind Finchampstead Ridges, over the Sandhurst-
Wokingham road and railway, past Ravenswood golf course

and through Crowthorne; then between Cæsar's Camp and
Wickham Bushes to the edge of Bagshot Park, where the
road changes direction for the first time since it left Silchester,
turning up to Duke's Hill and Virginia Water and thence by
Egham to the Thames. Virginia Water is, of course, artificial
and was constructed round about 1752, so the Romans had
merely to ford the small stream running from west to east.

The second Roman road from Silchester in Hampshire to
Dorchester in Oxford runs straight through the middle of
Berkshire. Leaving the capital by the north gate, it runs
through Kiln Farm, crossing on the way the little stream
which runs from Baughurst through Aldermaston Soke,
traverses the Mortimer road and dives into the woodland
between Mortimer and Padworth. Somehow it goes through
the Ufton Woods, but is not recognisable again till Ufton
Green; here it shows in a field and the crop is said to fail
year after year where the road passes beneath. It crossed the
Kennet somewhere west of Theale, and, although we can only
guess it, no doubt ran straight to Pangbourne, much as the
modern one does, skirting Englefield Park, over the Pang
stream and through Tidmarsh or through the Park, through
Great Bear Wood and down through Basildon Park to the
river. From here to Streatley it must have followed the prehistoric track beside the river through Lower Basildon, where,
just below my house, a Roman villa was discovered by men
preparing the land for railway construction. From Streatley
the road runs on to Moulsford, being at one time recognisable
as it crosses the lane running down to the Beetle and Wedge,
where on hot summer nights the chink of glasses comes from
somewhere in the dark, the lights twinkle in the boats moored
along the bank, and the air is heavy with night-scented stock.
Roman travellers would have been surprised almost as much
as the modern ones who discover this heavenly place. But I
wander, though who would not here? From where we left it
crossing the lane the road runs under the manor house and
under the church and on towards Cholsey, crossing an ancient
trackway which is probably a branch of the Icknield Way and
known as the "Papist Way"; on through Hill Green Farm
and Heathcroft Farm it is thought to have gone, over, or

rather through, Mill Brook, where a ford with a hard bottom suggests the line, and, skirting little Mackney, it follows a lane into Brightwell, where it crosses the Icknield Portway. Up towards Brightwell Barrow, where for some reason or other it turns north-east past North Farm, making for the Thames well below Dorchester. Why it should not have continued straight into that town (city then, of course) I do not know, for its line would have run to the Thames at Wittenham Wood where the Thame runs in, and perhaps this was the reason. Anyways, to use the Berkshire expression, we can rest assured that the Romans knew the reason, for they did not turn aside without good cause.

We must not follow this road any farther, but it goes on to join Akeman Street, the great road from Tring or St. Albans to Cirencester.

The third great road from Silchester runs from the west gate to the unknown Spinæ and thence to Bath and Cirencester. Its course was at one time believed to run through Brimpton and Greenham to Newbury, over the Kennet and up to Wickham. So like a Roman road is this that one feels disinclined to ignore it, even though it may not have been the road we thought it to be. But as in all things scientific, a *status quo* cannot be admitted, new findings upsetting rock-firm apple-carts with a single push. Archæological theories more than most, perhaps, are liable to overthrow, since so much has to be squeezed from so little. And how much really depends upon absolute chance, how much has been lost for ever, because it was not understood at the time of finding? But back to our road. Researches by Mr. Crawford have shown the Silchester Spinæ road to run through Aldermaston Soke, through the heatherland (so often burned black by small boys and grown men who should know better, invading from over the border) and crossing into Aldermaston Park between the "Soke road" and "'coy pond"; sweeping through the Park, the road goes into Wasing Park and down to Brimpton Mill. Here it must have come against the Kennet near Thatcham, which it crossed at Quaking Bridge. Outside Thatcham the road vanishes and cannot be found again before Stockcross beyond Newbury. Somewhere between the broken ends at

Shaw Bridge, west of Thatcham and Stockcross, must have
been Spinæ. Being no more than an amateur archæologist, I
will not presume where "angels fear to tread." Suffice it to
say that though Spinæ and Speen may be the same in name,
they need not be one and the same place, though we are safe
in locating the former somewhere close in that area. From
Stockcross the road can be traced as it passes through Hunts
Green Farm and Ownham Upper and Lower Farms, after
which it runs into Sole Wood, or Sole Common as you'll find
it called on the map. The road then disappears under Wickham rectory, but can be found again a bit past the Five Bells
Inn on the cross-roads. Until now the road has run parallel to,
but to the east of, the modern road from Newbury to Wickham; but from here to Cirencester it takes practically the
same line as the modern road to Bayden, which is just over
the Wiltshire border, and it goes under the title of "Ermine
Street." The present kinks in the road at Shefford Woodlánds
and the two right-angle bends before the border were taken
straight in true Roman fashion.

We must now step back to Sole Common and pick up the
branch road which runs to Bath. It has been spotted, though
not very clearly, near Benham Burslot and at Elgar's Farm;
after which it becomes more definite, running through Radley
Farm and Stibbs Wood, through Heath Hanger Copse and
along the northern edge of Oaken Copse, past Great Hidden
Farm and down to the cross-roads. It cannot be found farther
than this, but if it continued along the same line it would reach
the Kennet below Leverton and run through Cake Wood to
reach the Wiltshire border above Froxfield.

Naturally the Romans took advantage of any roads existing at the time, thus the northern branch of the Icknield Way
was "Romanised" and became a Portway. There must have
been other Roman roads in Berkshire, but, except for supposed
traces of them here and there, they have disappeared even
more completely than those which I have just traced out.
From the amount of Roman coins found at Bray, there must
have been a numismatist living there—Antoninus Pius, Faus-
tina, Constantine, Commodus, Phillipus, Postumus, Crispus,
Vespasian, Julian, Magnentius, Gallienus, Gæta, Helena,

Constantius, Arcadius—according to Peake. 120 coins in all
and found together, not in a nice cabinet, but in a small thumb-
pot of New Forest ware. Another numismatist, or miser
perhaps, evidently lived at Compton, where some 2,000 coins
of gold, silver and copper were found in jars.

Supposed traces of Roman roads have been found near
Bray, but the suggestion that a road led from Bray to Silchester is not supported by most authorities on the subject,
who also discredit the supposedly Roman imp-stone on the
edge of Silchester Common. Roman roads, of course, were
not intended to be of service to any but the military, and to
assist the weary soldier they were given a firm stone base,
and to keep his feet dry they were built up out of marshy
places. The hard base of a road, now hidden beneath the soil,
is sometimes reflected in the sparsity of the vegetation above
it. Even in Roman days there was a system of road classifica-
tion, the red, yellow and white roads of modern maps. The
viæ militares were the most important and were equivalent to
the "autobahn" of Nazi Germany rather than our first-class
roads. *Viæ vicinales* were branch roads, *viæ agrariæ* were
country roads, and *viæ deviæ* were lanes. But I must leave
the subject here. For those who are interested in ancient roads
I advise a thorough perusal of Hippisley Cox's *Green Roads
of England*, in which they will find much about Berkshire
and on the cover of which they will find our White Horse.
For those who are really inquisitive about ancient roads no
book could be more interesting, put forward more ideas and
theories, and be more likely to drive the enthusiast into a
frenzy of alignments and leys, of mark stones and sight
notches, than Alfred Watkins's *Old Straight Track*. I can
understand a man casting all aside to follow up some of the
theories set out in this, the most intriguing book one could
choose to read.

CHAPTER IV

BARROWS AND HILL-TOP CAMPS

I N the chapter dealing with the prehistoric story of Berkshire I decided to deal separately with those phenomena of ancient life which are above ground and which can be seen without the aid of picks and shovels. Anyone who has travelled the downland roads will be familiar with the little knob or the group of knobs so characteristic of the downland horizon. Probably most people have a vague idea as to their original purpose, but the passage of time has apparently removed their rather sinister significance, for who would choose a graveyard for a picnic spot or who would sleep peacefully in the hot summer sun in the knowledge that numbers of dead bodies were beneath the sward? Many barrows, of course, have been opened by archæologists and their contents removed to museums, and in the past many others have been raided for the gold coins or jewels which may have been buried with their owners, in which case the barrow has been ruined so far as archæological observation is concerned.

Barrows are classified according to their shape and structure, neither of which is always obvious to the unskilled eye, yet where the barrow has not been seriously mutilated, with very little textbook knowledge it is possible to name its type and make a pretty good guess as to its date and likely contents. The main division is between long and round barrows. The long barrows are the older of the two and were made by the long-headed men of the Late Stone Age. They may be chambered with stones or they may be earthen, and they approximate to our modern family vaults. "Wayland's Smithy" is the most famous long barrow we have in Berkshire and it is one of the most famous in the country. Standing in a grove on the very crest of the Downs, not far from Uffington Castle and the White Horse, this barrow is of the chambered type, the stones forming the chamber being the only part remaining. A properly organised investigation of "Wayland's Smithy" was carried out in 1919 by the two archæologists Smith and Peers, who found the remains of eight skeletons in the chambers and another one outside. They also found two iron currency bars, which I have referred to in a previous chapter : neither these, nor the legends, nor, for that matter, the name by which this barrow is always known have anything to do with its original purpose. (It is referred to as *Welandes Smidthan* in a charter of A.D. 955.) There are two square-sided chambers and a central passage which ends in what may be a third chamber. The sides of the barrow are 185 feet long and were originally supported by a walling of large sarsen stones set with a pronounced ramp. The actual chambers and passage part of the barrow are relatively small, being about 20 feet long and about the same width across the two side chambers. There are, as I have said, legends attached to this barrow, and these I will keep for another chapter.

A second long barrow, but of the non-chambered type, is at Combe, near Inkpen, in the extreme south of the County. So far as I know it has never been opened up scientifically, though it has been well examined by rabbits. Its main claim to fame is that on it stands a gibbet, now fortunately without its clanking chains and swaying bodies. There is a most marvellous view from the gibbet, looking out over the Kennet valley, across the Downs to the haze beyond, a view which was probably wasted upon the poor chaps hoisted up into the ever-blowing wind. This barrow is nearly 200 feet long and about 70 feet wide, and there are ditches running along the sides which are 15 feet wide. Easily accessible from the Hungerford-Inkpen road, this barrow should be visited by all who want a good view amid the bones of long-headed ancestors and the tortured souls of those whom the gallows claimed. I spent a night there once just to see if chains creaked in the wind, but more of this anon.

A chambered long barrow was discovered in 1935 by Mr. L. V. Grinsell, writer of a book called *The Ancient Burial Mounds of England,* who was wandering among the Lambourn Seven Barrows one sunny September day. It may sound amazing that a barrow 220 feet long and 50 feet wide should have passed unnoticed until 1935. But the thing was not so obvious as it sounds, for one end of it was ploughed up, and a cart-track and a grassy bank ran across the other end. It was, in fact, pretty well hidden, and it took a "barrow detective" like Mr. Grinsell to spot it. The sarsen stones which originally formed the passage and chambers lay beneath the cart-track and had become exposed.

In addition to these three long barrows there are three possibles, but these have been demoted by most archæologists. Two of them are on Blewbury Down and one is on Abingdon Lane Down. There may be other long barrows awaiting discovery, but those that have so far eluded us will probably continue to do so. It has been pointed out that long barrows represent a mere 3 per cent. of the total number of barrows in the County, and from this it has been deduced that the long barrow part of the Neolithic Age was very short compared with the Bronze Age (when most of the round barrows were made); that long barrows being as it were "collective graves," not so many would be needed, and that with the introduction of bronze there may have been a great increase in population. It is interesting to recall that the percentage is the same in Hampshire, where there are more than thirty long barrows.

We now come to the round barrows, made by the round-headed people of the Bronze Age. In Berkshire there are nearly 200 of them, and in addition there are a large number of suspected barrow sites, indicated by circles seen only in aerial photographs. While referring to aerial photographs, I cannot omit mention of the wonderful help to archæology given by the air photographers and print interpreters, G. W. G. Allen, O. G. S. Crawford and A. Keiller, who have written several books upon the subject. It is quite extraordinary the way ancient things show up in photographs, even though entirely obscured under growing crops, how rings show up where nothing can be seen upon the surface of the Downs, how ancient trackways, buried walls and the like are discovered by a method our fathers, let alone our grandfathers, would not have believed possible. The principle, of course, is that any alteration beneath the soil affecting its depth or chemistry is likely to be transmitted to vegetation grown over it, either as a better crop or worse crop or a

One of Aldworth's giants

different coloured crop; most farmers are accustomed to seeing mineral deficiencies alter the appearance of some part of a crop, or the fungus *Marasmius oreades* make fairy rings in the fields. In either case, the effect is much better seen from above.

Round barrows are of several types—namely, bowl-barrows, bell-barrows, disc-barrows, saucer-barrows, ring-mounds, and pillow-mounds. In addition to these, certain types of bowl-barrow belong to the early Iron Age, while conical, steep-sided bowl-barrows are of Roman origin, and what are known as grave-mound clusters are of Saxon origin. Even when one can recognise the type of barrow, it is often necessary to excavate, because the contents will give additional clues to the age. I do not suggest that anyone with a passing fancy for barrows should start digging. Far from it. And anyhow, many barrows have already been opened legally or illegally, as the case may be, so nothing would come of much laborious spadework. If there are some 200 round barrows in Berkshire now, there were probably many more at one time, for ploughing, land levelling and road-making have all taken their toll. We know from Saxon charters that many barrows have disappeared, for they were often used as boundary marks and were mentioned by name in these charters. Many of the lost barrows are being rediscovered as rings in aerial photographs, and identifying them with barrows mentioned in the charters is proving no easy task.

Much folk-lore and many legends are associated with barrows, for what better place for giants and devils could be found when the wind whistles through the scrub and the cry of the thick-knees haunts the twilight air? And on a still winter night when the grass is crisp with frost and the barrow casts a shadow in the moonlight, what is more natural than fairies dancing round the hidden golden coffin? Some of these tales I will tell you later; for the moment I must tell you where to look for barrows so that you may become barrow-minded, for without this no treasure will you find, no giant will toss mighty sarsens across the valleys for your pleasure.

Bowl-barrows (inverted bowls really) are the most common of the round barrows. Originally all were surrounded by a

Yattendon

ditch, but time has often filled this in, or farmers have
ploughed right up to the slope. If you want to see bowl-
barrows you must go up to the Downs, where there are plenty
of them. The Lambourn group, known for some reason as the
Seven Barrows, or the Idstone three barrows, are good
examples of the inverted bowl. Many of these barrows are
close to the Ridgeway, and we can feel quite certain that at
this time, the early Bronze Age, this famous trackway was
constantly in use.

The site of many round barrows suggests that the middle
Bronze Age people used parts of the County not previously
suited to their needs; the reason for this put forward by
eminent archæologists is that the Bronze Age people were
sheep breeders and could make use of the heathland, whereas
the Neolithic people were cattle breeders and could not find
pasture among the heather and bracken country. For bell-
barrows you must look again at the Lambourn group and on
Blewbury Down. To change the district, there is a well-
preserved "bell" on Mortimer Common in Holden's Firs, and
at Brimpton, not far from the Pineapple Inn, there is a group
of what are probably bell-barrows known as the "Borson
Barrows."

Disc-barrows are like bell-barrows, with a tiny central
mound and a bank outside the ditch. The method of construction is quite simple and the reader can build a barrow for
himself at any time. All that is required is to mark out a
circle about 180 feet in diameter and dig a ditch 6 feet wide
and 2 feet deep around the circle. With the soil removed
build a central mound 6 feet high and about 80 feet in
diameter : this will leave a flat space between the mound and
the ditch, which is technically called the "berm," and is
intended to stop the central mound slipping into the ditch. A
bell-barrow can be converted to a disc-barrow by decreasing
the size of the central mound and using the soil thus made
available to build a low ring outside the ditch. So as not to
waste all this labour, it would be advisable to persuade
mother-in-law to visit the scene when the ditch has been dug
and the central mound only roughly constructed. After cre-
mation the cinerary urn containing her ashes should be pushed

into the centre (upside down, of course, to prevent her ghost escaping) and the mound completed; a surrounding circle of pine trees would be nice, and the quicker the brambles cover the mound the better.

As a model there is a beautiful disc-barrow among the Lambourn Seven Barrows. It is known as Number 13, and, being close to the roadside, it is easily examined. Incidentally, disc-barrows were at one time considered to be graves only of women, on account of the beads and other female bric-à-brac found during excavation. (It would be as well to remember this point, and suitable beads should be cremated along with the owner.)

Saucer-barrows are like discs, but the central mound is flattened out to cover the whole of the area inside the ditch and the central platform is thus only slightly raised above ground-level. There are two saucers in the Lambourn group, and there is another on Hodcott Down, near East Ilsley.

Ring-mounds are often of doubtful origin and many of them may never have been barrows at all, just mounds intended for temples or the like, and excavation is always necessary to determine their origin. A large example is on Wash Common; ring-mounds are being found from time to time by aerial photographs, but it is a long, slow job.

Of Roman barrows there are few examples in Berkshire; in fact, most of England's examples are in East Anglia. In these barrows the cremated remains are usually found in glass jars or urns, each placed inside a sarcophagus of stone or wood; the barrows themselves are so like the Bronze Age bowls that considerable difficulty is experienced in separating them, but generally speaking they are steeper sided, higher and often have a flattened top. There is one such barrow at Fawler, north of Kingston Lisle, which from its situation and shape is considered more likely to be Roman than Bronze Age; in addition, there are two "pillow-mounds" on White Horse Hill which on excavation produced a large number of skeletons and other objects supposed to be Roman.

In Saxon times there were two types of barrow used—a large, steep, conical barrow for chiefs and small, low mounds, usually found in cemetery-like clusters, for ordinary people.

Skeletons, not ashes, are found in Saxon barrows; in Berkshire our only definite examples are near East Ilsley, but a fine example of a chief's barrow is just outside the County in the grounds of Taplow Court; this contained a male skeleton and a wonderful assortment of ornate swords, spears and other jewelled objects. Cuckhamsley or Cwichelmeshlaew, once described as "the boast and glory of our downs," was for long thought to be the burial-place of Cwichelm, a Saxon chief, but in 1934 Mr. Harold Peake, after a thorough excavation, came to the conclusion that most probably this was not a burial-place at all and had been constructed for some purpose during the early Iron Age.

Although these round barrows were originally intended for one person, as often as not excavation reveals other bodies of quite different periods. These are referred to as secondary burials and they tend to confuse the date of the original "owner." No doubt it saved a Saxon sexton a great deal of time if instead of throwing up a brand-new barrow all he had to do was to open up an existing one.

Unlike barrows, hill-top camps were never intentionally used for burial purposes, though often enough they had to be used as such. Of all prehistoric remains, excepting the mega-lithic monuments perhaps, these camps are the most impres-sive, their mighty ramparts and ditches silhouetted against the blue of the downland sky. Their isolation, their very position, perched often at the head of some perilous slope, and the unquestionable immensity of the task of constructing them, must always make us pause and speculate what like of man designed them, what terrible slavery or co-operative effort made them. It has been stressed by archæological writers that these places must have been defensive, their construction and their usual lack of communications not fitting in with offensive tactics. Defence against what, we may ask, and defence for whom? From excavations it is certain that they assumed their mighty proportions during the first part of the early Iron Age, though there is often reason to presume that the site with its natural defensive characters was in use much earlier, probably for cattle. Bitter tribal warfare first and then collective defence against the invading warriors from

northern France, these were the causes; the mighty earthworks
the result. But when one climbs their ramparts, chasing blue
butterflies or spying on the chestnut and white wheatears, one
is inclined to forget that centuries have smoothed the harsh
outline of the ramparts and rounded off the partly filled-in
ditches. No attacking soldier saw the camp as we see it to-day.
His was indeed a different view, of deep, straight-sided
ditches, of tall walls of timber lashed to timber; and the gate,
now a mere gap where clover covers the trodden path, must
have looked to him like the mouth of hell, the funnel-like
approach to it presenting the most perilous part of the attack,
under fire as he would be from the gate ahead and the mighty
walls beside him.

One may reasonably ask why these forts were so large, why
such lengthy walls were built, so many acres of downland
enclosed. The answer is that whole communities with all their
flocks and herds rushed there in times of danger, and may
have had to live there for some considerable time. Excavations inside these forts suggest that there were long periods
when the forts were not used, when they fell into disrepair,
timbers rotting and ditches filling in, and the refuse pits closed
with chalk rubble; then one day came news of impending
danger, of invading armies on the march. For a while confusion and chaos, cows with calves at heel, flocks limping,
footsore and fly-ridden, women and children carrying pots
and pans, while their men brought up new timbers for the
ramparts or cleared the overgrown ditches. One somehow
thinks of wailing air-raid sirens, the whistles of the wardens
and clanking tin-hats, of mothers shepherding their children
to the shelters, to the "Underground," under the stairs, under
the beds, and then, later, the news that the enemy had changed
direction, had destroyed some other town. As it is in A.D., so
it was in B.C., and one can visualise the fear of the women
huddled with their children close under the ramparts or out
of range, camped in the centre of the enclosure, and the relief
with which the gates were thrown open and the herds driven
out to the downland grazing once again.

There are some twenty hill-top camps in Berkshire, the
majority of which are associated with the Downs or their

southern slopes. Some of them, such as Uffington Castle, Letcombe Castle and Walbury Camp, are most impressive to see,
while others have been so smoothed out by time as to be of
little interest to any but archæologists. Uffington Castle, as it
is called, measures some 250 yards long and is nearly 200
yards wide, and stands nearly 900 feet above sea-level. From
it there are lovely views into more than one dozen counties.
The entrance gate, at the west end, lies at the inner extremity
of the narrow passage, formed by the abrupt ending and
joining of the inner and outer ramparts on either side, forming such a difficult place to force that one cannot imagine
anyone trying to do so. The stockading, of course, has gone,
but in the rampart walls is a double row of holes in the chalk,
showing where the upright supports so long ago stood.

So easy to reach, for one can drive up almost to the western
gateway, I suggest that everyone should visit Uffington Castle.
The road passes Dragon Hill, where St. George killed one
of his many dragons, and then runs beneath the precipice into
which the White Horse is cut, the awful drop into the Manger
below, causing many a driver to wish he had never started
the journey, and when two cars meet, as they usually do
beside the bowl of the Manger, the downward journey is
made doubly unpleasant! But once at the top the clearness of
the air, the nearness of the sky must surely compensate for
any nervous moments on the way up. Even the larks—and
there are hundreds of them—do not fly high; what need when
the heavens are so close? A walk along the northern rampart,
a scramble through the ditch, and we are soon upon the most
famous and probably the oldest of all White Horses. He
takes a bit of understanding from so close, but if you can
discover his eye it is lucky to wish thereupon. My wishes do
not normally come true, but once I walked to his eye with a
very special wish to make and, to the best of my knowledge,
the proposed television station on White Horse Hill no longer
threatens the solitude of this place, more tied to heaven than
to earth.

While Uffington Castle contains some 8 acres, Segsbury
Camp or Letcombe Castle, whichever name you prefer to use,
is built on a larger scale and contains nearly 27 acres. It

stands not as high as Uffington, and to my mind is not so imposing, for it seems to give the impression of being under the surrounding hills. The bank and the ditch are not so good, but a sarsen stone, covering a flint cist which contained some human fragments, was found in the south rampart in 1871; originally the whole rampart may have been strengthened by sarsens which have long since been removed and put to other uses.

Another camp which is easy to reach is Sinodon Castle Hill. The Sinodon Hills or Wittenham Clumps are well known to all who travel between Reading and Oxford, and a camp so placed must have had ample scope to guard against attack from the river Thames. A favourite approach is from Day's Lock via Wittenham Wood. The earthworks of Castle Hill can only be described as stupendous, and well repay a visit, the three circular ramparts, separated by deep ditches, providing excellent scrambling. The camp itself was in use over a long period, and the whole district is full of prehistoric interest.

One cannot leave this part of the country without reference to Blewburton Hill, since it has figured recently in the papers and is about to be the scene of a "dig" by the Berkshire Archæological Society. Standing just outside Blewbury village at Aston Upthorpe, the fine terraces are best seen from the Hagbourne road in the evening light. These terraces have obscured such defences as the camp may have had. Early Iron Age pottery fragments have been found in the past, and very recently rabbits have thrown out some more fragments; the exact spot is being kept very quiet, as the attention of casual collectors is not wanted, and during the summer trained archæologists will live and work on the hill. It is to be hoped that something positive will emerge, for the definition of this place is still speculative, and some trace of artificial ramparts and storage or refuse pits would go a long way to settle the matter. Blewburton is a pleasant spot, but has not the views one associates with hill-top camps, being closed in by the ridge of the Downs to the south and the corallian ridge from Oxford to Faringdon on the north.

Sweeping down to the Hampshire border there is the

mighty Walbury Camp, standing almost 1,000 feet above sea-level. It towers over Combe and Inkpen and is built upon a part of the Hampshire Downs protruding into Berkshire territory. I say protruding rather than intruding, because in 1895 Berkshire slightly altered her boundary line here to take Walbury out of Hampshire when it had been found that this hill was higher than Inkpen Beacon! It is a wonderful journey from Hungerford to Walbury and on to Andover, for here the rugged grandeur of the Downs is more felt than seen. The winding road sweeps down into narrow valleys and climbs over the hills; the views are magnificent and the evening air echoes the cry of the stone curlews and the vibrations of the peewits. And suddenly one leaves this scenery and dives into a world of trees towards Linkenholt and Hurstbourne Tarrant. From the road the climb to Walbury Camp is pretty stiff, but the end certainly justifies the sweat, for standing on the rampart one sees across the forest of north Hampshire to Winchester and St. Catherine's Hill, while in the other direction the scene includes the Kennet valley and the background is the ridge of the Berkshire Downs. The camp is enclosed within a single rampart and ditch, and a walk right round is about one mile in length. A Neolithic axehead and a Bronze Age urn have been found within the camp, indicating that it was in use for some purpose before the Iron Age.

I cannot take you to more camps, for space is short and little is to be gained by listing them; a visit to the famous Maiden Castle in Dorset is perhaps worth more than making at least a dozen voyages to our lesser Berkshire ones, though I would still prefer to climb once more the great White Horse and dream again of the days which have meant so much in the building up of Berkshire.

PART II

Not so Dusty Past

CHAPTER V

A BRIEF HISTORY OF BERKSHIRE

1. ROMANS, SAXONS, DANES

IN the chapter dealing with ancient men in Berkshire I have told the story of Berkshire's beginnings, long before the countryside we know had aspired to territorial rights. Now I propose to carry on the story, which will deal largely with men and places known to us to-day.

Somewhere about 2,000 years ago our old friend Julius Cæsar came to England determined to subdue a people who had helped the Belgæ on the other side of the Channel. He crossed from Gessoriacum, which we now call Boulogne, into Kent and fought his way north as far as the river Thames. After this he retired to France, carrying with him hostages and promises of submission. The following year the Romans again invaded our island, this time crossing the Thames and defeating King Cassivellaunus, and thus bringing about a collapse of the tribes of Southern England. Of the next hundred years we know nothing, but in A.D. 43 the Romans invaded again, conquering and subduing wherever they went. This time they had come to stay, and England was under Roman rule for the next 400 years. The Berkshire tribes, Segontiaci, Bibroci, Ancalites and Atrebates, all surrendered and the Roman conquest of our country was complete. The city of Calleva grew on the site of the old stronghold of the Atrabates and became one of the major Roman garrisons in the south of England. Like the rays of the sun, roads were built from Calleva to other Roman strongholds, and, although Calleva (now called Silchester) is just over the border into Hampshire, at the time of which we are thinking it was definitely of as much importance as Reading is to-day, and must have been infinitely more intimidating. You can find most of these roads marked on the Ordnance Survey maps, running towards Hungerford and Cirencester via Spinæ, to Dorchester in Oxfordshire via Theale and Pangbourne, to Staines, where the Roman Pontes appears to have been an island in the Thames. Archæologists have long squabbled over the exact position of the Roman station of Spinæ, some placing it at Speen, just outside Newbury, while others locate it in a variety of other places.

From the *Itinerary of Antoine,* written about A.D. 320, much has been learnt about Roman Berkshire, and some place at or near Speen certainly fits in with the facts better than most other suggestions. There were, of course, roads from Silchester running through Hampshire to Winchester and Salisbury, but we are not concerned with these here, and, Silchester no longer being our capital, I must refer my readers to Reading Museum if they wish to see the collection of "finds" from this once important place. To-day our old capital is a quiet country village, with turkeys sitting on the mighty walls, history meaning nothing to them, nor to the cows which crop the grass within.

Back in Roman times the County was largely forest and swamp, and, as one might expect, the Roman pottery, tiles, coins, oyster shells and other remains of this period have been found near to the great roads; Roman remains have been found in plenty and many of them may be seen in the museums. Villages have been located at Ashbury, Long Wittenham, Lowbury, Beedon Hill, Oareborough Hill, Wickham (north-west of Newbury), Speen, Thatcham, Wickham Bushes, and at Rapley's Farm, near Bagshot Park. Isolated villas have been found in a number of places in the north and west of the County, and coins likewise. If these are all marked on a map in the way that Peake has done in his *Archæology of Berkshire,* it will be seen that the County as we know it today was already taking shape. Some curious objects have been recovered from the bottom of a Roman well at Thatcham Newtown, including old shoes, a coin of Constans (about A.D. 340) and some pewter plates, a flagon and a bowl, all of which seem to have been padlocked into a wooden box and hidden down the well.

About A.D. 410 the Romans departed, called urgently to defend their fatherland, leaving Britain to look after herself. With the Romans gone, Saxons invaded, and somewhere in the middle of the fifth century they had penetrated up the Thames into Berkshire, raping and pillaging everywhere they went. Cerdic became their King, and his land was called Wessex, or the land of the West Saxons, and he and his son Cynric had fought their way up from the Hampshire coast. Winchester became the capital of Wessex and Calleva (Silchester) was destroyed. Just when the mighty walled town was burned down is not clear, and one fanciful story tells of Ælla, the South Saxon, tying firebrands to sparrows' tails in order to set fire to it. But destroyed it was, and weeds grew on the great roads leading to and from it.

Those armies, or hordes as they more likely were, which pushed up the Thames made settlements at Cookham, Reading, Long Wittenham, Sutton Courtenay and Wallingford; their remains and their tools and ornaments have been found in a variety of places throughout the County, especially in the gravels along the Thames and in the Lambourn valley. At Frilford, in the Ock valley, a cemetery has been found containing burials of Romano-British people, pagan Saxons and Christian Saxons. For those who are interested in the Kings of Wessex, their names and dates are as follows—A.D. 519 Cerdic, 534 Cynric, 559 Ceawlin, 592 Ceol, 597 Ceolwulf, 611 Cynegils, 614 Cynegils and Cwichelm, 643 Cenwalh, 672 Sexburga (a Queen), 672 Æscwin, 676 Centwine, 685 Cædwalla, 688 Ina, 728 Ethelred, 740 Cuthred, 754 Sigebryht, 755 Cynewulf, 784 Beorhtric, 800 Egbert.

At this time the two old enemies, Wessex and Mercia, came to terms, for the Danes were invading the south coast of England. In 871 the Danes arrived in Berkshire, attacked and overran the little town destined to become Reading, and setting up a great defensive rampart on what is now the Forbury, the old Great Western and Southern Railways' stations and yards and the ground between them. A battle took place at Englefield, the Danes being driven back to Reading. An attack on this stronghold failed, however, and our Saxon forefathers were put to flight, the Danes pursuing them over the river Loddon towards Whistley. The victorious Danes then marched on Englefield, and thence to Bradfield, Ashampstead and Aldworth, where they reached the Ridgeway. Somewhere up on the Downs the famous battle of Æscesdun was fought, the battle which has been referred to

as one of the turning-points of our national history. Asser
has recorded the story of this battle as told him by an eye-
witness, and it is quoted in Cooper King's *History of Berkshire*. It must suffice here for me to say that King Ethelred
held up the advance of his armies, while he heard Mass in
a tent, to such an extent that his brother Alfred would wait
no longer, and bloody conflict, leading to complete and utter
rout of the Danes, took place while the King was on his knees.
Alfred was a made man after this, for he led his men like a
wild boar, so that "never before or since was ever such
slaughter known."

It matters not a great deal exactly where the battle of
Æscesdun was fought, but the various places suggested are
not without interest. Outside the County, Ashdown in Sussex,
Ashdown in Essex and Ashendon in Bucks have been put
forward, but can all be excluded. Ashdown Park, in the parish
of Ashbury, had long been favoured, partly on account of its
name, partly because of a number of iron swords and battle-
axes found there, and partly because of its proximity to the
famous White Horse. All these can be discounted, for the
name Ashdown was in Saxon days applied to the whole ridge,
running from the White Horse to Aldworth; swords and
battle-axes are not definite proof of a battle, and certainly
not of any particular battle, while the White Horse was in
existence long before and was not, as local tradition indicates,
constructed to celebrate this battle. Another theory points to
King's Standing Hill, near Blewbury, for a battle-axe has
been found at Ashbrook House nearby, and axeheads have
been discovered in Grim's Ditch, near Aldworth. A third
theory, and the one with most to support it, is based upon the
possible association of a thorn tree, mentioned in Asser's
account of the battle, with the ancient Hundred Nachededorne
or "Naked Thorn" of the Domesday Book. Nachededorne
refers to Compton, where there was a Manor of Assedone,
Nachededorne Manor possibly being West Ilsley. (Ilsley,
incidentally, means "battle clearing.") King Alfred is reported
to have gone into Aston Church to give thanks after the
battle, and, according to Robert of Gloucester, Cnut built a
church at Nachededorne to commemorate the victory.

In 872 the Danes retired to London and King Alfred the Great made preparations to defeat them; in this he was unsuccessful, for in 893 Danish armies swept through Hampshire and Berkshire and once again a year later. In 900 King Alfred died, a man mighty in battle yet a lover of peace and learning. He it was who saw the advantages of written records and who organised the writing of the Saxon Chronicle, and he it was who fixed the boundaries of the County, and, it has been stated, fixed its name. The monks of Abingdon kept the records at the Abbey founded by Cissa in A.D. 675. Cissa had given his nephew Heane some land upon which to build the Abbey, and Heane himself became the first Prior; by 850 the Abbey had grown enormously and was wealthy in land and money, but in 893 it was destroyed by the Danes, who left nothing more than the walls standing; there is no evidence that the Abbey was restored before 929, when we know that a certain Cynath was Abbot there.

In the year 1006 the Danes came again, burning Reading, Wallingford and Cholsey, after which they marched to Cuckhamsley Knob. In 1014 King Cnut became King of England, and we learn that he granted a charter to the Minster at Lambourn, and he is reputed to have built a royal hall at Cherbury Camp; Cnut died in 1035 and was followed by his son, Harold Harefoot (what a lovely name!). In 1042 Edward the Confessor became King, and in 1065 he built a palace somewhere at Windsor, though the actual site is not known, and ever since that year Windsor has been the seat of kings.

During the years of war between Saxon and Dane Berkshire had grown apace, and innumerable villages are referred to in the Saxon Chronicles. Many of these references show that land must have been cleared of scrub and that planned agriculture had finally taken a place in life. Flax was grown for making clothes, and woad and madder grown for colouring them; wheat, oats, barley, peas and beans were grown, and cabbages, turnips, lettuce, onions, leeks and garlic too. Honey, poultry and pigs could be found on all farms, and no doubt there was a black-market of some kind. From the Chronicles we know of the following villages and towns :

Abingdon, Appleford, Appleton, Ashbury, Aston Upthorne, Bagley Wood, Barkham, Basildon, Baulking, Bayworth, Benham, Bessels Leigh, Blewbury, Boxford, Bradfield, Brightwalton, Brightwell, Brimpton, Buckland, Burghfield, Catmore, Chaddleworth, Charlton, Chieveley, Childrey, Chilton, Cholesy, Compton Beauchamp, Cookham, Cuckhamsley, Cumnor, Curridge, Denchworth, Drayton, East Hanney, East Hendred, Easthampstead, Faringdon, Farnborough, Frilford, Fyfield, Garford, Goosey, Ginge, Hagbourne, Hardwell, Harwell, Milton, Hawkridge, Hinksey, Kennington, Kingston Bagpuize, Kingston Lisle, Kintbury, Lambourn, Leckhampstead, Leverton, Littlewick, Lockinge, Longworth, Lyford, Oare, Padworth, Pangbourne, Peasemore, Pusey, Reading, Seacourt, Shellingford, Shrivenham, Sotwell, Sparsholt, Stanmore, Streatley, Sutton Courtenay, Swinley, Thatcham, Uffington, Wallingford, Wantage, Wargrave, Welford, West Hanney, West Ilsley, White Waltham, Whistley, Windsor (old), Winkfield, Wittenham and Wytham.

2. WILLIAM THE CONQUEROR, 1066

We have now reached the stage when so many history books begin a succession of royal births and deaths, like one glorious front page of *The Times*; scandal and intrigue hidden in the "marriages," illegitimacy, changelings and infanticide carefully concealed in the "births," murder, torture, death in battle, death after breakfast and sometimes death in bed in a normal manner, all so decently obscured that "History" ceases to interest after the first page or two.

Very little about any particular county can be got out of an ordinary history book, but with Royal Windsor in our County it is inevitable that royal personages should figure in its past, their presence, and that of their friends and foes, contributing no small part to its story. William the Conqueror, after his successful entry into England at Hastings, found himself unable to cross the Thames near London and was forced to follow the Thames as far up-stream as Wallingford before he was able to reach the other side. At Wallingford, Wigod, the Saxon, surrendered and allowed the Norman armies to

Frilsham Church, dedicated to the Saxon princess Saint Frideswide

move over the river to attack London; William thus got his first view of Berkshire, and he found it good. Defensive castles were erected at Windsor, Reading, Wallingford and Oxford to guard against possible dangers from the Thames, while at Newbury a castle was built to look after the roads across the Kennet. At Windsor he saw the Forest, and his thoughts turned to hunting; he made strict laws in order to keep it to himself.

One is inclined to think that the Normans subdued the Saxons by sheer weight of numbers, but this is not so; in fact the Normans were so few in number that they built no villages, occupying Saxon holdings and fortifying them, and in all walks of life, except perhaps the meanest, Saxon was replaced by Norman in much the same way as we have seen a peaceful penetration in modern times. Other things being equal, it makes relatively little difference to the worker for whom he works, and the Saxon peasant probably suffered least from the Norman occupation. Noblemen who lost their estates were not so pleased, quite naturally, but were unable to do much about it.

William was a man of method without a doubt, and he set about his inventory in such a manner and with such efficiency that no hide of land, no single cow or ox or pig was not recorded. Thus began the first farm census, and I doubt if the Saxon farmers were any the less crafty than their modern counterparts! This mighty tome, or tomes to be correct, was nicknamed Domesday Book, and two volumes remain to this day to show us what our country was then like. Berkshire was divided into twenty-two hundreds, and there were some 56 churches, 65 mills, and, believe it or not, 43 fisheries. There followed a great age of church building, stone replacing the wooden Saxon walls and roofs. Most guide-books explain how to recognise Norman work in churches, and there is plenty to be found in Berkshire, including the almost entirely Norman church at Padworth, which is complete with rounded apse and stone altar. At Remenham and Finchampstead there are churches with the rounded apse almost unaltered, but in most churches the rounded end has been squared off and the typical Norman arch and building material alone point their history.

A thatcher at work in Bucklebury

Not only churches, but priories and abbeys, were built, and Reading and Abingdon Abbeys and Hursley Priory (attached to Westminster) were Benedictine; Poughley Priory, erected in 1180, belonged to Augustine monks; the knights of St. John of Jerusalem held "Commanderies" at Brimpton and Greenham. Reading Abbey was founded by Henry I, brother of William Rufus, and its story I propose to write about elsewhere in this book. A great deal of good was done for Berkshire by the monks, for they were industrious and interested in agriculture, rivers were dredged and widened so that boats could carry corn to the mills, and much wet and valueless land was drained and put into production.

Henry I was educated by the monks at Abingdon Abbey, and quite a good job they made of him, for his reign was largely one of peace and advance, during which he reintroduced some of the old Saxon laws. Peace there was for some thirty-five years, but Henry's death set things off again, and once more Berkshire became the scene of intrigue and fighting. Two new castles were built, one over at Faringdon and one at Brightwell. Robert, Earl of Gloucester, built the former in 1142 to command the junction of five important roads and to cover the Thames crossing at Radcot Bridge. In Stephen's reign a four-day siege won this castle and it was completely destroyed, leaving nothing for us to see to-day. Brightwell's castle, in the shadow of the Sinodun Hills, was built by Stephen, its purpose to keep an ever-open eye on Wallingford Castle, where Maud Matilda's supporters were. There is a nice story of Maud Matilda, clad wholly in white, escaping from Oxford Castle, crossing the frozen river and waltzing through the snow to Abingdon via North Hinksey and Cumner and thence to Wallingford Castle by horse, kindly provided by the abbot of Abingdon! That lady was tough, for it is a goodish walk without the snow and flowing white raiment.

Stephen attacked and almost destroyed Newbury Castle and then went back to Wallingford, determined to subdue this hotbed of rivalry. In this he was only partly successful, coming to terms by which it was agreed he should be King until his death, with Maud Matilda's son Henry to follow on.

We know relatively little about Berkshire in the reign of

Henry II, though we do know that it was a time of law-making, of schemes for better justice and government, of attempts to reduce "power of Church and barons," and to this end we know that the great castles of Reading, Brightwell and Faringdon were destroyed. There seems little doubt that the peasant people of Berkshire had a spell of peace in which to make good the damage done by Stephen's battles over their countryside. Towns grew in size, for there was not the constant worry of siege, and farming once again claimed the land; a more just form of government, with a reduction in the power of the barons must indeed have made life more agreeable. And then came Heraclius, Patriarch of Jerusalem, speaking in the great hall of Reading Abbey, where he outlined the case for Christianity so well and the need to defend it against the Turks with such exactness that King Henry started weeping, big tears rolling down his cheek when Heraclius gave him keys to Christ's Sepulchre and to Jerusalem. But it was of no avail, for Henry, weighing in his mind the pros and cons, decided that, whatever his desires might be regarding the defence of the Holy Land, he was King of England, and in England he must stay.

Henry died while organising the Crusade, in which he himself would not have taken part, leaving Richard, his son and heir, the opportunity to go where his father had refused. So Richard Cœur de Lion became King of England and went away to amuse himself fighting almost overnight. The troubles which then arose between various bishops and the plotting which went on are well known; Richard's young brother, John, was for ever scheming his elder's downfall and seems to have done a good deal in Berkshire, working mainly from Windsor Castle. We hear of him calling a meeting in Reading in 1191 and acquiring land near Shrivenham, where it is thought he spent a considerable time. Of Richard there is little more to say. He reigned for ten years and spent about ten months of them in England. A great fighter, a suitable hero for maidens to dream about and a good example for the cause of Christianity, but as a ruling king a wash-out.

John's only claim to fame is that in 1215 he signed the famous Magna Carta at Runnymede, where the "Bells of

Ouzeley" now keep watch across that lovely stretch of
Thames. One cannot pretend that John was a good king, for
he had many of his brother's faults without any of his virtues;
he was like a shuttlecock, tossed about between bishops and
barons, at times shooting off at unexpected angles, to return
just as suddenly, ricocheting off the Pope or Prince Louis of
France. He need not concern us further; John's son Henry
was nine years old when his father died, and the country was
before long in the throes of civil war. Berkshire castles were
constantly in the news and Henry and his son Edward were
at one time prisoners in Wallingford. Henry ruled for fifty-
six years, and his reign has been described as one of the
brightest periods of mediæval history; interested in architecture and building, he gave encouragement to others, and
many of our Berkshire churches and houses were constructed
at this time. The development of the lancet window is one of
its features and so is the pointed arch, which is stronger and
lighter than the typical Norman arch. You will remember
Simon de Montfort, the "Provisions of Oxford" and the first
Parliament, the appearance of country gentry, knights of the
shire and the "Provisions of Westminster." You may think
that all this had little effect upon the people of Berkshire, but
that is not so, for by 1295 Reading, Windsor and Wallingford
were sending knights of the shire to Parliament and were
paying for the pleasure. Sir Thomas Hungerford was the
first Chairman, or Speaker as we should call him to-day.

At this time—and we have by now entered the prosperous
days of Edward Longshanks—a great thing happened for
Berkshire, for the Flemish cloth-makers agreed to buy their
wool from England. One can imagine the prices of ewes and
rams soaring up with the suddenly increased demand, and
one can almost hear the sheep-bells tinkling across the Downs
and the clamour of the great sheep fairs. Perhaps it was too
good to last, yet no one could guess that away in the east
something was happening that would sweep away prosperity
and turn a happy land into a filthy, stinking charnel-house.
Black Death. Creeping steadily along all the trade routes,
through Asia and Europe, the little flea—*Xenopsylla cheopsis*
we now call it—was spreading the plague. In China, it is said,

some thirteen million people died and twenty-four millions in other oriental places. We cannot assess the damage done throughout the world, the civilisations set rocking if not completely ruined; via the Black Sea and Constantinople, Italy, France and Germany the little flea came, bringing with it the plague germs, distributing them like largess. Rats abounded and rats were the reservoirs of plague bacilli—rats and fleas, what a charming combination! But there was nothing charming about it, and unfortunate people who had never learned to wash, nor to clean their houses, went down like ninepins.

Reaching England by Weymouth in 1348, it swept along like a heath-fire, until five million people, nearly half the population of England, had been destroyed. In Berkshire whole villages were decimated and starving herds and flocks wandered about the untilled land. For three years history stood still, while in the towns and villages a poverty descended such as had never been experienced before. At Thatcham all the free tenants and peasants died, and nobody was spared in Padworth; in Crookham the same tale. In fact, one could say the same for much of the County, but compared with the cities and large towns the countryside got off lightly.

An interesting development in medical practice occurred as a result of the Black Death, for in Italy a system of quarantine was evolved. "Quarantina," of course, means nothing more than forty in Italian, and for forty days ships suspected of carrying the plague had to lie in special docks away from everything else; but, apart from this, medical practice as we understand it was almost non-existent, and unfortunate sufferers were simply carted to the outskirts of the town and jettisoned, where they may or may not have received attention from the nuns, who cared for lepers disposed of in a like manner. And so the great wave of trade which brought such prosperity carried with it its own death, and, like much of England, Berkshire suffered badly. In stricken districts trade and industry almost vanished; food increased enormously in price and decreased in quantity and quality; large landowners could get no one to work in fields, and the few available men demanded higher wages. We have seen the same thing happen again and again, as though prosperity must inevitably crash from some cause which was unforeseen.

With the wretched Richard II on the throne, England was thrown into a wave of battles, one of which took place at Radcot Bridge, north of Faringdon. The Earl of Oxford, with some 5,000 men, was on his way to assist Richard when he was attacked by John of Gaunt's son, and it is said that the Earl escaped only by putting his horse at the guard rail of the bridge and jumping down into the river—an achievement which few of our hunting men would undertake to-day! Henry of Derby, winner of the Radcot Bridge episode, fought out another skirmish, this time on Maidenhead Bridge, though the bridge was successfully held by Richard's supporters.

Henry became King Henry IV (or Henry Lancaster) in 1399, having seized and murdered his cousin Richard, and Berkshire settled down to a period of peace and trade, which lasted through the reigns of Henry V and VI. The devastation caused by the Black Death was largely made good and sheep were once more to be seen and heard on the Downs. A bridge was built over the Thames at Abingdon to assist trade between Reading and the west, and it was built by co-operative effort. Sir Peter Besils of Besilsleigh presented the stone required and other local Berkshire people paid for the labour. Strange to relate, the monks of Abingdon gave no assistance; in fact, they hindered the good work and even demanded money (£115) in payment for the land upon which the bridge stood. Portraits of the bridge-building benefactors hang to this day in Christ's Hospital almshouses in Abingdon. Much of the forest which covered Berkshire was cleared and land which formerly had been waste was brought under cultivation. New roads were built, more bridges spanned the riverways, serfs and villains were winning their freedom, and craftsmen were assuming an importance new to them. In Parliament the power of the House of Commons was increasing, due very largely to the increasing power of the middle classes. And while nobles and kings murdered each other, the people of Berkshire went on developing their land, relatively unaffected by such goings on.

Windsor saw more of the unrest among the upper circles than most of Berkshire, for Edward Mortimer, hereditary heir to the throne on the death of Richard II, was a prisoner in the Castle until 1413; James I of Scotland was imprisoned there for nearly ten years, when he wrote his book, *The King's Quhair*; Henry VI was born there in 1421 and was reburied there in 1484, having been buried originally elsewhere. Edward IV, the undoubted murderer of Henry VI, was also reburied there, having been moved from his original resting-place at Westminster. Reading had a small share, for several Parliaments were held there by Henry VI, and he is supposed to have announced his intended marriage with Elizabeth Woodville there.

Wallingford was the scene of a nasty piece of injustice, for here the widow of Henry VI was imprisoned after her husband and her son had both been murdered. Richard (III) Crouchback is not known in Berkshire so much for his atrocious murder of the two young princes in the Tower as for his connection with Stanford in the Vale and Fyfield, for by his marriage to Anne Neville, daughter of Warwick the Kingmaker, he obtained the manor at Stanford; when his son died he pronounced John de la Pole of Fyfield Manor to be his heir. De la Pole was killed in an attempt to seize the crown when Richard had fallen in battle. Later, Perkin Warbeck's widow lived at Fyfield and was buried in the church there; she was Lady Catherine Gordon, the White Rose of Scotland, and Warbeck was her fourth husband. (This husband, you will remember, was executed for pretending to be one of the two young princes supposed to have been murdered in the Tower.) Warwick the Kingmaker was buried at Bisham in 1471 after two days of lying in state in St. Paul's. Sir William Norris, of Yattendon, and Sir Thomas de la Mare, of Aldermaston, both raised forces to support an insurrection to depose Richard III, and at Newbury in 1483 they and others like them met to proclaim Henry Tudor, Earl of Richmond, King of England.

When Henry VII came to the throne he found, much to his relief, that many of the powerful barons had been killed off during the Wars of the Roses, and he at once set about reducing the power which those remaining still possessed; their estates were quickly confiscated if they refused to obey, their private armies were forbidden, and the Star Chamber dealt with any of them who contravened. We are not much concerned with Henry VII in Berkshire except that under him the County increased in prosperity and there was a swift development in learning. Under his son, Henry VIII, the dissolution of the monasteries was carried out and carried out thoroughly. Henry, in fact, saw to it that he became Supreme Head of the Church and the Pope was told where he got off. Land was taken away from the ecclesiastical bodies and given to Henry's ministers, to country gentry, to universities and other places of learning. In 1525 the Benedictine Priory of the Holy Trinity at Wallingford gave in and was granted with all its possessions to Wolsey. The Monastery at Poughley was dissolved by Wolsey in 1524, Hurley Priory in 1535, Bisham first in 1536 and finally in 1539, when it was given to Anne of Cleves. The convent and church of Greyfriars, Reading, was surrendered in 1539 by the last guardian, Peter Schefford. The great Abbey at Abingdon surrendered to Henry in 1539, Rowland de Penthecost, the last abbot, being allowed to finish his life, hardly at peace, one imagines, at Cumnor Hall. The manor, which had been the abbot's country estate, was given to Sir Thomas Seymour, Henry's brother-in-law. The Abbey of Reading surrendered the same year, but the abbot, Hugh Cook, of Faringdon, was not so fortunate; no country house for him, but a rope round his neck outside the abbey gate. They hanged him and quartered him and he became a martyr, and two of his monks, Rugg and Onion, went with him. Heretics were hunted out and put to death; in 1518 Christopher Shoemaker and three others were burnt at Newbury for reading the Bible, and Filener, Peerson and Testwood were burnt at Windsor in 1543. Testwood's heresy was that with a key he struck off the nose of an image in Windsor Church.

One cannot omit mention here of the vicar of Bray, for he stood in the crowd watching Testwood dying at the stake; so moved was he by the dreadful sight and so frightened for his own skin that he vowed never to take any risks by standing up for his beliefs. It was perhaps not an unnatural decision for a man to make, but it is not one which produces martyrs. As a result of this horrible sight at Windsor the vicar agreed with the Reformation while Henry and Edward ruled, turned Roman Catholic for Mary's benefit (or was it his own?) and turned Protestant under Elizabeth. The song which we all know about the illustrious vicar must have been written a great deal later, in the eighteenth century certainly, for it gives the succession of crowned heads as Charles, James, William, Anne and George.

Such was life under Henry VIII, who loved wine, women and song; not altogether the great, bovine Bacchanalian of the paintings, nor perhaps the ruthless glutton, but without a doubt a man who meant to have his way whatever the cost. But despite the religious troubles, trade was doing well, especially the wool industry. Newbury for some time had been the centre of the cloth world and as a result had grown very considerably. Every house had its loom and unemployment was unknown, employers became wealthy and even the working people lived better than before.

Two men who became wealthy through connection with the cloth trade were John Smallwood and Thomas Dolman. Smallwood was born at Winchcombe in Gloucestershire and came to Newbury to serve an apprenticeship; he married the widow of his former master and thereby inherited the most wealthy cloth business in England. Better known as Jack of Newbury, he gained the King's favour by sending men to fight at Flodden. His quota was really only four pikemen and two horsemen, but instead he arrived at the head of fifty men mounted on good horses and fifty footmen with pikes and bows. An old song tells of the "Newberrie Archers" at Flodden and no doubt ascribes to them more glory than was justified, for there is considerable doubt that they ever reached the battlefield. Henry once visited Jack of Newbury, taking his queen Catherine with him; Jack rose to the occasion and carpeted the streets with cloth from his own looms! Jack, always with an eye for business, persuaded Henry to reopen free trading with the continent instead of conferring upon

him a knighthood! His house in Northbrook Street has gone,
so, too, has the inn which replaced it and was called The Jack
of Newbury, and now the green and gold emporium of Marks
and Spencer's occupies the site. His son, John, was given the
manors of Thatcham and Bucklebury when Reading Abbey
was dissolved. Thomas Dolman came from Yorkshire and
seems to have worked with Smallwood or Winchcombe, who
left him the princely sum of £10 in his will (much more
princely then than it would be now). Dolman lived at the
manor of Shaw, and when his son inherited his wealth he
retired from the cloth trade. A saying of the day goes:
"Lord, have mercy upon us miserable sinners, Thos. Dolman
has built a new house and turned away all his spinners."

Under Henry's son, Edward, the reformation proceeded,
and under "Bloody Mary" receded once more. Newbury
again figures with a burning, this time of the Protestants
Julius Palmer, Thomas Askew and John Gwin. Palmer,
unlike our friend from Bray, having seen men burned for
their beliefs, concluded that no man would suffer such agony
for nothing and set himself the task of finding out about this
belief that gave such strength. Resigning his Fellowship at
Oxford, he came to Reading, where he became a master at
the newly founded Grammar School, but news of his heresy
reached the town and he had to fly. Apprehended, he was
sent to Newbury for trial. The story is written how Sir Richard
Bridges, of Great Shefford, offered Palmer meat, drink and
books, £10 yearly, a wife and a farm if he would change his
religious opinions and acknowledge the Pope. John Winchcombe, son of the famous Jack of Newbury, likewise pleaded
with him, while the Chancellor of Salisbury threatened him
and Clement Burdett, parson of Englefield, called him names.
But these were of no avail; he had not witnessed the death of
the Oxford bishop for nothing, and, chained to the post with
Askew and Gwin, Palmer, at the age of twenty-four, followed
them to martyrdom.

With Elizabeth at last on the throne the country settled
down to grow rich quickly and there was less time for marching armed men up and down the countryside; instead, the men
who still wanted thrills went to the great ships, sailed under

Sir Francis Drake, Sir Walter Raleigh and others, and got as much excitement out of the Spaniards as they required. This new business of robbing the Spanish Main was a profitable one and many a man returned wealthy. As we all know, Elizabethan England was the cradle of great developments in learning, in art, in the sciences and in what to-day is generally known as culture. Elizabethan architecture shows a change for the better, to more space and more windows; the need for country houses to be miniature castles was gone and men wore swords less for fighting than for show; brick houses became fashionable, and many of the country houses we now know were erected at this time, with pleasure gardens and discreet shrubberies where no doubt nightingales sang. Elizabeth, who lived a great deal at Windsor, loved visiting, and travelled through Berkshire frequently. She came to Reading in 1572, 1575, 1592, 1602 and 1603. Henry VIII had made Reading Abbey his private residence; in 1552 Edward visited Reading, and in 1554 Mary passed through. So Berkshire people were quite accustomed to the sight of royalty on the move. Elizabeth was by far the most frequent visitor, and a part of the Abbey, or palace as we should call it, was known as the Queen's House, while a special pew was built for her in St. Lawrence's Church. Incidentally, it was Elizabeth who provided the mulberry trees to encourage the silk industry in the east part of Berkshire, and probably many of the trees now to be seen in Berkshire gardens are descended from Elizabeth's gift; as an entomologist, and having once been a small boy, I delight to think of the silkworm trade there must have been in the Wokingham district and also in an offshoot west of Newbury. Silk stockings were made in Wokingham—the raiding fleets of Drake were visiting America a bit too early for nylons!

Elizabeth visited other parts of the County too, partly, it is said, because she was very mean and by living in other people's houses she and her large retinue were kept for nothing. To Bucklebury she went to call on Jack of Newbury's son, to Englefield to see Sir Francis Walsingham, to Caversham to dine with Lord Knollys, and to other houses of wealthy and influential people—possibly also to Bisham, where as a small girl and a princess she had been kept in close custody by Sir Thomas Hoby.

Windsor must have been a hotbed of Elizabethan "culture" and saw many of the great men of the day. Hudson, Davies, Frobisher, Hawkins, Drake, Raleigh and Sidney the explorers, Shakespeare, Bacon and probably Marlowe the writers, and Byrd the musician who wrote for the lute, a favourite serenading instrument, all knew Windsor. Farming saw the light of a new day, for the horses formerly used only for military purposes were now without a job and could be put to civilian uses. The great oxen used for ploughing decreased in numbers as farmers discovered that horses were a better proposition; poultry increased in popularity—ducks, geese, hens and pigeons, swans and peacocks and turkeys newly introduced from Mexico. Arable farming was much as before, but root crops were still unknown, and, although the potato was brought to Europe about this time, it remained a curiosity, a kitchen-garden wonder, for quite a considerable time. Pigs still grunted in the streets, sorting over the refuse in the central gutter.

But the peace of Elizabeth's rule faded out with her death, and, during the reigns of James and his son Charles, Berkshire became once again a battlefield and Berkshire men and women heard the tramp of marching feet, the boom of the new cannons; much of the responsibility for this rests upon Archbishop Laud, a Reading born and educated man. His new Prayer Book caused a bigger bang than the barrels of gunpowder would have made if Guy Fawkes and Robert Catesby had not been foiled beneath the Houses of Parliament. The outcome of this was severe persecution of the Catholics, and it was about this time that the Eyston family of East Hendred secreted the hunted Catholic priests in their lonely house at Catmore. The wool trade was flourishing, and men in Reading, Abingdon and Newbury were making fortunes. One of these, John Kendrick, left money to build Reading a large house for the employment of poor people in the clothing trade. But with the arrival of Charles I on the throne things took a turn for the worse. Charles continued his father's religious persecutions and, in addition, he started taxing both people and towns so that he should be powerful enough to dissolve Parliament. In 1625 we find the Law Courts removed from London to Reading, owing to the Plague; there had been several occasions during James's reign when "plague" had flared up in Reading. It was never so bad as the Black Death, but medical knowledge had advanced very little and sufferers were isolated but little else done for them; special houses or huts were built on Whitley Hill to act as isolation hospitals. Then Civil War, which was, like the Black Death, to bring Berkshire's wool trade very near crashing, for men cannot be involved in battles and carry on their work at the same time.

Charles and his dandies, or Cavaliers as they called themselves, marched upon Reading, occupied it and set all the tailors to work upon a thousand suits of clothes for his men. The town was converted into a fortress and something like 3,000 soldiers were added to Reading's 5,000 population. Brawling soldiers filled the streets, attacking, robbing and even killing anyone who was stupid enough to venture out. The wool trade was finished, ruined, for cloth could not be moved without it being stolen, and many of the working houses had been turned into sleeping quarters for soldiers. Charles meanwhile went off to Oxford to rally troops and strengthen his grip on Berkshire. For Berkshire was important from a military point of view, and Charles held Basing House, Donnington Castle, Wallingford Castle and Faringdon House; Oxford, Abingdon, Wallingford and Reading controlled the Thames; Reading's bridge across the Thames at Caversham became of paramount importance, and the Parliamentarians under the Earl of Essex, determined to separate Oxford and London, attacked Reading. Reading was to be starved out. For ten days there was skirmishing all around, while Roundhead cannons knocked down church steeples; then a mighty encounter on Caversham Bridge and the Royalist holder of the town surrendered. Marching out, the defeated army were set upon by the Roundhead forces waiting to march in; then the town was ransacked and drunken men lurched through the streets. At Newbury the King suffered a sad loss, for the Earls of Sunderland, Carnarvon and Falkland were killed, together with many other noblemen. The victorious Essex marched from Newbury through Brimpton and Aldermaston to Padworth, down to the road at Theale and so on to Reading. Reading changed hands several times as it was captured and abandoned. Abingdon likewise was constantly changing hands and was the scene of many a battle. The great strongholds of Donnington, Basing and Faringdon were stormed and captured. Oxford was besieged and later King Charles was captured and his head removed. Religious ups and downs shook the country and political differences of opinion did the same. Cromwell, the "levellers," the "diggers," Long Parliament, New Model Army, all squabbling among themselves, while Prince Charles was creeping around in France spending money with which he should have buried his father.

Confusion all around ended in the death of Cromwell and the recall of Charles from the night-life of Paris, and in 1658 the day of Restoration (May 29th) was celebrated throughout the County, some people quietly wearing oak apples, while others—for example, those in Newbury—went mad with excitement. In that town it is said that the church bells were rung for two days and great bonfires were lit upon the neighbouring countryside, while the Corporation feasted, distributing wine, ale and cakes to the soldiers, who fired off volley after volley. Three years later Reading and Newbury had cause for further rejoicing, for Charles and his Queen, brother James and his duchess and Prince Rupert travelled through Berkshire.

For a few years all went well and the County which had seen so much fighting settled down to its agricultural existence, but throughout the towns and even the villages a great Puritan "hate" was going on; no longer allowed to worship in public as they wished, and prosecuted for trying to do so, Nonconformist meetings were held in cellars and other secret places. The Reading Nonconformist Chapel in Broad Street was founded by one Thomas Juice, a Baptist congregation met in a house on the banks of the Kennet not far from the old Bear Inn, and the Society of Friends, the Quakers, were exhorted from time to time by George Fox, the originator of the Society. John Bunyan used to visit the Kennet-bank Baptist meeting-house, and it is said that he came disguised as a waggoner so as to avoid capture by the "law"; it is also said that he gave his last sermon in Reading, for on the way back to London he developed a fever from which he died.

Another outbreak of "plague" rushed through the County, not so disastrous this time in the countryside as it was up in London, but bad enough for all that, and the fertility of the orchards round Blewbury and Harwell was increased by the bodies of Newbury's dead.

In 1685 Charles died and his brother James, blind to everything but his own Catholicism, commenced his three years' reign. In the same year the King's forces, 150 Life Guards and a body of Foot Guards, passed through Reading and Newbury on their way to put down the Duke of Monmouth's rebellion; the story of the battle of Sedgemoor, the capture and beheading of Monmouth, Judge Jeffreys and his "Bloody Assize" do not concern us, except that the Royal Artillery was commanded by Dr. Peter Mews, formerly vicar of St. Mary's, Reading, and Archdeacon of Berkshire, and that at least one Berkshire man, William Marshall, of Newbury, was convicted at the Quarter Sessions for joining Monmouth's partisans; he was committed to Reading Gaol.

In 1688 James committed his final blunder by producing a son; under normal conditions the arrival of an heir to the throne is the signal for rejoicing, but these were not normal times; instead of flags and salvoes in every town, a single flag was called out—the standard of William of Orange—heralding the arrival of Dutch troops in answer to the English people's cry. Once again James's troops marched through Reading and Newbury, though this time he lost so many of his men by desertion to the other side that he was forced to retreat by Wallingford to Windsor, to London, and then in disguise to France. His final act was to drop the "Great Seal" in the Thames, hoping this would make things difficult for William and Mary!

The Dutch troops marched to Hungerford, where, on December 6th, at the Bear Inn, Protestant leaders met William to discuss the calling of a Parliament. They arrived in Newbury on December 9th, 1688, where there were great celebrations, and where many volunteers rallied to the standard of William, Prince of Orange. From Newbury they marched via Farnborough, West Ilsley and Drayton to Abingdon and thence by Wallingford, Hurley and Maidenhead to London. Some of the Dutch troops marched through East Hendred, where they ransacked the Catholic chapel in the great house of the Eystons, drinking themselves drunk from the chalice and making a "guy" from the priest's vestments, which they carried to Oxford and burnt in a bonfire. Other troops went into Reading, where they attacked and defeated James's Irish troops in the Market Place. The people of Reading were overjoyed at this, because they loathed these Irishmen, who they believed had been sent to carry out a massacre; and so great was their fear that many of them fled. Irish guards were at once placed on all the exits from the town. In Castle Street a troop of horse was standing ready in the yard of the Bear Inn; St. Mary's Churchyard was lined with infantrymen, and a sentry was posted on the top of St. Mary's tower; a force was placed in Broad Street covering the main body in the Market Place. But the Dutchmen had cunning and they had previous warning of the disposition of the Irish troops, with the result that they effected a surprise attack from the Oxford road; the result was chaos in the town, increased by the appearance of faces with guns in all the house windows; it was all over quite quickly and fifty Irishmen were killed. The affair was known as the "Reading skirmish," and a ballad of that name was written to commemorate it.

During the reign of William and Mary there was a good deal of Jacobite bubbling, but it came to nothing until William fell with his horse and was killed. Then, with a splutter like a sulphur match, an abortive attempt was made to get James II's son to the throne; you will probably remember the questioned legitimacy of this child and the warming-pan theories, but Anne held the throne successfully for twelve years.

Despite the efforts of Lord Bolingbroke, who lived at Bucklebury, the Hanoverian Georges followed Anne in

The chalk-pit amphitheatre, Bradfield College

regular succession, though one of them, George II, was nearly unseated by the Jacobite rising of 1745; this uprising was squashed by George's son, William, Duke of Cumberland, who became Ranger of Windsor Forest; he lived at what we now call Cumberland Lodge, and he was responsible for the construction of Ascot Racecourse and the lakes of Virginia Water.

Many great advancements were made in Berkshire under the Georges. The waterway of the Kennet was improved so as to be navigable between Newbury and Reading, and the old wooden bridge at Newbury was replaced with a stone one; roads were improved and the Kennet and Avon Canal was started; the Reading *Mercury*, Reading's first newspaper, came into being, and the first attempts were made to improve Reading's streets with lighting and with paving stones. Banks were established (one of which failed, causing untold hardship and loss of trade in town and country), Simonds' Brewery, Cocks' sauce manufactory and Sutton's seed establishment appeared in Reading, bringing with them employment and prosperity. A steamboat ventured down the Thames towards London, but was stopped beyond Reading by the Lord Mayor, who was fearful that it would throw London's watermen out of work. Soldiers and sailors abroad were winning us an Empire, while at home rich men were living lives of luxury with dozens of servants to look after their needs. Poor men, on the other hand, were still living almost like animals, particularly out in the countryside, with scarcely enough food to keep them alive. Occasionally they behaved like animals too, and riots of one kind and another were not uncommon, such as the "bread riot" in Newbury in 1766, when a mob, maddened by the exorbitant cost of bread, broke into the market and attacked the sacks of corn, throwing many of them into the river. Such things are not surprising when one reads of the excessive meals eaten by the wealthy, yet just now and again one finds the poor being looked after. For instance, to give one example, when the news of Bonaparte's retirement to Elba was received, among Reading's celebrations was a great banquet for 6,000 poor people, subscribed to by the public; this banquet must have been a won-

The Blue Pool, Stanford-Dingley

derful sight, for eighty tables were spread, extending from
the top of London Street to the end of Friar Street! In
Newbury, too, the poor were given a celebration meal, Mr.
Coxeter (famous for the Throckmorton coat) presenting a
plum pudding 24 feet long, which was carried to Greenham
Mills upon a timber wagon drawn by eight oxen; 800 poor
persons sat down to eat it, while in Newbury itself 4,000
more were feasting in the main streets. But one good meal in
a lifetime is of little account, and in the reign of William IV
the agricultural workers rose up once more. This time they
feared the machinery which farmers were installing and which
would, they believed, throw them out of work. Night after
night fires showed where the rioters were burning farms and
ricks throughout the countryside; law and order was restored
by the use of force, many men were transported, one was
hanged and the farmers bought new threshing machines.

And so we reach Victoria, the Queen that many Berkshire
men can still remember. Perhaps the greatest development of
all is the arrival of the railway. The Great Western Railway
Company, formed in the reign of William IV, had put down
a line from London to Maidenhead by 1838; by 1840 it had
reached Reading, and in the following year it was possible to
travel by rail to Bristol, not through Newbury as you might
expect, but, because of the opposition of the Newbury landowners, through Didcot. The line to Newbury was not opened
until 1847. All along its route you can see where similar
opposition has taken the lines a mile or so away from the
towns, and you can also see the little dead-end lines constructed when the towns had discovered their error.

The decline of the waterways before the railways and now
the rivalry of road transport have each in turn affected the
appearance of our County; the modern roads are without a
doubt more pleasant to behold than any railway line, but
neither of them can hold a candle to the old lanes and waterways for beauty; perhaps it is the peacefulness of the old lane,
wandering beneath stately elms or the decaying lock gates of
the canals that appeal to us, while our children, not yet old
enough to be wearied by the speed of everything, still love to
stand on bridges and watch the trains rush by.

Much has happened since Victoria came to the throne, and a county as agricultural as Berkshire has had its ups and downs. National emergencies have probably been the greatest cause for change, and we have seen the Downs growing corn and the pastures of the Vale and even the commons of the south under the plough. Woods have been felled and not always replanted, rivers have been cleared and their banks piled high with mud and a dozen aerodromes or airfields have used up thousands of acres of farming land. Factories and housing sites there are galore, yet Berkshire remains predominantly an agricultural county. Education has gone ahead in leaps and bounds, and the Reading University College that was founded in 1892 and was then scattered through Valpy Street, Blagrave Street and West Street, has moved to its present more compact and very lovely premises off the London Road and has become by royal charter a full-blooded university; and very recently it has been made known that the university will move again, this time to the lovely Whiteknights Park, where in beautiful surroundings of some 300 acres a programme of expansion is planned that will allow a huge increase in the number of full-time students. In addition to Reading University, the Imperial College of Science has now purchased estates outside Ascot, where entomologists of the future will be trained and where research work on insecticides will be carried out. At Sonning, Reading and at Streatley the Royal Veterinary College has pursued an evacuated existence, and at Harwell the Atomic Research Station is coming into existence. In Reading also are the headquarters of the South-east Province of the recently formed National Agricultural Advisory Service, applying science to farming problems; and at Shinfield is the National Institution for Research in Dairying and the Ministry of Agriculture's Artificial Insemination Centre.

So Berkshire looks like being one of the important counties for scientific learning and achievement; but "learning" is not limited to the universities, for there is a remarkable number of schools and colleges of first-rate importance : Bradfield College (founded 1850); Douai Abbey (founded as St. Mary's School, 1833); Leighton Park School (1890);

Nautical College, Pangbourne (1917); Radley College (1847); Royal Military College, Sandhurst (1812); Wellington College (1853). Priority of age goes first to Reading School, which was founded either in 1486 or as far back as 1121, opinions differing as to the actual date, and secondly to the Reading Bluecoat School, founded by Richard Aldwort in 1646. (This school has recently moved from the Bath road to Holme Park, Sonning, occupied during the war by the Royal Veterinary College.)

A great many of the buildings we know so well in our towns were erected during Victoria's time : in Reading the Municipal Buildings (1875), the Assize Courts (1861), the Corn Exchange (1854) and the Royal Berkshire Hospital (1839); in Newbury the Municipal Buildings (1876) and the Corn Exchange (1861); in Abingdon the Corn Exchange (1885), the Public Library (1896), the Cottage Hospital (1885); in Faringdon the Corn Exchange (1863) and the Hospital (1892); in Hungerford the Town Hall and Corn Exchange (1870); in Maidenhead the Town Hall (1879) and the Hospital (1880); in Wallingford the Corn Exchange (1856), the Free Library (1871) and the alterations and improvements to the seventeenth-century Town Hall (1887); in Wantage the Cottage Hospital (1885) and the Victoria Cross Gallery, which was built for a Corn Exchange (1865). To commemorate those days of happiness and prosperity for a section of the community you will find a statue of Queen Victoria, a picture of Queen Victoria, a street or a building named after her in most, if not all, of our Berkshire towns; you will certainly find a plum named after her.

The South African War and the two World Wars have come and gone and some people appear to be arranging yet another, when perhaps Berkshire will not be so fortunate as it has been so far. While looking into the future I might perhaps refer to one or two proposals which, if carried out, will considerably affect the County. The first, which so far as I am aware is still rather nebulous, is the scheme to make certain alterations and adjustments to certain English counties; Berkshire may well lose bits of itself this way, particularly in the west, where Hampshire and Wiltshire can put forward some quite reasonable claims; but one may rest assured that such adjustments will not be made without the greatest possible consideration and will certainly not lead to the incredible parcels or islands of Wiltshire scattered within Berkshire during the late twelfth century, such as one sees in the many old maps which are now so popular, so popular indeed that one nice one I had was stolen—or perhaps it just strayed! Incidentally, there is a nice collection of old maps of Berkshire outside the Assize Court in Reading.

Perhaps the fashionable likening of Berkshire to an "old boot" will of necessity die out; deliberately I have refrained from making such a comparison, not because I dislike old boots, for I prefer them to new ones, though the "Berkshire boot" looks remarkably uncomfortable, but because nobody in Berkshire thinks about the shape of the County at all. The second proposal, which is not at all nebulous, and which rightly or wrongly has brought forth a howl of protest from those concerned, aims to construct an enormous lake in the Emborne valley. This proposal, known to newspaper men as the "Emborne Valley Scheme," but to farmers and others as something quite unprintable, is nothing new, having come before Parliament once before, when it was discreetly shown the door. This time, *quien sabe*? as the Spaniard says. As I understand it, this lake, extending from Newbury new town to Brimpton, where the Emborne and Kennet rivers meet, will be filled with winter water pumped from the Thames at Pangbourne, and in summer when the river runs low the pumping will be reversed and the lake poured back into the Thames. A cunning scheme, without a doubt, and one that is to cost between fifteen and twenty million pounds to put into operation and about three million pounds each year to keep going. Several thousand acres of irreplaceable farmland will go beneath the waves, together with farmhouses, business houses, dwelling-houses, public-houses, workhouses, schools, police stations, sewage farms, churches, and one might perhaps mention that many miles of roadway will also disappear and will, of course, no longer be required; travellers from Basingstoke to Newbury may have to cross by dugout canoe like their ancestors, who paddled about in the swamps and lakes

of the Kennet valley. But it is all too easy to criticise, to
imagine terrible scenes of mud and mist making an area far
larger than nine square miles quite unbearable for those who
have to live nearby, and one must bear in mind that the great
lake may not be so unpleasant as people expect; after all,
artificial lakes in the Elan valley in mid-Wales have become
one of the beauty spots of an already beautiful country, and
in Scotland the hydro-electric scheme, which is going to turn
an enormous area of the Tummel valley into a lake, will surely
not be an unpleasant sight. One can only hope, if the Metro-
politan Water Board insist upon prosecuting the Emborne
Valley Scheme, that the several thousand people whose homes
and livelihood are being sacrificed to give London more water
will be adequately compensated.

Other proposed changes in the County are that there should
be a new town at Bracknell; that the lovely little village of
Letcombe Basset should be done away with, apparently not
coming up to the requirements of modern times; that the
municipal centre of Reading should be transferred from its
present site, where it has been since the days of the Abbey,
back to an even older, though naturally very much enlarged,
site bounded by St. Mary's Butts, Castle Street, Carey Street,
Zinzan Street and the Oxford road; finally, there is the proposal to establish a Thames-side walk, which in the course of
its meandering will make one hundred miles of lovely Berkshire scenery available to one and all.

CHAPTER VI

READING AND NEWBURY : AN ABBEY AND AN ORGY

IT is about as easy to visualise the streets of Reading paved with gold as it is to picture the muddy tracks between the few hovels which clustered round the great Abbey. Likewise it is difficult to bear in mind that this Abbey, which visitors to modern Reading inspect from time to time and which the bona fide inhabitants care little about, once completely over-shadowed all else in the town and countryside. Now, on a hot summer afternoon when one wanders among the flowers and deck-chairs of the Forbury Gardens, the ivy-clad walls of the once great Abbey remain almost unnoticed, except perhaps by the few people who prefer to sit in their shade, or by those whose hands are firmly clasped and whose conversation is too secret and important for more public places.

To understand and to appreciate the Abbey one must go there many times; one must stare up at the great walls, ignoring the guide-book, erasing from the mind the fact that it is no more than the rubble lining of the ancient walls that one sees; one must poke about here and there and get the "feel" of the place; one should see a frosty moon shine through the arched windows, throwing sharply outlined shadows on the walls and ground; one should cast a blind eye upon encircling buildings, on spiked iron railings, even upon a recent presentation of "Summer is icumen in"; in fact, one should get to know intimately the walls and the places they enclose, and then only should one read the guide-book.

Way back in the twelfth century, in 1121 to be precise, eight monks arrived in the little hamlet destined to become Reading, from the mighty Abbey of Cluny, near Mâcon on the Grosne in France. Accustomed to their quarters in the Benedictine Abbey of Cluny, these monks must have found the muddy hamlet among the rivers not entirely desirable, for the damp mists which rose nightly must have caused terrible aches and pains. But aching joints in no way diminished their zeal, and in a very short time the monks had marked out the site of the monastery to be, and craftsmen had been imported to carry out the construction. The foundation stone was laid by King Henry I on June 18th, 1121, before a large party of nobles, and in 1123 Hugh de Boves, Prior of St. Pancras at Lewes, was appointed first Abbot of Reading.

Under Abbot Hugh the Abbey developed apace, and on March 29th, 1125, the foundation charter was signed by King Henry in Rouen. It is in this charter that we discover why King Henry was so interested in the foundation of an abbey : the salvation of his own soul, his father's soul, his brother's soul, his son's soul, his wife's soul and the souls of all his ancestors and successors—aspirations somewhat similar to those of a Spaniard addressing a gentleman who has trodden upon his pet corn in a bus queue ! So great was his interest that Henry sent over to Reading the dried hand of St. James the Apostle, to be kept in the Abbey enclosed in a shrine of gold, and in addition he conferred a second charter, which exempted the Abbey from payment of Dane-geld and other taxes, while at the same time allowing the privilege of a "moneyer" with the right to mint his own money. At his death in Rouen King Henry I was suitably embalmed and carried across the sea to Reading, where he was buried with great pomp and circumstance before the high altar in the Abbey of his founding.

So much for the instigation of our ruined Abbey, and now what was it like and what were its bounds? To investigate this we must delve into the guide-books, for the ruins which can be seen to-day give very little idea of what once constituted the Abbey and its grounds. An excellent little visitors' guide, costing a mere 6d., has recently been compiled by Messrs. Morley and Smallcombe, names too well known in Reading and Berkshire to require comment, in which the positions of the Abbey buildings can be seen superimposed upon a street map of modern Reading. The Abbey precincts consisted of no less than 32 acres, enclosed upon the south by the river Kennet and by the Holy Brook, which of course runs below ground now, while the other three sides were bounded by a wall running from the South Gate near the

The tiny church of Tidmarsh in the trees by the Pang
The Street, Aldermaston

telephone kiosk at the back of Suttons' in Abbey Square to
the main or Compter Gate against the wall of St. Lawrence's
Church. The wall continued through the town halls, museum,
art gallery and public library, across Valpy Street and straight
towards the railway line, but turned sharply right to the
North Gate, which looked down Vastern Road towards the
river, and which stood more or less where the roundabout is
to-day; from here the wall ran along the edge of the railway
goods yard and North Forbury Road, swinging southwards
down East Forbury Road past the Prison to the East Gate,
which faced the river crossing, with the southern boundary
running west along the Kennet to its southerly bend; from
this point it followed the north bank of the little Holy Brook
beneath William Ridley's timber yard, beneath Abbey Street
and beneath the buildings between the King's Road and Abbey
Square to the South Gate, where we began our perambula-
tions.

    And now we will walk round again, this time imagining the
buildings that once lay upon the periphery. Starting as before
at the South Gate, we would pass the inner court and the
Abbey gardens running up to the porter's lodge of the main
gate; incidentally, the gateways in the outer wall, none of
which remain, were probably similar to the inner gateway,
which stands to this day and which we shall visit later. Next
to the gateway stood St. Lawrence's Church, erected early in
the twelfth century and therefore not in existence when the
Abbey was being built (older than St. Lawrence's is St. Mary's
in the Butts); next was the Hospitium of St. John, the guesthouse, an essential part of every monastery, and consisting of
a refectory, an almshouse and a dormitory; the almshouse
held twenty-six poor persons, thirteen men and thirteen
women, and thirteen other poor men from the town were
provided with alms daily; the refectory consisted of a large
hall measuring 120 feet by 30 feet, with a row of pillars
down the centre, and stood where the Town Hall now stands;
the dormitory, a building nearly 200 feet in length, stood at
right angles to the outer wall and projected inwards almost to
the West Forbury Road; at the west end of the refectory
were the kitchens, bakehouses and a buttery. (This part stood

Entrance to Douai College, Woolhampton
Ancient chapel in a farmyard at Brimpton

until 1882, when it was pulled down during the erection of
the new Town Hall; it was, however, rebuilt again in 1891.)
There was nothing more that we know of in the walls save
the North and East Gates with their lodges, until we are
almost back to the South Gate, before which was a mill
bridging the Holy Brook, with a bakehouse behind it and
adoining the gateway was a long row of stables.

We must now turn in towards the main mass of the Abbey,
and as we are at the South Gate our easiest route lies up
Abbey Square, past the old bakery, now a mill, round into
Abbey Street towards the inner gate; on our left is the County
Police Station, standing where Abbot Aucherius founded a
Leper House dedicated to St. Mary Magdalene; the lepers
and persons suffering from lupus and other complaints were
not allowed to enter church, mill, bakehouse nor refectory,
but were apparently free to wander elsewhere clad in distinc-
tive garments and announcing their approach with clappers.
On our right was once the abbot's house and garden, now lost
beneath car parks and prefabricated office buildings, and
ahead of us is the lovely gateway, spanning Abbey Street and
showing a glimpse of the Forbury Gardens beyond; it is the
best-preserved bit of the Abbey and in the hall above the
abbot held his courts—the last abbot was condemned to death
—and many of Reading's learned societies now hold their
meetings there. With a glance at the flowers and fountain in
the Forbury Gardens we pass through a little arch into the
ruins proper. Ahead of us are the remains of the great cruci-
form church covering an area of some 35,000 square feet
and consisting once of a long central nave and two transepts
divided into apsidal chapels, the mighty roof held aloft upon
two series of eight piers and semicircular arches; a great
central tower arose from the interception of nave and transepts, and a lady chapel dedicated to the Virgin Mary lay at
the east end beyond the high altar, before which Henry I was
buried; at the north-west corner of the church is a memorial
cross erected in honour of its founder. Behind the lady chapel
was the cemetery, and behind that the infirmary, where sick
monks were nursed either to health or probably more often
than not to the adjacent cemetery. From beneath the towering

walls of the church we pass to the quadrangular cloisters
nestling for protection against the south wall of the great
nave; here once sat monks and novices, abbot and prior, reading and writing, teaching and being taught, the abbot and prior
sitting on either side of the door from cloisters to church;
from the south walk of the cloisters one enters the refectory
past the place where the monks washed before meals; the
refectory measured nearly 170 feet long and nearly 40 feet
wide; at the west end was the kitchen and washing-up depart-
ment, and at the east end sat the abbot, the monks sitting at
two long parallel tables before him, while on the south side
was a pulpit from which a monk read aloud during meals.
Behind the east wall of the cloisters was the chapter-house,
said to be one of the largest in England, measuring 79 feet in
length and 42 feet in breadth and about 40 feet in height, with
benches running round the walls for the monks to sit upon.
Between the chapter-house and the south transept of the
church was the little sacristy and treasury, where were kept
the vestments and ornaments and probably the bejewelled
case containing the hand of St. James, while running towards
the Kennet was the day room, and above it the dormitory
where the monks slept fully clad, and beyond it, over a branch
of the Holy Brook, was the "gents," so nicely termed the
necessarium in the Latin tongue. (The waters of both the
Holy Brook and Kennet must have been well polluted higher
up, so what did it matter so near its opening into the Thames?)

And so we have finished our tour of the Abbey as it was,
and what have we really seen? Practically nothing more than
ivy-clad walls where sparrows and spiders nest. And why is it,
you may ask, that a stately place, once one of the three
greatest abbeys in England founded by a King and considered
to be one of the most important seats of learning, why should
it have been brought so low?

Now, in order to understand the ruinous state of the Abbey
we must go back to the twelfth century and see what was going
on. You will remember that the foundation stone was laid by
Henry I in 1121, and that it received its first charter in 1125;
the inner gate was built in 1150, and the great church was
hallowed in 1164 by Archbishop Thomas Becket, though the

lady chapel was not added until 1314. The man in command over all this building was the abbot, who without question was the most important and powerful personage in Reading. He owned manors scattered over the County at Cholsey, Blewbury, Hendred, Burghelbury, Greenham, Midgham, Cookham, Calthrop, Pangbourne, Basyldon, Shyningfield and Sonning; he owned many farms; he was a busy man and from time to time he needed rest, so he owned country houses here and there where he could go and recover; the favourite house was Bere Court, on the hill above Pangbourne. In the Abbey he lived like a fighting-cock, with no less than thirty-seven servants at his beck and call, not to mention the monks, numbering as many as two hundred, who would do anything for him; a list of the Abbey servants has been drawn up by Dr. J. B. Hurry, and it is interesting for the number of cooks—a master cook, an abbot's under cook, an abbot's third cook, a prior's cook, a head cook and an infirmary cook, each with one or more boys in attendance; in addition there was a panterer, a cup-bearer, an under cup-bearer, a chamberlain who carved the abbot's meat, a keeper of the wine cellar who brought drinks after dinner, and a boy who waited in the refectory. One can only presume that the broth was often spoiled! Another list describes the abbot as controlling marshal, master of the horse, two keepers of the pantry, three cup-bearers, four janitors, five pages, eight chamberlains, twelve hostellers, twenty huntsmen, thirty-one running footmen and an almoner.

The monks, of course, were not "fighting-cocks" and were bound to poverty, chastity and obedience; seven times each day they went into the church to pray, commencing at midnight, when for more than half an hour they had to keep themselves from wishing they were back in bed again. The remainder of the day was devoted to breakfast of bread and beer or wine (alternatives of time rather than menu), dinner in silence listening to one of their number reading aloud, supper with dessert; between meals and when not in the church the monks were addressed by the abbot in the chapter-house or instructed in reading, writing and illuminating in the cloisters, or worked in the workshops, gardens and fields—

a full day and a dull one, you will say, and I agree. Even so, it seems that the younger monks found time to play games and to indulge in other forms of amusement, while those who liked to play "snob" had ample opportunity, for many were the kings and queens who visited the abbot, and many were the titled heads which lay upon abbey linen : Henry I, Stephen, Henry II, Richard I, John, Henry III, Edward I, Edward III, Richard II, Henry IV, Henry VI, Edward IV, Henry VII and, after the dissolution, Henry VIII, Edward VI, Queen Elizabeth and Charles I. Among the important visitors were many nobles who came with Stephen to bury Henry I; the Empress Maud (1141); Henry de Essex, who, after fighting and losing a duel with Robert de Montford in 1163, was nursed back to health in the Abbey infirmary and subsequently became a monk; Thomas à Becket, ten bishops and many nobles (1164); the Earl of Cornwall (to be buried in 1175); Heraclius canvassing for help with the Crusades; John of Florence, legate of Pope Innocent III (1206); John of Gaunt, who was married in the church (1359); and Elizabeth Woodville (1464). There was one monk who had no time for playing the snob; his name was John Fornsett; he lived about 1240, and to him goes the credit of having written the earliest known musical "round" :

> "Sumer is icumen in,
> Lhude sing cuccu;
> Groweth sed and bloweth med
> And springth the wode nu,
> Sing cuccu.
> Awe bleteth after lomb,
> Llouth after calue cu;
> Bulluc sterteth, bucke verteth,
> Murie sing cuccu,
> Cuccu, Cuccu.
> Wel singes thu cuccu,
> Ne swik thu nauer nu."

The tune is well known to most people, but the old English words are not easy to understand. For those who wish to sing, the modern wording is as follows :

> "Summer is a-coming in,
> Loud sing cuckoo;

Groweth seed and bloweth mead
And springeth the wood now,
   Sing cuckoo.
Ewe bleateth after lamb,
Loweth after calf cow;
Bullock sterteth, buck verteth,
Merry sing cuckoo,
    Cuckoo, cuckoo.
Well sing the cuckoo,
Nor cease thou never now.

This has been described as the most remarkable ancient musical composition in existence, one of the world's oldest preserved pieces of music, one of the oldest known pieces of music in canon, the oldest example of "ground bass," the oldest known piece in six parts, one of the oldest known pieces of music in the "major key" and the oldest piece of choral music in the world that is still in the repertory! It has been argued, with every reason, that it can be no isolated freak of genius, but is simply an indicator of the level of musical composition in this country at that time. Those who wish to see the original must visit the British Museum, but those who are content with a very beautiful copy can see one on the wall of the chapter-house in the Abbey ruins.

But it is not because of this that the Abbey is in ruins. It is a long story, which starts in 1125 when Henry I signed the first charter giving the abbot power over the people of Reading. They resented this and by 1253 were almost at open war with the abbot, at which stage the latter called in the King's judges to settle the dispute. The abbot had forgotten that he was not the Almighty, and the people of Reading felt obliged to remind him by lying in wait day and night in order to seize his servants and beat them. Right or wrong, the King's judges sided with the abbot and the people of Reading lost the day, but, smarting under the blow, they balanced things by getting a charter during the following year which returned them their Guildhall, which the abbot had seized. But this charter really settled nothing and the town was constantly trying to stick pins into the abbot.

In 1240 the Pope's monetary demands were refused by the clergy of East Berkshire, and in 1258 the abbot refused to

lend the King (Henry III) money which he demanded. A
condition therefore arose in which the people refused to assist
the abbot and the abbot refused to support the King. By 1275
the Abbey was so heavily in debt that King Edward I appointed Roland de Harlegh to investigate and thereafter to
control the Abbey expenditure. In 1303 the Abbey was in
debt for £1,227 7s. 8d., a very large sum in those days, and
the number of monks had dropped to sixty-five. The Abbey
capital was further depleted in 1339, when Edward III borrowed (on long loan, it seems!) many of the valuables, and
a few years later the same King borrowed £100 from the
monks (there are modern equivalents of this!). By 1360
something had gone seriously amiss and the people of Reading
had complained to the King of the irregularities, not to mention the vices, of the monks in the Abbey; this was swiftly
followed by the appointment of Thomas de la Mare, President of the General Chapter of Benedictines and Abbot of
St. Albans, to investigate the matter and by the subsequent
punishment of several monks. In 1413 the Leper House was
shut down, there having been no new cases of leprosy for
some time. This meant that cases of lupus and cancer, both
common enough, could be no longer attended to, and the
following year the abbot was "on the mat" for having
sequestrated the hospital moneys! In 1446 John Thorne,
the twenty-eighth abbot, closed down the almshouses of the
poor sisters, heaping further coals upon the Abbey's head.
By 1458 things had come to such a pass that, in rank defiance
of the Abbot, the burgesses of Reading town had bought their
own mace from the goldsmith Richard and were using it
openly. In reply the abbot obliged the King to place a ban
upon the use of this mace, allowing the mayor no more
dignity than two tipped staves carried (with great indignity)
by two servants of the abbot! The burgesses countered in
1487 with a charter allowing once again the use of their mace
and, in addition, certain other privileges. The abbot replied
by refusing to appoint a mayor, his right by the original
charter, and for the following seven years no mayor was
appointed—not by the abbot, certainly—but by then the burgesses cared little for the abbot's wrath, and in 1488 they

appointed their own mayor; he was Richard Clerke, and he soon fell foul of the abbot by discharging two constables who had been chosen by him and not by the Guild. In 1500 the abbot, John Thorne II, took the matter to the King's court and won the day, and consolidated it in 1507 when two of the King's judges came down on his side, suppressing most of the Guild's privileges and upholding most of the abbot's. And so, until the last abbot was dead, his limbs stretched, his body drawn and quartered before his Abbey gateway, the people of Reading suffered in smouldering silence.

This was in 1539, in the reign of Henry VIII, by which time all the smaller abbeys and monasteries throughout the County had fallen. Like the coloured petals falling from a flower-head, they had seen their day, had passed their prime, were decaying and their benefit to life had ended; in full flower many had been the unsuccessful attempts to pluck the blooms, but in decadence these jaded heads were robbed of seed and cast aside. Between them Henry VIII and his minister, Thomas Cromwell, ably supported by "get-rich-quick" friends, robbed the abbeys and monasteries of their possessions and their power, and those that followed dismantled their beautiful buildings and pushed over their disfigured walls. And in Reading, upon a gibbet outside the gate, hung the ghastly remains of Abbot Hugh Cook of Faringdon and two monks who died with him. During 1539 Thomas Vachell and members of the King's Commissioners had assumed possession of the Abbey and had impounded the valuable gold and silver plate and the rich garments and fabrics for the King's use. Vachell, who was at that time M.P. for the borough, was given charge of these valuables, and Girdamo Penizon, one of Cromwell's supporters, was put in charge of the Abbey buildings. Penizon and Vachell were immediately at loggerheads, each in turn writing complaining letters about the other; this unpleasantness was to some extent straightened out by Vachell being appointed to the offices of Overseer of the Abbey possessions and Bailiff of the town of Reading, while Penizon was made Chief Steward of the Borough and of the Berkshire possessions of the Abbey. The actual work of demolition started on February 10th,

Sonning, a riverside idler's paradise

1549, and if anyone should think that the dismembering was done in a "bulldozing" sort of way he would be sadly mistaken. From certain accounts discovered by chance in the Public Record Office and reproduced by Mr. Arthur E. Preston in the *Berkshire Archæological Journal* for 1935, it is clear that no modern firm of contractors could have done the job with more care and thoroughness. There was none of the Roundhead "smashing for the sake of smashing," and a team of men was employed to reduce the Abbey into "lots" suitable for sale. The work was carried out under the supervision of George Hynde, of the Court of Augmentations, a court which had been set up in 1536 specifically for dealing with possessions coming to the Crown from suppressed monasteries. Of the men employed, about seventy are mentioned by name, and it might perhaps be interesting to Berkshire readers if I were to list them.

Accomptaunte—George Hynde.

Clerk of the Works—Robert Huggens (also Huggons).

Carpenters.	*Carpenter's Laborers.*
George Barefoote (also Barfote).	George Bawle.
John Nayse.	William Deane.
Henry South.	William Waller.
Thomas Daye.	Thomas Tanner.
John Cottrell.	Walter Syngleton.
John Martenley.	Robert Mouneford.
John Tallarde.	Richard Combey.
William Gybbes (also Gibbes).	
John Tailler (also Tayllor).	
Richard Bowyer.	
Richard Cottrell.	
William Scargell.	
William Magytt (also Magett).	
John Revel.	
John Barfote.	

Comon Laborers.

Thomas Lightfoote.	Richard Marten.	John Hyde.
George Gettons.	Thomas Barthelett.	Thomas Cocker.
Robert Tayllar.	John Wallys (also	William Hemmyng.
John Wallyngton (also	Walles).	William Waller.
Wallington).	John Morgan.	Thomas Tanner.
Henry Counsell.	Richard Tayller.	Edmund Wright.
Robert Hytchens.	Thomas Bredes.	Thomas Baylye.
Walter Bernam.	John Trowe.	Robert Foxe.
William Roberts.	John Wyat.	John Browne.
Thomas Sussex.	Henry Penny.	Water Henyell.
William Deane.	Dennys Chylde.	

The Thames at Sonning Lock

Sawyers.
Thomas Cotrell.
Jeamys Welberd (also Wylberde).
Henry Reade.
John Payne.

Tylar.
William Samforde (also Sampforthe).

Tylar's Laborers.
William Twynne.
Richard Combe.
William Teven.

Fremason.
Henry Mercer.

Fremason's laborers.
John Morgan.
Robert Tayller.

Plombers.
Robert Spaffolde.
Henry Deacon.
Thomas Ratclyff.

Fynar.
Henry Hall.

Gate Keepers.

William Lightfote.   John Wright.   Henry Counsayll.

Nightwatchmen.

Robert Spaffolde.   Henry Deakyn.   Thomas Ratclyf.
Richard Derelove.   William Hande.   John Haywood.
Robert Deacon.   Robert Martyndale.   Robert Sturrye.
William Goodyere.   Thomas Hyllar.   John Morgan.
George Gyttons.   John Wayte.   William Hemmyng.
William Lightfote.

In the course of demolition purchases of this and that were
no doubt made locally as occasion demanded, and in the
account George Hynde refers to such as follows :

> itm payde to Wyllyan Lightfote for vj baste Ropes
> itm payde to John Rychardson for iij hande maunds
> itm payde to Richard Smythe for a basket
> etc. etc.

The following names appear as in receipt of money for com-
modities sold to Hynde :

Edmonde Sherewood for "loodes" and "lodes" of sand.

Peter Gonstone for quires of paper and quires of white paper.

John Breche for "handle Ropes," a "gyn rope" and numerous lbs.
weight of ropes.

William Hanare for a "berying tubbe."

Thomas Sussex for "ryngs and bolts."

Thomas Lightfote for "axe and a bowle."

Richard Gylbarde a quantity of "pennye nayles" and "lathe
nayles."

John Fawsebye for "Tyle pynnes" and "penny nayles."

William Bayllye for "long spryggs."

Lypskom for "lyme."

Thomas Baylye for "new stocke locke, a staple and nayle"; and
for a "newe crowe of Iron" and also for "steeling" a number of
"crowes."

In addition to the afore-mentioned purchases, George Hynde
bought from persons not mentioned "stocke locks," "ryngs
for waights and a cole rake," a "skommer for the lead," a
"howke and a dryf pyn and ij harde chyssells," "ij crowes of
iron," "iiij pynnes to the dronge," a "lock and a dryff pyn,"
a "new stoke locke," a "keye" and a "newe keye and mending
of an old locke," a "gryndestone," a "crowe of Iron," a "newe
Buckett," numerous "lodes of sand" and "lodes of poles," a
"marking Iron and a plate for the skales," a "fyer forke,"
"Rings of the leade molde," a number of "draggs of iron to
drawe leade," an "Iron staff for to knytt the conduite pypes,"
a quantity of "staples of Iron" and "boltes for the gynne"
and a number of "pykeaxes." Then there was carriage to be
paid for the bringing and removing of odds and ends;
Tomasyn Nicholas, Mr. Mayer, John Cowper, Edmonde
Sherewood, Mr. Rowte, Richard Rowe and Richard Thome
were paid for carrying "leade, Tymber and Sande," while
Peter West and Nicholas Warde, "Collyars," were paid for
conveying "coles," and Richard Turn was paid for bringing
"Henry Halls tooles to Redinge." Henry Hall, perhaps an
ancestor of "guest-night," required his "tooles" for "fynyng
leade" from the Abbey roofs. The lead, which was one of the
most valuable assets of the Abbey, proved to be in the region
of 406 fothers—that is to say, about 450 tons, and equivalent
to £30,000 in modern currency. So far nothing has been discovered as to the disposal of this lead, though many have
been the guesses.

Now let us see what happened to the "lots" which were
not lead. Such a large "sale" may well have attracted buyers
from places far from Reading, and certainly one came from
London and one from Windsor, but we know from George
Hyndes's account that many "lots" went locally to men who
were no doubt builders and repairers. Literally tens of
thousands of tiles were disposed of to Henry Skynnar,
Thomas Alworthe, John Redges, Thomas Chamberlayne,
Fraunces Beyke, John Fawsebye, Richard Mathewe, Mr.
Rocklyff, Mr. Dobskott, Sir John Gresham, John Nixon, and
finally to Mr. Chauncellor of the Augmentacyons. The glass,
and presumably therefore the stained glass, went to William

Draper, a London "Ironmonger, who also purchased all the Images and stones standing at the Highe Altare." And loads of old iron also went to John Revell, Mighell Hopen, the King's smith at Windsor, William Orpen and to the afore-mentioned Mr. Chauncellor. Gravestones both broken and "hole" went to Thomas Alworthe, John Heythe, Master Anthonye Brygame, Thomas Seyntman, and some marble stone went to a Mr. Fen. Stonework from the walls, etc., went to John Sands, Mayster Greye (later described as Mr. Graye and identified as William Gray, M.P. for Reading), Mr. Beke and Mayster Alworthe, Thomas Malthouse, Richard Watlyngeton and to Mr. Chauncellor. "Olde lathe bourdes" were bought by Thomas Alderw'othe, Henry Hawthorne, Richard Smythe and William Hande.

Having now disposed of most of the smaller items, we can proceed to the sale of large lumps of the Abbey. Let's take the roofs first. Mr. Greye bought the "lytle rofe standing at the ende of the Fratrye"; Mr. Fawchyll bought the "rofe of the lybrarye"—this is interesting because it is the one and only indication of the Abbey owning such a place. Bernarde Moore bought "a lytle roofe" and the wardens of St. Mary's Church bought "the olde Chapel roofe," Mr. Dabskott bought the "prior's halle roofe" while Messrs. Henry Hynde and William Draper bought the "Roofe of the spere steple," and thus provide us with the only known reference to the existence of this steeple. The Duke of Som'sett and Mr. Chauncellor of the Corte of Thaugementacyons (Sir Richard Sackville) picked up most of the better items, notably "the rofe of the Bodye of the Church," "the rofe of the Chaun-cell," "the rofe of the lower Dorter," "the rofe of the higher Dorter," "the fenistre rofe," " the Fermery rofe," "the rofe of the Northe syde of the quyer," "the rofe of the south side of the quyer," "the rofe of the Chapter house," and finally "the rofe of the Ladye Chapell." From the valuation of the roofs we know that they were worth having, especially as there is no record of their being paid for by the two gentle-men concerned.

Some of the remaining parcels are not without interest. John Nyxson bought the frame that the "organs stode upon,"

Thomas Alworthe bought a number of "broken sells in dortare" and a "pticon before a chappell." John Redges bought
several lots, including some "olde bedsteds and an olde Table,
iij formes and an old portall, and an olde organ case"; and
then he paid 33/4d. of his money for "an olde chamber"!
Not exactly as it reads, I think, but John Redges must undoubtedly have kept a junk shop ! Robert Style collected some
"monks selles in the dorter" and Mr. Riggs bought up "all
the cabens in the Fermerye wherin the sycke monkes laye."
St. Mary's Church purchased the "monks stalls in the Quyre"
and some "pillors of stone standing in the olde Chapple."
Thomas Mawks bought the "Comen Jakeses of the dortare"
and Mr. Greye bought "the plaster of parrys that wente
about the Quyere" and a number of "Jakes stokes." Mr.
Warde bought "an olde halle" and Mr. Bradshawe bought
up the "tymbre of the North Ile of the Church."

Finally, the outbuildings were sold; Mr. Redkowte buying
a "lytle lodgynge," Mr. Warde "an olde lodgynge behynde
the Fermerye," John Cowper "the Jaks howse," Messrs.
Bregame and John Redges "a lytle howse standing by the
water syde called a slaughter howse." Maister Venare "an
olde lodgynge" and Stephen Christyan "a litle howse by the
water syde." And so at last the once proud, arrogant Abbey
stood naked and ashamed, clutching at a figleaf that was kept
as an "Occasional Palace" until 1625. Before Hynde had
finished his task a piece of constructional work was carried
out, in "conveying of the water from the King's place at
Reding to the King's stable there." Appropriately enough,
one Water Reyman was employed for "digging and casting of
the Trenche, and filling it in agayn and for pavyng certayne
placs wheare need was"; William Hande (an ex-night-watch-
man) was paid for "buryeng and layeng of the pypes" and
John Sewell provided a "cocke"; in addition 32 lb. of
"sowder" was purchased from an unmentioned source. The
cost of the whole job was 70/-d. The carpenters, sawyers,
plumbers, freemasons, tylers, refiners, gatekeepers and nightwatchmen had all gone, to return only to execute some private
looting of wood and stones.

At some later date, boat-loads of stones from the Abbey

were sent downstream to Windsor where they were used in
the construction of the Hospital of the Poor Knights, while
others went to Henley to build a bridge at Park Place. Much
of the panelling from the Abbey walls went to Merton College, Oxford (perhaps the idea of getting hold of the panelling for Oxford began in 1209, when about 3,000 students
and teachers from that town came to Reading as a protest at
the lynching of two innocent students accused of murdering
a girl!). The walls began to crumble, some tottered and fell,
and the sparrows and spiders took control. In 1643, during
the siege of Reading, the Abbey walls were considerably battered by Roundhead cannons and were apparently blown up
with gunpowder, though for what reason I know not; and if
the Compter Gate had stood until 1943 it would have been
damaged by the German bomb which defaced St. Lawrence's
Church, the Old Town Hall and the premises of Messrs.
Blandy and Blandy.

In conclusion, I should point out that in the Reading
Museum there are some Norman capitals found at Holme
Park, Sonning, and presumed to have come from the Abbey,
the abbot's seals, a few rusty keys, some silver coins minted
in the Abbey, a mediæval badge, a pair of compasses and a
variety of tiles, probably from the church floor. Absent from
the collection is a box containing the hand which was dug up
among the Abbey ruins by workmen in 1810. The hand was
said to be "a perfectly formed fleshy hand holding a slender
rod surmounted by a crucifix. It is in perfect preservation, a
plump and well-shaped hand, small, and with taper fingers,
and almond-shaped nails, so small it might well be a
woman's." So wrote the author of the *History of Shiplake*.
Apparently she had seen the hand, which was then in Mr.
Scott Murray's Roman Catholic Chapel at Danesfield, where
it was presumed to be the hand of St. James, presented to the
Abbey by Henry I. Another school of thought allots the hand
to the second wife of Henry I, Queen Adeliza, who was
buried in the Abbey. Also absent from the museum is the
collection of sacred bits and pieces which at the time of the
Dissolution were catalogued as follows :

THE ENVENTORYE OF THE RELYQUES OFF THE CHURCHE OFF REYDNG

Two peces off the Holy crosse.
Saint James hand.
Saint Phelyps stolle.
A bone of Mary Magdalens.
Saynt Anastasius is hande.
A Peece of Saynt Pancrosts arme.
A bone off Saynt Qyntyus arme.
A bone off Saynt Davide is arme.
A bone off Saynt Edward ye Martyr is arme.
A bone off Saynt Hierome.
Bones off Saynt Stephen.
A bone off Saynt Alasse.
A bone off Saynt Ismonde.
A peece off Saynt Ursula stole.
A chawbone off Saynt Ethelwol.
Bones off Saint Leodigorie, etc.
Bones off Saynt Margarett.
Bones of Saint Arnel.
A bone of Saynt Andrewe and ij peces of his crosse.
A bone off Saynt Fredysayde.
A bone off Saint Anne.

A fine collection, you must agree.

NEWBURY—COACHING DAYS AND COACHING WAYS

When one wanders around that rather unattractive part of Newbury which sprawls along the Bath road by the old clock-house, how very little there is now to remind one of the importance of Newbury in the coaching days; and important Newbury was, too, for here the London to Bath coaches stopped for the night, discharging their cargoes of ladies and gentlemen who were off to take the cure. Some sort of cure was really necessary after more than a hundred miles in a stage coach, and the night of drinking and revelry in Newbury in no way diminished the need.

Before we inspect the night-life of Newbury, however, we should investigate the reason for it. Somewhere about the end of the seventeenth century there came a demand for better roads, caused by the change-over from the pack-horse to the wheeled wagon. This demand was, of course, very reasonable, because the roads really were shocking; we call roads "shocking" to-day that would have amazed our ancestors by their smoothness! Who nowadays, driving from London to Bath, anticipates overturning in the ruts sometimes four or five feet deep, or becoming bogged or losing the way, thus adding an extra night to the journey? Even the roads damaged by the winter of 1946-47 could have been nothing compared with the roads of 1647.

Improvements to the old roads had to be paid for by someone, and the turnpike system quite reasonably handed the baby, bit by bit, to the users of the roads. The users of the roads naturally resented having to pay, but without a shadow of doubt it was the old turnpike system that made roads fit for wheeled traffic at all possible. Even so, it was many years before main roads approached the condition of our modern cart tracks, and the journey from London to Bath must have been one of unmitigated hell. First of all, the coach left London at five o'clock in the morning! This meant a night in London, at or near the "Bell Savage" on Ludgate Hill, the appointed place from which the coach would start its journey. This was in 1667, when King Charles II was on the throne. The cost was twenty-four shillings (not our modern shilling, of course), fourteen pounds weight of luggage was allowed, and the journey completed, all going well or no worse than usual, in three days.

In 1752 John Clark and Company of Newbury put on the road a vehicle which undertook to complete the journey from that town to London in twelve hours; four passengers only could be accommodated, and the cost was ten shillings. By 1761 the journey to Bath could be made in a single day, leaving London at eleven o'clock at night and arriving in Bath late next evening. It seems that such disgusting haste was met with stones from the horrified onlookers and with ugly grins from the highwaymen, who looked forward to overturned coaches.

Until 1744 the Bath road beyond Newbury passed through Chilton Foliate, past Littlecote Park to Ramsbury and on to Marlborough, but by an arrangement with the Duke of

Somerset the road was carried through Savernake Forest.
We are not concerned here with the journey to Bath, but the
"New Bath road," as this section was called, affected Newbury not a little, greatly increasing the popularity of the road,
for the "Ramsbury Narrow Way," as the old route was later
called, was devastating to comfort of passenger and to the
well-being of vehicle alike.

Nearly one hundred years after our coach left the Bell
Savage on Ludgate Hill a new coach was running to Bath
from the Saracen's Head in Cheapside, leaving London at the
same ungodly hour, breakfasting in one of the many inns in
Colnbrook; it was too early to stop when the King's Head
was reached—you and I know it now as the Peggy Bedford—
it was the returning coaches which pulled up there and made
it famous. Highwaymen permitting, the coach reached Reading for dinner. The George, the Bear, the Crown and the
King's Arms were the fashionable places, and one of them
remains so to this day. Between Reading and Theale the
effects of a good meal became apparent, for gallant gentlemen
produced drinks, told stories (awfully nice ones, of course)
and sang songs to keep up the spirits of the party. In Theale
the coach stopped for tea at the Crown—tea then consisted of
cakes and ale—where gentlemen and ladies stretched their
legs and said how nice it would be to reach Newbury and
finish with all this jolting. And so on through Woolhampton
and Thatcham to Newbury, though if the coach had been
much delayed, say, by a wheel setting fire to its axle, a stop for
supper would be made at Cooper's Cottage at Thatcham;
Cooper's was a popular place to feed because of the "spread"
and the excellent service. And so at last we reach Newbury's
Speenhamland—tired, sore, cross and perhaps robbed.

Speenhamland was a veritable oasis, and soon all the aches
and bruises of the journey were forgotten in the good cheer
with which the place abounded. The most famous, and presumably therefore the most expensive, coaching hotel was the
George and Pelican, already nearly two hundred years old;
many well-known or well-to-do people stayed at the Pelican,
as it was familiarly known, one of whom was Mr. Quin, an
Irish actor who had retired to Bath; Quin, who had travelled

the Bath road time and again, composed the following lines
and wrote them on one of the windows :

> "The famous inn at Speenhamland
> That stands below the hill,
> May well be called the Pelican
> From its enormous bill."

Upon another window some other wag wrote :

> "As often as ye bell ye handle
> Ye'll have to pay for snoffing of ye candle."

The Pelican, despite its "bill," remained the most popular of
all the inns. Nelson used to stay there when visiting his father
in Bath, and William Cobbett addressed a meeting there
after attending a market-ordinary at the inn; in 1839 the
Duke and Duchess of Cambridge and Princess Mary ate
luncheon there on their way to stay with the Duke of Beau-
fort at Badminton. For those who did not wish to use the
Pelican, but at the same time wanted something first class—
5 star, as we might call it to-day—the Chequers and the Bear
were close at hand, the former remaining to this day. The
Bear, which had housed the lifeless bodies of the three lords
—Carnarvon, Sunderland and Falkland—after the first
Battle of Newbury and had seen Cromwell, Charles II,
James II, William of Orange, saw many a weary traveller
helped from the coaches of the late eighteenth century and
had known many a boisterous night of drinking and cock-
fighting in the cock-pits behind. The Bear was eventually
closed down as a result of some kind of disturbance during
which the unfortunate cook was hurled down the stairs and
killed. (This might well be taken as a warning by some of the
so-called cooks who ruin our food for us day after day!)

The Bacon Arms, the Angel, the Cross Keys, the Lamb
and Flag, the King's Arms, were all huddled together close to
the Chequers and the Pelican, so that drunken parties returning home from the other attractions which Newbury offered
may well have had difficulty in finding the correct courtyard.
Further away upon Speen Hill stood the Castle, frequented
by Royalty and possibly a little superior to the mass of inns
down below.

Now, what were the attractions of Newbury which made
the night so pleasant for weary travellers? Sing-songs in most
of the inns, blind fiddlers, fortune-tellers, exhibitions of one
kind and another, cock-fighting contests, gambling and probably a good deal of brawling. Wealthy widows might be successfully wooed upon the bridge over the Kennet, or one might
flirt with the supposedly coy serving wenches in any of the
taverns. Or one might spend the evening in the theatre, with
its imposing entrance, enormous pillars supporting a gigantic
lion and unicorn. This theatre was erected in 1802 and, according to Mr. Money in his *Popular History of Newbury*,
many celebrities of the stage performed there, including John
Philip Kemble, Edmund Kean, Mrs. Fanny Kemble, Mrs.
Jordan (mistress of the Prince Regent, later George IV),
Miss Brunton, Incledon and Braham, the Infant Roscius,
John Banister, Mrs. Powell, Mr. and Mrs. Middleton, and
Miss Foote.

A typical programme is quoted by Cecil Roberts in his *And
So to Bath*, which commences with a representation of the
"desperate and glorious engagement" by which the British
and Dutch Marines blew up the Town, Fort and Shipping of
Algiers. This was performed at the desire of Captain Mon-
tagne, the officers, non-commissioned officers and privates of
the Woodley Troop of the Berkshire Yeomanry Cavalry.
After this, a Mr. Wilson was down to give an exhibition upon
a tight rope, his "unrivalled Exertion commencing with his
celebrated gavotte, with several Equilibriums, during the performance of which he will throw an Extraordinary Somersault over the Orchestra." Finally, Mr. Wilson, assuming
that all had gone well and that he had not come to grief
among the instruments of the orchestra, would dance his
"much admired Fandango, accompanying himself on the casta-
nets, as expressly composed for him by Signor Baptiste, first
violin of the Theatre Royal, Madrid, concluding with his
justly admired Tambourine Rondo." I admire Mr. Wilson,
not so much for his Extraordinary Somersault over the
Orchestra, but for being able to perform his Fandango and
Rondo without the modern necessity of styling himself Don
Garcia or Don Pedro.

And so they stumbled back to their hostelries either to lie in bed trying to sleep and trying not to scratch, or to stretch out their legs and call for drink after drink, until the shouting of ostlers and post-boys and the stamping of hooves upon the cobbles forced their banging heads to realise that they must be on their way if they were to breakfast in Marlborough and reach Bath before midnight.

CHAPTER VII

PASTIME ON WHITE HORSE HILL

NEARLY a hundred years ago, in 1857 to be precise, the old
White Horse was "scoured" for the last time and the hills
and valleys rang with the happy voices of men from near and
far. For in those days mass amusement was hard to come by,
and the Pastime on White Horse Hill was waited for with
excitement throughout Berkshire and the neighbouring counties. The story has been told by Tom Hughes in his *Scouring
of the White Horse, or The Long Vacation Ramble of a
London Clerk and What Came of It*. This author is better
known for *Tom Brown's School Days*—what boy has not
read this and loved it? And if he has read it he will already
have come across the White Horse and the ridges and vales
of Uffington. The less known book is equally delightful,
though perhaps without the same appeal to the schoolboy; it
is a book I keep by my bedside, to browse through in those
delightful moments before sleep.

What was the purpose of "scouring" the White Horse,
you will ask, and how often did it happen? First of all, I
should explain that a "scouring" was a wash and brush up for
the Horse and it was a traditional affair. When it was first
done no one knows, but rain storms, which are not uncommon
on the hill, wash away the chalk lines of the Horse and dirty
the whiteness, so every seven years the Horse was tidied up
and men took the opportunity of celebrating.

The first "scouring" of which we have any details took
place in 1736, and apparently being nothing unusual, we can
presume that there had been many a "scouring" before this;
this was followed by a "scouring" in 1755, when an Uffington
boy turned highwayman, Tim Gibbons by name, suddenly
appeared on the scene and won the prize for backswording
from the acknowledged champion of the day, after which he
jumped upon his horse and rode off. Of the next "scouring"
there are no details, not even the year is known; 1776 is the
next "scouring" we are able to read about, for Hughes prints

the programme in his book. The items in this are interesting, for they show a similarity to many a modern gymkhana, though at the same time they show a great difference where prizes are concerned. Here are a few extracts :

"A silvercup will be run for near White Horse Hill by any horse, etc., that never ran for anything, carrying 11 stone, the best of three two-mile heats, to start at ten o'clock."

". . . will be run for by Poneys, a saddle, bridle and whip, the best of 3 two-mile heats, the winner of 2 heats will be entitled to the saddle, the second best the bridle and the third the whip."

"A Thill harness will be run for by cart-horses and in their harness and bells, the carters to ride in smock frocks without saddles, crossing and jostling, but no whipping allowed."

"A flitch of bacon to be run for by asses."

So much for the horse events, which were accompanied by events such as these :

"A good Hat to be run for by men in sacks, every man to bring his own sack."

"A Waistcoat, 10/6d. value, to be given to the person who shall take a bullet out of a tub of flour with his mouth in the shortest time."

"A Cheese to be run for down the White Horse Manger."

And so that the womenfolk should have some of the fun, a single event was aimed at their attention :

"Smocks to be run for by ladies, the second best of prize to be entitled to a Silk Hat."

These events were for the amusement of the locals, but were not what the burly drovers from far away came for. The first events were for amusement only and nobody cared who won the prizes. But now we come to the *pièce de résistance*, the business of the day, taken as seriously by its adherents as village cricket to-day. Local honour was at stake.

"Cudgel-playing for a *gold laced Hat*, and a pair of buckskin Breeches, and *Wrestling* for a pair of Silver Buckles and a pair of pumps."

Finally, the programme ended in the conventional manner :

"The horses to be on the White Horse Hill by nine o'clock."
"No less than four horses, and/or asses to start for the above prizes."

The next "scouring" took place in 1780, and according to the "write-up" in the *Reading Mercury* of May 22nd, 1780, upwards of thirty thousand people were there, including most of the nobility and gentry from several counties. The next "scouring" was in 1785, and then comes a gap until 1803. Hughes could get no line on anything between these dates but supposes there were at least two "scourings"; 1808 produced a new event, much disapproved of by Hughes but no doubt highly amusing to those who saw it, for a gallon of gin or half a guinea was given to the woman who could smoke most tobacco in an hour ! Only two gipsy women competed, and according to Hughes, who after all wrote in 1858, "it seems to have been a very abominable business. . . ." The 1812 or 1813 "scouring" was marred by one of the champion wrestlers falling into a canal on the way home; a jury returned the strange verdict of "killed at wrestling" ! In 1825 the White Horse was given a miss and the Pastime was held at Lambourn Seven Barrows. There seems to have been no further "scourings" until 1838, when it was once more held above the White Horse. This was followed by another in 1843, and finally, the last of all, in 1857, which Hughes attended himself and of which he has written so amusingly and thoroughly. Without wishing in any way to steal his thunder, for I hope that many of my readers will search the shelves for his book and wipe away the dust, I cannot leave the subject without giving you some idea of what happened on that day in September, 1857.

But we must go back to the day before the Pastime when the London clerk went up on to the hill with his friend Joe

Hurst of Elm Close Farm, Uffington. The "scouring" was
then under way and there were many men from nearby farms
sweeping with besoms and shovels and trimming up the edges
of the ditches cut into the chalk. When they had finished, the
men settled into a large can of beer sent up by the squire.
One of the men sang a song which Hughes calls "The Ballad
of the 'Scouring' of the White Horse"; it has four verses in
broad dialect, the first of which runs as follows :

"The owld White Harse wants zettin' to rights
And the Squire hev promised good cheer,
Zo we'll gee un a scrape to kip un in zhape
And a'll last for many a year."

Next morning Elm Farm was humming with activity at an
early hour, as the men tried to get their work done in order to
get away to the Pastime, which was timed to begin at ten
o'clock. The journey up to the castle via the Blowing Stone
was full of excitement, all manner of vehicles competing with
horsemen and walkers to reach first the Ridgeway and then
Uffington Castle. In the castle were booths and show-tents,
each one making its own music to the best of its ability. Bank
Holiday on Hampstead Heath couldn't have beaten the noise,
and the farmers and their womenfolk, decked in "Sunday-
best," shouted at each other above the din. And then, after the
sandwiches had been consumed and the bottles emptied, the
ring in the centre of the castle became the focus of all eyes.
An old gamester, John Bunn, of Wedinore in Somerset,
jumped up and was challenged by George Gregory of Strat-
ton. Bunn won this event, bringing blood from the Wiltshire
head with a mighty blow of his stick. Then Harry Seely of
Shrivenham goes in to fight against a rather bad-tempered
man from the west. In the fifth round, or bout as they called
it, Seely brought blood pouring from his opponent's hair.
When asked why he took so long to do it, he answered,
"There's no 'cumulation o' blood belongs to thay cider drink-
in' chaps as there does to we as drinks beer. Besides, thay
drinks vinegar allus for a week afore playin' which dries up
most o' the blood as thay has got, so it takes a 'mazing sight
of cloutin' to break their yeads as should be." Between the

The Bell, Hurley

bouts, competitors took the hand-guard baskets from their sticks around the audience collecting pennies and watched the wrestling which then occupied the ring. The wrestling was as great an attraction as the backswording, and from what Hughes says of it I gather the audience shouted much the same suggestions to their favourites and hurled the same abuse at their opponents as one has heard more recently at "all-in wrestling" competitions. Then there was the carthorse race, the thill harnesses jingling and jangling and the carters in clean smocks and "break-o'-day" hats, as proud of their mounts as any Ascot professional. The cheese prize for running down the manger after a wheel must have been well earned, as anyone who peers over the edge will see. On skis one might perhaps set up a jumping record here, and running down on foot would surely be as quick a way of breaking something, but though many men fell we hear of no serious disasters. Jonathan Legg of Childray won the race, having taken a straight line from top to bottom, an almost unbelievable feat, but no doubt at each Pastime there was someone with the courage to go straight and the luck to get away with it. The wheel was made by Henry Jones of Ashbury and was solid, the size of a cartwheel and with a ten-foot pole through it for balance. It usually broke long before the heads and legs which were chasing it! A pig was chased by a mob and almost lynched, but was rescued in true cowboy fashion by Farmer Whitfield and galloped away to Wayland's Smithy, where he was once again turned loose, chased and won by some fellow who could run faster than his colleagues. And so to the committee's tent, where at one end the committee were giving away prizes while at the other end the squire and another Justice were doing summary justice on two pick-pockets.

Outside it was dark now and all the booths lighted up little lamps; tired but happy people thronged the refreshment places, getting themselves into condition to start on the homeward journey. There was a good deal of singing, and Hughes records a number of songs in Berkshire dialect, including the "Barkshire Tragedy," which tells the sad tale of a beautiful girl who was pushed into the river by her sister, rescued by a miller who took her tip (10 guineas) and pushed her in again;

The Thames, near Bisham Abbey

the miller was hanged beside his own gate and the wicked and presumably ugly sister fled to foreign lands where she died among black savages! Then they sang "Tovey's Tap" and the Gloucestershire song "Gaarge Ridler" and a dozen or so more before it was decided to get away home, leaving the showmen and the gipsies to sleep the remainder of the night up in the camp, beneath the stars which had kept watch on generation after generation of men unknowingly keeping alive the ancient custom. And so we come to the end of this Pastime and wend our way to the farms and cottages of the vale, to the junipers and barrows of Wiltshire, the cider of Somerset; the dozing men leave their horses and asses and donkeys to find the way for themselves and the women crumple their fancy dresses, huddled together in sleep. They did not know that they had attended a funeral, that another ancient custom had died that day, as they cheered the gamesters and wrestlers, the cart-horses and asses, as they tossed their coins in the baskets and bought their fortunes from the gipsies, and at dusk, when they sat in groups singing their songs, they could not hear the sighing undertone, the last gasps of something infinitely old.

PART III

Open Air

CHAPTER VIII

NATURAL HISTORY

1. SLAVES ON THE HAMPSHIRE BORDER

ANY afternoon in full summer I could show you slaves, small black people toiling in the homes of their overlords, whose great red torsos shine in the sun as they hurry about their business. Who will believe me that here in the heather and pine trees there is no "servant problem," no need for the ladies of the establishment to do chores they had never been brought up to do. It is all quite simple; you just send the estate servants off into the countryside and lo! they return with slaves.

Who are they, these feudal overlords, and who are their slaves? If you will go to a spot before the house I lived in you will find a rotten pine stump—you will find thousands, but you must concentrate to find the one. Here you will see the red men and their negro slaves. *Formica sanguinea*, the slave-making ant, the blood-red robber ant, call it what you will, looks for all the world like the big wood ant of the heathland, but, unlike the latter, the slave-maker does not build a mighty dome of pine needles, preferring to live beneath stones, in clumps of grass, in rotten dusty stumps. He is not common, this slave-maker, and on the whole of my thirty-five acres I knew of but three nests. The slaves are little black or grey fellows, cousins perhaps and *Formica fusca* by name, nests of which are always abundant on this dry and acid land.

I have never watched the slave-makers sally forth upon a raid, and very few such raids have been seen in England; according to continental observers, the red men send out scouts first and later small bands of warriors, who, as though under the direction of some officer, wheel around, attack, retire, retreat (according to plan) and receive reinforcements when the position looks hopeless. This little battle rages for a considerable time, the dry twigs crackling like a miniature artillery; and if the attackers are too strong the *fusca* camp will be thrown into confusion, ants rushing hither and thither, carrying their precious pupæ, their infants, throwing them ruthlessly aside in the final effort of self-preservation. The invaders reach the ramparts, tearing at the bodies of the defenders and bearing away their now immobilised captives. But these captives are not to be slaves; they are for the pot. For slaves must have no preconceived ideas, must not resent captivity. So *sanguinea* takes away the pupæ, the embryonic ants who have never seen the light of day, who have never tasted freedom. These pupæ, often called eggs in error, are carried back into the victorious nest to be reared into captivity.

This battle I would dearly love to have seen, but in the course of five or six summers I have not been lucky. The attack is said to start about noon, probably a function of the sun, and often continues into the following day. During my own observations I have seen *sanguinea* workers carrying *fusca* bodies, but never pupæ. One or two raids each season will probably provide sufficient slaves, and the chances of stumbling on these raids is therefore pretty slight.

Now, what of the slaves? What manner of life does a slave live? These are questions that can only be answered by opening up nests and by setting up observation *formicaria*. The first duty of the slave is that of parlourmaid, doing the dusting, so to speak, and opening the front door; a second equally onorous duty is nursemaid, feeding the larvæ and tending the pupæ and looking after the food supplies. Sometimes the *fusca* ants, which are all workers of course, have a day off and are free to wander outside the nest, but if the whole colony is moving from its winter nest to its summer quarters the slaves are carried by their owners. Naturally there will be a lot to do in the new nest, and the *fusca* workers must not arrive too tired to get down to it. And this thoughtfulness is typical of *sanguinea*, who treats the slaves with every kindness and attention. No frog-infested dungeons and no chaingangs are to be found; in fact, except that they were stolen at the start, the *fusca* slaves have nothing to complain about.

A strange thing about *sanguinea* is that slaves are not always present in the nest and are not necessary for its efficient running. Why is this? One probable reason is that young colonies of *sanguinea* require assistance that can only be got through slaves, whereas an old-established colony may well be able to cope on its own. The queen *sanguinea,* that royal lady who is really the heart of the nest, sits about in glorious decadence, laying eggs but doing little else; so dependent is she upon others for help that the only way for her to start a new colony is to go and stay in a *fusca* nest, leaving *fusca* workers to bring up her babes. And these, when they are present in sufficient numbers, will turn upon their hosts and clear the nest—Peaceful Penetration it has been called in other spheres—and not all is peaceful when Her Highness, shorn of her wings and fertilised, tries to sneak in by the back door; and many's the Queen who dies the death upon her honeymoon, for the *fusca* colony likes not the intrusion and resents the presence of the uninvited guest.

How very like human beings ants can be at times! How many of us have suffered the guest who dominates our house, drinks our sherry and pinches the newspaper at breakfast. But ants, unlike human beings, are fascinating creatures and are always worth an afternoon of observation. The *Formica* ants, by the way, cannot sting but can inflict a savage bite which, when sprayed with acid from their poison glands, can drive one almost frantic.

2. DUMBLEDORE

Who knows what this is? An ancient Berkshire name for humble-bee! It is rather a nice name, like flittermouse the bat. The dumbledore has always been my friend and my bee village has given me immense pleasure.

What and where is my bee village? It consists of nests carefully housed in wooden glass-topped boxes standing on a windowsill. For humble-bees can be thus kept under constant observation, like the hive-bees in the Reading Museum.

Humble-bees make very little honey, for, unlike the exploited hive-bee, only queens survive the winter, hibernating and not needing food. So there is no chance of getting a sugar allocation for humble-bees! Humble-bees do an immense amount of good, pollinating flowers and trees, even being kept in experimental glass-houses for pollinating purposes. It has been said that if all the wild bees and hive bees were exterminated we should be left with nuts and cereals only to feed upon. But this is not likely to occur even with the most irrational use of certain new insecticides, so one need not pursue the matter further.

Few people really know what happens in the life of a humble-bee, so I will explain. We must start in winter with a queen, immobile and creeping with leather-coloured mites, hidden under bark or snug in a mouse's run. Here she stays until the hot summer sun calls her forth to visit the golden flowers of the gorse and the catkins of the willow. Then she makes a nest, one can hardly call it building, though some species which nest above ground have to do a little more constructional work. Underground, however, the nest is little more than a ball of grass, left there by some mouse or vole the previous year. Returning from a foraging expedition, she makes a floor of pollen damped with nectar and lays half a dozen eggs upon it; then with wax from her body she builds a roof over the eggs and makes a honey pot near the door. Four or five days of brooding and she hatches out the larvæ which she feeds on regurgitated pollen and honey; in due time the larvæ pupate, the pupæ are broken open and a generation of worker bees come forth. As soon as these are hardened off they go off to forage in order to help their queen produce another batch of eggs, and to feed the developing youngsters. And so throughout the summer more and more workers are produced, the nest increased in size, the honey pots in numbers. Finally, towards the autumn, males and females come out of the nest and drift away, the male to die when the cold weather comes, the females, or queens as they are called, to hibernate and start their job of reproduction the following year.

So much for that—now let me tell you more about my village. Humble-bee nests are not difficult things to steal, but some of the underground nests require a lot of digging, for the passage may go down several yards. What is more, returning workers do not make the digging any easier. A little practice, however, goes a long way towards assurance and then it is as easy as pie. Workers coming from the nest are caught in jam jars, while their returning comrades are caught in a butterfly net and transferred to jars. The queen may come dashing out in a fury and can usually be recognised while still down below by her deeper rumbling buzzing. It is most important to catch her, for if she flies away one has to await her return—a somewhat tedious business !

The nest itself must be undermined and removed *in toto,* though the scavenging and parasitic creatures which live at the bottom can well be spared. The nest is now transferred to a wooden box of a sufficient size and in the dark of evening the jars of workers are tipped in. In the morning the cork which plugs the entrance hole must be removed and with luck one has the first house of the village. Once they are working contented, honey pots can be inspected, the old lady can be brought out with an angry buzz when the box is tapped, and later the appearance of the males and queens will be spotted through the glass. This is all theoretical of course and naturally things do not always go to plan. But I say again, it is not difficult and at Aldermaston I have had nests of seven different species living side by side upon my windowsill, and woe betide a bee which went into the wrong box. When really agitated in the nest humble-bees grow wet all over and considerable damage may be done to the health and strength of a colony this way.

I have never had any of the cuckoo-bees (*Psithyrus spp*) invade my window-sill nests but I think that this is due to the unsuitability of the nest site. Nests placed under flower-pots upon the ground will sometimes be invaded but one is rarely able to see the mortal battle which takes place between the cuckoo and the rightful owner. On the other hand, I have caused fights by introducing *Psithyrus* females into *Bombus* nests and it is well worth watching; the buzzing is terrific and the soft sides of the nest bulge and burst as the adversaries roll around locked together. *Psithyrus,* the cuckoo, does not appear in spring until the humble-bees have got their nests in order and the females then hunt the banks and grassy corners most methodically. Upon finding a suitable nest the cuckoo boldly marches in and has a drink from the honey pot. Meanwhile, the little workers watch as though knowing ruin is at hand. The *Bombus* queen knows just when the intruder is about to lay eggs in her nest and waits till then to attack. In doing so she is usually killed and what are left of her workers hang about the nest rearing cuckoo youngsters, not so much against their will but through simple ignorance. And so *Psithyrus* lays her eggs and produces her males and females; no egg of hers ever produces a worker.

Of the bees which I have kept on my window-sill, I like *B. jonellus*, the heath humble-bee, as much as any. At Alder-maston it was common in the heather and was very readily domesticated. *B. hortorum,* with its long dismal face, I have frequently kept and *B. pratorum,* which shows up so early in the spring, is another. The red-tailed *B. lapidarius* is also an early spring bee and not difficult to domesticate. Nests should not be taken too early in the season, or they are liable to fail; in fact the larger the colony the better. It is a very interesting game and one that I strongly recommend.

3. BAZE AND NATHAGALUM

Bee-keeping in the County is quite a thriving and lucrative hobby, as is shown by the attendance at the various lectures and meetings organised by the Berkshire Beekeepers' Association, and by the excellence of the honey exhibited at the various summer shows. A considerable amount of intelligent investigation into swarm control is going on and is often responsible for poor yields! While talking of swarms, the Berkshire words for the various casts which emerge from a hive after swarming are smart, cast and hitch, in that order, though they are nowadays collectively known as casts.

It is the geology of a county which is largely responsible for its bee-keeping and Berkshire has a lot to be thankful for. Along the Hampshire border the silver birch in spring is alive with bees and other insects, in the same way that later on the heather and the pine trees will be. But the heather is a doubt-ful quality, for it can be too dry for it, too wet for it, or more often than not, just when it is available, the weather breaks and the bees go nowhere near it. In early autumn here the bone-dry, peaty ground smells hot and dangerous and the purple pink of fireweed stretches away in the distance; this is ideal for bees, allowing them to build up good reserves and bee numbers increase in parallel. And holly also rings to the tune of busy bees, its florets swaying beneath their weight. In gardens pretty flowers are not of much avail, though they need the pollinating visits, but round the towns and leafy parks the limes send a sweet sticky call to the bee-keeper and many a hive is moved to fill with the popular lime honey.

The moving of hives has only been practised to a small extent, most people preferring to keep their bees somewhere down the garden. But the movable apiary can do great things, travelling round the orchards, the clover, the charlock, the lime and the heather. But one wants time, money and petrol, all of which are singularly lacking nowadays.

Bee-keeping of course is a really ancient habit and there is evidence that mead, a fermented honey drink, was the earliest of the man-made intoxicants. No doubt at first wild colonies were robbed for their honey, then came the straw skepp and the sulphurous extinction of the colony at the end of the season. All very wasteful, but Rome was not built in a day, and even now the practice still persists in villages, though the skepp has given place to the wooden hive. For those who would like to make mead here is a recipe which I can vouch for, it being my wife's practice to use the cappings and washings for this purpose each season. Like all counties, Berkshire bees have to be kept in touch with domestic events, particularly the cottage colonies which live in hives little better than the straw skepps of old.

(1) To make "Sack Mead." "To every gallon of water put four pounds of honey and boil it for three-quarters of an hour, taking care to skim it. To every gallon add an ounce of hops; then boil it for half an hour, and let it stand till next day; put it into your cask, and to thirteen gallons of the liquor, add a quart of brandy. Let it be lightly stoppered till the fermentation is over, and then stopper it very close. If you make a large cask keep it a year in cask."

(2) To make "Cowslip Mead." "Put thirty pounds of

honey into fifteen gallons of water and boil till one gallon is wasted. Skim it, take it off the fire, and have ready a dozen and-a-half lemons quartered, pour a gallon of the liquor boiling hot upon them, put the remainder of the liquor into a tub, with seven pecks of cowslip-pips; let them remain there all night, and then put the liquor and the lemons to eight spoons of new yeast, and a handful of sweet briar; stir all well together and let it work for three or four days. Strain it, and put into the cask, let it stand six months, and then bottle it for keeping."

These both without question make a very excellent mead but not exactly a cheap variety. Nor is it the thick sticky stuff, but has a thin wine-like consistency. To make the sticky liquid stuff, the following instructions should be sufficient and are those which the cottagers of the "Vale," both Wiltshire and Berkshire, used to make under the strange name of "Natha-galum," similar names but with different vowels occur in other counties. As you will see this is quite a cheap mead, quite different from the others which smack of Mrs. Beeton but come from another ancient tome. Once the honey has been drained from the combs, these are put into a vessel and water added according to the quantity of comb available. After a good soaking the wax is removed and the remaining liquor is tested for its sweetness. To do this an egg, presumably a hen's egg, is put into the liquid and like the witch in the village pond either sinks or floats; if the egg floats the sweetness is correct but if the egg sinks, it must be rescued—a sticky business if the vessel is deep and the honey crop has been good—and the liquor diluted until the egg does float. Then comes the boiling, which takes half an hour, after which it is strained and casked. Shortly the liquor becomes ripe and strong, "seductive to the taste" and highly alcoholic. The wax, which was removed early in the proceedings, was dried and sold to the dealers for a shilling or one and twopence a pound, and if there was honey to spare, this was also sold, at sixpence a pound. The mead on the other hand was not sold, but kept at home for high days and holidays. Things have altered since then and with all the expense of modern bee-keeping and the shocking summers we are blessed with, the black-market price of five or more shillings a pound for honey alone makes bee-keeping a profitable concern.

4. SNAKES AND LIZARDS

All three British snakes have been recorded from Berkshire and both lizards, though the smooth snake and its prey, the sand lizard, have been found only on the heathland near Wellington College; I myself have never seen them outside Dorset, where they are not uncommon. The slow-worm, which of course is a lizard and not a snake at all, is common everywhere, frightening delicate ladies but otherwise carrying on in its own quiet way, each year producing a batch of about nine youngsters, hatched from the eggs within the body of the mother. Grass snakes there are in plenty especially in the wooded valley of the Pang, where on a fine spring afternoon a dozen or more may sometimes be seen curled up asleep in the leaves just outside the woods, though the best place I know of to see them is across the Thames to Mapledurham and the Hardwick woods, but this of course is Oxfordshire and I must not trespass.

As everyone knows the grass snake lays her eggs in dung heaps and other fermenting places so that the heat may incubate and hatch them. The eggs are peculiar things, white and with a paperlike shell. At Woodhay I once ran over a female, bursting the eggs from her body; such eggs as were not damaged I collected and kept in my laboratory incubator on damp cotton-wool; for a while all went well, the eggs increasing in size as they absorbed liquid, but then one day they collapsed and that was that. A pity, for I would have liked some baby snakes, but the full incubation period of nearly ten weeks makes constant attention rather difficult.

Snakes swimming in the Thames are no uncommon sight, though I suspect that these are from the Oxfordshire bank; swimming is not only for fun, for grass snakes eat newts, tadpoles and frogs, but it is always a wonder how snakes get through the water in the way they do.

To see adders you want to go to the Mortimer and Padworth commons along the Hampshire border, where in summer there are hundreds of them curled up in the heather or hissing at your shoes. The cross or inverted V on the head will be sufficient to tell you when you see an adder, and it never has the grass snake's yellow patches. And although he will hiss frightfully and undoubtedly will bite your finger if you poke it at him, he is not so dangerous as we are led to believe. His mouth is too small and socks and trouser-legs absorb the poison; but for all that, I would not have children running around with bare feet. Dogs do from time to time get bitten and the result is usually fatal; a goat of mine was once bitten and developed a head nearly as large as its body, but after suffering a good deal of discomfort it recovered.

Lizards are not so often seen as snakes, but the common lizard does occur along the Hampshire and Surrey borders and in the heathland areas around Newbury and Bucklebury. In colour they vary from fawn to dark purple on the back, and from pale yellowish green to red beneath. It is largely due to their colouring that they are so rarely seen; one's eye really has to be in to do much good lizard hunting—the lizard's eye, of course, is always in and he can tell exactly where you are looking and is not in the least deceived if you put your hat on the wrong way round, or wear your shoes back to front. Flat on a stone or on the hot sand nothing moves except—and this is what you must watch for and see without looking at it—the sides of his neck, alternately contracting and dilating. Having spotted him, the only way to keep him under observation is never to look at him! The first time you do will be the last for suddenly he'll be gone, goodness knows where. This sounds very Irish, but that is quite reasonable, for this little lizard is Ireland's only reptile!

If the fat ladies are caught early in summer, they will obligingly produce their young in the glass accumulator tank you provide for them, and fascinating little pets they make too. The sand lizard lays eggs and trusts to the sun to incubate them. What a wonder the species survives! And when you pick up a wild lizard for goodness' sake don't make him shed his tail. The stump is not pretty, and the new tail, which takes several years to grow, is a poor thing when compared with the original.

5. BADGERS AND OTTERS

"Brock" is a great deal more abundant than people imagine, but he is a chap who likes to travel about "incog.," snuffling around after dark. He is much more strictly nocturnal than the fox, who is often on the move while the sun shines; "Brock" on the other hand sleeps during the day, deep down in his "set." Sometimes he may be discovered asleep above ground, curled up in the sunny corner of some field, but this is a rare occurrence.

Most of our Berkshire woods hold a badger or two, as anyone who likes to prowl about at night can discover for themselves. And as he lives by night, crowded towns have no terror for him. I know where badgers live within ten minutes' cycle ride from Huntley and Palmers' factory—and foxes too!

There are day-time signs of badgers which the trained eye will quickly spot; near a "set" there will be innumerable lavatory scrapings, for, cat-like, the badger is house-trained, but unlike the cat he does not bother to camouflage afterwards, leaving his pits open for all the world and all the flies to see. Again cat-like, he loves to stand against a tree and sharpen his claws, leaving the trunk to tell its tale. And the nests of humble-bees and wasps scraped out and devoid of grubs—who else but "Brock" would do this?

Badgers have been accused of poultry thefts, and they are strong enough to overturn a quite sizeable chicken house. Eggs they love and will leave little of both "setty" hen and eggs or for that matter a pheasant or partridge. Keepers don't like them because they are so infernally difficult to trap, and digging out is a dreadfully long job, for the badger can dig quite as fast as any keeper. In olden days, terriers were kept for badger digging; wretched they looked, those undersized little fellows, but like the hunt terriers we know to-day were just about one hundred per cent. "guts." You won't see many of these dogs around nowadays, though the German badger-dog—dachshund—is common enough. And only very occasionally, tucked away in some cobwebby corner of the cottage kitchen, you may discover the old tongs used for

pulling badgers out of dark damp earth. And what a bite one
of these animals can give; it is even said that a human hand
or foot can be cut clean off in one snap! Look at those
shoulders, running straight into his head—talk about bull-
necked! If you ever see a skull take a look at the great keel
at the back, remember the muscles and vow never to touch a
wounded badger!

In the cottage where you saw those tongs they'll probably
remember the taste of badger hams and they may even
remember some of the other uses to which this poor animal
was put. Badgers and foxes, by the way, are the wild hosts of
our human flea! Domestic hosts are pigs, goats and dogs and,
horrible to relate, human fleas can live and breed on pig
manure without any blood meals! Hence the alarming infesta-
tions of fields and orchards, not to mention houses. It has
been suggested that man first picked up fleas when he lived
in caves, since he had first of all to drive out certain other
animals with whom he refused to share the cave.

Like badgers, otters are generally considered to be much
less common than they really are. They also move at night
and, unless disturbed, spend the daytime sleeping, curled up in
some hole beneath the river bank. Otters must have visited
all of Berkshire's streams at one time or another and I have
heard many tales of them, but once, only once have I seen
one. Those who fish the rivers in the early hours of morning,
or walk the banks before the day is light, are the most likely
to meet an otter, for during the night he travels far, and
returns home when the first curlew wakes the lark and dogs
start barking in the farmsteads.

The one occasion I saw an otter in Berkshire, I was doing
a bit of private fishing sitting huddled up in an old coat,
wondering why I was not comfortably at home in bed.
Suddenly I saw a wave, V-shaped, passing ahead of me,
against the current; I followed it down the bank a bit but in
the dark I made noises and it dived. There was no question
what it was, for I saw the long dark body behind that wave—
a bitch I guessed and not a large one at that. And that was
all I saw; none of those exhibitions of aquabatics one reads
about and which are not uncommon in wilder parts of England.

Boulter's Lock

6. HEDGEHOGS, MOLES AND SHREWS

I have had several household hedgehogs but I cannot pretend they have been a success, and one after another they have been shown the door. The young ones are perhaps the most interesting, especially if the mother has been caught at the same time. When asleep she snores like a "grampus" and when the young lose her they shriek in the most impressive manner. Once their spines have darkened the young are easily reared without mama, but before this, when the spines are nearly white, they will almost certainly die if taken away from her. The babes are born in July and August, five or six of them, and a family out for an evening stroll is a sight to see.

One summer when my evenings were free I used to sit with a rifle waiting for crepuscular rabbits; often, then, I saw things which I was not looking for; hedgepigs there were in plenty in the woods and they used to venture out into the meadow in the dusk, the young ones sqeaking when mama ran ahead of them. They would proceed in a line, like a "crocodile" of schoolgirls off to church, but out, I think, more for exercise than for anything else. There were not many slugs and snails here, but there were plenty of beetles of one kind and another, and at the right time the heather was full of birds' nests; the hedgehog is a great lover of eggs and will, given time, deal with all the partridges' nests in nearby ditches; he will also reduce the small bird population quite considerably, for has he not the evening, the whole night and early morning free for bird-nesting? Incidentally, he can climb bushes and trees like an expert, and if he falls, why, he simply rolls up and bounces like a ball.

The hedgehog is relatively free from surprise attack, though both the fox and badger have their ways and means of opening him up. I have never seen this happen, nor met a man who has—in fact, it is not a very likely thing to stumble across. Perhaps it has been tried out in zoological gardens or with tame foxes—but it makes a good story, so why worry? My dog did it once, but then he'd do it anywhere; the effect was nil, unless the hedgehog closed up tighter; dogs, of

Maidenhead Bridge

course, are no longer carnivores, particularly not gun-trained spaniels, and have not the art with which to charm.

I should think that death on the highroad is the hedgehog's greatest fear, judging by the number of nasty "pressed copies" one sees. Finally, if you want to do something useful with hedgehogs, just "pepper" one with DDT dust and quickly wrap it in a napkin. You'll be surprised when you unwrap it a few minutes later, and I am always interested in examining fleas!

Now as to "Wants, wunts, or wands" and "shoe-mize," I have never kept any of them as pets. "Wants"—moles you probably call them—are said to have given their name to Wantage, but there's no need to believe that. (Wantage is actually an ancient river name, though whether the river gave its name to the village upon its banks, or vice versa, is unknown, and anyhow, the name has no intelligible meaning.) Moles, of course, are common throughout the County, annoying farmers and gardeners alike. Not that they eat anything but worms and insect grubs, though they have been accused of sucking partridges' eggs; and hedgehogs have been accused of emptying cows' udders, and nightjars of doing the same to goats, don't forget. And gypsies sit in their caravans all night, reading the "Good Book" I suppose.

It is difficult to weigh up the "pros and cons" of the mole; it doesn't matter how many grubs he eats if he gets into a lawn or bowling-green, nor if he uproots young plants and leaves the ground hollow beneath; and we can't really approve of all the earth-worms he eats either; in meadowland he may do some good by his drainage, if his mounds are not too numerous; "mole drainage" is a recognised agricultural practice, of course, but how many farmers know that it is the male mole which is emulated, the runs of the sow twisting and turning quite unlike the long straight tunnels of the boar.

Moleskin caps and waistcoats are out of fashion now and what happens to the thousands of moles which are caught each year I do not know. Expensive fur linings? But the dead mole becomes flyblown more quickly than any animal I know, and that must dispose of a lot of them.

The common shrew or "shoe-mouse" is often heard though rarely seen until the autumn, when many of them are found dead on garden paths—though why they are dead nobody seems to know. During their lifetime, shrews never stop eating for more than the odd half-hour, and it is said that starvation for one hour will kill them. Insects they eat and nothing else, their tiny snouts for ever on the move. Often I have heard their squeaking in the grass but rarely have I discovered one by following up the sound, which, like the "chirrups" of the great green grasshopper, are remarkably difficult to place.

Now about these dead ones; zoologists have decided that they are all of about the same age, that is to say, approaching their second winter—by the way, I refer only to those shrews which lie dead, showing no signs of what might be called "unnatural death"; males killed in mortal combat earlier in the year show a quite different appearance. One September I gathered together all the dead shrews I could lay my hands upon; both common and lesser shrews were there, and both sexes in near enough equal numbers. I intended to dissect these shrews but I could not find the time. My idea was that in their old age they became incapable of catching insects at the necessary rate and thus died of starvation. That being the case, their empty tummies should be visible in dissection. But whatever the cause—and all sorts of theories have been advanced—the most amazing thing is the number which die at the same time, for they don't die only on garden paths I'm sure.

Because they feed throughout daylight, these little animals (the lesser shrew is the smallest of all our mammals) are often captured by birds of prey, while at night owls take their toll, and the easily recognised skulls are frequently found in pellets.

7. "HARNETS"

Because of my profession I often get called upon to deal with swarms of bees, and nests of wasps and hornets. While I cannot look upon these expeditions as part of my official "job," I have never refused because I know what a nuisance these things are to those who do not enjoy them, and I know that I myself do enjoy the whole business even though it may be rather "prickly."

But I cannot pretend I enjoy destroying hornets' nests. Ethically the thing offends me and I prefer not to be invited to take part in such vandalism. But occasionally it has to be done, where the nest is a real inconvenience or where the hornets are frightening children. Believe it or not, hornets are much less "prickly" than wasps and hive-bees, and though I've investigated many nests I've not yet been stung, whereas it is no uncommon thing to be attacked by some stray wasp or bee which should know better. But there we are, and the hornet for all its size and fearful appearance is just longing to be friends!

I've seen hornets from all parts of Berkshire and if anything I should say that they are on the increase, especially in the Windsor Park region, where numbers of hollow trees provide ideal nesting sites. Various other insects are mistaken for hornets, the most interesting, perhaps, being the horntail or wood-wasp, which was not uncommon at one stage during the war in the anti-tank ditch between Calcot and Theale; here, also, the gigantic ichneumon parasite *Rhyssa persuasoria* was to be seen, searching the soft-wood props for wood-wasp grubs; it is quite incredible that this ichneumon should be able to locate the host grubs within the wood, and even more incredible that it should be able to insert its one and a half inches of ovipositor into solid wood in order to lay its egg on the wood-wasp grub.

Please dont hurt hornets unless you really must, for they are so much less dangerous than bees; and if you do ever handle a hornet, notice that it is not black and yellow like the other wasps.

A large hornet's nest is a truly wonderful affair—one I saw hanging in an outside "privy" reached from the roof almost to the seat and had put that place out of commission most of the summer! A nest like this has a yellow paper shell covering the tiers of cells, but in a hollow tree or in thatch the shell is dispensed with, and the cells are exposed to view. The smaller wasps always surround their cells in a paper envelope;

the "paper," of course, is made from wood shavings chewed from or off posts and railings. One nest I investigated was made largely of fibre-board chewings. But hornets are not so fussy and they normally use rotten wood from which to make their pulp and the colour of the "paper" varies with the wood used. It is usually much coarser than the "paper" made by the smaller wasps and at the same time is much more brittle.

Hornets hunt both day and night, though on a really rough night, when the moon is hidden behind scurrying clouds, when trees sway from side to side and rotten branches come crashing down, discretion is considered the better part of valour, and all sensible hornets remain at home; and, of course, the night-flying insects they prey upon are all at home too, so there would be little point in venturing outside.

8. POTAMOGETON

What is it that makes a river so dear to us? Surely it isn't the shouting holiday crowds at any of the fashionable riverside places, the splashing of paddles, the throbbing of engines. But no, this is not the river, no more than Hampstead Heath bank holidays crowds represent our English countryside.

To understand the River, or any river for that matter, you must go to Constable, a painter who really got the feeling of an English river. And what did he see, what did his brush produce which is so special? Peace, the peace of old mills, of old trees, of cows lazily flicking flies with their tails, legs and udders deep in the cooling stream, of water-lilies and sedges, of moss and lichen, the lazy heat of a summer afternoon. He paints a peace as old as the streams themselves, where the only sounds are part of the picture and strike no discord.

I could show you places along several of our Berkshire rivers quite as lovely as Flatford and East Bergholt, where an artist could spend a lifetime, where a naturalist could spend more. And I know the secret of the river—the little backwaters like chapels opening off some majestic nave, where redpolls twitter among the red-galled osier leaves, and reed and sedge warblers keep up a never ending chatter. Almost, one can see the "reed pheasant" sitting, beautifully moustached, in the silent rushes, and over the bank, where the water is shallow, a heron, old as time itself, examining its own reflection. And just occasionally a plop and the stillness of the surface is broken by a V-shaped ripple as a water vole—why call him rat, poor fellow—goes about his business, inspecting the roots of horsetails and sedges, his basic diet. And sometimes a sound, part rustling, part clicking, denotes a dragonfly moving with a speed quite absurd in the heat of the afternoon. Shafts of sunlight play upon a water-lily, upright and white, yet languid, like some bride princess in a film, the leaf her train and all around the *Potamogeton*, Nature's confetti. This is the river-peace which Constable knew, which Peter Scott hints at so tantalisingly in many of his paintings, the peace into which Seeby painted birds and Robert Gibbings quietly and determinedly thrust his broad shoulders. At bottom it is the peace of being lazy.

9. TREE-RATS AND SKUGS

I have to-day seen a red squirrel—no, not in Berkshire, alas, but in Scotland. But it reminded me of a few paragraphs in the *Victoria History of Berkshire*; these paragraphs refer entirely to the red squirrel, quite simply called squirrel (though in dialect called by the singularly unpleasant name "Skug"), for there was no need to call it otherwise, no more than there is need to refer to the "red fox"—the reason is plain enough.

At that time, the end of the nineteenth century, it seems that squirrels could be divided into two types—those which lived mostly in private gardens and were so unafraid of human beings that they would enter houses by open windows, and would steal the nuts while you were dreaming over the port; the other kind lived in the woods and were round the back of the tree before you could say Jack Robinson. So when you next see a grey squirrel, remember that you have something to avenge. They do a lot of damage too, so there is every excuse. Personally, I always shoot the rotten things if I can—feed them to the ferrets or to myself, or leave them to the flies; and have you noticed how the skin comes off the tail when you swing its owner round your head? No wonder they are called tree-rats.

10. INSECT INTRUDERS IN A BERKSHIRE BEDROOM

During the so-called summer of 1948, I was struck down by the adult manifestations of a childhood disease. For a while human visitors were forbidden, but no one said that insects should be kept away. So with little else to relieve the boredom of those days, I watched my insect visitors like Bruce his spider. There was a static population of house flies, though not, I think, always the same individuals; the lamp bulbs were their Mecca, and they seemed to do little else but play around them; occasionally a bluebottle came in and once a green-bottle, but neither was interested in anything but getting out again. One morning there were several cluster flies upon the window but I did not see them arrive; that is a habit of cluster flies and I knew there would be hundreds of them on the yellow umbels in the field below.

One afternoon, when the sun shone and it was really very hot, a drone-fly came in and, settling on a book, proceeded to scratch his tummy and his back with his legs; the same afternoon a small black and yellow hover-fly ventured in and was soon tied up in a spider's web—I did not see his going but he was not there next day. Of mosquitoes there were not many, thank goodness, for if anything really annoys me it is that maddening whine which ends in loss of blood and a lump on the nose; one great fellow with long banded legs gave me some trouble; his name was *Theobaldia*, but that is not what I called him and eventually he died a bloody death.

The moths were quite an interesting selection; the greatest force came out of drawers and cupboards, leaving their hide-outs in my trousers and pullovers to look around for pastures new. On two successive nights, beautiful swallow-tail moths fluttered on the window-pane but failed to find the way in. Often pretty buff and pink ruby tigers came to the lights, and it was no uncommon sight to see four or five of them at one time—their tufted caterpillars I had seen before on the golden-rod in the garden. Cinnabars, with lovely pink hind wings, once or twice came in, but July is late for them and their black and yellow caterpillars were common on the ragwort before I retired to bed. They made a pretty sight flying with the ruby tigers. A dismal Noctuid, the heart and dart moth, crept down my neck one night, cooked silly on the lamp above my head. One morning there was an Old Lady sulking in the roof of my four-poster bed—I had not set eyes on one since I came to live in Berkshire, just on ten years ago. And one morning my wife picked up a male lappet, much worn and quietly passing out on the window-sill. A white ermine came one night and, unusual for this species, forsook the lamp and went away. The largest of my visitors, a privet hawk, appeared one morning on the velvet curtain; it never moved all day, nor did it move during the night; some time during the following day I foolishly asked my wife to put it out of the window, but it was very dopy and fell to the ground where I expect the chickens or the cats killed it.

A thousand little moths flew around the lamp each night, but I did not know their names. The only butterfly that came in was a peacock, which fluttered at the window until pushed out. Every afternoon wasps came in and inspected the room and its occupant; perhaps it was my sprouting beard which intrigued them—if it was I'm glad because it intrigued no one else! These wasps never came during the morning, and they entered through the windows on one side of the room only, and one day, when I deliberately had those windows closed, they did not come at all. Other wasps, the solitary ones, came in from time to time; some wasted their energy hunting for greenfly on the curtains, while others searched the furniture for nesting-holes; the carved columns of the old four-poster were particularly attractive to the mason wasps. A brilliant red and green chrysid wasp, I guessed it to be *Chrysis ignita,* the commonest of the ruby-tails, came about two o'clock one afternoon and was quite frantic to get out again. The only hive-bee that came in got trapped between the open window panes; considering that ten hives containing so many hundreds of thousands of bees stood less than a few seconds' flying time from my window, this was disappointing;

I know my wife was very busy and perhaps she never "told" them.

With beetles I was unlucky, a single specimen of one of the smaller dung beetles which arrived late at night being the sole representative. If I had only gone sick a fortnight or so earlier I should have had a lot of fun with stag beetles, for every evening for at least a week hundreds of these creatures floated down like paratroops, their great mandibles sticking up and their legs waving about in front of them. Where they came from I know not, but they buzzed down into the nut hedge behind the house, where the cats hunted them, occasionally leaping and screaming as though possessed of evil spirits, when those great jaws closed on tender nose or lip. But the cats used to win in the end, for morning showed heads and mandibles everywhere, the bodies safely inside the cats! I found only one female, and in all the dozens of males I caught there was tremendous variation in size, from mighty "royals" measuring four inches in length down to mere "prickets" of little more than two. The larvæ live in decaying oak, gate-posts being a favourite site and it takes them five years to attain maturity.

In another wood-feeding beetle to which I at one time devoted my attention, I found that small individuals were caused by larvæ pupating at an earlier stage than was normal, due to undernourishment, among other things.

One gets this sudden appearance of insects in overwhelming numbers in creatures which take a long time to develop; the reason is quite plain, for the females of one horde produce another every so often. No burying beetles sat around me, vulture-like waiting for the end, neither did I hear the awful tapping of the death watch; being an entomologist saved me that amount of worry, but burying beetles or carrion beetles, to give them their other name, are filthy creatures at the best of times and I should loathe them in my bedroom.

11. SWAN SONG

The people of Reading and other Thames-side towns are well accustomed to swans floating gracefully on the river, proud and haughty, long neck erect and tiny head forever watchful, eyes snake-like, so that one expects a forked tongue; or at midday, when working men eat sandwiches where the Kennet cuts through the ancient town, a dozen or more swans stand, one-footed and headless, one snake-eye scarcely distinguishable but none the less watching that none should disturb the postprandial sleep of anatid royalty. And fortunates like me have stood on Caversham Bridge and seen the courting, heard the love-song of this bird and, entranced, have let the hours slip by watching the dipping breasts, the arched wings, the serpentine necks twining and crossing. How proudly does cob woo pen, what promises he makes as he dips his head to meet hers beneath the water, heedless of the crying gulls, whose swooping flights are surely nothing less than peeping, their voices a "Lohengrin" to the courtship, a background of music to remind of wild places where ancestral swans made love in thousands, no less proud than these of our rivers and lakes. And on winter afternoons, when snow clouds fill the heavens and rivers sough in their banks, measuring the reed stalks and angrily awaiting the freedom of the meadows, then the great swans fly low across the countryside, necks extended, the sound of their mighty wing-beats penetrating the lighted cottage kitchens so that men look out, and wonder how long before the snow begins.

Why are they on Berkshire waters, these great birds that men say belong to the King? They are here because some seven hundred years ago at least this majestic bird was given royal patronage or perhaps to put it more explicitly, none but the King should taste its meat, should know the flavour of a cygnet's breast. The earliest definite reference to Berkshire swans is a demand from King Henry III to the Sheriff of Berkshire and Oxfordshire in 1247, that ten swans should be sent to him for a feast in Winchester (the Royal Order included 10 boars, 50 hares, 12 peacocks, 600 chickens and just as many wild duck and wild geese as the Sheriff could manage !).

Rather more than one hundred years later, in the reign of the third Edward, a King's Swan Master was appointed, who had control over all swans upon the Thames and its tributaries for twenty miles on either side between London and Oxford, and he was given powers to effect this control. Then, as now, all unmarked swans flying at liberty belonged to the King, and in 1356 Edward III granted for seven years his right in unmarked swans to the "Warden and College of the King's Free Chapel of Wyndesore." A statute of Edward IV restricted the ownership of swans to owners of property of not less than five marks, probably because the proud distinction of owning swans was being jeopardised by the practices of unworthy people. To augment this, a swan-mote was held in various places to enquire into the matter and to bring to justice any man found guilty of taking swans and cygnets with hooks, nets, "lymestrynges" and other engines or by taking eggs. From the Rolls of the Swan Masters, the names and marks of the lawful owners have been brought to light, largely due to the efforts of Norman Ticehurst, so well known to all serious ornithologists. The "marks" were the only means of determining ownership at the annual "uppings" and were located on the upper mandible, the leg or the foot. Thames swans were marked only upon the mandible, though there is some reason to suppose that where, for any reason, the King confiscated a marked swan, his own mark would be made upon the leg, since two marks upon the bill were unlawful. One might suppose that the "mark" would be the owner's arms, but in Berkshire at any rate this is not so, for it is known in three instances only.

I cannot here attempt to describe the Berkshire swan marks; in an article in the *Berkshire Archæological Journal* of 1932, Ticehurst illustrates 140 and I must direct the curious to examine these for himself. It must be sufficient for me to say that the marks consist of lines both longitudinal and transverse, roundels and annulets, semi-circles, triangles, rectangles, chevrons and small triangular side-gaps. The religious houses usually marked with priors' staffs in a variety of positions and with the addition of annulets and roundels, an established mark could be "differenced"—that is to say, made different, by addition or subtraction or by conversion (for instance, changing annulets to roundels and vice versa). "Differencing," a custom discovered by Ticehurst from a study of the Swan Rolls, was a means of slightly altering an existing mark prior to upping and before marking free (*i.e.*, unmarked) birds so that swans thus marked could be separated from others bearing the parent mark. This seems to have been practised largely by successive generations of a family all using the same parent mark, and by the successors of abbots' and priors' marks after the dissolution of the monasteries.

Now who in Berkshire owned swans? For remember it was an honour to do so and was a sign of wealth and heritage. The Royal Family first, with six distinct marks, the abbots of Abingdon and Reading (3 and 5) using priors' staffs and annulets. The priors of Bisham (2), Hurley (3), Wallingford (2), using either priors' staffs or crosses. The convent of Reading used gaps, transverse bar and rectangle. It seems that the mayor and burgesses of Reading owned swans at least as early as 1501 on the Thames, Kennet and Calcot Brook, the number of birds reaching eight by 1521. The mayor and burgesses lost their interest and in 1543 let their swans out on lease, the "rent" being paid in cygnets to be handed to the mayor when required. Things went wrong after this and by 1642 the stock had dwindled to one old bird and four cygnets. Reading used five marks, all "differenced" from the original.

The mayor and burgesses of Windsor had tired of swan-keeping by the beginning of the sixteenth century and had let their swans die out and had forgotten their mark, but through the enthusiasm of one John Scott, of Dorney on the Buckinghamshire side of the Thames, a fresh start was made and a new stock built up. The ancient mark was sought for and discovered in the "King's Standing Roll" and John Scott presented the borough with one of his male birds marked with his own mark, which was "differenced" at the next upping by the addition of an annulet so that the bird should not be confused with his other birds. Some sixty years later the "game of swans" belonging to the Borough of Windsor stood at fourteen birds, not counting cygnets.

The list of Berkshire swan owners is lengthy and I cannot give it here, but I will mention a few of the names which will be familiar to anyone who has probed into the County's history.

The Earl of Salisbury at Bisham takes pride of place followed by Lord Norreys and successors at Bray, Wytham and Yattendon. Sir Thomas Englefield, followed by his son and Mistress Englefield; Sir William Essex of Lambourn; Sir John Fettiplace of Besselsleigh; Sir Thomas Fettiplace of East Shefford; Sir John Forster of Aldermaston and his son; Sir John Golafre of Fyfield; Sir John Kentwood of Childrey; Sir Francis Knollys and family of Reading and Stanford; Sir Thomas de la Mare of Aldermaston; Sir John Langford and Sir William Stafford of Bradfield; and, among others, John Winchcombe—Jack of Newbury.

Finally, let us just glance at the places where swans were kept and were free to travel the waterways; working the Thames downstream were Faringdon, Buckland, Kingston Bagpuize Fyfield, Besselsleigh, Abingdon, Sutton Courtenay, Little Wittenham, Wallingford, Basildon, Reading, Sonning, Wargrave, Hurley, Bisham, Cookham, Bray, Windsor. On the Kennet were Benham, Newbury, Woolhampton, Aldermaston, Englefield and Burghfield. On the Loddon were Arborfield and Ruscombe and Wokingham via the Emme Brook. On the Lambourn were Lambourn and Shefford, while on the Ock were Stanford, Denchworth, West Hanney and Childrey via its Brook leading to the river. On the Pang were Yattendon and Bradfield, and on the Emborne, West Woodhay; associated with the Broadwater were Binfield, Warfield and Winkfield. Thomas Harrison, who lived in Finchampstead about 1550, may have kept his swans upon the Blackwater and thus via the Loddon they swam into the Thames. There are a number of places where swan owners lived which cannot reasonably be associated with any water and in all probability these birds were kept upon the nearest river. It is on record that the Thames once carried an enormous population of swans; one could scarcely say that to-day, and any swans you may see belong to the King or the Worshipful Companies of Dyers and Vintners.

CHAPTER IX

BIRDS AND BIRD HAUNTS

L i k e all our English counties, Berkshire is poorer in bird species than it used to be. This is largely due to the growth of towns and villages and to the cultivation of the land, but at the same time one has to admit that the ornithologist of a hundred or two hundred years ago must shoulder some of the responsibility. I use the word "responsibility" rather than "blame" because the "bird-man" of those days did his job remarkably well if one allows his different approach.

To-day, in England, to shoot a bird in order to name it must surely be an unusual happening. Fortunately, we no longer think along those lines, for our field-glasses and books have made it unnecessary. In fact, we now tend to scorn the old collector, forgetful of the fact that our modern books and museum collections were founded for us by him and his gun. But Berkshire, like other counties, has now several ornithological clubs, bird-watching clubs and natural history societies, and it is to be hoped that the protection afforded by these will enable us to retain as Berkshire birds many of the species most threatened by the gradual merging of town and country.

I have an interesting old book on the birds of Berkshire and Buckinghamshire, published in 1868, by Alexander W. Clark Kennedy. It is dedicated to H.R.H. Prince Leopold, with whom the author had spent many happy hours at Windsor Castle, and from it we can draw a fair picture of the ornithologist of that time. The craze for converting one's house into a private museum was in full swing and the English countryside was, indeed, a dangerous place for a bird. There was then a brisk trade in birds for eating, birds for stuffing, birds for sporting or taming, birds alive, birds dead. Big men strode round their estates blazing away at anything and everything, while smaller men covered in nets and birdlime crept round hedges casting covetous eyes at larks and linnets. Schoolboys with torn breeches and pockets stuffed with eggs fell out of gigantic trees and over tremendous cliffs, or in a

manner more befitting young gentlemen, bought their eggs
with a nice discretion from old Mother Lipscombe in the side
streets of Eton. Nor were ministers of the church exempt,
and many a country parson visited the nests of his feathered
flock at least as often as he visited those of his human charges.
Taxidermists' shops abounded in most towns, and it was a
simple matter to have a favourite bird stuffed and erected
in a corner of the billiard room, or to have some vast snake
wound round the handrail of the banisters; to-day it would
probably prove impossible to get a white mouse set up locally.

Kennedy mentions no less than eleven taxidermists by
name, Hasell, Hall and Bartlet of Windsor, Drye and Fisher
of Eton, Ford and Briggs of Cookham, Wilmot of Maidenhead, Hebbs of Burnham, Ferryman of Datchet and "Old
Osman" of Oxford. This takes no account of Reading, Newbury, Hungerford, Wantage and Abingdon, each of which
had its complement. In addition to the shops, Kennedy refers
to the Lipscombe family who sold eggs in the streets of Eton,
Mr. Lipscombe driving round the neighbouring villages two
or three times a week, bringing back about three hundred
eggs on each journey. (He apparently specialised in "classy"
goods, refusing to have dealings with blackbirds or thrushes.)
No doubt Lipscombe had his counterpart elsewhere in the
County and it is easy to imagine the damage these commercial birdnesters must have done.

The protection and rearing of game birds, without doubt,
was responsible for the slaughter of hawks and owls first by
trapping and later by shooting. Game-birds, of course, were
originally reared for eating, and the idea of shooting them
was as foreign then as shooting Light-Sussex cockerels would
be to-day. Gilbert White, who was born in 1720, refers to
keepers with spaniels and guns, and points out that black-
game used to be abundant before shooting on the wing became
so common. Just when shooting for sport became popular I
do not know, but in 1828 and 1831 Acts to prevent night
poaching and to protect "game" were introduced, although a
licence was required to kill hares and pheasants as far back
as 1100. But apart from a desire to preserve certain birds
which provided either food or fun or both, little was done for

wild birds in general. A licence was required to shoot woodcock, snipe, quail and landrail not classified as game by the
1831 Game Act, though woodcock and snipe became "game"
for the purpose of the "Poaching Prevention" Act in 1862.
The rearing of game birds, as I have already mentioned, cost
many a lordly eagle his life, and from Berkshire we have
records of the deaths of golden eagle, white tailed eagle,
osprey, peregrine, buzzard, honey buzzard, Montague and
hen harriers, hobby, sparrow hawk and kestrel in the interest
of game preservation.

Somewhere about the middle of the nineteenth century,
certain naturalists began to take an interest in the preservation
of some of our wild birds which seemed to be in danger of
extermination by sportsmen and collectors. Bit by bit the idea
spread and in 1880 the first Wild Birds Protection Act came
about, making it unlawful, between March 1st and August
1st, to take the life of any wild bird, and mentioned in a
schedule some birds for which special protection was desired.
There were eighty-six names in the schedule, but many of
these are synonymous—for instance, fern owl, goatsucker,
nightjar, night-hawk—while others are collective, such as gull,
owl, tern, plover. The lark was added to the schedule by an
Act of 1881, and the sandgrouse in 1888. In 1894 and 1896
adjustments to the 1880 Act made it possible for the Secretary
of State to prohibit the taking of eggs and the killing of birds
not on the schedule, at the request of any county in England
and Wales. This was a great step forward and showed that
some people at any rate realised where the continued persecution of many wild birds was leading.

In 1895 several counties, but not Berkshire, applied to have
various birds added to the schedule and thus protected, either
temporarily or permanently. Birds of prey immediately came
in for protection as the following list, with the number of
county applications, will show: hobby (18), osprey (13),
merlin (9), buzzard (20), honey buzzard (16), Montague
harrier (2), hen harrier (3), marsh harrier (3); in addition
to these, the following interesting birds also were protected
from the egg collector : bearded tit (9), bittern (6), nightjar
(18), and great bustard (1—Suffolk, where the last breeding

Scene in Maidenhead thicket
Bray Church

record is 1832 !). All four birds formerly bred in Berkshire, the last great bustard having been seen near Lambourn in 1802; the bittern may still visit the Kennet banks, but as a breeding bird, I am afraid it is gone for ever; the nightjar on the other hand is abundant in several parts of the County, but I shall have more to say of this later.

No one can deny that the many Wild Bird Protection Acts which follow their 1880 leader have done much for our birds, yet I am convinced that they are not the answer, for they assume that an egg collector knows what eggs he is taking, that the shooting man can recognise a protected bird in the heat of the moment and, finally, that some policeman is aware of the killing and can identify the species. Also, it is the wrong way round, for the eggs are taken and the bird dead before any protection is afforded. As recently as 1947 Lord Winterton stated in Parliament that the existing law was strong enough to protect our wild birds if properly interpreted, and enforced and run. But how is this law to be enforced? Not by displaying lists of bird names outside police stations surely. Small boys don't take policemen bird-nesting with them and neither of them would be likely to recognise the eggs of a rare and, no doubt, hitherto unencountered bird. And keepers going their rounds can shoot what they please and who is the wiser? Perhaps there is no answer, but this is not the place to delve into the ethics of egg collecting and the shooting of non-game birds.

It is obviously not possible here to refer to all the birds which have set foot in Berkshire. A good list by Mr. H. Noble appears in the *Victoria County History,* and various other lists have been published before and after this, including one in 1926 on the birds of the Oxford district by the Rev. F. C. R. Jourdain, and there is a useful report by the Oxford Ornithological Society. I might perhaps mention a few of the more unusual birds, some or all of which have turned up unexpectedly in most English counties : dipper, bearded tit, blueheaded wagtail, golden oriole, woodchat, pine grosbeak, barred crossbill, snow bunting, rose-coloured pastor, chough, great black woodpecker, hoopoe, Tengmalm's owl, eagle owl, scops owl, marsh harrier, hen harrier, buzzard, golden eagle,

Abbey Gateway, Reading
Bull pens in the Artificial Insemination Centre at Shinfield

white-tailed eagle, goshawk, kite, honey buzzard, merlin, osprey, purple heron, night heron, bittern and little bittern, glossy ibis, long-tailed duck, eider duck, scoter, velvet scoter, Pallas' sand grouse, quail, spotted crake, crake, Carolina crake, great bustard, little bustard, avocet, black-winged stilt, grey phalarope, ruff and reeve, greenshank, bar-tailed godwit, whimbrel, black tern, sooty tern, Sandwich tern, pomatorhine skua, Richardson's skua, little auk, puffin, great northern diver, red-throated diver, red-necked grebe, Slavonic grebe, eared grebe, Manx shearwater, stormy petrel, Leach's petrel.

This imposing array is made up largely of birds which have very little reason for being on the Berkshire list, for immigrating or storm-bound birds will often break their journey and cause astonishment, like the puffin must have done which was discovered in Northbrook Street, Newbury, way back in 1816! I hope I shall never forget the lovely sight of terns hovering over a flood-pool near Blewbury in the spring of 1947. I was returning at dusk from a walk on Blewburton Hill and spotted a tern "fishing" in the pool. I was more than surprised to discover four more sitting on unsubmerged lumps of soil. I sat and watched them for some while, a redshank joining them; in the growing dusk two hares appeared and stone curlews started calling in the valley; it was cold and I was thirsty but I stayed there until too dark to see more.

A golden eagle was shot in 1924 on the Lambourn Downs and now adorns Reading Museum. Surely a ghost must haunt the conqueror, a proud arrogant ghost circling on outstretched wings, not an effigy condemned for ever to sit in a glass-walled case.

So much for the protection afforded our noblest British birds—a glass coffin and a brass plate, and this in 1924. And I have heard through Brian Vesey-Fitzgerald of an osprey which was shot much more recently in an adjoining county. I wouldn't shame my gun by so much as pointing it at an osprey but there you are, we are not all made alike.

If I were asked which I considered my favourite Berkshire bird, I should find it difficult to decide between nightjar, stone curlew and hobby. Chance has favoured me with the opportunity to watch all three, hobby and nightjar from my house in the Aldermaston Woods, and the stone curlew within a few miles of my present home in Basildon.

I count myself lucky, for how many have been able to sit in the kitchen doorway and see hobbies feeding their young. Hobbies were not uncommon in that part of Berkshire and we often saw them in the woods or circling high above pines in spring. I never saw one hunting the heather like the sparrow hawks, nor the hedges and meadows like the kestrels. Definitely a bird of the belts and spinneys, this little falcon would dash through the tree-tops like a mad thing, setting the magpies chattering and the jays cursing. Said to be the fastest of all our falcons, the hobby can outfly even swifts and swallows, and will leave a kestrel behind like some clumsy lout of the countryside. I never saw one attack a swift, in fact it was not often that I saw one attack any bird, but when it did the victim was more often than not a meadow pipit. Unlike the much larger peregrine, the hobby does not send its victim crashing to earth to be retrieved and eaten on the ground, but gripping it in its talons, carries it away to eat in some favourite tree. One misses the peregrine's "stoop" and sudden upward climb, for although the hobby will "stoop" it more often "gathers" its prey in the way a Rugger wing three-quarter will "collect" the ball while gaining speed and without any apparent change of direction. But insects form the main food, especially chafers, which are caught and devoured without alighting, dragon-flies of the "demoiselle" type are readily captured, for their flight is slow and floppy, but the darting here one moment and there the next flight of the larger *Æschna, Annax and Libellula* dragon-flies is often more than a match for our little falcon. This is not so much a matter of speed, for the bird is easily the faster, but is due to the dragon-fly's almost supernatural ability of being in two places at once! To recall once more the Rugger-field, it is the sudden side-step at speed that counts, that leaves the tackler stretched full length, his fingertips just touching what he hoped to hold; so with the dragon-fly, and many other insects too, for the moment they set off to run away they are lost.

For two years in succession a pair of hobbies nested near my house, but the second year a gale blew down the nest soon

after the young were hatched; the following year I was unable
to find a pair breeding. They are interesting birds to watch at
the nest, but owing to many other calls, I was never able to
devote much time to them. Some excellent photographs of
nesting hobbies, by Eric Hosking and Cyril Newbury, can be
seen in the 1947 volume of *Country Life*. Of the youngsters
which came down in the gale I have the fondest memories.
There were four of them, which is unusual, three eggs being
the normal number, and for about three weeks they all lived
apparently content in an out-house. Then unfortunately I was
called to a conference in London and when I returned, with a
supply of books on falconry, for I had made up my mind to
rear and train these birds, they were all dead. This was a
great blow and remains unexplained to this day, for they had
received just the same attention in my absence but from a
different hand. After the nest came down, the parent birds
hung about for several days, flying through the trees calling
loudly . . . kew kew kew kew. . . . Although the youngsters
could hear their cries, they showed no interest and the parents
apparently left the neighbourhood, for I neither saw nor
heard them again.

The nightjars were our evening companions each summer,
turning up on May Day, or soon after, and having gone by
early September. There were usually six or seven pairs on my
land, but I rarely found more than three nests each season.
One I well remember, for it was immediately below the bottom
strand of an electric fence and in my routine walks to cut
away bracken touching the wires, I narrowly missed decapi-
tating this bird with my hook. It was a late nest and she sat
until August 24th, after which she gave it up and left, the two
eggs disappearing one after another, probably into the
voluminous stomach of some magpie.

All through the summer evenings the nightjars used to float
around like gigantic butterflies, clapping their wings, rising
up to meet each other, turning away and circling round, rising
and falling, weaving and wheeling, as graceful as any ballet,
and without the slightly nauseating male in tights. What a
pity that these attractive birds fly in the dusk, when so much
of their display is missed; but like *A Midsummer Night's*

Dream in Regent's Park, the setting is so perfect that one fears to alter it, to lose the warm evening air and the smell of pines, and the grasshoppers in the heather. And of course the "churring" of other nightjars in the trees, almost continuous, like the tom-toms of some African tribe, rising and falling, driving the dancers into a frenzy of exertion, their wings clapping in the centre, their bodies meeting.

During the dance the male constantly calls "coo io" or "quick quick" as he floats with wide-spread tail and raised wings, and sometimes he will "hang" in the air, his open tail depressed. Many's the evening I have spent propped against a pine enjoying this courtship, smoking pipe after pipe, dreaming of the things I would do one day, and forgetting the income tax forms waiting to be filled in. Those who have not lived among nightjars may find it difficult to appreciate the fascination of their evening flight, the companionship of that churring song.

Nightjars breed in several parts of the County, but are most abundant in the south, along the Hampshire border, where on any summer evening they can be heard, if not seen. I know one road, now, alas, submerged beneath the clamour of an aerodrome, where I could meet nightjars "churring" in the middle of the highway and watch them in the glow of my headlamps. I had not realised till then that all this noise is made with a closed beak, somehow imagining a beak wide open, like the pictures one sometimes sees designed to illustrate the hairy mouth. This is definitely so, and the bird hunts insects with a closed beak, snapping at its prey rather than engulfing it. Occasionally the "churring" would be heard in the early dawn, drowning the voices of those miniature nightjars, the grasshopper warblers. Sometimes, especially when the nights were too hot to sleep, these little warblers would keep up their metallic trills for hours on end, but more commonly they would start with the first light of dawn, when the mist lay low in the gully and the pheasants were still in the trees.

This tiny bird, whose voice is said to carry more than a quarter of a mile, sings with beak open wide, the whole of its little body vibrating and its head moving from side to side. To

watch it one feels that it is taxing itself beyond the endurance
of so small a frame, that it must shake to pieces, its bearings
seize, so metallic is the sound it makes. In the course of several
summers I found but one nest, though two or three pairs breed
in that gully each year.

Turning now to the Downs, I cannot name a bird I love
more than the stone curlew. Locally it is known as a "curlew,"
but of course it is quite unlike that bird except for the plain-
tiveness of its call. It is essentially a bird of the wild open
places, of the junipers and warrens. Its weird call at evening,
"curlee, curlee, curlee," haunts the bottoms and the Ridgeway, the coombs and the hangings, and is answered by echoes
and by birds perhaps a mile away. To those who yearn for
the saltings and the marshes, who know the cold of gun
barrels and the last glimmers of day, I recommend this bird,
for its cry will stir up memories, perhaps almost forgotten,
of wild scenes, of wind and snow, the call of widgeon, the rush
of wings, and the acrid smell of drifting powder. How it all
comes back, that memory of days now gone, and places far
remote from Berkshire's earliest highway.

Up on the Downs among the barrows and the stunted
thorns, these birds live a life of relative security; few people
know their haunts, for who walks the Downs at dusk but the
poacher or the lover? Few hearts beat faster at that distant
cry "curlee, curlee, curlee" though some may feel afraid who
walk that road, where ancient man once shuffled through the
dawn of civilisation. Those who love the Downs by day should
try this experience in the dusk of rising summer. A short walk
up the Fairmile from the Blewbury road before the sun is
gone, and smoke a pipe while the evening chill is stealing
across the valleys. Peewits wheeling round in flocks, wings
vibrating, calling; a rabbit thumping as you move; a mouse
rustling in the ditch; and when you can see but a faint outline
of Unhill Wood you will hear them. First a single bird up by
Roden Down and Lowbury, then another and another, and
after that silence. Again a single bird and then a sudden
clamouring, perhaps twenty or thirty birds. Silence once more.
A bird so close that even in the dark you think you can see
him, answers from across the bottom, the cry taken up by

others behind you; occasionally some bird will fly across the track, probably a carrion crow and silent as the night itself; suddenly another clamouring and then silence. And if you wait and see the moon throw shadows half across the valley, shine on the flints and on the mist, you may perhaps hear them again, but if the night is dull and the moon obscured you will not hear again their voices.

I have met this bird often before on the Suffolk "brecks," where its eggs were no uncommon sight, but I have never come across a nest on the Berkshire Downs. Notices suggesting the presence of unexploded—and presumably unrequired—bombs and land mines do not encourage an expedition into the land where the stone curlews undoubtedly breed! Who knows, there may be neither bombs nor mines, but the stone curlews must have reaped the benefit of the doubt. Here on the Downs the great bustard once lived, and here the little wheatear spends the summer, nesting in rabbit-holes and beneath overhanging banks, and larks, buntings and pipits fill the air with music. And on a winter afternoon when the wind races through the dry grass and the crippled oaks, and the pigeons come over the scattered woods like rockets, turning to face the tempest before dropping to sleep in rows along the branches on the leeward side, then one sees the Downs in a different light; gone is the rolling curving "sea" of grass, the blue sky and the summer song of birds, gone is the purple of the pasque flowers and the background whine of bees and flies; instead, one might be on the very rim of Hell, so furious is the gale, so deafening the noise, so blinding the rain, and when the lightning sears the sky and thunder adds its weight, making the very ground rock, modern man may well tremble and crouch to gain protection, conscious, as was early man, of forces so tremendous that he could but hide and wait, no puny strength of his the least avail.

CHAPTER X

HORS D'ŒUVRES

SHORTAGE of food during the war sent people searching the countryside for additions to the rations. For the moment I am not concerned with the walking-stick gun and collapsible ·410, nor with the gentlemen who remove your henhouse as well as your hens under cover of dark, but with those people who, casting traditional "mumbo-jumbo" where it belongs, collect toadstools and eat them.

Berkshire could, and still can, boast of several groups of mycophagists, based largely upon the University and the Reading Natural History Society. My wife and I have been eating toadstools for many years and we know many who have done likewise, but it is rare to find a genuine country-man, a cottager, who would eat one. Perhaps we who have lived in towns and travelled abroad are accustomed to a greater variety of food, and are more prepared to experiment. I have met people who "didn't fancy" rabbit, wood-pigeon, venison and even pheasant, and this during war-time when most butchers' meat was so bad that the smallness of the ration was more of a relief than a disappointment; all these people would eat mushrooms—unless they were offered the toadstool, *Psaliota campestris*! Few people realise that a mushroom is every bit as much a toadstool as the more beauti-ful red-capped *Amanita muscaria,* with a gnome sitting cross-legged upon it, or the deadly *Amanita phalloides,* that wolf in sheep's clothing that not even a gnome can tolerate. It is also not generally known that one toadstool alone in Great Britain is a killer, and that this obeys all the silver-spoon tests of decency. It is the cad of the toadstool world, and its old school tie is so like that of the mushroom that the unwary are easily deceived and as easily die. This fungus, *Amanita phalloides,* is undoubtedly responsible for nearly all the deaths we read of associated with mushroom eating. There are about a dozen other toadstools which can produce horrible pains and very occasionally the death of otherwise healthy bodies, but the rest, and there are literally hundreds of them, are all edible, though not all are pleasant. I do not want to lead anyone astray by anything I say here, but the less like a mushroom a toadstool looks, the less likely it is to kill. The safest way, of course, is to buy one of Dr. John Ramsbottom's books and learn a bit about mycology for yourself.

Now toadstools, like flowers and birds, can be linked with types of countryside. Some grow in woods, some in fields, others in heather country, etc., and before starting out on an expedition, one can have a fair idea of what to expect. A large flat shopping basket or butter basket is the best container, and though fungi may be mixed when collecting they should never be mixed in cooking. Let us wander forth, armed with basket and knife (toadstools should be cut, not pulled out of the ground lock, stock and barrel) to some of the best Berkshire grounds.

The first area to be considered lies between Mortimer, Burghfield Common, Padworth, Silchester and Aldermaston. Starting at the Three Firs Inn, where a pint of beer will undoubtedly assist the coming search, the "horn of plenty" should be found within, say, three hundred yards of the Inn. It is not a common toadstool but where it occurs it is usually present in quantity. In looking for it we shall probably have picked up a number of *Boletus,* the caps of many nibbled by rabbits and grey squirrels. Three highly edible species occur commonly throughout the district, *Boletus edulis, Boletus versipellis* and *Boletus scaber*. The former is known as the "Cep" and has a bun-like dark brown cap on a thick pinkish stalk; *Boletus versipellis* is a taller and more elegant fungus and has a nice orange brown cap on a more slender white stem which is flecked with black. *Boletus scaber* is like *versipellis* but without the dull brown cap. All of these occur abundantly and their spongy tubes should be removed before cooking. I am not a great lover of *Boletus,* unless in an omelette, when it is delicious.

Proceeding again towards Padworth, there is a deep ditch where some years Chanterelles grow, looking for all the world like orange peel carelessly thrown away. It was this that caught my wife's eye, for during the war years orange peel was indeed a rarity, and in our house at any rate was never thrown away, but carefully retained for a variety of uses. This find was a great joy, for previously we had to journey to the New Forest to find it, where it occurred with a delightful *Hidnum,* to my mind even more lovely to eat than the Chanterelle. Unfortunately, the *Hidnum* does not occur in Berkshire so far as I know.

A short walk will take us to the Round Oak Inn where another pint will do no harm. If in luck, there will be horse mushrooms growing within a few hundred yards on one side of the road and parasols on the other. Some people will not eat horse mushrooms, I can't imagine why. But who would not eat the parasol, the queen of toadstools? For delicacy of flavour I would pit it against all your cultivated buttons. A little farther on, on the edge of Aldermaston Park, *Coprinus,* the ink cap, used to grow. Twice every day I drove past this spot and was able to choose my moment for cutting. All who have dealt with this toadstool will know that there is a critical date in its life, when it has reached its maximum size but not yet turned to ink—this is the time to cut and cook, washing out the grit which its road-side habitat provides. (I have noticed that country dogs, lost for inspiration, turn to this road-side fungus for routine inspections. The old roadman must have wondered why I drove a stake into the verge a few yards away!)

Turning into the woods by the footpath opposite Decoy Pond, crossing the brook and mounting the rise, one comes into a paradise for fungi. *Boletus* of several kinds, some of which turn a nasty blue-green, by oxidation, on breaking, suggestive (but not always correctly) of tummyache and pains; *Amanita rubescens,* a relative, a decent one, of the deadly *Amanita phalloides,* whose pink-flushed cap and pinky stem have many times made my breakfast taste the nicer; *Sparassis,* the cauliflower, that curious fungus clustered round some pine stump, full of pine needles which must be forced out under a tap before cooking; *Amanitopsis,* the "griselle," a delicate little toadstool, with slender stem and deeply striated periphery of cap, makes a lovely savoury, grilled on toast with red pepper and scraps of bacon fat. In one wood,

Tricholoma nudum, the wood blewit, grew a pretty violet colour against the leather brown of dead pine needles and fallen oak leaves; it was usually associated with favourite browsing spots for our goats. And in another wood, where timber had been felled to fight an earlier war, and heath fires had more recently cleared the heather and bracken, we sometimes found *Helvella esculenta*; spring was the time for this, and it was a glad day when we found it; more like a "marron glacé" than a toadstool, this close relative of the *morel* often eluded us, it seemed to depend so much upon suitable weather conditions. But when it did appear it was always in places where we had learned to expect it—I cannot tell you where because I have sold that wood and the present owner might not like to lose this fascinating and temperamental addition to his rations.

Armillaria mellea, the honey fungus or bootlace which is said to make wood luminous, was often found in huge quantities, and, though perhaps not in the top class, is certainly worth the trouble of cooking. As well as those already mentioned, there were a score of other toadstools which we ate and survived, but there were one or two which we never tried. The first and most abundant was the red-capped *Amanita muscaria,* a fungus considered poisonous in England, edible (when suitably cooked) in some Scandinavian countries and in some parts of Germany, and reputed to be useful as an intoxicant and aphrodisiac in some parts of Russia; whether one would totter or rush to bed, or painfully twist to death there, I have never felt inclined to investigate. Another is the stinkhorn, which looks a trifle odious and in the height of its bloom certainly is odorous. Actually, it is the egg (the immature fungus, sticky, shiny and egg-like in shape) which is said to be edible. Two kinds of this occurred in our woods, both equally offensive to behold; perhaps some reader of this will try out these eggs and let me know the result—for the time being I am content to take it on trust that they are not as horrid as they look.

Another locality from which I have fed freely is the land lying between Sulham and Oxford. Except for the heavily wooded area round Tidmarsh and Sulham, the land is chalk,

downland for the most part. The woods referred to contain
the usual woodland fungi : wood-blewits; *Boletus*; *Amanita
rubescens*; large numbers of *Russula*, a reddish- or purple-
capped species predominating, and said to be selective in its
poisoning abilities; several kinds of *Polyporus*, the most
common kind of which forms brackets on birch trees; this
and other species are not poisonous, but to my mind are .as
nice to eat as old football boots ! The cream of the Sulham
district is the *morel*, which is sometimes to be seen on sale
(but more often as a gift to some knowing local) at an inn in
Tidmarsh; I have never found it there and the spot is a
guarded secret. Turning from the woods out into the fields,
Marasmius oreades, the fairy-ring toadstool, is often abundant and is well worth drying for future use. Several fungi
respond to this treatment, and are often to be seen strung up
on threads around our kitchen fire. Toadstools may also be
bottled, as my wife has discovered, and they come in very useful when the fungus season is over. St. George's mushroom,
which forms rings like *Marasmius*, is frequently met with on
the Downs near Compton and Streatley during April, and
makes a delicious addition to a meal. *Lactarius deliciosus*, the
saffron milk cap, is not common, but I have found it in the
coniferous belts below the Ridgeway. This toadstool has a
sweet smell and when crushed exudes a milk, saffron-yellow
in colour. It is delightful to eat and is easily preserved in
brine. "Jews' ears" are often found in great quantities on old
elder trees and are nicer to eat than their rather gelatinous
appearance would suggest. I have found these commonly at
Basildon in my garden, and elsewhere in overgrown thickets.
Tricholoma personatum, the blue-leg or blewit, is not uncommon in meadows between Pangbourne and Streatley, and
high up above the latter village the "horn of plenty" is found.
Pleurotus ostreatus, the oyster mushroom, is not uncommon
in the woods; it is a rather shiny fungus which tastes better
than it looks. So do oysters for that matter. *Sparassis*, the
cauliflower, I have not found in this district, though it was
common enough in the pine woods at Aldermaston. The beef
steak fungus, *Fistulina hepatica*, is met with from time to
time on oak trees; I believe it grows on other trees too, but

I have yet to see one not on oak. It causes a staining of the wood, the "brown oak" beloved of carpenters and pretty box makers. It is much sought after by some toadstool eaters, but I look upon it as one of the nastiest I have tried.

Perhaps the greatest joy of all the Downs is the giant puff-ball, one of which from West Ilsley weighed eight pounds! What a meal, fried in thick slices with plenty of butter and home-cured ham! It is worth the trouble of cows and pigs to eat this, the grand old man of the fungus world. According to Dr. Ramsbottom, it was used in olden days, smouldering, to drive bees; as a means of carrying fire from one village to another; and when dried as a means of stopping bleeding. I have tried the last remedy after shaving and found it rather unsuccessful, but the square of puff-ball assumed a lovely pink!

So much for toadstools, a much-maligned group of eat-ables, for remember, it is nearly always the mushroom hunter who dies, though the toadstool man may have some awful pains.

The urge to augment rations has discovered other local products. The grey squirrel, for instance, that insolent robber of every woodland, provides an excellent meal. Known in Berkshire and in many other counties as the "tree-rat," there is a great deal more meat upon him than on a young rabbit of equivalent size, and in addition each squirrel killed is a bless-ing to the country. Keepers use them for "ferret grub" and thousands of skins are sent up yearly to earn a few pence each from the fur trade. One cannot pretend that our Berkshire ancestors ate grey squirrels, for these animals did not reach our woods until some few years ago, and for quite a consider-able time were more of a novelty than a nuisance.

The red squirrel, which I believe and hope is increasing in numbers in some parts of England, was an everyday sight in Berkshire, but I doubt if anybody ever thought of eating him. Not so the hedgehog, however. I have known the "hedgepig" or "hotchi-witchi," as it is called in some parts, eaten in a number of houses. This is no wartime novelty, but is a well-known dish of the gypsies, gyppos, dids or didicies, whichever name you care to use. I have been offered such a meal many times but have never accepted. I do not doubt "she eats a treat," but the thought of the little snuffly fellow wrapped in clay and cooked alive does not appeal to me.

Somehow this squeamishness does not hold for shell-fish, for I can eat my lobster as well as the next man, which makes me think of crayfish, another addition to the rations at certain times of year. These little lobster-like creatures live in several of our Berkshire rivers, and I know of excellent "fishing" spots in the Kennet, Emborne and Loddon. The whereabouts of the "spots" are usually carefully guarded secrets, known only to certain "locals" who will often fish at night so that they may not be seen and their favourite grounds "poached." The procedure is quite simple; an ordinary garden sieve, baited with kipper heads and carrion is gently lowered into the water at the end of a long pole. It is left down for the time of one or two pints (hence the clandestine behaviour of some fishers) and then gently raised full of crayfish. It is really quite simple to write about, but try it out in practice and see. The crayfish can move remarkably fast backwards and if at all alarmed will certainly not be in the sieve when it comes to the surface. They are allowed, or perhaps more accurately forced, to spend a night in salt water to clear out the muddy taste, after which they are treated like lobsters and taste just as good, especially if there are enough of them.

Eels, though not so abundant as they used to be, are still to be caught in the Thames and other rivers where once upon a time eel trapping was a not unimportant sideline for many a riverside cottage. I have tried various methods of eel catching which I learned long ago from an old Norfolk waterman, who could drink so much beer that even in those balmy days of threepenny pints, an expedition with him seemed quite expensive. He showed me how to sniggle an eel in shallow water, and how to bob for them in deeper water. I have never been very successful as a sniggler on the Thames, and anyhow it is a puerile method of fishing for food purposes, as only one eel at a time can be caught; bobbing on the other hand, which by the way consists of threading innumerable worms on innumerable lines of thick wool on which it is hoped innumerable eels will thread themselves, sometimes produces consider-

able numbers in a fairly short time; bobbing is done at night
when the eels are on the feed, whereas sniggling takes place
during the day, preferably a fine day, when eels protrude
their heads from holes in banks and muddy bottoms; eels,
of course, are sometimes caught when bottom fishing, but I
am convinced that there are far fewer now than there used
to be.

I have met people who ate adders and said they were good,
and the same applies to foxes and badgers. I have tried none
of these, though foxes' heads boiling have a most appetising
smell and, perhaps excluding a dog-fox carelessly skinned, I
do not see why they should not be eaten.

Moorhens are eaten in many Berkshire houses, and very
good they are too; they should be skinned, as they do not
pluck nicely and the skin is bitter. Jays I have often eaten and
they are well worth trying; although "vermin" to the keeper,
the jay is a gourmand in reality, and lives on the fat of the
land; during the war years jays increased enormously in
numbers, due to the shortage of keepers and the cost of
cartridges, and to-day most shoots hold more vermin than
game.

The rook is another bird which might well be mentioned
here. I am one who believes that a rook does a great deal
more harm than good, and I am sure that all rookeries should
be shot hard every year, for it is only by keeping the numbers
down that we shall eventually save our English rook from
extermination. Shooting young rooks when they can fly provides many a pleasant evening, and though one may not call it
"sport," young birds strong on the wing can provide some
very tricky shooting. Shooting young birds sitting around the
nest is nothing less than murder and can be justified only as a
sure means to an end, the reduction of numbers. After the
shoot, perhaps two or three hundred rooks are tied up in
dozens for anyone to take who likes, and rook pie is a
favourite country dish at this time of year. Breasts and legs
are literally torn off, there being no attempt to pluck or skin.
One very often accumulates far more rooks than are required
for immediate consumption and my larder is always well
stocked with breasts and legs bottled against a rainy day.

My wife certainly surprised the Women's Institute by exhibiting bottled rooks' breasts at one of their shows! No less surprising was to see cormorants (called "sea-goose") and curlews hung up for sale in a Reading shop! Sea-goose I tried once and rather liked, but a second attempt ended in a nasty, oily failure.

Caversham Bridge

CHAPTER XI

GAME BOOK

BERKSHIRE may not equal some other counties in its shooting propensities, but its downland partridges must surely rival
the little brown birds from anywhere else. Its pheasants, too,
are not to be despised, curling as well over the Pang and the
Kennet as over more famous places. Rabbits and hares
abound, and duck—mallard, teal, widgeon, pochard and
tufted—provide excellent shooting in several parts of the
County. Wily pigeons in their thousands flop into the softwood plantations, and woodcocks spring from the dry bracken
and, owl-like, flit round the tree trunks; twisting snipe are in
the meadows near most of the rivers, and occasionally geese,
when the winter is hard and the floods are out; deer too, in
some parts and, at any rate during the war when hounds were
reduced to a handful of couples, foxes, great red fellows who
slept at night and hunted largely by day, more accustomed to
the air-raid siren than the huntsman's horn.

I think in Berkshire I have shot at everything a man may
decently shoot at, but I am a naturalist at heart, and cannot
get into the deadly frame of mind which shoots first and looks
later—I miss innumerable duck in this way, for I would rather
miss a widgeon than kill some rarer bird. I long for marshes
and punts, long guns and waders, but one cannot have everything—one partridge torn out of the sky may be worth all
the duck a puntgun can kill. Punt-gunning, like deer-stalking
and shooting the neighbour's cat, depends upon the approach
for its thrill, the actual shot being rather a tiresome necessity,
an attempt to vindicate one part of the conscience against
another. But up on the Downs, one has no conscience in bringing down a left and right. One's conscience is not easily put to
test, so fast and high do the birds fly; the wind screams in
one's ears, each shot fills the eyes with powder, and occasionally, just occasionally, two little birds drop from the covey,
and fall half a mile behind. That is the sport of kings, and
whacks all your walked birds into a cocked hat. If you cannot

Three Mile Cross, Mary Mitford's village

hit a bird in the bottom, you'll never hit one in the head. Take these rifle people who call us "spray-gun merchants," take them to the Downs and show them birds. Real live birds, like sparrows in the sky, no time to think of wind allowance or range, they're gone before they come, those little targets speeding with five hundred balls of lead a mile behind them. Take them back to their firing-points, to their slings and tele-scopes, wipe the dust from their eyes and let them go on shooting millimetre groups, for they can do that better than you and I, and mark my word, they'll remember that day, and the clumsy cannon they thought could never miss.

Not all our partridges live on the Downs, of course, and many a good day's fun is had elsewhere. Down in the valley stubbles the hot September dust rises in clouds when birds take off or land, dogs find little scent, and shirts and coats grow heavy with perspiration; by midday many birds will have found their own way into the shelter of the roots, while others will have been persuaded to do so. Taken slowly, with many pauses to wipe the stinging sweat from dusty eyes, the stubble walking reaps its own reward, for covey after covey is sent whirring towards the roots from which they will be flushed and shot, albeit in the backside.

Partridges, like most of our island's wild creatures, are not so numerous now as once they were, and those we have are gifted with a caution which would have surprised and aggra-vated the simple birds of fifty years ago. What partridge now sits quietly in the stubble till man and dog are ready to spring it? Some young bird, perhaps, before September 1st.

Through the kindness of my friend Mr. Chapman, I have been able to examine an old game book of his father's. Nearly all the shooting referred to in this book took place near Hungerford and provides much interesting reading. For instance, the first day of partridges from 1882-1893 pro-duced 548 birds, an average of just on 6 brace per gun. The best day, September 1st, 1893, produced 89 birds to 4 guns, or 22 birds per gun, in addition 10 hares and 4 rabbits were accounted for. Between the first and last dates in the book, September 1st, 1882, and September 5th, 1893, 16,870 head of game was killed; no birds were reared, no birds were driven, walking up was the order of the day. And this was an ordinary shoot in those days—nothing fancy, no special days, just honest-to-God shooting. Times have changed since then and our ordinary shoots now could not show such a record. The totals from this Game Book might interest those who, like me, fumble about on a small shoot to-day, trying to make the best of a bad job :

Partridges.	Pheasants.	Hares.	Rabbits.	Woodcock.
3,603	2,503	2,367	8,236	26

In addition, there were duck and other wildfowl, pigeons and rooks and innumerable days with ferrets—none of which are recorded in the book. What a lot of cartridges fired without any beaters, what miles of walking and what tales to tell afterwards. But I'd still rather take my place behind the artificial shelter in the road-side hedge, or stand beneath the berried spindle listening to the beaters' tap and shoot my birds as they jink and curl headfirst towards me, than kick them out of roots and blow their tails away.

"Big days" at pheasants were common enough at one time on all the larger estates, especially in the more wooded parts of the County. When keepers and eggs cost something within reason, birds by the thousand could be reared. But the numbers of birds killed each season bore no relation to the wild pheasant population and cannot be compared with the numbers in Mr. Chapman's Game Book. And each bird accounted for in the two or three days' shooting had cost a pretty penny, even then, when one thinks of head keepers, keepers, under keepers, beaters, pickers-up, game waggon staff, luncheons staff, loaders, gentlemen's gentlemen, etc., etc. And in those days, the greater part of the total bag was got before the alfresco lunch, the sumptuous fare both liquid and solid being the cause of much "tail feather" shooting in the afternoon. Little wonder that the head keeper, like the butler, was really more important than "his lordship," for the success of the day depended largely upon his handling of this army of men.

But those days have gone, I think never to return. Pairs of guns have been split and one half sold, the empty place in

the heavy leather gun-case like a grave, like an empty bed in
the nursery when one of twins has died. Little need now for
a practised loader except perhaps on the grouse-moor, no sale
for the trays to hold a hundred cartridges. My own gun is one
of three, made with all the skill and tenderness of a London
firm in the last century; No. 3 is mine, but where, I wonder,
are 1 and 2? What days those guns must have seen, for they
shot at Royal shoots, what stories they might tell, to make me
feel ashamed of blank days or bad misses through lack of
practice. But never mind about those big days, for they were
never the kernel of shooting, never the utopia of the ordinary
man, and for a long time yet there will be rabbits and pigeons,
partridges and duck, an excuse to carry a gun and to train a
dog.

DEER SHOOT

I have mentioned deer shoots, and those of my readers who
are not country dwellers may find it hard to believe that deer
live wild in many of our Berkshire woods; live wild, and
damage farmers' crops too. Fallow deer, both plain and
spotted and just now and again, roe, may be seen by the
patient observer. Most frequently they are seen by woodmen,
going about their business with their horses in the early morning; a dozen does and a stately buck (for you must never call
the male Fallow a stag) will stand with ears erect and watch
a horse team pass them by, a keeper sitting still across the
pole could easily get a right and left. But why? Why should
we shoot these lovely animals, a glimpse of which is a thing
to enjoy, to treasure like the song of the first blackcap on a
summer morning, unforgettable, and bringing back a host of
other memories?

The countryman, living among the songs of many birds,
trampling the spring flowers beneath his mud-caked boots,
passing the "blues" and the small copper butterflies without
ever a glance, has never the time and rarely the inclination to
enjoy the pleasures of the land. His corn is nibbled by rabbits,
the glorious red and yellow of poppy and charlock serve only
to show that new wire is required, new fencing stakes, to
remind him of the cost of weed control. And his turnips, which

should have stood into the new year, were chewed and broken, the rabbit wire around the field providing no protection from the deer which came at night. The forester, too, had complaints to make, of young trees barked and shoots nipped off. Food was scarce and money was scarcer and the haunch of venison, dark brown against the currant jelly, seemed a fair reprisal for the damaged turnips. So there was an excuse for shooting deer, and everyone was happy at the idea of shooting something quite so large.

After a few experiences of deer shooting, most people come to realise that it is almost as dangerous to themselves as to the deer, for the cries of "deer coming forward," the body-level height of the aim, the excitement of the moment and the inexperience of some of the guns, are apt to cast caution to the winds, and buck-shot is an unpleasant visitor in the face and ribs. The "guns" are mainly local farmers, their men and their friends armed with fire-arms ranging from ancient and rusty hammer-guns, the barrels tied together with wire, to modern sidelock ejectors, four-tens, sixteens, twelves, buck-shot, 4, 5 and 6, even the Home Guard ball, anyone with the courage to fire a gun (and it takes more courage than I've got to stand near some of the weapons, let alone discharge them). No dogs, unless the keepers', trained in this sort of work. Hats, caps, bare heads, breeches and leggings, flannels and wellington boots, no rules, no ceremony. The same crowd of men who would have turned out, in slightly more uniform costume and with slightly less up-to-date weapons to meet the invading enemy! We would start by lining up round that wood where Fred shot that fox that time, those of us present on that occasion remembering where the fell deed took place and lining out our guns accordingly. If this drew blank we would move over the "Saw-mill Piece" where another Fred had shot another fox. This often proved the best draw of the day, innumerable jays, an occasional fox, and a rabbit or two coming under gunfire; the deer normally turned back in this wood passing between the beaters under cover of their shout of "deer forward."

I once shot a deer here, the only deer I ever killed; it dashed out into a ride some thirty yards ahead of me. It was a doe and I jumped on it and cut its throat like any one of us would have done. It was dead, its eyes glassy and nothing like the lovely creature that had stood before me, its ears pricked, its nostrils wide.

After "Saw-mill Piece" perhaps we moved up to "Cow-pond Piece." There were hollies here and nut bushes where rabbits lurked. The shooting became safer. A few pigeons out of the firs gave us something to watch for, the scream of a jay sending the safety catch forward. I never knew a deer in this piece, but it bordered the chewed turnips and one never could tell. In the heather and valley, which lay below it, a hare lived, and we hunted that hare with as much excitement as we might have hunted a tiger. Someone always saw him (he is known as her, or puss by harriers and beaters), someone fired at him, but we never got him. Sometimes we followed a deer by the slot, but we rarely caught up with him, and we drew small clumps of trees where deer had been seen. More often than not we never saw a deer, sometimes we saw one but could not shoot it, and occasionally, just occasionally, we shot one. If this was early in the day, we were filled with joy, shot more jays and rabbits than usual and hung about around the keeper's cottage when all was over. The deer was hung up by the hind legs and skinned, the steaming body examined by all to see the shot marks. A bucket for the paunching and the smallest boy present was blooded and given a part we do not eat; the brains were sent off to a local gentleman, and the rest allowed to cool and distributed among the guns the following day. The head, chucked into the hawthorn hedge, used to provide me with beetles for many a month. And that is deer shooting. Many a day was blank, the fingers frozen in useless expectation, the deer seen so often during the week gone somewhere else; perhaps their ears burned on Friday night, for many a man in the district went to bed to dream of the shoot on the morrow.

Deer shooting with shotguns is not a very kind sport; the normal killing range for deer is somewhere about twenty yards with buck-shot, and firing No. 6 at three times this range rarely does more than hurt and perhaps cause death at some later date. Some aim at the head, some at

the heart, some don't aim at all; some have buck-shot
in one barrel and six in the other, and usually manage to
fire the buck-shot at a rabbit or a jay. Many foxes were shot
—"long-tails" or "charlies" they were called—during the
deer drives, for the hunt rarely came there during the war
and there were far too many foxes anyhow.

Deer shoots usually ended with a cup of tea with the keeper
and his wife, and we spent a pleasant half-hour looking at
guns and dogs, or counting his collection of squirrel skins
waiting to go off to earn a little extra. Then off to the "local"
to spend the evening at darts and bar billiards—and so to
bed. This kind of deer shoot never accounted for many deer,
which was really just as well, but in the course of a winter it
did thin them out a bit. Those who think it a cruel business
must remember that it was the only possible method in a
district where the proximity of roads put rifle shooting out of
the question.

DUCK SHOOT

During the winter months much fun can be had flighting
duck on the Kennet and Loddon, as well as on some of the
little lakes and "coy" ponds, and the many gravel workings.
One has to have the right contacts, for shooting on other
people's land was never encouraged in Berkshire. I am
fortunate in my friends and have spent many happy evenings
at their invitation.

There is one place I shall always remember, though I have
not shot there for several years, where a duck drive was part
of a day at "various." The birds, mostly mallard, but occasionally a teal or two, and once, when I was not there, a
shoveller, are put off a couple of lakes and usually fly straight
down a valley; the three or four guns stand in this valley and
shoot as the duck come high over the oaks. It is a scene like a
Peter Scott, the blue sky for background, the colouring of the
birds showing as it so rarely does in morning and evening
flight. But this is quite unlike ordinary duck shooting, when
darkening skies and freezing winds, or perhaps the death-like
stillness of a snow-covered countryside, add an eerie touch.
This is what I really love, the stand beneath the leafless

willow, waiting for the birds to come off the river to feed in the shallow flood-pools. The cry of a snipe overhead, the call of a moorhen homeward bound, and the rustlings of the reeds —this is music for my ears—suddenly stopping, in that curious way it does when winter snow lies thick, and just as suddenly starting up again. A quacking of domestic ducks in some distant farmyard makes one tense for a moment and then the real thing begins. Two or three drakes have come in unnoticed and are splashing and talking somewhere behind, and the weird call of widgeon is approaching from out in front. Another gun fires from another pool and up go the mallard. Shoot and reload as fast as fumbling fingers allow, and for the next quarter of an hour or so there is shooting as exciting as any man may wish. Then it is all over, for no more birds will come that night. Birds are picked up, the light off the snow proving a great asset and assuring that no bird is left to creep away and die; the noise of the guns is gone, the smell of powder has drifted away and the quiet of a winter's night once more reigns supreme.

ROOK SHOOT

Whatever may be the rights and wrongs of the rook, whatever the truth in the "shoot the rookery for the good of the rooks" theory, rook shooting has been a popular Berkshire sport for years untold. Nests are carefully watched to decide the day, and when the youngsters are sitting on branches near the nest is usually considered the best. For myself, I do not care about this sitting-bird business, though no doubt it does account for many kills. Much more fun can be had when the birds are flying though not too strong on the wing.

Rook shoots are usually organised by the farmer on whose land the rookery stands, and there may be as many as thirty or forty guns. Like the deer shoots, there is little ceremony, except perhaps a "cap" for the boys who gather up the corpses. Shot-guns of all sizes, air guns, ·22 rifles and even revolvers are used; there is much noise and much slaughter, and everyone has enjoyed a pleasant evening and used far more cartridges than he expected. After shooting the rookeries, those with any ammunition left usually have a go at jackdaws coming in to roost. Flying high and strong, it is a good man who can get a left and right despite the stiff neck which always comes on in the rook "season."

All over the country, many thousands of rooks are killed at this time of year, yet this most persistent of birds, perhaps because it is large, perhaps because it is black, perhaps because it nests in colonies for all to see, always manages to survive, to eat the farmer's corn or the farmer's wireworm, whichever theory you believe.

CARDBOARD AND CLAY

For those who prefer, there are several rifle clubs scattered throughout the County. Although the war did much towards the death of many such clubs, rifle shooting did receive considerable support, as one might expect, and ammunition, almost unobtainable in the shops, was available to the Home Guard for target practice. In addition, there are one or two clay pigeon clubs where on highdays and holidays there are competitions open to the public, drawing large crowds anxious to show their skill, though not always successfully doing so ! Cartridge scarcity during the war put clay pigeons off the map, and their ever increasing cost is likely to do so again, but in the off season many a keeper will spend his beer-money at this sport, which, while providing nothing for the pot, undoubtedly gives many a shot.

PART IV

Open Mind

CHAPTER XII

BATS AND BELFRIES

I T comes so naturally to think of bats together with belfries that there seems no good reason for not writing of them together. For bats love rivers, especially the Thames, and bell-founding was, until not so very long ago, a good old Berkshire habit.

The belfry, of course, originally had nothing whatever to do with bells. The word comes from *berfroi*, an old French word taken from the Latin *berfridus*, meaning a watch-tower. The addition of a bell to the watch-tower is a fairly obvious development, and the *ber* was somewhat naturally turned into *bel* in English. Few people now-a-days would look upon a New Forest "fire-watch" tower as a belfry, and it is equally doubtful whether a bat would. For, of course, it is the dark, cave-like effect of the church tower which really appeals to bats, and they care not if the bell be treble or tenor, nor if it were presented by some local dignitary or were paid for by the corporation.

The exact origin of the saying "bats in the belfry" is not clear; it may indicate a "cracked" sound from the bell caused by bats upsetting the acoustics of the bell-tower, or it may refer to the behaviour of the bats when the bell sounds. To such sensitive creatures the vibrations within the bell-tower when a great bell rings one would think must cause extreme discomfort, but it is possible that such low notes are not heard at all by bats.

In England we have some twelve kinds of bats any one of which may be the original "bat out of Hell"! Few of them are rare, but nearly all are local and are unlikely to be found where their particular insect food does not abound. Eight species have been recorded from Berkshire, but few people can recognise our British bats in flight, and mistaken identity may increase or decrease this Berkshire number. The greater and lesser horseshoe bats flit their weird faces around many parts of the County; the first is often to be seen hunting beetles

along the Ridgeway, its low flight making it difficult to follow
in the gathering dusk; during the day it may occasionally be
found hanging in some farm building. The long-eared bat is
not at all uncommon, though I think it is most frequently seen
in wooded districts, such as that between Pangbourne and
Coldash or near Windsor; high among the branches one
moment, in and out among the boles the next, showing an
ability to pass between leaves and twigs quite equal to its
horse-shoe colleagues. The barbastelle has been recorded
from Berkshire, but I do not think I have ever seen it in this
County. It is a bat with longish ears, not quite so long as the
long-eared bat's, but like this species the ears are connected
across the forehead; it likes to fly high and often appears
some considerable time before dusk. Daubenton's bat, which
looks so like the common pipistrelle, is in reality a common
river species, although at one time it was thought to be rare
and was, no doubt, mistaken for the pipistrelle. It loves to fly
up and down a few inches from the water, now and again
seizing some insect from the surface, causing a ripple to
appear on the darkening water. I have seen what I take to be
Daubenton's bat hunting the canal between Bridge Street and
Watlington Street in Reading.

The pipistrelle, in towns at any rate, really is the common
bat. It is the bat which everyone must have seen, and which
has sent many an old maid scuttling out of her boudoir in a
panic. What with bats and mice some dear old ladies must live
a terrifying existence; it has always surprised me that no-one
ever invented button boots fitted with anti-mouse cones! But
electric lighting has largely removed the bat "danger," and,
anyway, a candle-lit face drifting uncertainly through the dark
of a country night may look quite alarming to the bat. I have
known several of these bats personally, that is to say, I have
visited their "homes" and even have shared a four-poster bed
with one for several days—it reminded me of stories of child
labour and the mills, for this bat and I took it in turns to use
the bed, I by night and he by day. I say "he" in order to
observe propriety but it may well have been a "she." Hung
upside down in the carved wood of the bed, he faded into the
woodwork and was safe from domestic interference, but he

was untidy about the house and had to be evicted and the window kept closed. The whiskered bat is not uncommon, I fancy, in the many Berkshire woods, where the long-winged red-grey bat (Natterer's bat) can also be seen. Bechstein's bat has been found in Berkshire, and it is said to be the rarest British bat, but I do not know what this really means. Neither the serotine nor the noctule are mentioned in the *Victoria County History* which is strange, but nor is the pipistrelle for that matter. I know that the noctule occurs, and I have shot one in Basildon Park, when we were rook shooting; it is a species which flies very high, a fact which was commented upon by Gilbert White in 1769, before it was generally recognised as a British species.

I expect the serotine is a Berkshire bat, though I have not caught one myself. I knew it well in both Surrey and Hampshire woods; it has an ugly face and reminds me of a landlady I once met. But joking apart, one cannot pretend that bats are attractive creatures; some, like the horse-shoe bats, are remarkable in their ugliness, while others, like the serotine, are just evil. Many of them smell and most of them harbour fleas and curious wingless flies. For all that, they are most fascinating creatures and their ugliness is sometimes made up for by their delightful names. What better could one want than *vespertillio, myotis,* pipistrelle, noctule, while flitter-mouse one may sometimes hear in Berkshire. I wonder just how many people realise that our largest bat, the noctule, that terror of the night, has a head and body measuring only three inches in length, though its wings measure about fourteen inches from tip to tip? What would the old ladies do if confronted with an Australian fruit bat? But enough of bats; let us turn to the bells, for which Berkshire was at one time famous.

Most churches have a bell-tower, which may house one or more bells. Just as in modern times, the bells of long ago were made by quite a small number of "bell-founders," with the result that the products of a Reading foundry of the thirteenth or fourteenth century are found not only in Berkshire, but in many other counties, and bells cast in London, Wiltshire, Norfolk, etc., are found in our county.

Many bells are extremely old, and in Berkshire we have several dating at least as far back as the latter half of the thirteenth century. The art of deciphering the history of a bell is an interesting as well as a skilled one. Most bells are stamped with the founder's mark, and often with his name, initials or crest; the date and place of casting may also be there, and very often there may be an exhortation to the Lord or to the bell-ringer. The type of lettering used and its position on the bell may give a clue to the founder's name or at any rate to the approximate date of the bell. The oldest known bell in England with a date on it is at Claughton in Lancashire, and it bears the date of 1296. At West Challow in Berkshire is a treble bell cast by Paul the Potter, a London bell-founder, bearing the date 1297. This is believed to be one of the earliest English bells to carry the founder's name.

The oldest bells from a Berkshire foundry are known from Appleford, Arborfield, Aston Upthorpe and Didcot, and they all came from a foundry at Wokingham early in the fourteenth century. None of these carry dates, and are stamped with a coin, a lion's head and a trefoil, in that order, at Appleford and Arborfield; at Aston Upthorpe with a trefoil, the lion's head and a coin; and at Didcot, on two bells, with a coin, lion's head and trefoil. The next oldest from this Wokingham foundry is at North Moreton, and is stamped with the three stamps and in addition a crowned cross. After this there was a bell at Chilton (now recast) which was stamped with a crowned cross, lion's head and coin but the trefoil replaced by another stamp. The inscription "AVE MARIA" was in large letters and each letter crowned. The date of this bell from the Wokingham foundry is estimated to be late fourteenth century. Next we come to another bell at Appleford which is considered to be of rather later date, probably early fifteenth century, which has the crowned cross, lion's head and coin and the inscription "SANCTE GABRIEL ORA PRO NOBIS," each word starting with a crowned capital, the following letters being smaller. At Farnborough there are two bells of the same age (fifteenth century), another at Brightwalton, and at Combe and Fawley there are two more, the letters not having the crowned-cross stamp.

Silver birch and bracken at Cold Ash

All these bells from Wokingham so far mentioned were cast by unknown hands. It is likely, from the various changes and alterations in the stamps, that several men were involved at different times, and that the originator of the foundry either came to Wokingham from London or had worked previously in the London foundries, for his bells show certain similarity in design to fourteenth-century London bells. In 1448, however, we are certain from old manuscripts that a Roger Landen had a foundry at Wokingham, and we know that in addition to the lion's head and coin he used a stamp in the form of a shield with a bell in the centre, the letters "R. L." at the top on each side of the inscription band and the letter "W" beneath the clapper. There are no known bells in Berkshire by Roger Landen, but some still exist in other counties.

Somewhere in the middle of the fifteenth century the lion's head stamp changed and was replaced by a copy which, like so many copies, was distinctly inferior to its model. This change suggests that Roger Landen died, and we know that he was succeeded by John Michell, who cast bells for Stanford Dingley and Warfield, stamping the coin, new lion's head and the Roger Landen shield; the inscription "TE DEUM LAUDAMUS" at Stanford Dingley and "SANCTA KATERINA" at Warfield are without the crowned capitals. John Michell died about 1495, and for some reason the foundry was moved from Wokingham to Reading, where William Hazylwood took charge. Hazylwood's will was proved on December 10th, 1509, and his son, John, took over the foundry. There are no bells in Berkshire by either father or son, nor by John White, who followed and died in 1539. It has been suggested that William Hazylwood cast the great tenor bell "Harry" for St. Lawrence's Church, Reading, some time before 1499, but it is equally likely that it was cast at the Knights' Reading foundry or even at Wokingham. "Harry" lasted until 1567, when "he" was recast.

The next founder, John Saunders, is known in Berkshire from bells at Hurley, Tidmarsh and Drayton, the last now recast. Saunders' name is known until 1559, after which the curtain drops temporally on the Reading foundry.

Some time later we read of Vincent Gorowage, William

Ruins of Donnington Castle

Wells and William Knight in an old undated book called *The Book of the Names and Ordinancies of the Cutlers and Bell Founders Companye.* Vincent Gorowage was evidently not an energetic man, for we know nothing whatever about him. William Wells has left no bells in Berkshire, but there are two in Buckinghamshire. It seems that Joseph Carter took over from Wells. He died in 1609 and was buried at St. Lawrence's Church, leaving some sixteen bells in Berkshire, ranging over some thirty years. In 1579 Joseph Carter recast "Harry," St. Lawrence's tenor, the bell having previously (1567) been recast by William Knight of Reading. Carter recast "Harry" yet again in 1595, and Ellis and Francis Knight recast "him" once more in 1646. In 1662 it was decided by a committee of seven gentlemen and two church-wardens to melt down the five bells of St. Lawrence and cast eight smaller bells. Knight of Reading did the job and what was left of old "Harry" was spread through the new bells. In 1703 the tenor bell was recast again (it may also have been recast in 1664, but this is by no means certain). In 1748 all eight bells were recast and two bells added, making a ring of ten. Robert Catlin cast these bells, four of which remain to this day. By 1881 the tenor bell was in trouble again and was recast by John Taylor and Co. of Loughborough in 1882.

But we must go back to Joseph Carter, who, it will be remembered, took over the Reading foundry from William Wells. Joseph was appointed a churchwarden of St. Lawrence's in 1593 and again in 1594. He was succeeded in 1609 by his son-in-law, William Yare, who kept the foundry going until his death in 1616, after which it was closed down for ever. There are eight of Yare's bells in Berkshire.

We now move from this foundry to that of William Knight, who, it will be recalled, was one of the three Reading founders mentioned in *The Book of the Names and Ordinancies. . . .* Although this book is undated, the matter within it suggests 1565 as being its latest possible date. The Knight family's connection with bells may go back considerably further than this, for a John Knight made a "bawdrick" for St. Lawrence's Church in 1499. William Knight was a churchwarden of St. Lawrence's in 1519, and was definitely a bell-founder. Until this foundry was moved to London in 1710 it remained in the family, sons following their fathers in succession. During this time there were two Williams, three Henrys, two Ellises and a Samuel. The Knights were a most industrious family, particularly Ellis I, whose name is associated with the bells of a great many Berkshire churches.

The demand for bells must have been fairly great because another foundry was started up in Wokingham in 1565, or thereabouts, by Thomas Eldridge. Just before the end of the sixteenth century Thomas was succeeded by his son Richard, who was in turn followed by his son Bryan, whose two sons, Bryan and William, were concerned with a branch of the foundry at Chertsey in Surrey. Both foundries disappear at the end of the seventeenth century; there are not many bells in Berkshire cast by this family, and a mere handful have come from their Chertsey foundry. It is doubtful if the Eldridge foundry at any time rivalled the Knights of Reading.

After this, bell-founding in Berkshire dies out except for one or two attempts by men whose names are little known. In 1723 Henry Bagley, whose parent foundry was in Northamptonshire, cast a bell in Reading at Tilehurst; in 1734 or so, Thomas Dicker, who was a clockmaker in Reading, cast a few bells, two of which are known in Berkshire; one, a treble bell at Basildon, was recast in 1876, the other is at Inkpen; John Hunt of Cholsey, who was a smith by trade, occasionally did an odd job on bells, and cast two for his own village and one for Blewbury. It is recorded that he had three shots at the Blewbury bell and Sharpe quotes a local rhyme:

> "Three times run and three times cast,
> Blewbury's tenor's cast at last!"

John Hunt inscribed this bell NIL DESPERANDUM and I take it he lived happily ever after.

So Berkshire bell-founding faded out and bells were purchased from the large London foundries of Mears and Stainbank, or from the famous foundries at Aldbourne, Wilts, or from other places when required.

Anyone who is interested in bells or in the founders'

marks should inspect the illustrated articles by Mr. F. Sharpe, which have been appearing since 1939 in the *Berkshire Archæological Journal* and in which an enormous amount of detail is given. I have gleaned a lot of otherwise almost unobtainable information from these articles and also from A. H. Cocks' article in the *Victoria County History*.

One cannot leave the subject of bells without mentioning the White family of Appleton, who for generations have been intimately concerned with our Berkshire bells. Alfred White, who lived in the first half of the nineteenth century, came of an Appleton family well known as smiths. Alfred's interest lay in bells, and what he did not know about bells and their ringing was not worth knowing; he eventually founded a bell-hanging business and many of our Berkshire bells have at some time or other been repaired by himself or by members of his family, for bells sometimes crack, sometimes want tuning, sometimes want recasting, or the wooden fittings may need replacing. At bell-ringing, Alfred White set the pace for his successors, for in 1818 he was on the third bell when, on March 4th, Appleton village celebrated a gift of six London bells from Robert Southby of Appleton Manor. March 4th has ever after been celebrated in Appleton with much ringing and dining. In 1854 the peal of six was increased to eight and in 1861 to ten bells when the tower had to be altered to provide greater space. Alfred White was instrumental in achieving these alterations and undertook the hanging at his own expense.

Appleton, as a centre of bell-ringing competition, has not looked back since Alfred White was on that third bell in 1818, and there are many tablets on the tower walls to commemorate notable achievements in the field of campanology; in 1855 William, Alfred, Henry and Frederick White were among the eight who, conducted by Henry White, rang a peal of Grandsire Trebles of 5,040 changes in 3 hours and 30 minutes. In 1861 a team containing three Whites (Alfred was missing) rang 5,040 changes in 2 hours and 54 minutes. Ten years later, on ten bells, 10,080 changes of Grandsire Trebles were rung by a team containing four Whites, Alfred being present this time. This peal was composed and conducted by Frederick White, and took 6 hours and 21 minutes to execute. In 1888 the Appleton Ringers secured four world records, 10,080 changes of Double Norwich Court Bob Majors in 5 hours 58 minutes (F. White on the treble), 13,041 Stedman Caters in 7 hours 26 minutes (F. White treble, F. S. White tenor), 13,265 Grandsire Caters in 8 hours 5 minutes (F. White on 6, F. S. White tenor), 15,041 Stedman Caters in 9 hours 16 minutes (Oxford Diocesan Guild, F. White treble, F. S. White tenor). In 1921 10,043 Grandsire Caters (Oxford Diocesan Guild) in 6 hours 5 minutes (F. S. White treble, C. G. White 5, A. H. White 6, R. White 9 and F. White tenor). In 1922 the Oxford Diocesan Guild and an old London ringing society rang 21,363 changes of Stedman Caters in 12 hours and 25 minutes (R. White 9 and F. White tenor). Again in 1932 the record for Grandsire Caters was captured (regained) by the Oxford Guild, for in 9 hours and 20 minutes, 16,271 changes were rung (C. G. White treble, R. White 9, F. White tenor).

Alfred White, the founder of the bell-ringing business, and the leader of the band, so to speak, died in 1876, his death being an enormous loss to the villages of Appleton and Besselsleigh. Frederick, his son, followed him, and in repairs and alterations was his father's equal. His father, whose heart was of oak, had brought him up to understand English oak as the only material for bell-frames, but son Fred was forced by circumstances to apply many a rough iron frame; it is on record, however, that he thoroughly disapproved of this material. Frederick was succeeded by his son Richard, who discontinued the rough iron frames, and tried out cast-iron frames mounted on rolled-steel joists. Since then English oak has again been available and most of the cast-iron frames have been replaced by oak. The White family still exist, and for hanging and ringing there is no one to beat them. The White family did not only ring in Appleton and among others, one might well refer to a ring at Drayton in 1880, when F. S. White, F. White, J. White in a team rang 5,040 Grandsire Triples. Drayton bells are also famous for 5,056 changes of Cambridge Surprise Majors, 5,088 Superlative Surprise Majors, and 5,184 Double Norwich Court Bob

Majors, and 5,040 Stedman Triples, executed in 2 hours and
42 minutes, also for 11,328 changes of London Surprise
Majors in 6 hours and 6 minutes (1896). The success of many
of these was due to Mr. Robinson, who held the living of
Drayton and who, when he retired, had performed 1,261
peals of 5,000 changes in 456 towers for 32 guilds and associations. From 1881 to 1910 Mr. Robinson was Master of
the Oxford Guild of Church Bell-ringers; Mr. Robinson, in
1861, gave two tenor bells to Appleton to increase the then
ring of eight to ten. Before leaving the subject of bells and
the name of White, one must mention the 1867 newspaper
advertisement, quoted by Sharpe :

> "A. White and Sons Belhangers were made,
>   Because it was their fancy trade;
> In hanging bells they take delight
>   To make them go with all their might.
> They in their brasses don't confine them,
>   Or else no man could ever rise them.
> In clappering they're quite expert,
>   For in the bell they put the work
> That makes the clapper to rebound,
>   Which brings the true and proper sound.
> In tuning they are competent,
>   To tuning fork, and instrument.
> In ringing bells also they're right,
>   For they're a band whose name is WHITE :
> They'll ring the bells with any band,
>   To Treble Bob, Grandsire, or Stedman;
> Hand Bells they make; are skill'd in tuning,
>   Can ring some tunes that are amusing;
> If you've a peal that's not quite right,
>   Just drop a line to ALFRED WHITE,
> And with his SONS he will come down,
>   Re-hang the bells, and make them sound
> The proper note, that's not been heard
>   Perhaps for as much as twenty years.
> His SONS the clocks and chimes can do,
>   Make them play tunes and keep time true.
> If you've a job that's worth attention,
>   They will do their best to give satisfaction."

A White and Sons, Besselsleigh, near Abingdon, July, 1867.

And the song written by John Harding of Appleton to celebrate March 4th, 1818, with its last verse added in 1854 :

"May friendship and freedom this day much abound,
May mirth and good humour go jovely round;
May the young, and the old, the grave, and the gay,
Remember this is our March the Fourth Day.

In this present year which we have now all seen,
The number one thousand, eight hundred, eighteen;
The six well-tuned bells that by Southby were given,
Rang their first Merry Peal our hearts to enliven.

Then come all your aged, and witness this scene;
Bring your Sons and your Daughters, to dance on the green;
You are heartily welcome to take of the fare,
Which will drive away sorrow, and banish all care.

So fill up your Bumpers, be this toast given:
'Here's Southby for ever, may His Soul rest in Heav'n.'
For his bounteous hand it has made us all sing:
'Old England for Ever and God save the King.'

But when thirty-six years had quite altered the date,
The peal of six Bells was transposed into eight.
For a Treble, and Tenor, are put up quite right,
By the Friend of all ringers, that fam'd Alfred White."

Chapter XIII

BEER AND BISCUITS

M y friends will understand that I have nothing but an alphabetical reason for putting beer before biscuits, though I might add that beer should be placed first for a variety of other reasons. England drank mead and cider long before the coming of beer; it is pretty certain that beer was almost, if not entirely, unknown before the Romans arrived, after which barley was grown and used for brewing. Hops were not cultivated, so far as is known, until the middle of the fifteenth century, and not on any scale until nearly a hundred years later, though the hop plant was known and used long before this, in fact, probably by the Saxons.

In Berkshire, hops were at one time cultivated at East Hagbourne and at Little Wittenham, and have left their mark in local field-names, such as Hop Garden Field and Upper Hop Garden; to-day, the small hop industry is centred on Kingston Bagpuize.

For many hundreds of years ale has been brewed in this County, the abbeys of Reading and Abingdon brewing for the monks and retaining cellarers and tasters to supervise the quality of their ales. By the time of Henry III, each borough kept an ale taster and brewing had reached the stage when vested interests began to be threatened; accordingly, rules were made tying down the making and sale of "maulte," and requiring an intending "licensee" to bring forward evidence as to the "juste length, bredth and depth of the casternes or steepinge fatts" which were intended for use in "mauletinge." In 1369 William de Harwell and Henry Redynge were each fined 3d. for not adhering to the letter of the law. By the time of Henry VIII, new rules were in force, and all brewers were obliged to sell thirteen gallons to the dozen of ale for 22d., so long as a quart of malt was not more than 8d. At the same time all "tipsters" were to sell out-of-doors a quart of ale for $\frac{1}{2}$d. while malt was 8d.

From various records a bit is shown about the brewers of

long ago; for example in 1510 Henry White was a "bruere" and Nicholas Nicolas was a "bere bruer." At this time most brewers were "ale bruers" and Nicholas was probably a go-ahead chap, for he flavoured with hops, and what is more he was quick off the mark, for Henry VII, who died in 1509, had passed an Act forbidding the mixing of hops with beer. I have a soft spot for Nicholas!

In Elizabeth's time, when men such as Walter Raleigh and Philip Sidney were exploring and fighting one moment, and dancing and reciting poems the next, hop cultivation started its career in many parts of the country. By 1622, when James I was nearing the end of his reign, Reading boasted three brewers, Mr. Ironmonger, who must have forsaken his family calling, Mr. Winche and Mr. Harrison, who, after being Reading's mayor for three years, went bankrupt; probably being three times mayor cost him a bit, but no doubt the Civil War and the siege of Reading really finished him off. From Charles's reign we have a record of what a pub-crawl or a party at home might cost :

			Double beere.	Single beere.
The Barrell	...	...	viiis	iiijs
The Kiderkyn	...	...	iiijs	iis
The Firkyn	...	...	ijs	xiid
The Pipkin	...	...	xiid	vid
The Duzzen of Ale	...	iiijd	—

Messrs. Simonds, without doubt, have the largest beer trade in Reading. Towards the end of the eighteenth century, William Simonds set up a brewery in Broad Street, Reading, and was so successful that in 1790 he moved to larger premises in Bridge Street, where the brewery stands to this day. It is now an enormous affair, covering many acres, not only supplying drink to the thirsty in Berkshire, but owning hotels and catering establishments throughout the south and south-west of England. Their sign, a red hop-leaf, hangs outside unnumbered pubs in Berkshire, and would be pleasant to look at if it were not so often more like one of those rail way-side advertisements for Virol or Tangye Pumps than an inn sign.

Another Bridge Street brewery belonged to Blandy and

Hawkins; it was known as the Castle Brewery and was destroyed by fire in 1888. The modern Castle Brewery is run by the South Berks Brewery Company and has an offshoot in Newbury. Earlier than this, the Mill Lane Brewery was owned by Messrs. Willots, John Stevens and William Blandy, while Ferguson brewed in Broad Street and Higgs brewed in Castle Street; Dymore Brown brewed at the Royal Abbot Brewery in Queen's Road and lived in the house that is now the "Queen's."

Abingdon, that town of many inns, has a great brewing history. Little wonder there were so many places to sell beer, for in 1585 there were no less than nine men brewing: Messrs. Braunche (William and Antony), Bostock, Fyssher, Rysbye, Teysdall, Blacknoll, Welling and Bolte. By law they had to exhibit their malt on market day and were subject to a fine for selling beer for retail purposes to unlicensed persons. Innkeepers were at that time a crowd of rascals, often brewing their own beer; this was black-market beer and the fine was 10s. per bottle, no matter whether pinte, quarte or gallon potte was sold. With this huge trade in Abingdon, much barley was grown in the district, and a lot of malt used to travel up to London by river. By 1830 Abingdon had increased her brewers to eleven in number, and cider was being made as well, the apples very likely coming from Appleton and Appleford. Of the innumerable inns in Abingdon I shall write later.

This whole district of fair agricultural land, with the Thames at its highroad, went in for brewing in a large way. Wallingford was also a "hive" of brewing; by 1830 Edward Wells, James Bennett, Charles Morrell, Job Lovelock, William Hilliard were producing nearly 2,000 bushels of malt each year. Edward Wells had brewing interests in Abingdon, and his namesake had started the Wallingford Brewery Company in 1720. The Morrell family, well known to-day in the brewing world, are remembered in Wallingford by a Morrell Charity, instituted in 1855 by the will of Charles Morrell to assist ten poor persons, and by the Morrell Memorial Hospital originated by Mary Morrell who died in 1880.

Moving now to Newbury, John Edmunds, Thomas Martyn and Thomas Manning were beer brewers there in 1643, and by the beginning of the nineteenth century there were thirteen maltsters and six brewers. By 1830 there were three breweries at Hungerford, and one at Kintbury. Stephens and Kingston each brewed at Aldermaston, the latter also at Woolhampton. In 1883 John Thomas Strange took over the Aldermaston brewing, and recently Strong of Romsey have taken over the business, although at the time of writing the Aldermaston brewery is still producing Strange's beer.

Lambourn had a brewery and maltsters, of which there were five in Faringdon, and Wantage, also, had several breweries. We then come to the Ilsleys, where the Homers and Morlands had breweries; later the Morland family took the breweries of John Thornton Morland and Edward Morland in Abingdon, and the West Ilsley brewery of Edward Henry Morland. In addition to these, Morlands took over Saxby's Brewery in Abingdon and Field's in Shellingford. Morland's headquarters are now in what had been the Eagle Brewery run by Mr. Belcher. Recently Morlands have joined forces with Dymore Brown and Company, of the Royal Abbot Brewery in Reading. Morland's Brewery in Abingdon is one of the few breweries I have been over from A–Z, the tour ending in a little holy of holies set aside for the liquid refreshment of visitors.

Travelling eastwards across the County, just outside Reading, there were small breweries at Twyford and Hurst, while Cookham had four brewers, and hops were at one time cultivated there. James Hayward, maltster, and Thomas Lock, brewer, functioned in Wokingham, while John Barton supplied the needs of Bray. Windsor, as one might suppose, has nearly always brewed considerable quantities for soldiers, and retinues of great men are usually thirsty folk. At one time brewing was the most important industry there; in mid-sixteenth century there were twenty-one inns; in the seventeenth century Mills, Chapman, Galland, Sweetzer, Pennington and Quartermaine were building up a reputation for Windsor ales, and early in the nineteenth century John Jennings and Company produced what they chose to call

"King's Ale," while their rivals, Ramsbottom and Legh, played back with "Queen's Ale." A third brewer, Nevill Reid and Company, being too late to have a "royal" ale of their own, bought out Ramsbottom and Legh. Other brewers there were too : Mr. Twine in Peascod Street, where Noakes now brew; Lovibond's and Burghe's, both of which are still working; and in addition to these there were other breweries scattered throughout the County at Theale (Blatch), Mortimer (Mosdell and Pagze), Donnington (Palmer), Ashbury (Carter) and Harwell (Beesley). And so we finish our tour of breweries past and present; but before we finish, with beer we should visit a few of the places where it is sold.

Before I wrote this chapter, I thought it would be nice to visit every pub in the County and have a pint and a chat with the landlord. I still think it would be nice, but it would cost a fortune in time and beer, for one pint only leads to another. I have done my best, however, and in the course of my wanderings I have tasted the "maulte" in a great many places. Nothing can have changed so much in the last hundred years as the "pub"—except for low dives round our ports and in some parts of our larger towns, the pub is no longer a sink of iniquity, frequented by rough men who swear, spit and get noisily drunk; this is largely a matter of "gravity" as any beer drinker will know, but it is also due to a fundamental change in our outlook. To-day there is scarcely a pub in the whole County where a girl could not go—she is much more likely to cause offence than to receive it. Not so very long ago if a girl went into a pub, she no doubt got all she went there for, and more besides.

Inn signs belong, of course, to the days of over-indulgence and under-education. In fact, there was no use writing Ye Bull if no-one could read, but a great red bull nicely painted, or the emblems, crests, devices and what you will of nobility, could strike chords where words would fail. Inn signs can be divided up into several large groups, of which the heraldic group accounts for more than any other division. Under this heading we start with coloured lions, and boars; the Red Lion occurs twenty-one times and the Blue Lion twice; the lion, as a part of our national badge, dates back to James I, and red, white and blue and black specimens occur in Hampshire, but black and white, so far as I know, are absent in Berkshire. There are various explanations of the "Ure Lion," or "Lion Azure" as I should call him, none of which have any bearing in Berkshire. The White Hart occurs nineteen times and in most cases refers to the badge of Richard II, though it may also have a purely sporting significance dating back to Henry VII, when "Albert," a favourite white hart, gave the King such good sport in the New Forest that hounds were called off, the "Albert" presented with a gold collar and Halliday Wagstaff, keeper of the woods and forests, was knighted there and then; "Albert" was then sent to Windsor for a holiday. The King's Arms dates back to James I, who insisted that the Royal Arms should hang in all churches and public places to remind men of the Royal Authority; Charles II issued the same order. We have four examples of the Blue Boar, some or all of which, no doubt, started life white, for the White Boar was the cognisance of Richard III, and was easily altered after his death. "A Blue Boar, with his tusks and his cleis, and his members of gold" was the cognisance of the Earl of Oxford. In addition to these boars, we have the Boar's Head, twice in the County. Most people will have struck this little rhyme :

> "The Cat, the Rat, and Lovel our Dogge,
> Rule all England under a Hogge."

The Cat was William Catesby; the Rat, Sir William Ratcliffe; the Dog was Lord Lovel; and the Hogge, of course, was Richard III. William Collingbourne, who wrote these words, came to a sticky end. Lord Lovel, incidentally, was at one time Constable of the Royal Castle at Wallingford. The Bear and Ragged Staff is another heraldic sign, representing the arms of Warwick and Leicester; it occurs only once in Berkshire, at Cumnor. The Feathers, the Fleur de Lys, of course represent the Black Prince. In addition to these signs of men high up the social ladder, there are lots of "arms" of a baser sort, bricklayers, carpenters, millers, tanners and the like, and sometimes these are represented by symbols, but more often by a description of the symbol; for instance, the

Boot, which occurs several times, naturally represents the "shoe-makers' arms." I wonder how many people realise that the arms of the Company of Cordwainers (shoe-makers) consist of three goats' heads?

The arms of local gentry were often used in the great man's neighbourhood—we have several ways of describing that sort of theory nowadays, and "currying favour" is the only one that I can write here. It is also possible that when important people, like butlers, retired from service, they removed a sufficiency of crested spoons and plate to set up in a tavern. Anyhow (or anyways, as we say) there are numbers of such inn-signs in Berkshire. The Wellington or the Wellington Arms and the Waterloo are, no doubt, due to the proximity of the Duke's estates; the Craven Arms occurring at Newbury, Hungerford and Faringdon commemorate Sir William Craven who, while Lord Mayor of London, is said to have deserted that city upon the approach of the "plague" and retreated to Ashbury, where he built Ashdown Park. Barrington (Shrivenham), East (Hurley), Eyston (a family of considerable historic interest at East Hendred) and, of course, the Winchcombe family commemorated "Jack of Newbury," the wool manufacturer—the Jack Hotel stood in Newbury where Marks and Spencers shop now stands—but enough for the moment about Jack Winchcombe as he will appear in another chapter. There is a Winchcombe club in Newbury and the name of Jack of Newbury is retained at Binfield. Another Newbury family is commemorated in the Bacon Arms next to the Chequers on the Bath Road, Anthony Bacon being at one time lord of the manor of Donnington and part of Speenhamland, and this hotel, for it was an inn, not a tavern, must have seen much gaiety and colour in the coaching days.

What might be described as "loyal" signs are innumerable, as the King's Head (usually Henry VIII), Queen's Head (usually Elizabeth), Prince of Wales, Princes Albert, Alfred and Christian, and the Royal Oak in memory of Charles II, who, you will recall, hid in an oak tree after his defeat at Boscobel in 1651. The Round Oak at Padworth may be a corruption of Royal Oak, or it may commemorate some old tree long since departed, and which gave name to the hamlet now included under the name of Padworth.

The George, or George and Dragon, occurs several times in the County. The myth of St. George goes back to Saxon days when he was honoured by a festival; in Berkshire, below White Horse Hill, we have the spot where St. George actually encountered and slew his dragon, witness the bare top of the hill, ruined for all time so far as vegetative growth is concerned by "dragon's blood." Among the various Georges and George and Dragons, the George in Reading must be mentioned; described as a "commercial hotel," in the modern telephone book, this inn goes back to 1506, and must have seen many an interesting sight. The ancient visitors' books are full of names of well-known men who travelled the Bath Road long ago. It is a fascinating old place with a cobbled courtyard, off which open four bars, offering different brewers' products, for the George is a free-house, and each with its nucleus of "regulars," who rarely visit the other bars and who meet unveiled hostility when they do so. In one of the bars you will find old photographs of the place and, much older, the original charters dated 1506 and 1571. In the "men only" bar is a fine old Act of Parliament Clock dated 1797. The George is, no doubt, the oldest inn in Reading; the Bear, almost a contemporary, has now gone and Gilbert White wrote in 1774 : "In the garden of the Black Bear Inn in the town of Reading, is a stream or canal running under the stables and out into the fields on the other side of the road; in this water are many carps, which lie rolling about in sight, being fed by travellers, who amuse themselves by tossing them bread." Another old Reading tavern, the Crown, has long since disappeared. It stood at the junction of Crown Street and London Street, and is said to have been the "snob place" at one time; it was the meeting place of the Whigs— the Tories meeting at the Bear. (The modern Crown, in Crown Street, does not stand on the site of its ancestor.)

Of ecclesiastical signs, we have nine Lambs. More often than not the Lamb here referred to is the Holy Lamb, but in such places as Wantage, Faringdon, Newbury, East Ilsley and Hungerford, one is inclined to think otherwise. The

Shears and the Woolpack at Wantage support this inclination. We also have Mitors, Angels and a Golden Cross (of St. Peter, and the Papal See). The Crispin occurs four times, and recalls two Christian missionaries, Crispin and Crispian, who were adopted as patrons of the shoe-making trade, both of them having worked as shoe-makers before the call to Christianity. The best of them all is at Woodside, on the edge of Windsor Park and within a stone's throw of the Ascot racecourse. The White Horse, which has a particular significance in Berkshire, should, no doubt, be considered ecclesiastical, going back to Saxon times; it is also the sinister supporter of the Howard family, and at one time a white horse was a not uncommon and useful animal; the inns so called at Uffington and Woolstone cannot be difficult to explain, but others scattered through the County are less obvious if not similarly explained.

One would expect a county with a bell-founding history to have inn signs recalling this, and we need not be disappointed, for there are some twenty-five inns whose signs are bells or something connected with them. Five, Six and Eight Bells occur in proportion, and the Ringers at Maidenhead is, I think, the only one of this name in the County—incidentally, rings of five bells are not common in the County, though six and eight are. The mysterious triad does not, I think, occur in bells, but three Brewers, Crowns, Elms, Firs, Frogs, Horseshoes (the farriers' emblem), Kings and Tuns (the vintners' emblem) occur throughout the County. Apparently the bell-founders of old were not organised, for there is no bell-founders' arms—perhaps there were not enough of them or they did not approve of "collective security."

The Three Kings, also known as Jack's Booth, on the Bath Road, reminds me of the various inn signs relating to travel. Probably the oldest of these are the Pack Horses and Pack Saddles, which are usually found on or near some ancient track. The only Berkshire example I can recall is the Old Pack Horse at Milton Hill, near Steventon. The Coach and Horses and the Horse and Groom suggest a more advanced form of travel, while the Traveller's Friend and Traveller's Welcome might suit any period. The innumerable Railway

East Ilsley

Hotels speak for themselves and can have, as yet, no great antiquity. Most of them, like the railway stations they serve, were created with that rare beauty one has learned to associate with the railways of Great Britain. The Row Barge indicates another form of travel, and is known from Abingdon and Wallingford on the Thames, and Woolhampton on the Kennet.

Agriculture, naturally, is well represented, and there is scarce a village and surely no town without at least one inn sign of an agricultural type. I have commented earlier on those signs related to sheep. In a county which grew so rich at one time largely because of these animals, it is curious how few inns remain that recall those days. The Shepherd's House and Shepherd's Hut occur in the Maidenhead part of the County, not up on the Downs where one might expect them. Ploughs and Harrows are common enough, but the Steam Plough in Abingdon is an unusual one. There are a dozen or so examples of the Wheatsheaf, but only one Oatsheaf. Why the oatsheaf should be so uncommon I cannot tell, and, so far as I know, it is absent from Oxfordshire and Buckinghamshire, and occurs, or did occur, only once in Hampshire, near Farnham. The Barley Mow is not uncommon, and of course refers to a stack of barley sheaves, while the Malt Shovel at Lambourn links up with barley and the small brewery business centred in that town. The Bull may, in certain instances, have an agricultural bias, for at one time it was the custom for a town to own a bull or two for stud purposes—even in those days it was appreciated that a communal bull, such as we now have in our artificial insemination centres, costs less than a private one. But more often than not, the Bull must have been associated with the sport of the times.

Now we come to those signs related to sport, and from their number and variety of subject, it is easy to see that Berkshire, long ago, was even then filled with a sporting enthusiasm such as nowadays sends thousands to stand uncomfortably in football crowds, racing crowds, three-day drives to see (or not to see) the "National," all-night standing for the centre court at Wimbledon or, something even more difficult to explain to a foreigner, the silent shrouded figures,

The little downland village of Farnborough

inwardly cursing the weather, evenly spread along the Thames
bank for a Sunday morning fishing competition! But to our
pubs—falconry, that grandfather of our field sports, is represented by the Falcon and the Bird in Hand; the Falcon, on
the southern outskirts of Aldermaston, is locally called the
Fuzzbush, though no one seems to know why, except that
gorse is abundant in the district; the Bird in Hand should
probably be the Bird on Hand, the falconer carrying his
hawks and falcons on his left wrist. (The difference between
hawks and falcons, by the way, is a matter of sex, for a falcon
is the female of any hawk, the male being called a tiercel—
scientists, on the other hand, call long-winged hawks falcons,
while short-winged ones they call hawks : confusing, is it not?)
Hunting the stag, the fox and the hare has provided ideas
for many an inn sign, though the Fox and Punch Bowl at
Windsor sounds less like hunting than carousing, and the Fox
and Castle, in the same town, is merely a local combination.
The Bramshill Hunt, a sign to be seen near Arborfield, was
the subject of some discussion in *Horse and Hound* at one
time; it seems that there was, at one time, a hunt bearing
this name and hunting the Garth country of the present day.

Shooting is represented by the Pheasant, Pigeons and Dog
and Partridge, though the Dog and Duck does not refer to
shooting ducks over dogs, but to chasing ducks with spaniels
in special ponds arranged for the purpose, and although it
was considered a sport then, well worth a Saturday afternoon, it must be classed with the more brutal sports unlikely
to return to any popularity in this country. When passing
judgment on our forefathers, we must remember that even
to-day the countryman is naturally rougher than the towns-
man. He is constantly killing things, rabbits, birds, pigs,
poultry and the like, and the idea of any pain being associated
with his killing rarely enters his head. The pheasant with one
leg down, the rabbit shot in the bottom and lost down a hole,
these are looked upon as bad shooting and nothing more. Not
that I condone such things, but rather that, perhaps, than
some of the "cissy" ideas of to-day.

The Bull, occurring in a dozen or more places, the Bear
and the Black Bear, the Cock and the Cock and Tree, all

refer to the "brutal" sports. The last named, in Abingdon, probably refers, not to cock-fighting but to cock-shying, in which the unfortunate cock, tethered to a post or tree, took the place of our modern (pre-war) coconut. Badger-baiting appears to have skipped the notice of the beer trade in our country, which is odd since the woods are full of badgers. The Dog and Badger, at Medmenham in Bucks, is the nearest reference to a once popular sport. Fishing, as one might expect, is well represented, the Complete Angler on the Berkshire side of Marlow Bridge being, perhaps, the best known, and then there are the Angler's Arms, the Fish, the Trout and the Fisherman's Cottage. There are innumerable Greyhounds, for coursing is a very ancient sport in England, going back to the days when the Belgæ inhabited the south, breeding these dogs for hunting deer as well as hares.

Natural history forms the basis for many a name, the Elephant, the Reindeer, Ibex, Fawn, Mole, Squirrel, Swan, Eagle, Dove, Griffin, Baytree, Yew Tree, Holy Bush, Three Firs and the Old Elm Tree. Some of these, the Griffin for example, have heraldic significance; the Maybush, at Kingston Bagpuize, no doubt owes its name basically to the prehistoric festivities associated with spring, for the Maytree was the forerunner of the Maypole. The Grapes and the Vine, occurring at Reading, Windsor, Abingdon and Cumnor, point to a small wine trade in the County, while the Beehive probably refers to mead, that most ancient of drinks, still made in a few country kitchens and on the threshold of "rediscovery" on a commercial scale in south-west England.

Finally, there is an assortment of more or less unintelligible names; The Happy Dick in Abingdon may refer to the downfall of Richard Cromwell in the same way as the Hampshire Tumble-down Dick, but more likely, I think, to some inebriated customer; the Pin and Bowl in Wokingham refers to the old pegged tankard used for "level-pegging," and the Hole in the Wall, an inn which at one time stood just outside Pangbourne on the Oxford road, refers to the little hole in the wall of a debtors' jail through which relatives pushed food, the only food, incidentally, which the unfortunate inmate was likely to get ! The World Turned Upside Down, or

the "Upsydown" as it is called locally, stands facing the
sewage farm outside Reading on the Basingstoke road—the
"influence of alcohol" seems to be the only possible meaning
of its curious name. The Land's End, near Woodley, is well
named, for in winter when the moon shines on the Loddon-
filled meadows and the wind and rain beat furiously against
the windows, one might well be facing out to sea, and on
really stormy nights World's End might be a better name.

Of biscuits there is much less to say, for they are a much
more modern commodity, and the retailers' premises are less
interesting historically than those which sell the barley drink.
By 1830 Joseph Huntley and his son were manufacturing
biscuits in London Street, Reading. At this time there were
no fancy things, but only Captains' Biscuits, made from wheat-
flour, salt and water—not unpleasant but definitely uninteresting. Some ten years later, George Palmer came upon the
scene, an energetic man with a flair for inventions and focus-
ing his attention upon biscuits, brought out a wonderful piece
of machinery which mixed up the flour, kneaded the dough,
"braked" the mixture, that is to say, ran it between rollers
which squeezed it out into sheets, cut it up into shapes and
sizes and took them away to be baked. Altogether an
admirable machine and, coupled with the exhilarating effect
of abolished corn laws and the introduction of free trade in
wheat, Huntley and Palmer's grew, bringing considerable
prosperity to the town of Reading. Biscuits could now be produced in large quantities and at a low price; the demand for
the Reading biscuits increased, and soon a whole range of
ingredients were filling the trucks to Reading, and George
Palmer was joined by his two brothers, Samuel and William;
in 1857 Thomas Huntley, the grand old man of the firm,
died. Since the introduction of the first rather "Heath Robin-
sonish" machine, the biscuit trade has never looked back. The
enormous factory in King's Road is said to cover nearly thirty
acres and has supplied the armed forces of two wars, at one
time between those wars turning out four hundred different
kinds of biscuits and cakes.

One tends to look no further than Huntley and Palmer's
for biscuits but there is another firm in Reading which makes

biscuits. In 1851 in Plymouth, H. O. Serpell's were busily making ship's biscuits, the proprietors being Messrs. Frean, Daw and Serpell. Frean left the firm to join up with a Mr. Peek who was likewise interested in biscuits; then Daw faded out, leaving Serpell in sole command. A great fire in 1869 demolished the factory and Serpell bought out Meaby and Company of Reading in 1899. Serpell still makes biscuits, and the name of Meaby is well known in the Reading baking trade. But biscuits are on points, and the man in the Reading street has forgotten half the different kinds of Berkshire biscuits which, before the war, were available in every grocer's shop throughout England, Wales and Scotland, and which frequently turned up in unexpected places abroad.

CHAPTER XIV

INDUSTRIES, ANCIENT AND MODERN

To a large extent, the natural assets of a county determined its trades and industries. This works as a negative rather than a positive, for not always were these assets utilised. A land with no rivers could have no water-mills, no coal-mines if the geology was not suitable, no kelp industry if it had no seaboard. So much depended upon the initiative of the people, for those who saw an opening and rode hard at it were often in a position to make a fortune.

To-day, this matters less and less, and many, if not all, of our English counties carry industries whose main interest is proximity to their respective markets. But in the past Berkshire was not slow to use her greatest natural assets, her river systems and her Downs; there is not much to be exploited beneath our countryside, though a fair use has been made of what there is. Fortunately, perhaps, we have been spared the blast furnaces, the slag heaps and all the other horrors some counties have to bear. Instead, the peaceful cultivation of the land, the tinkle of sheep-bells, the sweet smell of malt. Yes, an agricultural land, its little valley fields and great rolling downland pastures side by side in the summer sun. And yet, beneath this veneer of bliss, this reflection of heaven upon earth, little girls working eighteen hours each day in the whiting factories and in the fulling mills; women with frozen hands and frozen bodies "bolting" the rods in the beds along the Kennet banks; the poor and unemployed obliged, under threats of severe penalties, to report for work in the cloth and silk industries. And, meantime, men grew rich and turned a blind eye upon the hardships of the life they had escaped. No wonder there are trade unions!

Berkshire, having once been largely forest, was well favoured with trees, and good use has been made of them from an early date. Way back as far as Henry III, Berkshire trees were showing a profit, travelling to London down the Thames. Windsor Castle claimed many of our trees, likewise Eton and doubtless many of the stately mansions. The mighty trees of Windsor Forest have built many a proud ship, and it is on record that in 1649, 2,640 trees were marked for this purpose alone.

What a joy it is to lie and look up into the very heart of a big oak—what a glorious green world for little birds, the tits and so forth that creep about exploring, so high up that their little voices are scarcely heard down below, and the beautiful chestnut and blue nuthatch, which is inseparable from mighty trees, searches every crack and cranny. But these are not man-made trees, so to speak. Successive generations of Berkshire men have inherited them, looked after them, at times neglected them, but always had them in the bank, as it were.

And what about other kinds of trees—willows and so forth —that men cultivate, from time to time taking what they want? Willows are pollarded along the Berkshire rivers just as they are anywhere else. The purpose of this is often questioned by townsmen, who do not know the intricacies of hurdle making and mending, nor the formality of spicks and spars needed for rick thatching. And then the "rods," what are they for? The rod-beds or withies of the Kennet valley are as much a part of the landscape as the river itself, and have been so for hundreds of years, the reds, oranges, browns and greens, a kaleidoscope of autumn colours. Almost anywhere between Calcot and Hungerford you will find them, and not always close to the river, either, for the rods can be persuaded to grow in strange places like hillsides and in the corners of fields. Withies grown in a clay soil are said to produce the best-quality rods, because it provides a good insulation for the roots. Where the soil is suitable, withies are planted during the winter months. The ground must be ploughed and harrowed, though not much of a tilth is required; the "sets" are planted at the rate of between ten and twenty thousand to the acre, according to the type of "rod," and there follows the same amount of hoeing as any nursery crop receives. But this is no nursery crop to be transplanted, for by the second winter the men will be cutting the rods of all colours except blue, and carting them to the sorting yards. The bundles, or bolts as they are called, measure 42 inches in girth at 14 inches from the butts. The bright-red bolts are the shortest and are the first to be cut; the green rods of the common osier, twice or three times as long, are cut last, often as late as March. At one time the womenfolk worked in the yards as well as in the beds, for in the spring all hands were required for stripping the coloured rind from the rods; even children were put to this task, which was neither arduous nor unpleasant when the sun shone and the yards were a blaze of colour.

Starting as a cottage industry, for baskets and eel-traps were made in many of the river-side villages, the rod industry grew until the rods were sent off along the waterways to supply the London basket-makers; and then, when the industry was at its height, imported rods from foreign lands knocked the bottom clean out of the industry, which has never recovered, and though there are rod-beds functioning to this day, the whole thing is on a small scale and I doubt if there is much money in it. As part of a shoot these rod-beds are ideal, for pheasants love them, and the glorious colours of a winter cock rising from the greens and reds of the beds into the clear blue of a frosty sky is a sight not to be missed.

Further from the river, in the same valley, we have the brakes of alder, ash and hazel. These are sold once every eight or ten years for faggoting, but more frequently when required for hurdles. The wood is used for a variety of purposes, such as thatchers' spicks, hurdles, handles for tools and walking-sticks, both ash and hazel making good walking-sticks but neither really equalling blackthorn for lasting power; formerly there was a great demand for these woods for hoop-making, for when split and trimmed they are very pliable and can be bent round barrels and casks.

Naturally, there was a fair demand for hurdles where sheep were kept, and most of the vale villages had their own little trade. Sheep-hurdles were made from hazel and willow, split and twisted together, and for cribs and hay-cages ash and willow were used, but, like the sheep, these village industries have disappeared. Incidentally, while their men were making hurdles and the like, the village women used to plait straw, both wheat and rye, and make hats, or bonnets as they called them. And not only straws were plaited, but strips of willow as thin as straws were worked into strips or woven on looms into sheets a yard square. These were sent off to London to be made into bonnets; lime was sometimes used but was never available in the same quantities as willow.

You will find plenty of these coppices all over the County, and with them you will find primroses and bluebells; partridges love to nest in them, among the bronze of last year's leaves and the twisting tentacles of the ever-spreading brambles, while in the prickly depths of the hollies scattered here and there jays scream and scold and sometimes nest. Mentioning holly reminds me of an "industry" which appears round Christmas-time each year. I call it an "industry" with considerable diffidence. The whole trouble is due to the absurd amount of money townspeople will pay in order to decorate their houses with holly. The result is that unscrupulous people go about hacking the crown off every accessible tree. The removal of young conifers from plantations is a wicked waste of future timber, more wicked than the desecration of holly trees, which, after all, have little value; attempts by the authorities to put an end to this Christmas "industry" have not, I regret to say, been very successful.

Birch plantations, of which there are many along the Hampshire border, are sold and cut every three or four years. The trees are cut right back to within an inch or so of the ground, and walking through a newly cut plantation is a dangerous business. The long pliable tops are tied into bundles and so are the poles, and lorries laden with such bundles are no uncommon sight. At one time Aldermaston was the centre of the broom trade, but that was when water transport was important; then, Aldermaston wharf was the scene of constant activity, what with withies and besoms and peat and the brewery. But now the besom business has almost departed from Berkshire over the border into Hampshire, where it is very much a cottage industry even though the prerogative of but a few families. Another type of broom is made here, binding heather to a shaft of birch; and hay-rakes too. And so the leaves and the catkins go, leaving for a year or two the heather and the moss, the bracken and the toadstools in command; but slowly and surely the birch comes back, spreading over everything, sticky with greenfly and nibbled by weevils, but always gaining on the other vegetation until it stands as tall as a man and the deer can stand in it unseen; then it is cut again, and each time it is cut it grows thicker. Acres and acres of birch are destroyed each summer by fires which run through the heather roots for days on end, but like the inevitable willow-herb, the birch soon comes again.

Tanning at one time was a flourishing Berkshire industry. This was largely due to the natural supply of oak trees, the bark from which was much coveted. The stripping of the bark has to be done when the sap has begun to rise—that is to say, in April and May, and though it can be done somewhat later than this, once the tree is in leaf it is too late; for one thing, the "fallers" don't like "falling" trees in leaf, and they have good reason. You will notice I call them timber "fallers"; in Berkshire you may "fell" a tree but the men who do the job are not "fellers" but "fallers," and this is not entirely a matter of dialect; the wedge of wood, which is cut out at the base of the tree on the side on which it is to crash, is known as the "fall," and, strange as it may seem, one talks about "putting in the fall," not cutting it out. Having got the tree down, the limbs are sawn off and the bark, or rind as it is more often called, is peeled off. This is done with a small axe and a broad flat tool which is pushed in beneath the bark and used as a lever. The bark is chopped into suitable lengths on the tree so that once it is peeled off it is ready for stacking. The drying process is a tricky one, for both rain and sun will damage the bark; one somehow thinks more in terms of rain than sun in England nowadays, but one must remember that in the days when the oak-bark trade was at its height, perhaps one hundred years ago or more, the seasons had not yet merged or reversed or whatever it is that has happened, and winter really was winter and summer was summer. And the sight of a "peeled" tree travelling to the saw-mills is rare enough to-day, except perhaps for softwood trees, which are always "peeled" where they fall.

What of the tanneries themselves? Well, most of us have known the smell and it isn't very nice, and one can well imagine that a hundred years ago it was a good deal worse! The oak bark, by the way, is cut up into little blocks in the

tanneries and sometimes ground up into powder. No wonder
the place stinks, for here are piles of fresh skins waiting to be
cleaned of fat and hair, of more interest to the flies than to
anybody else, and hanging up like Monday's washing are more
skins, or hides as we should call them, drying off. Where then
does the oak bark come into the picture? For this you must
venture into the sheds if you can bring yourself to do so.
Here there are tanks containing horrible-looking liquids, the
tannic acid or tannin content of which varies from very weak
to very strong; and this is where the oak bark does come into
the picture, for tannin can be extracted from the bark of
many trees, the oak heading the list for its quantity and
quality; willow, larch, Scotch fir, birch and alder can also be
used. Once the hide has had a lime bath and has been scraped
clean of hairs it goes to float on logs in the weakest bath.
Gradually the hide is moved along to stronger liquids. Some
hides spend a year or more in the tanks before their tanning
is complete; sometimes in days of old they were bathed in a
witch-like brew of pigeons' dung : it is not really surprising
that the places smelt ! Once out of the tanning liquids the hides
undergo all sorts of treatment, with which we are not concerned here, but eventually they become the leather for which
England is so rightly famous. And it really was leather, not
the sort of wasp's-nest paper that boots are made of to-day.
But there is really very little demand for oak bark now, and
the trade is definitely on its last legs wherever in the County
it has survived so long.

Oaks were even pollarded to produce more young and
tender bark. In 1297 a certain Thomas le Tannur performed
in Newbury town; but although there may have been tanneries
here and there as early as the thirteenth century, it was not
until several hundred years later that the tanning business
could be called an industry. There are records of one Richard
Boles, who employed large numbers of men in his tanning
yards at Mortimer, and there were other yards in the Kennet
valley at Shaw, Donnington and Coldash, in the vale of the
White Horse at Wantage and Abingdon, in the Thames
valley at Reading, in the loop of the river between Marlow and Maidenhead, and at the base of the downs at Blew-

bury. At Hungerford the tanning business was of sufficient importance for the Hock-tide Court to appoint "searchers and seakers" annually. The "searchers and seakers" were official "snoops" whose duty it was to see that none but properly tanned leather appeared for sale.

It was only natural that, with a thriving tanning trade, craftsmen in leather goods should appear on the scene, and in 1828, in the neighbourhood of Cookham, there was a boot and shoe industry employing nearly two thousand workmen. It seems that most of the work was done in the cottages, the leather being supplied from a central depot at Cookham where the cutting was carried out, the finished products being brought back and sent off to London. Bootlaces and harnesses were also made in several parts of the County, but eventually the trade flopped owing to the go-ahead chaps in Northamptonshire and Leicestershire. But even after that Berkshire oak bark remained popular.

The very ancient trade of charcoal-burning existed wherever there was a forest, and somehow one can no more think of Windsor Forest without its little clearings and its grimy charcoal-burners than without its trees. In a sense it was a skilled job, though once the principle was mastered it became a simple, if arduous, routine. The wood was chopped into yard lengths during the winter, and a deal of wood was wanted to keep the "hearths" burning throughout the summer —four tons of chopped wood to produce one ton of charcoal! Different kinds of wood were found to produce different grades of charcoal, and once the trade had developed to this stage the charcoal-burner's wife and children were required to sort the wood, while he himself was building his "hearths."

This building was an art in itself and upon it depended the success of the whole thing. A chimney was first built in the centre of the clearing and sticks laid against it to form a circular mass; more sticks were then laid on top, radiating from the central chimney, and the whole thing covered with earth and wood. It was fired by throwing smouldering charcoal down the chimney, packing the chimney with unlighted charcoal, and finally sealing it with a lump of earth. After a week or so of constant attention, for the fire must smoulder

but never flare up, the "hearth" would provide a nice quantity
of good charcoal; if too much air had got in and, unnoticed,
had allowed the wood to burn, there would be nothing left
but ash. And what was the purpose of making charcoal you
may well ask. There were several uses for it, each demanding
a different grade and kind; brewers wanted it for drying
hops, and required it to be made from alder; blacksmiths and
iron-founders wanted it made from oak and ash; the silk
trade wanted it, and I don't think they cared what it was made
from; while lords and labourers wanted it for fuel, for
remember this was long before coal had been heard of. Other
woods were used for a variety of purposes, the most popular
being beech, birch and chestnut. Nowadays charcoal-burning
is somewhat a rarity, but charcoal is sometimes made, in the
vicinity of sawmills, from off-cuts and otherwise unsaleable bits
of wood (I use the word "unsaleable" in the pre-war spirit!).
The old-fashioned "hearth" is no longer used, the wood being
charred in iron furnaces. The ashes also were disposed of,
largely to soap-makers, to wool merchants and to tanners and
brewers.

The beechwood trade is on a much smaller scale than in
the Chiltern counties, though some timber is supplied to the
High Wycombe furniture factories. There once was a small
wooden bowl trade at Bucklebury, and it is said that some of
the larger Bucklebury bowls are still in use at the Mint. Bowls
of this kind were the forerunners of the mass-produced and
not unpleasant wooden plates, fruit bowls, saltcellars to be
seen in many shops to-day.

Sawmills there are in plenty and there is a considerable
timber trade in Reading. Oak and elm are probably the most
important trees, and in the County sawmills, gates, posts and
fencing stakes are made. Elm, by the way, is in great demand
for cart bottoms, because it dents rather than cracks when
heavy objects are dropped upon it; coffins are more often
made of imported timber than of elm nowadays. Talking of
elm for cart bottoms reminds me of yet another Berkshire
industry that is struggling to hold its own against the march
of time. Farm carts, or any kind of cart for that matter,
required wheels, and the wheelwright's trade was indeed a

skilled one. Dunlop tyres and tractors have hit this industry pretty hard, but wheels are not the only things a wheelwright can make. Berkshire wagons were famous throughout the south of England, not only for the high standard of their wheels, but also for the craftsmanship put into each part so that they stood up to the rough usage occasioned by rough roads, drunken carters, enormous loads and all the misuse a farm vehicle gets in the course of its life.

There were many wheelwrights throughout the County, and as likely as not the village blacksmith was also a wheelwright. And what woods are used for wheel-making? First of all the great hub has to be made from well-seasoned timber, probably elm which has been stacked around the workshop for many a year; so important, in fact, is the seasoning of this hub wood that a man may never use timber which he himself has laid down, working only blocks his father prepared before him, his own selection passing to his son. This block is shaved down and lathed nowadays, though before the arrival of lathes the whole thing was shaped by hand. The holes to take the spokes are drilled or gouged out and the hub prepared to fit an axle. For the spokes only split oak is used, for great strength is needed, and the accurate bedding of the spokes in hub and rim is the factor which decides how soon a wheel will shake to bits. The rim is composed of a number of "felloes" or "felleys," curved pieces of wood cut preferably from ash, though sometimes from other woods, particularly from elm. The sawing is done with a gigantic fretsaw, and the "felloes" must be accurately drilled to receive the outer ends of the spokes, and they must all fit snugly together to give the wheel firmness. Then an iron tyre is cunningly fitted to bind the whole thing together. The cunning part is that the tyre is made a bit too small to fit over the "felloes" until it is expanded by heat, and when cooled down it fits as firm as a rock. Finally, the tyre is nailed to the "felloes," the woodwork is sand-papered and the wheel is painted to your requirements.

I think that I have said enough about wood and I must push on to another group of natural products, which have been, and some of which still are, made use of in Berkshire. First of all, the chalk. Having such a nice amount of chalk spread right across the County, it is not surprising that from time immemorial uses have been found for it. Houses have been built with it, though many of these have long ago fallen down and have been replaced with brick and tile buildings. Chalk cottages can still be seen at the north-west end of the County, their thatched roofs and the various iron devices tying their crumbling walls together being conspicuous. There is chalk in Windsor Castle and in many of the chalkland churches. Flints, likewise, have been much used both for building and for road construction.

In days of old, when time was not of great importance, men and women used to pick flints out of the arable fields at the rate of one shilling for twenty bushels; according to Alfred Williams in his *Villages of the White Horse*, the work was not uncongenial, and a comfortable eight or nine shillings could be gathered in a week! Flints were also gathered from the Downs where the top soil had to be turned back, and the work calling for greater pay, the princely sum of two shillings and sixpence was paid for twenty bushels. The work up on the Downs was less congenial, and the man sat beneath a shelter of hurdles which he moved about with him like a snail-shell. And more flints were got from the whiting factories, where their presence was definitely not wanted. To-day, flints are obtained from chalk quarries and are screened off in the process of chalk grinding; they are in great demand on farms for yard bottoms; they are also used by some farmers for repairing their private roads—when loose they are terrible to walk on, but are not so damaging to pneumatic tyres as one might think; it is when they get well bedded down that nasty cuts appear in otherwise good tyres!

In chalkland every village has its quarry, though most of these are now overgrown and are haunts of rabbits and bird-nesting boys. But once they were an important, one might say an essential, part of village life, for here flints were got to make the roads, chalk was cut for building purposes, while softer chalk was used for yards and farm tracks. The chalk used for building had to be hard and was cut out in large blocks, which in their turn were sawn into smaller blocks and

stood aside to weather under a roof of thatch. Winter frosts
were relied upon to separate the good from the bad, and in
the spring the blocks which had stood the test went off to
the builders. In building it was important that the grain of
the chalk should be laid horizontally, in which position it
would last almost indefinitely, whereas if the grain was set
vertically the block soon started crumbling away. From the
same pits, chalk was burned for lime, or was spread on the
land in lumps as a dressing. But when one sees for how many
years lump chalk will remain apparently untouched by
exposure, one can guess how much good it can be as a dressing. A more modern way of handling chalk is to screen out the
flints and nodules, and grind it into a powder, which, when
spread, has a much more beneficial effect than the same sub-
stance in lump form.

In certain parts of the County the soft upper chalk was
turned into whiting, a material used by the paint trade. Kintbury and Warren Row, near Henley, were the centres of the
trade. The chalk was dug, broken up and sieved to remove
flints, after which it was soaked in water and allowed to
settle; the so-called "slurry" was then run off and dried in
open sheds; most of the "whiting" from Kintbury was sent
off by waterway to the paint manufacturers in Bristol, though
there was a small demand for it in Reading and Slough. The
old prison-like silk factory in Kintbury was turned over to
whiting production in 1850, but in 1896 it was pulled down,
people having at last realised what an eyesore it was. There
is talk of the industry starting up again in Kintbury.

Other building materials have been dug from local deposits;
limestones and sandstones from the corallian ridge in the
north of the County have been considerably used in the building of churches, farmhouses, barns and field fences, and the
coral rag is still quarried for road materials.

Sarsen stones, the "grey wethers" of the downland pasture,
have been used for building where they have been available,
as, for instance, round Lambourn and other villages near the
Downs, and sometimes layers of sarsens are separated by
chalk blocks or by flint layers; sarsens have been considerably
used at Windsor but they were probably brought there from

Cloth Hall, Newbury

the Bagshot area of Surrey. There were two objections to the use of sarsens for building, for in the first place they are extremely hard and, being, therefore, difficult to chip, took much time to dress; and in the second place houses built of them were always damp because the stones "sweated" such a lot; but for field fences and outside walls it was an ideal material, being almost indestructible. Eventually concrete came along to usurp the place of chalk, rag, flint and sarsens, and many of the countryside occupations dwindled out of sight. In their place, however, arose a great trade in gravel, which has flourished in various parts of the County ever since; these gravel workings are particularly noticeable just outside Reading, between the Loddon and Kennet, and through the Kennet valley at Calcot, Theale, Aldermaston and Beenham, Greenham, Newbury and on to Hungerford.

Berkshire bricks and tiles were justly renowned and still are, though, like so many of our industries, much of the trade has gone elsewhere. Several of the various clays with which the County has been favoured are suitable for brickmaking, notably the clays of the Reading beds worked principally at Katesgrove and Grovelands; but also at Tilehurst, Upper Basildon, Knowle Hill, Pinkneys Green, Maidenhead, Cookham, Kintbury, Shaw, Curridge and Wickham, the London Clay at Newbury, Bracknell, Binfield and Wokingham, the Kimeridge Clay at Abingdon, Faringdon, Cumnor and Drayton, the Gault Clay in the Vale at Childrey, Stanford in the Vale, Wantage and Uffington and the Highworth Clay of the Berkshire Oolites at Marcham, Cumnor and Kingston Bagpuize. Quite a number of these brickworks are still functioning; perhaps the earliest records are from Cookham, where, in 1287, tiles were sold at two shillings and twopence per thousand.

It just remains to say a few words about peat, and we have finished with Berkshire's natural assets. In the old valley of the Kennet, which, as anyone can see, was considerably wider than it is at present, much mud and the remains of mosses, principally *Sphagnum* (the bog-moss), sedges, reeds, rushes, heather, bracken and other plants were deposited in bogs, marshes and lagoons. These were relatively recent deposits

Clock House, Newbury

and in the course of time they have become partially mineral-
ised. Peat was dug until quite recently in the Kennet valley
between Theale and Hungerford, and was either sold for
firing or was burnt to produce fertiliser; peat is still dug but
no longer on a commercial scale, and one can no longer expect
to see the stacked blocks along the Kennet side.

Now I must turn to the man-made industries, first and
foremost of which, of course, was the great wool trade. Of
all the industries our County has ever had, the wool trade
was perhaps the most far reaching, and because of this, one
which carried the prosperity of the County like a switchback,
up to the peaks and down into the troughs, finally losing
speed and slipping backwards to its end.

It has been suggested that a wool factory was established
at Winchester during the Roman occupation; it is certain that
the Romans knew the art of cloth- and felt-making, for in the
ruins of Pompeii a complete set of scouring, fulling and pressing implements was found. Just when the industry reached
Berkshire we do not know, but theories, and not altogether
tenable ones, have been put forward suggesting the early
twelfth century. Be that as it may, we know for certain that
during the thirteenth century there was a fulling mill at Newbury and that considerable quantities of English wool were
being exported to Flanders, running the gauntlet of both
French and British pirates in the Channel. It is also known
that at about the same time English wool was being sent to
the merchants of Venice in exchange for sugar and spices.

The rolling Downs were ideal for sheep and the rivers provided power for the fulling mills and a convenient means of
transport. The home-made cloth was very coarse and was
more suited to sacks than human raiment. From time to time
infusions of Flemings reached England, and the Berkshire
trade benefited by the ideas and methods they brought with
them. Fulling mills there were all over the County, at Hungerford, Greenham, Newbury, Bagnor, Thatcham, Reading,
Wallingford and East Hendred to mention only a few. Fulling, of course, was the process of felting the woven fabric,
and was only one of the large number of processes between
the raw material and the finished article. Other processes were

scouring to remove the greasy yolk in the natural wool; teazing with teazel heads to separate the fibres; oiling to put back the gloss removed by scouring; scribbling and carding; condensing to roll the fibres into threads; spinning to yarn and weaving of warp and weft; followed by perching, knotting, scouring, milling, cutting, pressing, brushing, and finally marketing.

From the number of operations one can see that a very large number of workmen would be required, quite apart from the shepherds and shearers, hurdle makers and crib makers, and all the other members of the agricultural community whose skill and knowledge was from time to time required. And then there were the craftsmen who made and repaired the looms, the spindles, the whorls, the bobbins, shuttles and rollers, the fulling machines, the waterwheels and the teazle wheels. Yes, indeed, it certainly was an industry, and at one time there were more Berkshire men and women employed in the cloth trade than in all the other trades put together.

From the *Industrial History of England* we know that the Reading Mills produced a cloth of heavy texture, a "piece" being 30 yards long and 6½ quarters broad and weighing 66 lbs.

Reading, Abingdon and Newbury were the centres of the wool trade, the great mass of the Downs finding keep for thousands of sheep. The great Berkshire sheep fairs were famous throughout the land, and sheep from distant counties wearily plodded along the droves towards East Ilsley and Compton. And what of the ups and downs that finally brought the industry to a standstill? I have already pointed out that in the thirteenth century there was a nice, steady trade with Flanders, but that this was hindered by pirates. By the middle of the fourteenth century the Hundred Years' War with France was in full swing, the French King being determined to capture Flanders and the important weaving and cloth-finishing industry, for by doing so he would be able to forbid the buying of English wool, thus bringing ruin upon the merchants and the landowners, and disaster upon the King who levied taxes upon the trade. Although he did not entirely succeed, the French King certainly brought the wool trade down into a trough of depression, for men were required to fight instead of work on both sides of the Channel and everything was disorganised; then came the Black Death, sweeping everything before it, leaving the Berkshire sheep to wander starving through the fields, there being no one left to tend them. This was followed by a fillip to the trade in the form of the Inclosure Act of 1517, which, while suiting the landowners, drove the labourers away from agriculture and made them available for the mills and other departures of the woollen trade. It is said that at this time sheep grew fat and men grew thin, for sheep farming was so profitable that cereals and other crops for human consumption were scarcely grown at all. It was at this time that men like Kendrick, Dolman and Jack of Newbury appeared, towering above their colleagues and their rivals on account of their great wealth.

I have written elsewhere of Dolman who built Shaw House, and of John Winchcombe, alias Smallwood, alias Jack of Newbury; the old Cloth Hall in Newbury, now a museum, is a relic of their days. Kenrick, a Reading merchant who lived at the end of the sixteenth century, kept 140 looms in constant employ, with an army of pickers, sorters, carders, spinners, weavers, dyers and teazers. He died in 1624, leaving money to build a house of employment for the Reading poor. And then the discord grew, town being jealous of country and trying to wrest the trade from the cottage looms; a variety of stupid regulations were made in an endeavour to cut each other's throats; Kendrick's gift become a bone of contention, the cause of enormous trouble, and finally led to the complete crippling of the town trade. To make matters worse the Civil War came to Berkshire and Reading was sieged. What was left of the trade went all to pieces; the factories were closed or used for billeting soldiers. The cloth trade was requisitioned and tailors set to work on one thousand suits of army clothes for the occupying soldiers. And thus the wool trade, the mightiest industry the County has ever had, tottered to its fall.

It continued long after this in a small way in and around Wantage and Newbury, where in 1724 the looms were turning out nothing but shalloon, a kind of stuff used for the linings of coats, but the spirit had gone and the craftsmen were leaving the south for the mills of Yorkshire and Lancashire, where they were told that there was work for all. In Reading a ghost of the old trade was revived, and into the middle of the last century sail cloth was made from imported materials. In Abingdon the carpet and clothing factories are the sole relics of those good old days, when unemployment was unknown, and when on the Downs the sheep-bells tinkled like some corner of fairyland.

I cannot leave the subject of wool and the clothing trade without reference to a Mr. John Coxeter of Greenham Mills; Mr. Coxeter was a man with a machine-mind, whose aim and object in life was to get things done as quickly as possible, even if this meant using the new-fangled machines which people were constantly inventing. In support of his speeding-up schemes and because of a wager, he undertook to make a coat for Sir John Throckmorton between sunrise and sunset starting with two live sheep. Starting at 5 a.m. the two sheep were shorn, the wool cleaned and stubbed, spun and woven, the cloth washed and fulled, trimmed and dyed. By 4 p.m. the cloth was ready for the tailors, who succeeded in producing from it a fine hunting kersey well within the allotted time. The wager was for 1,000 guineas!

Turning now from sheep; I must take you to Wokingham to see some animals imported from abroad, which were to cause quite a stir in the County. There were thousands of them, living in warmed sheds and feeding on mulberry leaves. You can guess, of course, that they are silkworms, but do you know how they got to Berkshire?

The silkworm with which we are concerned is a native of China, where as long ago as 2640 B.C. silkworms were reared for silk making. Sometime during the sixth century two Persian monks, who were in China as missionaries, stole a batch of eggs and hid them within a hollow cane. They were safely brought back to Constantinople, where they were hatched and the caterpillars fed upon wild mulberry. The two monks, who had not wasted their time in China, knew all the details of rearing the caterpillars and of winding the silk from the cocoons. From Constantinople, eggs were distributed to Cashmere, Russia, Turkey, Egypt, Algeria, Italy, Spain and France, a considerable time, of course, being taken before France became involved. The Flemings, retreating to England, brought with them the germ of what was for a time to be quite an important industry, and Berkshire was to be one of the first counties to try it out.

When Elizabeth came to the throne, the silk trade was in its infancy, but showed such promise that mulberry trees were sent to Wokingham for planting in the district. The silk-worms were reared in sheds, the eggs being encouraged to hatch by the warmth produced from fermenting dung; it is even said that batches of eggs were carried in the bosom sewn up in little bags! Once hatched, the caterpillars were fed upon fresh mulberry leaves daily until they spun a nice golden cocoon. Once the spinning was finished, the cocoons were sexed according to their size, and a number taken out as breeding stock. The remainder were put in an oven to kill the enclosed pupæ and were then soaked in water kept warm by charcoal fires. When in a suitable condition, the threads of half a dozen cocoons were taken and twisted together through the glass eye of the reeling machine; the cocoons were then literally unwound, and a very tricky job this is, as many a schoolboy knows. Each cocoon yields about 1,000 feet of silk. The strands of silk thus produced then have to be cleaned and handed over to the weavers.

Silk stockings were made at Wokingham and at one time were the best in the country. So keen was the trade that local laws were passed forcing unemployed, unmarried, poor and otherwise unoccupied persons to work in the silk business. The labour costs were low, for the women and children who were largely employed were paid no more than five shillings a week! Later, continental silk was imported and worked into hatbands, ribands and bootlaces, but this importation crippled the trade, and the treaty with France, organised by William Huskisson, President of the Board of Trade in 1825, which allowed French silk to come into the country duty free, caught both England and Ireland on the hop, and, unable to compete, our Berkshire industry dwindled away.

Not only Wokingham, but Reading also went in for silk, and Robert Smart is said to have been the first manufacturer there in 1640. But the silk trade did not flourish in Reading until 1730, when there were factories near the Abbey wall, near the present site of Huntley and Palmer's biscuit factory, and a third in Brunswick Place. Kendrick's workhouse in Minster Street, called the Oracle, was used for silk weaving at this time, and in the same street there was a silk mill. The Oracle was pulled down in 1849 and its gate taken to St. Mary's Hill. At Twyford the trade held out until 1835, under the direction of the Billing family, and at Newbury and Kintbury there was at one time a thriving industry.

Another trade brought over by the Flemings was lace-making, and at one time there was quite a sound little concern around Cookham and Longworth, lace being manufactured in most of the cottages.

Sacking, rope and twine were made at Abingdon and Reading, and the hemp and flax was grown around many of the villages of the Vale. The preparation of the fibres was a cottage industry, but their conversion into rope and twine was probably beyond the capacity of most villagers, requiring extensive rope walks; on the other hand, a coarsish linen could be woven at home. With hemp the practice was, no doubt, to pull the male plants as soon as they had shed their pollen and make cloth from their fibres, and later to pull the female plants and send their coarse fibres off for rope and sail making, having harvested the seed. Flax, on the other hand, was all pulled at once, and both hemp and flax were subjected to certain processes, such as retting, grassing, breaking and scrutching, designed to separate the woody matter from the fibres. In the manufacture of linen cloth the fibres were heckled, the size of the teeth of the heckle varying according to the final material required, and then spun into yarn, after which it was woven on hand-looms. For making rope the hemp was heckled, spun, tarred, wound on to bobbins, formed into strands and finally the strands were laid into a rope. The "rope walk" is a necessity for spinning; the spinner wraps a quantity of the heckled hemp around his waist and, having attached some ends to a revolving hook, walks away backwards down the "walk," regulating the supply of fibres by hand. In most rope-making factories nowadays, everything is done by machinery as one would suppose.

Having now dealt with the materials made in our County what about some of the instruments used for sewing? Both thimbles and pins were made in the County; the former were made at Bisham, where by 1748 there was a flourishing copper-rolling industry; wire drawing was a going concern in Reading in 1619, followed by pin making in 1633, though pin making had been going on in Wargrave before this. Reading pins were made very largely by children, or by poverty-stricken old people, who were only too glad to earn a few shillings. Pin making continued until the end of the nineteenth century; the Reading pin was made in two parts, the shank and the head, and in the Reading museum there is a good exhibit showing some of the original pins and illustrating the way in which they were constructed.

Soap boiling and tallow chandling were village industries. Soap was made with the lees drawn from the ashes of potash and lime, boiled up with tallow and oil; it was boiled twice—the second boiling in order to purify it and make it ready for cutting up into blocks; soap could be bought "Black" at one halfpenny a pound, "Grey Bristol" at one penny, and "White," an imported soap, was even more expensive! For some reason a heavy tax was put upon home-made soaps, to the extent of 1½d. per pound! Candles the same, and in 1732 one John Sexton was fined £100 for keeping candles in his house, a deed that was forbidden. In the days of no other means of lighting, I suppose it was only natural for the authorities to tax candles and put unnecessary restrictions upon their use. The soap and candle works was, no doubt, a pretty smelly affair; and talking of smells, an ingenious gentleman called William Hayes got into trouble in 1634, not so much for making gut lute strings—for is not the lute a wholly delightful instrument?—but for the dreadful smell which seemed to be part of the business, and so the Berkshire Lute String Company, or whatever he called himself, disappeared just as suddenly as it appeared.

Paper making has in the past been carried on at Bisham,

Thatcham, Cookham, Sutton Courtenay, Arborfield, East Hagbourne (where blotting-paper is said to have been accidentally discovered), Bagnor, Twyford and Whistley. You will notice that all these places are in a position to use water power; it very often happened that an old corn-grinding mill was converted for paper making, and the history of Colthrop mill at Thatcham is a good example. Although it may have been in existence earlier, the first we know of this mill is in 1472, when it was a corn-mill; in 1540 the great stones had been removed and it was a fulling mill; with the collapse of the wool trade the mill lay idle so far as we know, and the next we hear of it is in 1805, when it started life anew as a paper mill; not the same building all the time, of course, but the same site on the river Kennet. This mill, with its odious chimneys (chimbleys, of course, in Berkshire dialect), produces paper to this day and so does the mill at Bisham.

From paper one's thoughts go to printing, and here Berkshire can claim a very ancient achievement, for in 1528 the first press in the County started work in the abbey at Abingdon. But someone influential saw the dangers of the "written word," and in 1583 an Act was passed forbidding the use of printing presses except in London, Oxford and Cambridge, where presumably they could be kept to heel. By 1723, however, things had changed and the first copy of the *Reading Mercury* appeared under the direction of one John Watts, the mayor of Reading. Rather different from the *Mercury* we know to-day, eight inches wide and ten inches long; it is a truly wonderful record that the *Reading Mercury* should have stood up to all the knocks in a world of competition and survived where others have fallen by the wayside. The *Mercury* is indeed to be congratulated on this fine achievement, and one can only wonder what size and shape it will be after another 225 years; there are times when one wonders if anything will survive the Scylla and Charybdis ahead! In 1744 the *Mercury* weathered the first storm when Mr. D. Henry failed in an attempt to "kill" it with his *Reading Journal and Weekly Review*. In 1770 the *Berkshire Chronicle* was inaugurated and has survived to this day.

Many interesting books have been published from Berkshire presses, but one that appeals to me most of all was printed in 1832 by the Snare family in Minster Street, Reading, and was a catalogue of the books current at that time ! John Man, who wrote that rather unreliable *History of Reading*, joined the Snare family, and with them printed *The Stranger in Reading* and the *Environs of Reading*.

As the knowledge of printing spread so did the machines, and, early in the nineteenth century, Reading, Newbury, Faringdon, Abingdon, Wantage, Wokingham, Windsor and Wallingford could all claim presses. The subject has been very well written up in the *Victoria County History*, Vol. I, and I would direct anyone there who wishes to further his knowledge of local activities in the printing world.

Returning to the rivers which have helped all Berkshire's industries to such an extent, we cannot omit mention of boats and boat building. Both Reading and Newbury were at one time great places for barge building. The Thames, the Kennet and Loddon, the Kennet and Avon Canal (projected in 1794 and completed in 1810, connecting London and Bristol), the Wantage-Abingdon Canal, joining the Thames and Severn Canal, made Berkshire waterways even more important than roadways. Because of this Berkshire has always been a barge-building County.

The earliest known Berkshire boat is a Bronze Age dugout canoe found near the Lambourn at Bagnor, and the remains of an Iron Age boat has been found in the Thames at Windsor. More recently, other boats have been made in the Newbury district, but none have been required for crossing the Lambourn at Bagnor, I imagine. Boats of all kinds have been built in most of the riverside villages from Windsor to Oxford and from Reading to Hungerford, though nowadays the demand for anything but pleasure boats and racing craft has changed the style of the industry, and the horse-drawn barge is, indeed, as rare a sight on the waterways as on the stocks in the builders' yards.

Another industry concerned with our streams is the growing of watercress. Although by no means a large industry at any time, Berkshire cress used to be well known and much sought after in the London markets. The largest concern of the present day is near Stanford Dingley, where the green of the young cress and the blue of the "Blue Pool" are sights worth seeing. At Blewbury, just where one would not expect to find cress, the little streams have been used to good purpose. There are other unexpected cressbeds, too, in the "Vale" at Letcombe Bassett and Ashbury, and over the border into Wiltshire at Bishopstone and over into Hampshire at Ecchinswell.

The secret of watercress cultivation has been jealously guarded by those in the "know," and there was, in the past, great rivalry between the various growers which has done considerable harm to the development of the industry as a whole. The same can be said for mushroom cultivation, a habit which is getting a hold on Berkshire and many other counties at the moment; secrecy and jealousy usually do more harm than good, although in an economy such as we have, to hold a monopoly of the market may be well worth an occasional crop failure due to unexplainable or unadmittable reasons.

A county so definitely agricultural as Berkshire, undoubtedly had at an early date a tool and implement industry, carrying with it an iron works and foundry trade. The first reference to this sort of thing comes from 1626 when we knew the County possessed at least one "nayle maker." Nails and iron tyres for wheels, bands for barrels, harrows and digging implements have been in use for a long time. During the last century practically every village had its "smithy" if not its small foundry. A village foundry, such as the one which still functions in Bucklebury, is always a wonderful sight of old iron, rusty ploughs and harrows, axles, wheels, pipes and a hundred other odds and ends half hidden in the grass which threatens to hide them completely while they wait until there comes a day when they are needed.

The agricultural implement maker was a most important person, and he usually had his "works" close to one of the larger towns. But he supplied only local needs. To-day in Berkshire we have implement makers supplying a demand from over the whole country and beyond. One might point out at this stage that the agricultural seed-drill was invented by a Berkshire man, one Jethro Tull, who was born in 1674 at Basildon, and who died there in 1741. It seems that at some time during his life he lived at Prosperous Farm, Shalbourne (Wiltshire). An Oxford graduate, he was called to the Bar, but ill-health demanded a country life, where he wrote about agriculture, carried out experiments and was a pioneer of our modern scientific approach to farming.

The subject of agricultural implements makes one think of those lovely shiny garden forks and trowels sold by Suttons in Reading Market Place; though not ancient, for it was not started until early in the nineteenth century, the seed trade has gone ahead like wildfire since the day when Martin Hope Sutton first opened shop. It is whispered that Sutton had built their house upon the rock of Irish famine in 1847, when they were able to supply seeds of turnips, beet and cabbage (more probably they were the only firm capable of so doing). One hundred years later Sutton's is a most enormous firm, with trial grounds all over the country and employing thousands of people. The "Royal Seed Establishment" is not the only seed concern in Berkshire, but by the virtue of its size, age and achievements it far and away surpasses the others.

Few Berkshire people realise that at one time there was a strong clock-making fraternity in the County. A very interesting note on this subject was published in 1926 by Mr. Ernest Dormer in the *Berkshire, Buckinghamshire and Oxfordshire Archæological Journal,* from which we learn that the earliest Berkshire clock-maker was Richard of Wallingford, Abbot of St. Albans, who, in the fourteenth century, made a clock which showed not only the time, but also showed the course of the sun, moon and stars, and the rise and fall of the tides. An achievement indeed for the fourteenth century! Next on the list comes Henry Seymour of Wantage, who made the clock still at East Hendred Church, in the first half of the sixteenth century. Richard Whitheare in 1648 and J. Hoddle forty years later, and in 1682 John Hocker, all made clocks in Reading. The Dickers, a great clock-making family, performed in Reading, Mortimer and Silchester (at the last mentioned there is a Dickers' Farm which presumably has some connection with this family of long ago). By 1660 William Wise was clock-maker in Wantage, and during the eighteenth century John Lord of Faringdon, Thomas Jones of Windsor, William Gunn of Wallingford, Peter Godlyman and Benjamin Cotton of Hurley and Bunce of Wantage, Joseph Kember of Shaw, John Player, Thomas West, Thomas Wild, William Randall, all of Reading, John Lee of Cookham and Horsnaile (what a lovely Shakespearean sort of name!) of Warfield. Finally, Mr. Dormer gives a list of nineteenth-century Berkshire clock-makers in which there are fifty-eight names, from Newbury, Windsor, Wantage, Wallingford, Reading, Wokingham, Maidenhead, Lambourn, Hungerford, Faringdon, Abingdon, Theale and Pangbourne.

In Berkshire one can trace the manufacture of weapons of sport and warfare from Stone Age flint arrowheads and axes through the Bronze Age and Iron Age swords and daggers to the spears and bludgeons of Romans, Saxons and Danes, past the clumsy arbalests of the eleventh and twelfth centuries, past the long bows of the "Newberrie Archers," past the ornate but inaccurate shoulder guns of the early Tudors and the pieces of canon of the Roundhead forces. And here we pause, for since 1636 Bartholomew Abrey had been making guns in Reading. By 1750 he had been replaced by John Mace, a small blunderbuss by whom is in the Reading Museum for all to see. Another John Mace, a descendant, was running the business in 1830. Now Turners have the whole trade in Reading and Newbury and over the border in Basingstoke.

From the sporting-guns of Turner's we pass to all the bits and pieces of far deadlier weapons produced in Berkshire factories during the recent war, and we end our tour with the final word in modern methods of destruction, for up by the Downs, at Harwell, where the Ridgeway and the Icknield Way run silently across the landscape and where wheat-ears and buntings can look back into prehistoric times, atomic energy is to be investigated, atoms to be bombarded, split; cyclotrons, electrons, neutrons, isotopes, uranium, plutonium and thorium are now the words of the district and one needs a scientific dictionary and a very modern one at that, to make out what it's all about—and then one wouldn't know a thing. You could only hope that the peaceful side of atomic energy will not be entirely lost from sight.

I have said very little about the modern industries, and this deliberately. Aeroplanes and motor cars, fountain pens and camera lenses, plastic tapes, insulated wires, cables and linoleum, they all bring employment with them and confer sometimes rather doubtful blessings upon the land of their choice; the time is not ripe to write of them, and many of them are with us only because of the war; though they are made within our bounds they have no real connection with the County.

CHAPTER XV

DIALECT AND PLACE-NAMES

SOMEBODY once said that in north-west Berkshire you could hear a language more akin to pure Saxon than anywhere else. That may well have been true once, for it refers to a long time ago. To-day, dialects are fast dying out, as one would expect when schools, wireless sets and cinemas are everywhere; not that this is a bad thing for it really would be most inconvenient to-day. Whether the American English which has largely replaced the Saxon is a prettier language I do not know, but it does mean that all Berkshire men and women who attend the local cinema regularly are able to understand one another, no matter from which part of the County they may come. As a most irregular cinema-goer, I find almost as much difficulty in understanding modern jargon as I would pure Saxon! That dialects are dying out all over England there is no question, and no harm is done so long as they are written down for posterity.

Travelling through Berkshire now you may hear many slightly strange accents, but you will not find the true "Berkshire dialect" without considerable difficulty. The Downs near the Wiltshire border and across the Vale of the White Horse will be your most likely hunting-ground. I could give you, but not here, the name of one jolly farmer who could cause you some consternation by his "nearly pure Saxon," though he talks this language only when he gets excited, and if he were asking you in his most shrill and polite Saxon to refrain from trespassing and leaving his gates open, you might fancy he were relating some comic tale to make you laugh. His sons, like most of the sons of these parts, have far less of the dialect in their speech, and the chances are that his grandchildren will know nothing of it.

Yet many of the strange words persist, those words, I mean, which are not merely strangely pronounced, but are strange in themselves. Who knows, for example, what a "want" or a "wunt" is, or a "hitchen", or a "louzy"? Yet words like these are still in use, particularly among farmers. In 1888 Major Lowsley of Hampstead Norreys put into print *A Glossary of Berkshire Words and Phrases*. There are roughly 2,500 words described, far more than I can possibly mention here. In 1933, when the dialect was fast disappearing, the Rev. G. W. B. Huntingford published another account of the grammar and a very much smaller glossary, which, however, contains many words not found in the earlier work. But if you want to read the dialect, turn to Tom Hughes' *Scouring of the White Horse*. Here you will find words to defeat you, phrases which don't make sense and a sort of teasing good humour all the way through. I quote from this book the following verses, which refer to a pig race on White Horse Hill:

THE LAY OF THE HUNTED PIG

"Vathers, mothers, mothers' zons!
You as loves yer little wuns!
Happy pegs among the stubble,
Listen to a tale of trouble;
Listen, pegs in yeard and stye,
How the Barkshire chaps zard I.

I wur barn at Kingstone-Lisle,
Wher I vrolicked var a while,
As vine a peg as e'er wur zeen
(One of a litter o' thirteen),
Till zome chaps wi' cussed spite
Aimed ov I to make a zite,
And to have a 'bit o' vun,'
Took I up to Uffington.

Up, vorights the Castle mound
They did zet I on the ground;
Then a thousand chaps, or nigh,
Runned and hollered arter I—
Ther, then, I, till I wur blowed,
Runned and hollered all I knowed,
When, zo zure as pegs is pegs,
Eight chaps ketched I by the legs,
Two to each—'tis truth I tell 'ee—
Dree more clapsed I round the belly·
Under all they fellers lyin'—
Pegs!—I thought as I wur dyin'.

Combe Gibbet, a warning by day and by night

> But the Squire (I thenks I zees un),
> Varmer Whitfield ridin' wi' un,
> Fot I out o' all thuck caddle,
> Stretched athurt the varmer's zaddle—
> Bless' em, pegs in yeard and stye,
> Them two vrends as stuck to I.
>
> Barkshire men, vrom Hill and Vale,
> All as ever hears this tale,
> If to spwoort you be inclined,
> Plaze to bear this here in mind—
> Pegs beant made no race to win,
> Be zhart o' wind, and tight o' skin;
> Dwont' 'ee hunt 'em, but instead
> At backswyrd break each other's yead—
> Cheezes down the manger rowl—
> Or try and clim the greasy powl.
>
> Pegs! in stubble yeard and stye,
> May you be never zard like I,
> Nor druv wi' greasy ears and tail,
> By men and bwoys drough White Horse Vale."

The following interpretation of some of the words may help, although the general meaning is clear enough : Zard means served, from zar to serve; Vorights, means opposite; Ther, then, I, means there I was then; Dree, of course, means three; Fot I out, means saved or rescued (this F should really be V); Thuck caddle, means that chaos; Athurt means across; Spwoort means sport; Zhart means short; Backswyrd is only backswords, a game of cracking heads with sticks; Drough (more often Droo') means through.

It isn't difficult once you've got the hang of it, but now try this one : "Ther was a rummy sterb up at verm, somebody took all the vawkses skuts away whilst um was at work." That's not so easy is it? For it means : "There was a funny happening up at the farm, someone took all the chaps' coats away while they were at work."

Mr. Huntingford has shown that although many of the Berkshire words are of undoubted Anglo-Saxon origin, many others are not, being derived from thirteenth- and fifteenth-century English, from French, Dutch and corrupted modern English. The most noticeable feature of the dialect is the

The victim's last view, from Combe Gibbet

many Zs and Vs, for Z covers S as well as Z, and V covers all the words which begin with F as well as V. Then again, the vowel A is pronounced as in Paay, Haay and Waay, making short words sound quite long. O often carries a W before it, as in Bwoy (boy) and Kwut (coat) or, just to be difficult, it becomes an A as in Harnet, Marnin', Tharn. E often gets shoved in before an A, lengthening a word, for example, Neame and Pleace. Then Th often turns into D, as Dree, Drout, Drow; the final G always fades out, as in "Marnin," though the end of a word is sometimes lengthened by the addition of T after a final N; also noticeable is the substitution of -er and sometimes -y for -ow, for instance my name would be Yarrer or Yarry.

The vocabulary is more difficult than the grammar because one can guess at the one, but get nowhere with the other. The following words were in use until fairly recently, and even now just occasionally one will hear them in the County: bottom, a valley, especially in the Downland; butt, a piece of land shorter than a furlong; bush, a bush in my arm is a thorn in my arm; cutt, a drain or ditch; hade, a ridge of land; hangin', the overhanging part of a hill; hitchen a field, part fallow part sown; louze, a verb, to turn cattle out to grass; louzy, noun, a meadow or pasture; piddle, a tiny field; quab, boggy land; slade, low ground; stabble (nothing to do with stubble), to kick mud about the house from dirty boots; shard, a stile; wunt, a mole.

And here is some pig anatomy from Lowsley's vocabulary: the "pluck" and "acelets" are parts of the offal, such as the heart, the "arley bwone" is the hip bone, "innerds" and "chidlins" are the small intestines. Brawn is called "collaredzouse," while the ears, trotters and hocks of a pig are collectively known as the "zouse." "Scump" and "cracklin" are used for what we call crackling in the roasted article. The "vley" is the fat used for making lard, and "crittens" are small bits of lean meat strained from the lard (crittens are chopped up and mixed with sugar, spice and with flour made up into a pudding). The "melt" is the spleen and is eaten with the heart, the valves and gristley part of the latter being called the "dewsiers." The "griskin" is the lean part of the

loin. A pig that is growing well is said to be a good doer and
one that is about ready to kill is a "me-a-ty peg." The part of
its neck where the knife is inserted is called the "sticking
pe-us," and when killed, the "zweelin" is the burning of the
hairs with wheat-straw. The "Vogger's Jint" is the piece of
meat given to the man who slaughtered the pig. "Hoppers"
are mites in bacon, and "rusty baaycon" is rancid yellow stuff.
The "hog-tub" was kept near the kitchen, for waste food and
the pigs taught to come to it at feeding-time. "Hog wash"
was the stuff in the tub. The "dall" and the "derlin" were
runts, the smallest pig in each litter. "Piggin ut" was to live
in a filthy manner. "Pig-ke-uping" consisted of driving pigs to
the stubbles after the harvest and having little boys armed
with whips to see they did not stray. "Stoor pegs" has our
modern meaning and a "peg muzzle" was a gate which an
animal could not push open. Pigs are "ringed" and "cut" for
obvious reasons.

Small boys must have had a pretty thin time, for Lowsley
gives more than forty words referring to chastisement, some
of which are still in use, but as the practice itself is fading
out so are the words and phrases employed. Small boys
should read this list and thank their lucky stars! Baayste,
baaystin', bate, cut, drap into, dresh, dust, dustin', hide, hidin',
laay into, laayce, laaycin', larrup, larrupin', leather, leatherin',
lick, lickin', monkey's 'lowance, quilt, quiltin', slash, spat,
stirrup grace (grease) strap oil, tan, tannin', thimble-pie (rap-
ping the head with a thimbled finger, a habit of school-
marms), towelin, trim, trounce, vlap (with a book), wallop,
wallopin', warm, welt, weltin', whackin', whittle, whop,
whoppin'.

Finally, a few expressions common enough even nowadays.
"Where be I?" "Who be she?" "Anyways, you'll come too."
"I expect he'll come anywhen now." "I be maain cross with
he." "There's a good gun, you." "Where's the old bwoy?"
(the "old boy" always refers to a child, not to the parent).

During the war Americans occupied many aerodromes in
Berkshire and they filled our towns with lorry-loads of men;
now they have gone and left behind a group of gum-chewing
maidens, who have a more pronounced accent than the

Americans themselves! No doubt this will wear off and we shall get some sort of standard language, not including, however, the dialects of Berkshire, Wiltshire and Somerset which once echoed across the Ridgeway and the Vale.

PLACE-NAMES

The study of place-names is difficult, requiring much time and thought, much browsing through old books and charters, and much scholarship. It is quite definitely not a job for the many, but is one for the few, who, armed with the right kind of education and happy in the still of great libraries, can ruthlessly pursue their quarry, from book to book, from language to language, back into the past. And pitfalls there are by the thousand for the unwary, waiting to engulf the tyro, as large and unfathomable as the past he seeks to explain. So leave the machinery to the suitably qualified people, and remember that they, for all their knowledge and reasons, can be completely stumped. But one can get much pleasure from their labours and enjoy the countryside the more, by understanding a few of the basic principles, the hard core as it were, of our common names.

I do not profess to be one of the wise men, having neither the time nor the inclination to pursue the subject far—life is short and one cannot do everything. According to Professor Stenton of Reading University, who is one of the acknowledged sages of place names study, about two-thirds of the Berkshire names have now been worked out, and are of Celtic or Anglo-Saxon and Anglo-French origin, though for some reason, one name and one only (East Garston) is almost certainly of Scandinavian background. Many, we cannot tell how many, of the old names have gone, making those which remain to us the more difficult to understand. Let me deal with our County name, Berkshire. Much has been written concerning its origin, many theories expounded; one of these makes *Berrocscire* from *Bibroci,* possibly a group of the *Atrebates,* living between the Thames basin and the river Severn. Another theory derives the name from the Anglo-Saxon *Bær ac,* meaning bare oak, while another theory carries this a stage farther and associates it with a sacred grove, and then further still, to a particular tree in a sacred grove; it was not a great step to tie this up with a sacred bare oak in Windsor Forest and Herne the Hunter's blasted oak. Yet another theory derives Berkshire from the Roman town *Bibracte*. Professor Skeat, who wrote many books on county place names, and I gather made innumerable though forgivable mistakes, follows Asser's *Life of King Alfred* and finds *Berroc* (or *Bearric*) the name of a wood where the box-tree grows most abundantly, and suggests that Berkshire simply means that the County was once much wooded and that box was abundant, naming the villages of Boxford and Boxgrove to support this. In those days most counties were "much wooded" and one might as well call Reading the town of "much houses." Another and perhaps the most likely theory finds *Berroc* meaning, in British (as distinct from English and Anglo-Saxon, in which it has no meaning at all) a little hill, as well as a wood, some place of importance where in all probability the Shire Court would meet. But I do not think this matter is really straight yet to everyone's satisfaction and I must leave it here.

For those who are interested in derivation, but who, like myself, have no time for further study, I will give as briefly as possible a sketch which the learned professors of the subject would, no doubt, eschew. There are a number of suffixes which can be understood, even by the most ordinary person, though the etymology of the first part of the name may be too much. I do not want to make this like a text-book, yet it is difficult not to "classify and list and write in columns." Perhaps I can group the suffixes by subject rather than adopting the straightforward alphabetical list. Take first, words related to farms and farming; the suffixes "-ham," "hamstede," "-ton" and "-worth" all refer to farms—Greenham, Thatcham, Ashampstead, Easthampstead, Finchampstead, Aldermaston, Appleton, Milton, Upton, Aldworth, Bayworth, Padworth. Many of these farm names refer to persons, the owners presumably, for Padworth is Peada's farm, Bayworth is Bæga's farm, but Aldworth, on the other hand, means old farm, while Aldermaston means alderman's farm; Appleton is the farm with the apple orchard. Milton does not mean mill farm as one might suppose, but middle farm, and, of course, Upton means the upper farm. The suffix "-field"—as in Bradfield, Burghfield, Englefield—does not mean "field" as we know it to-day, but has the significance of "wide open spaces." The suffix "-hay" comes from *haga,* an enclosure, and is found in Woodhay, the woodland enclosure; the suffix "-ley" is from *leah,* a clearing, as in Purley, the pear tree clearing, Streatley, the street by the clearing. Rivers have an importance as one can well imagine, and Pangbourne means Pæginga-burna, the stream of the sons of Pæga, and Shottesbrook, Shot's or Scott's brook. Cholsey means Ceol's island; Hinksey, Hengist's island; Tubney, Tubba island, for the suffix "-ey" is from the Anglo-Saxon *ig,* an island, and "-ford," of course, in Welford, the ford near the willows; Appleford, the apple tree ford; and Sandford, the sandy ford. The suffix "-well" means a spring and Brightwell means "clear spring," while Sunningwell means the well of Suna's people; "-mere," as in Catmore, means cat pond, whereas "-more," as in Stanmore, means swampy ground. The hills and vales are also represented— in "-berg," from *beorh,* the Anglo-Saxon for hill; hence our modern English barrow. Farnborough means Fern hill, the "-comb" in Ruscombe means camp or field, but in Letcombe it means Leoda's valley; "-dene" or den also means valley as in Yattenden, now spelt Yattendon, meaning the valley of the people of Geat; "-don" and "-down" mean hill as in Abingdon and Ashdown; Basildon is a bit deceiving as it goes back to the old English Bestlesdun and then further back to Bestles- forda, meaning Bestel's hill and ford respectively. Our modern hill comes from the old English hyll seen in Coles- hill and Sunninghill;—grove, meaning a wood, from *graf,* a grove, and not from *græf,* the French for grave; Blagrove, Blagrave, Wargrave are examples. Hyrst, or Hurst, also means a wood, as in Hurst, Sandhurst and Tilehurst; "-cote" in Buscot, Calcot, Didcot and others means small house or cottage; and the bury in Bucklebury and Newbury is from the Anglo-Saxon *byrig,* a borough or sometimes a fort. Finally, the termination "-ing," as in Sonning, Reading, comes from

Sunningas and Rædingas, with the meaning "of the peoples of Suna and Reada."

I must not spend much more time on this subject, but it should be possible to have a look round the County, and we could do worse than start with the rivers, because these and the hills above them are as old as time itself. We can divide the river names into three groups—(1) Celtic, (2) Old English, (3) names which are used for villages but which really belong to rivers. In the first group, we find Cern, near Charney, Ginge, near the Hendreds, Kennet, Kimber, Loddon, Pang and surprisingly Wantage, which does not get its name from the great number of wants (moles) there. These names are all of Celtic origin, and are therefore the oldest river names in the County. The Thames, by the way, has an exceedingly old name the origin of which is unknown. Of the old English names, the Cole is a back-formation from the village Coleshill and was called Lenta in A.D. 931. The Emborne, which in A.D. 944 had a different name east and west of Newbury, the former being "alder brook," the latter being "duck brook," Lambourn, the lamb's stream, and the Ock, which by some is said to take its name from the British word ehoc, a salmon. In group 3, we find Baulking (probably), Childrey, Lockinge from the Old English *lacu*, a slow flowing stream and there are certain other possibilities.

Of hill names, there are two kinds, hill names proper and names of villages which are really hill names. Of the hill names proper, Blewburton; Churn; Cuckhamsley, from the old English *Cwichelmeshlæw*; Hackpen; Harrowdown Hill, probably meaning "Temple Hill"; Kite Hill near Fawley, meaning the hill of kites (birds no doubt abundant then); Lowbury Hill; Titcombe Hill; and White Horse Hill will have to suffice. Of the village names, which are in reality hill names, Abingdon, Faringdon and Inkpen are examples. (Abingdon means Abba's Hill, Faringdon means Fern Hill; the old name Inkpen has nothing to do with writing, but means Inga's Hill.) There are more river names and more hill names than I have mentioned, and those who want to proceed further should turn up the various books and papers which have been written about our place names.

It will be quickly seen that the whole subject is very much more complicated than I have indicated in these few pages, and that no value attaches to anything so sketchy as this, unless it stimulates an interest in the more obscure. Yet I cannot leave this subject without mentioning some of our ancestors whose names were used for places. It very often happens that a personal name is the simplest explanation of a difficult word. In some names the personal element is obvious, for instance, Abingdon in A.D. 821 was written *Abbandune,* meaning Abba's hill, but the old English female name *Burghilda* for Bucklebury is not so easily seen. G. W. B. Huntingford in 1934 drew up a list of Old English personal names occurring in Berkshire, and I quote them here to show what sort of names people had in those far-off days—Abba, Baga, Beorhtwead, Bestel, Bryni, Burghilda, Burgweard, Ceadda, Cening, Ceol, Cilla, Clapa, Col, Colmen, Cusa, Dude, Duduc, Eadwin, Eardwulf, Frithela, Frithowulf, Geat, Hengest, Leoda, Peada, Scara, Seofec, Stifa, Suga, Tubba, Uffa, Wada, Wineca, Witta, Wulflaf and Wulfric. Our modern names are slightly different but no doubt quite as absurd!

CHAPTER XVI

OLD WIVES' TALES

A l l counties have their store of "old wives' tales," the whole of which are known to no one person. Even the same story is told differently from one part of the County to the next, though the theme may be the same throughout. Many of these stories have their counterparts elsewhere and some of them come from an international folk-lore, not bound by any limits, relics of days gone by, when there were no barriers, no officials to check or turn back a mass movement of peoples, taking with them to some unknown place not only their pots and pans, but their social and religious habits. One might well begin this chapter with an example which has its Scandinavian equivalent.

1. LEGENDS OF THE WHITE HORSE, DRAGON HILL AND WAYLAND THE SMITH

These three are tied together by mythology, though by 1948 the legends concerning them are losing their hold, even upon the men of the Vale who were brought up to believe them. Wayland's Smithy, or Wayland Smith's Cave or simply Wayland Smith, as we now know is no more than an interesting example of a Neolithic chambered long-barrow. The legend attached to this barrow probably goes back to the arrival of men from afar, who brought with them from Scandinavian sagas the tale of an invisible smith called Wieland who lived in a cave. The cave, of course, was the passage-way entrance to the barrow which was probably intact at that time.

Wieland's forge was down an underground passage where no one dared to venture. A horse requiring a shoe was taken to the mouth of the cave, the shoeing fee was placed on a stone and the rider withdrew a discreet distance. Provided that he did not approach he would find his horse shod and his money gone, but if he waited upon his horse, or stood nearby, nothing whatever would happen. Just how late in prehistory or even in history Wieland was spared to continue his good work we do not know, but the discovery of two currency bars of early Iron Age buried beneath the "payment" stone does more than suggest he had his clients long before historic times. The Scandinavian version is that Wieland fell asleep after a large meal of bear flesh and was captured by the Niding, who set him to work at an underground forge. He escaped, despite his hamstrung legs, and turned into a bird.

There is a second story about Wieland or Wayland who apparently was possessed of a mighty temper. He had a boy whose work it was to run his errands, and whose surprising name was Flibbertigibbet; one day, his nail supply exhausted, Wayland sent the boy down into the valley to buy some. Flibbertigibbet, like modern errand-boys, made no haste to discharge his duty, and being a country boy, started to do a bit of birdnesting. Wayland got cross at the end of two hours, for there was a horse waiting, and looking down the hillside, spotted Flibbertigibbet with his arm up to the shoulder in a thornbush. So infuriated was the invisible smith that he picked up his anvil-stone and hurled it at the boy some two miles off. Strong though he was the stone fell short but slid along the ground and hit the boy on the heel. Poor Flibbertigibbet started blubbing and limped off down the hill. The locals who saw him, christened the place "Snivelling Corner." And it is to this day so called, and Wayland's anvil-stone is there too, though the heel mark leaves a good deal to the imagination.

A theory, lacking the amusing element of Flibbertigibbet, is that the stone, where it lies at Snivelling Corner was in reality a "heol-stone" or sun-stone from "Helios," the Greek for sun. And this brings me to the whole possibility of sun-worship, for there is an old legend of white horses drawing the chariot of the sun, both in the Norse sagas and in classic mythology. On the basis of the Norse sagas, it has been suggested that our White Horse represents Grannie, a white horse ridden by Sigurd and shod by Wieland. The Norse invaders discovered at Uffington a sacred mound where sun-worship had been carried on, and they also found in the mound a secret chamber and an underground passage, so what more natural than the provision of a white horse for Wieland to shoe? But this was a very long time ago. Since then, tradition has provided another legend attached to sun-worship, for Dragon Hill, below the White Horse, is where St. George (the sun) is said to have slain the dragon (the night) in order to rescue a beautiful maiden (the earth).

The most popular, and at the same time probably the most incorrect belief regarding the White Horse, is that King Alfred, after his great victory over the Danes, caused the Horse to be cut in the chalk to commemorate the event; this is manifestly absurd if one thinks about it all, but neverthe-less, it is the most popular theory. Some amusing fellow, followed more recently by Lord Wyfold, put forward the idea that it was no horse at all, but some primæval monster carved up there on the hillside to commemorate a successful bout between prehistoric men and some such monster. But this is no good, however, because we now know that human beings and the last of the great Saurian monsters missed each other on earth by a pretty considerable time.

Then again, there is the theory of the coins. A small number, seven I believe, of coins bearing the representation of a horse and in date previous to 50 B.C., are in existence, and show a similarity in form to our Berkshire Horse; from these coins it is presumed that the White Horse was in existence before the earliest of them (about 100 B.C.), and from certain other things discovered close to the White Horse, it has been surmised that the Horse must have been in existence nearer 250 B.C. But whatever the legends and tales, there is no evidence whatever of its origin. Why it is where it is, and what it was put there for, is something archæologists cannot answer, though Grannie by her fireside knows better. And she knows about Dragon Hill too, for here it was that Pendragon was buried, or King George killed a dragon and let its blood run down the side where nothing now will grow —or was it Danish blood? She really wouldn't know which it was. Dragon Hill has also been called Uffington Castle on account of a supposed Norman Castle of which it was the mound.

2. THE FOLK-LORE OF SOME ROUND BARROWS

There are many legends about the round barrows of the downland, some of which I can tell you here. It was only natural, I suppose, that there should be weird and wonderful stories about these, for are they not somehow uncanny, so lonely up on the hills?

Fairies are perhaps the nicest people associated with them in this country and in Scandinavia. A round barrow at Beedon is certainly inhabited by fairies, for the story goes that a ploughman broke a ploughshare nearby and discovered upon his return with tools to make a repair, that it was already mended though nobody was there to explain just how.

The Devil, once upon a time, started making a ditch; near Cuckhamsley he cleaned his ploughshare and the lump of mud which fell off became Cuckhamsley Knob. Grim's Ditch, or the Devil's Ditch, lies between the Ridgeway and the Icknield Way. Another story of Cuckhamsley is that Captain Scutchamer, killed in the Civil Wars, was buried there. Other stories explain Cuckhamsley as the burial mound of Cwichelm's soldiers slain in battle and alternatively as the grave required after a battle with the Scots. This place I have referred to elsewhere; if for no other reason it is interesting on account of the variety of names it can boast. Grinsell, in an article on barrows in the *Berkshire Archæological Journal,* lists the following: Cuckhamsley, Cuckhamsley Hill (maps by Saxton, Rocque and others), Cuckhamslow Hill (map by Greenwood), Cuchinslow, Scuchinslow, Scuchamere, Cwichelmes-low, Cwichelms low, Cwicelemes Hlæw, Cutchinloe, Scutchamer Knob, The Knob, Scutchamfly Knob, Scotchamfly Barrow, Scotchman's Knob and Scratch my Knob. Other scrapings from the Devil's ploughshare are round barrows at Churn which were thrown up while the Devil was at work one night. The Devil crops up further along the Ridgeway, where his punch-bowl near Letcombe Basset gives the walker something to peer down into, and, of course, the Devil's Highway runs eastward from Silchester. Apart from these, Berkshire is free of Devils so far as I can recall.

A ghost, a headless one, lives in a barrow near Inkpen; at one time this barrow was being opened when a colossal thunderstorm is said to have stopped the digging. A similar event is locally supposed to have occurred at Beedon. The idea of treasure hidden in or around barrows goes back to Roman if not Saxon days, when barrows were frequently robbed of any "grave goods" worth taking. This habit ultimately resulted in empty barrows and the idea that the treasure once there had been hidden. Somewhere up on the Downs, between Wayland's Smithy and the White Horse, is a golden coffin; perhaps it is really hidden in the legendary underground passage from the "cave" to Ashbury coombs and that is why no one can find it. Another gold or possibly silver coffin should be near Beedon, for a man called Burrow is alleged to have been buried in such a coffin in Barrow Hill. Needless to say no such coffin was found upon excavation, but the cremated ruins of Mr. Burrow were there, complete with incense cup and dagger. A golden table is supposed to lie in a barrow on Inkpen Hill and golden treasure in another near Great Shefford.

At Idle Bush barrow or Idle Tump, a traveller, lost on the Downs and desirous of reaching Lambourn before dark demanded the way of a shepherd, lying half asleep in the afternoon sun. The shepherd, too lazy to speak, merely nodded his head to indicate the direction. A second and a third shepherd, busily occupied studying the heavens, languidly pointed finger and toe respectively. The traveller is said to have been so amused by the laziness of these shepherds that he nicknamed the place "Idle Tump." Time was little object I take it, even to the traveller. A different story tells of trees planted on the barrow failing to grow out of sheer laziness—hence Idle Bush.

It is surprising that there are not more stories of the Combe long barrow, crowned as it is with a grizzly gibbet, where bodies must have swung, chains rattled and flies buzzed. Here, on March 7th, 1676, George Bromman and Dorothy Newman were hanged side by side, for the murder of two children, the result of Dorothy's former marriage. It is odd that there are no ghosts here, neither related to the

Neolithic barrow nor to the more recent gibbet—George and Dorothy or even the two children might turn up, but ghosts appear at prescribed times and I have not yet managed to be in the right place at the right time.

3. SOME GHOSTS

The ghost of Lady Hoby wandered about at Bisham Priory, following a ghostly basin in which she was constantly attempting to wash her hands. No wonder she wanted to wash, for she beat her small son to death for smudges in his writing-book!

Another story of Bisham tells how a squire eloped with the Earl of Salisbury's daughter while the Earl was at prayer; captured in a small boat on the river at Marlow, the squire was locked up in a tower, from which he escaped only to injure himself when he crashed to the ground below.

Another ghostly tale comes from Bucklebury, where a chariot with six black horses, driven by headless postillions and a lady clad in white, haunts the site of Winchcombe House. Every time I wander under the great trees of this pleasant village, I can imagine the chariot, the horses and the lady in white, but the headless postillions are too much for me.

At one time a funeral procession haunted Bucklebury, the ghostly bearers clad in white carrying a white corpse between them. Some village tough waited one night for the procession to draw near, when dashing out and swinging a stout stick he caused the bearers to disappear; the corpse did not disappear with them, however, but lay there, horribly white in the moon-light. Plucking up his courage, our friend drew close to it and discovered—a sheep; the bearers were nowhere to be seen, naturally enough, for they were sheep stealers clad in white smocks to spare themselves inquisitive eyes! But they reckoned without Bucklebury Finn, or whatever that stout-hearted fellow was called.

Another tale about Bucklebury tells you of a gross monster, a mammoth which lived by the Kennet and used to "act very unpleasant" to people who lived in the valley; not being able to stand its depredations any longer, these people gathered together and slew the mammoth, burying it on the river bank. Hundreds of years later it was unearthed and a person living in Bucklebury collected the "bladebone," which he gave to his "local," on the strength of which the innkeeper rechristened his hostel.

In Aldermaston the ghost of a suicide haunts the vicarage, and in Buckland a lady ghost is sometimes to be seen at the manor. In a meadow near Yattendon, a ghost has been seen wandering rather aimlessly about, and the local story tells of a house which once stood proudly in the meadow, until one day in the Civil War it was destroyed; the owners, fleeing for safety, hid their treasures in a well, and so far as is known they never returned—but somebody did, for modern treasure hunters have found nothing, though several wells have been located.

On Wash Common, outside Newbury, the ghost of a sentry stood night after night at a lane junction hard by the cottage, Biggs' Cottage, where Essex slept before the battle of Newbury; he has not been on parade recently so far as I can gather, though when he was still "serving," his supposed presence at night was better than any "no thoroughfare" notice. Another ghost intimately connected with soldiery and bloody warfare appears at Chieveley. In the way that these things do happen, the daughter of Phillip Weston, a great Royalist, fell in love with a smart Roundhead officer; father arranged to send her news of the battle by trumpet—one blast if he were killed, two if her lover were killed and three if they were both killed; waiting by her open window her anxious ears discerned three blasts. With both father and lover gone what had life to offer? She sought peace in death by casting herself down the well; peace she may have found, but since that fateful day. her ghost has haunted the place. A slight variance of this story says that she ran out of the house on hearing the three trumpet blasts and accidentally fell down the open well. It matters not which version you prefer.

In Tilehurst there is a haunted house of which I can find no details, and at Appleford there is a ghost or devil which nobody has seen; this person, buried beneath an altar-tomb in the churchyard, dislikes the village schoolboys sharpening their pocket-knives upon his final home and sneaks out unseen to remove the offending but essential part of schoolboy furniture—some watchful vicar perhaps instigated this story!

Basildon owns two ghosts, Nan Carey, who haunts the hill of her name, and Nobes, who, so far as one can find out, was a local and probably eccentric farmer; Nobes had a fear of being molested after death, so he built a stone cell with a semicircular top, leaded to keep the weather out. His coffin was shut in and the key to the door thrown in to join him. But one does not buy security that way and his tomb has been broken into and is now empty and the lead has been taken from the roof. The date on the door is 1692. I cannot tell you when to look for Nobes because I do not know, but he may be riding his white horse, or looking for his white horse or not really keen on horses at all.

At Longworth is the ghost of the Ungodly Sir Harry Marten, known best, perhaps, for his shaky signature which adorned the death warrant of Charles I. Ungodly Harry was a terrible chap apparently, always drinking, gambling and "calling in the dancing girls"; despite all this he was M.P. for Berkshire, and some say he managed to spend more than £1,000 a year! His ghost, presumably searching for the key to the cellar, or perhaps for his dancing-pumps, still pays periodic visits to the manor.

At Streatley there is the ghost of a shepherd's wife careering round the garden in her nightdress, and at Hampstead Norris there is the ghost of "old Tanner" who strolls around the church in knee-breeches. Another ghost in this churchyard is said by Lowsley to have frightened many of the locals by raising up its head to a gigantic height and uttering unearthly noises; someone braver than the rest called his bluff and found him to be nothing worse than a large white turkey-cock!

In Bagley wood there was a highwayman's ghost, astride a white horse, and at Compton Beauchamp a ghostly lady spins incessantly. Until it was demolished, Billingbear House, Binfield, claimed a ghostly lady in white; she had at one time been the lady of the house and disappeared with it. At Radley strange things have happened, for two acacia trees at Wick Hall are not trees at all, being the transformed bodies of a

The old pigeon house at Eastbury

gypsy lad and a married woman! This lady, perhaps, had never been warned about the gypsies in the wood, but she paid the price of eloping with one. Monkish ghosts have been seen in the vicarage, and the one-legged ghost of old Admiral Boyer waddles up a staircase in Radley College, though no one has yet heard him come down again.

Nearer to Oxford, at Botley, there was at one time a haunted house; a previous owner had done a deal with the Devil by which his soul and some wealth changed hands; true to form the Devil returned later without the soul and dragged his unfortunate client out of his house through a chimney. Another Botley house is said to have been haunted by the ghost of a Cromwellian soldier.

At Charlton there used to be a ghost in the Hell Pits, and at South Moreton, Lowsley records the successful silencing of a poltergeist. It seems that the occupants of a particular house were troubled with gravel flying into their bedroom at night, while at the same time candles would go out or explode and the large family Bible would come to life and fly across the room. After a night of waiting for something to happen a loose floor board was discovered through which a person in the room below could throw a handful of gravel; by a similar device the Bible could be sent flying across the room and the candles were found to have been severed, filled with gunpowder and stuck together again. All this because the rent was about to be raised.

Another poltergeist played tricks in a cottage at Finchampstead, and experts, who travelled down from London to observe the furniture and books being hurled about, went away little the wiser; the local people would not believe that these happenings were caused by the ghost of a dear old lady who once lived in the cottage, as it seemed so very unlike her to do anything so unusual.

At Cookham the ghost of Hern the Hunter winds his horn and the music of his hounds can be heard from across the common; Hern hunts at night, of course. Lambourn has no ghost, though I cannot think why, since there is the making of a perfectly good one; once upon a time a man stole a sheep on the Downs, and tying it across his back he set off for home;

East Hendred, Berkshire's most fascinating village

on the way he grew weary and sitting down on a large sarsen-stone he fell asleep. The sheep was not so weary, for it had been spared the effort of walking, and struggling to escape it pulled the rope tight across the sleeper's throat and strangled him—the sarsen is known as Hangman's Stone to this day. But no ghost.

At Cumnor Place there was the ghost of poor Amy Rob-sart, mysteriously murdered wife of Robert Dudley, Earl of Leicester. The story goes that, running to greet her husband, she fell into a pit cunningly concealed at the bottom of the staircase; there were no witnesses of this, for all the servants had conveniently been sent off to Abingdon Fair. It seems that nine parsons attempted to lay the unquiet spirit in a nearby pond but were unable to do so, and it has been said that the water in the pond never froze again. The terrible noises which used to be heard at night kept the house untenanted until, decayed and deserted, it more or less fell to bits, and the ghost of the beautiful Amy found rest.

At Padworth, there should be a ghost, though I cannot find one, for here an Ufton man, William Billimore, was foully murdered in 1787 by two Padworth boys, aged 19 and 17 respectively, Abraham Tull and William Hawkins; they were captured, tried and hanged on a gibbet at Padworth (giving the name Gibbet-piece to the land where it stood); the bodies of the two wretched youths dangled there for many years, it is said, until a lady who was living at Woke-field Park, being greatly shocked by the horrible sight, gave orders for the bodies to be taken down and buried. Three bodies and apparently no ghost!

At Littlewick there are three ghosts, the White Lady, another lady called Dorcas Noble, who has no head, and the white Dog of Feens. And this is about the end of our ghosts, though I do not doubt there are some I know nothing about. As time goes on ghosts get more and more difficult to find, the need to believe in the supernatural no longer exists, and in the little cottages parents no longer find it necessary to spin yarns to keep their children amused—or in terror, for the wireless set and "children's hour" do all that is required.

4. SOME WITCHES AND WIZARDS

Aldermaston once owned a witch, Maria Hale to wit; her special trick was to turn herself into a hare, and "haunt" the Park; one of the keepers "upped his gun" and shot this hare in the leg one day and it was noticed that Maria Hale developed a nasty limp; in the guise of a hare she would spend hours sitting outside the Falcon Inn on the edge of the Park, like a policeman making notes of all the comings and goings. I wonder how long a hare could sit there now, in this meatless world? It's said that although she kept no pigs, she had two flitches of bacon beneath the mattress of her bed— surely there was no black market in those days! Maria was buried beneath a yew tree in Aldermaston churchyard, and the man who did the job took care to keep her beneath the yew tree, filling in the grave with bricks and stones.

There are some variations to this story, in one of them the witch being called Maria Chandler; in the road one evening a dog attacked her, whereupon she turned into a hare and ran away, not before the dog had snapped at her several times; next morning Maria Chandler was found to have been bitten by a dog. The same Maria had the power to make people ill and they did not regain health until she died. Yet another variation—if a large hare was seen in the lane there was no need to be afraid as it was only old Mrs. A., who was reported to be a witch. I have never met anyone who was frightened of a hare, and old Mrs. A. was probably much more awe-inspiring.

Kintbury has a witch story too : a great storm blew down the church-tower, depositing the bell in the Kennet; the local witch thought she should be consulted about getting the bell out again, but instead, the local wizard was approached. He arranged that a hook should be attached to the bell which should then be dragged up the bank by chains fastened to twelve white heifers, led by moonlight and by twelve maidens clad in white dresses with blood-red sashes; the business had to be conducted in silence or the bell would fall back into the river and be lost for ever. The story goes that heifers, moonlight, maidens and blood-red sashes had got the bell almost on to the bank when the witch appeared, consumed with jealousy and screaming in her nasty nasal voice : "Here comes the Great Kintbury Bell, in spite of all the Devils in Hell." Alas, the spell was broken and with a resounding plop the bell retired beneath the water again.

While touching on wizards, I can tell you of another who lived at Crookham. His name was Coudrey and he was much feared by the neighbourhood, and anyone who tried to steal from him was likely to get into trouble. Two people did try— one found himself surrounded by water so that he could not escape while the other discovered to his horror that he was standing in the wizard's room, holding the logs he had tried to steal. Coudrey was no one-trick man, and he demonstrated his versatility to a carter who had lost his pony on Crookham Common. "It's going to rain," he said, "so get away home and you will find the pony there." So off went the carter in the sunshine thinking old Coudrey mad, but on the way a terrific storm burst over him and his pony came down with the rain.

There was also a witch who lived at Newbury; one day she was spotted by soldiers of Lord Essex, crossing over the Kennet on a plank; apparently one of the soldiers had con- siderable trouble in killing her, because the bullet bounced off her head and came back to him, narrowly missing his face.

In 1654 the rector of Bradfield was in trouble, accused of having, among other things, familiarity with evil spirits; this rector, whose name was John Pordage, had the impression of a coach drawn by lions and tigers carved upon the wall of his chimney, and had an assistant, Everard by name, who was equally skilled in raising spirits.

A real broomstick kind of witch once used to deliver milk to a particular house near Newbury where her "witchiness" was tested out, for one of the maidservants placed crossed broomsticks in the doorway; the old lady jumped the broom- sticks thus proving herself a witch; but she was furious with the girl who had found her out and immediately put a curse upon her, after which everything the poor girl did went wrong and she lost her job.

"L. S.," in her *Untravelled Berkshire*, gives a witch story that would surely provide Sigmund Freud with food for thought. Two men, a carter and a thatcher, used to share a bed in a farmhouse; the carter was always tired out and at last admitted to having been ridden, night after night, by a witch. The thatcher, being a friendly soul, offered to change sides next night; the witch came and put a bit between his teeth and rode him off to the stables, where many other witches were putting up their horses. Being a big, strong man he turned the tables upon the lady and rode her off to the blacksmith where he had a new shoe put on her foreleg; in the morning the farmer was found to have murdered his wife for being a devil, and lo and behold, upon her right hand was a great new horseshoe! What a story!

Finally, a story for girls: a pretty maiden sat by the open window combing her golden locks; catching the comb in a tangle, she, pretty maiden though she was, let fly a stream of abuse both at her golden locks and at Him who made them. Instantly the comb fell, the locks fell and down she went, dead. In due course her relatives came to bury her and being surprised at the lightness of the coffin, took out the screws and looked within. Nothing but smoke!

Details of a case of witchcraft at North Moreton have been published, from which one gathers that a girl, Anne Gunter, aged fourteen, was seized with strange fits in the year 1604. In her fits she upbraided certain local cottage women, by name Elizabeth Gregory and Mary and Agnes Pepwell. Various wise doctors from Oxford pronounced the fits to be of supernatural quality, and John Wendore of Newbury, who was a specialist in diseases due to sorcery, diagnosed a supernatural disease from a sample of the girl's water. As a result of all this the girl's father, Brian Gunter, came to believe in witchery and confirmed his opinions when, suffering from a pain in his shoulder, he deliberately scratched Elizabeth Gregory upon the head, and found an instant relief from the pain. Both Anne and her father fell to reading books upon the subject and apparently were considerably influenced by what they read. Anne's spasms took on the form of body swellings, goggling eyes and foaming mouth, and, more extraordinary still, pins came out of her when she sneezed and she both voided and vomited pins and at times pins came from her fingers and breasts! She declared that Agnes Pepwell appeared to her as a white mouse with a man's face, that Mary Pepwell had dealings with a white toad and that Elizabeth Gregory had a black rat with the face of a swine. All the appropriate anti-witch remedies were tried, such as burning hair and thatch from their respective heads and houses and Anne always came out of her fit when this was done. But it looks as though Miss Anne rather overdid things for she was subjected to various tests to see if she was leg pulling! It goes without saying that she did not show up very well under examination. Her father, who was either "in the know" or remarkably gullible, went to court, however, and arranged for the arrest of the three ladies together with the white mouse, white toad and black rat. Mary Pepwell and her white toad fled I know not where; Elizabeth and Agnes were indicted of witchcraft and sent to the assizes in Abingdon, but thanks to a good deal of behind-the-scenes deliberation, they were not found guilty, though it seems that they remained in custody. At this time King James I examined Anne on three occasions, in Oxford, Windsor and Whitehall, for he was very interested in such things. Anne was definitely caught out when she vomited some marked pins and some kind of confession was wrung from her, in which she fairly implicated her father, who she made out a tyrant desiring the death of the three so-called witches. This may or may not have been true, but everyone in the case seems to have been handy with lies, and Brian Gunter and his dear daughter were brought before the Star Chamber, accused of conspiracy. An interesting witness for the defence was Gilbert Bradshawe, vicar of North Moreton, who stated that he had been in the girl's bedroom and seen her undies, shoes, stockings and garters come from under her skirt and creep along the ground like worms, after which they returned in a decent manner where they belonged! Repressed I would say! To complicate matters Agnes Powell confessed to having been a witch for fourteen years, complete with Spirit of Black Cat given her by a colleague, Goodwife Bishop; in addition, her mother-in-law, Katherine Gregory, was a witch and possessed spirits. Agnes much regretted having bewitched Anne Gunter, but could do nothing about it. The case caused a considerable stir in Oxford and London, and one presumes in North Moreton also. Some were for Anne, some for the three village women, some tried to explain it this way, others that way. The finale is not known, but oh that vicar! Mr. C. L'Estrange Ewen is to be congratulated on having unearthed such a story from the Record of the Star Chamber.

Chapter XVII

BERKSHIRE SCRAPBOOK

1. THE HOME DOCTOR

I n days of old, when professional doctors carried in their black bags little more than bleeding-knives and tins of leeches, it behoved the villagers to find their own remedies, at least for the minor ills of life. And this they certainly did, often with the assistance of sorcery; but I am not concerned here with the "finger of birth-strangled babe" methods, but with those which are derived from the flowers and the streams.

Let us in the first instance tour the medicinal waters of the County, and be it noted that water of this kind was in general use for sore eyes, a complaint which seems to have been common throughout the County. At Appleford, Bads-well, an ancient spring was in frequent use for afflictions of the eyes; near Bablock Hythe there was a physic well, and at Bisham, Princess Elizabeth's spring cured sore eyes. At Finchampstead there was a ferruginous stream to which people came from far and wide, taking bottles of water for their medicine-chests, the colour of the waters being taken for blood; Goring had a spring noted for curing skin diseases; at Frilsham there is a well on the common which never runs dry, the waters of which had healing properties as well as being good for the eyes; near Kingston Lisle, a spring called Black Jack gave water good for rheumatism and sore eyes; Padworth boasted two medicinal springs, and there was a renowned well at St. Leonard's Hill by Clewer; at Speen there was a chalybeate well near the church, known as Ye Ancient Ladye Well, and both Sunninghill and Sunningwell had waters for sore eyes; in Winkfield Park there was a Spa, where fashionable people disported themselves, and to St. Antony's Well, just outside Wittenham, people were sent who were sick or dying.

So much for waters, and now what about patent medicines? Basildon had its "salts," Bucklebury had in "Old John" a herbalist who supplied not only his district but also London with remedies, such as tansy tea for rheumatics, marsh mallow poultices for cuts and wounds, white lily-root ointment for "gatherings" and preparations of wood sage and hore-hound for a variety of ills. Here in Bucklebury warts are cured by cutting slits in alder or by making holes in walnut leaves; the leaves must be buried or put down a well, and as they decay, so do the warts disappear. A variation of this from other parts of the County, is to put the walnut leaves into the slits in the alder and wait for them to decay. Drayton cured whooping-cough by placing a few white hairs from the chest of a donkey on the patient, made a gargle with sage tea and vinegar, a tonic for adults from dandelions and for children from the juice of crushed snails; Kingston Lisle made an ointment from cowslips and a lotion from elder flowers, healed its cuts with lily leaves soaked in brandy and removed its thorns and splinters with bacon-fat; in Milton, whooping-cough was cured by grinding a thunderstone to powder and mixing it with milk, while shingles were treated with verdigris scraped from church bells and jaundice was cured with scrap-ings from berberis root. At Northcourt cuts were healed with cobwebs, and for sore throats a frog was allowed to hop down inside! Repulsive, but perhaps the slime really assisted! Pad-worth cured chilblains with goosegrease and coughs with either Good Friday Bread or with an infusion of hairs from a donkey's tail. Sandhurst, like many other villages, healed wounds with cobwebs, and Sonning had a chapel, a visit to which was good for madness; Stratfield Mortimer had a cure for rabies which involved the use of rue, garlic, Venice treacle, pewter scrapings, metidate and strong ale, the concoction to be taken within nine days of being bitten, and could be given to the dog as well. In St. Sebastian's, whooping-cough was relieved by the administration of a holly-berry drink. In the "Vale," soap pills were used as an aperient.

In addition to "the doctor," the village "Jack of all trades" often tried out his hand at cutting corns, bleeding and blister-ing; Isaak Factotem from near Reading performed at surgery and midwifery. John Briggs of Hurley drew all sorts of teeth, removed "motes" from eyes and cured the "itch." William Sorry of Brightwalton sold Dr. James' fever powders, genuine

Daffy's Elixir, Manna, Bateman's and Stoughton's Drops, Godfrey's cordial, Hooper's Pills, Dr. Hitchcock's Rochford Drops and pills, Eaton's Styptic, Friar's Balsam, double-distilled lavender and Hungary water, salts and cordial cephalic snuff. According to Mr. A. C. Humpherys in an article of whose I found this information about Isaak, John and William, when not playing doctors and dentists, these three were shaving, haircutting, teaching grammar, dancing, deportment, "jaggraphy", making wigs, shoes and horseshoes, selling mousetraps, stationery ware, blackin' balls, gingerbread, sausages and garden things, or maybe they were playing violins, or teaching the Hoboy or the Jewsharp. As well as "jaggraphy" Isaak admits to teaching other "outlandish kind of things," and John modestly states that he can cope with many other articles "too tedious to mention." Definitely Jacks of all trades! A very elucidating analysis of such things can be found in the 1948 volume of *Folk-lore*, under the title of "Some Notes on the Pharmacology and Therapeutic Value of Folk-Medicines."

2. FEASTS, REVELS, FAIRS AND THE LIKE

Instead of cinemas and football matches, which nowadays occur so frequently as to be almost a bore, our forbears went in for mighty days of drinking and dancing, fighting, acting, singing and climbing greasy poles in their fancy waistcoats, while their wives and daughters flirted in new straw hats and their best "toggery."

Some of these fairs were of a more serious nature and the sale of animals was all-important, and perhaps then there would be no games and dancing, though plenty of beer. In fact, the fairs were usually serious, more like our modern markets and "shows," and what we call fairs to-day would have been called revels or feasts before. There were the great sheep fairs of the Downs, headed in magnitude by the August one at East Ilsley, when the downland droves would be lost in clouds of dust beneath which the flocks were moving, their bells tinkling, the dogs barking, the shepherds plodding along flourishing their great walking-sticks. The shepherd's life was

a full one, day in day out, and when at long last he went to
the grave, he took with him in his coffin a lock of wool and
sometimes his stick or crook, so that the Almighty would
understand why he had never time to attend church on
Sundays!

There was a horse fair at Harwell, a cattle fair at Waltham St. Lawrence, and no doubt there were fairs for cattle
and pigs at places of which I have no record. There may even
have been bloodstock sales at Newbury, where horse-racing
had been going on since the time of Charles II, over Sandleford Priory, Enborne Heath, Wash Common and Woodhay
Common, attracting people from far and wide; the present
racecourse, which as a result of the recent war is no longer
fit for racing, was not in use before the early part of this
century, the old racecourses having been put out of commission long before the Enclosure Act. But I must turn back to
fairs and leave racing to its gambling and shouting and its
brightly coloured jockeys.

From old records it is not always an easy matter to separate
fairs from feasts, for, although their purposes were quite
distinct—the village feasts were usually to celebrate the
dedication of the churches—the "fun and games" of a holiday
in time swamped them both and the aims and objects of each
were soon lost from sight. Most of these village celebrations
have gone, no longer serving any purpose, but here and there
enthusiasts still try to retain the old traditions. And now let
us travel the County again, though I cannot pretend to have
collected anything like a complete list, but before we start
let us just review the things we should have seen if we could
have attended in person. At a fair, we should have found
sheep, horses, cattle and probably pigs standing in temporarily
erected stalls, surrounded by their owners and their "voggers,"
their shepherds, their herdsmen, their pigmen (swineherds at
one time) and their drovers, each with a dog and a stick, and
no doubt plenty of riff-raff hoping to earn a penny for holding
a horse or leading a bull; there would be a committee of
local "big-wigs" in a tent, and afterwards there would be
much drinking and maybe a fight or two. As time went on
farmers brought their wives and children for the day out, and

then the modern idea of a fair crept in. A feast on the other hand, would be quite different, for we would start the day in the village church, offering prayers to the patron saint; the religious part being over we would "feast," and in the afternoon proceed to the bazaars and stalls in the village street and to the sports and contests on the green; a feast, therefore, was rather similar to our modern fête, and as now, the vicar and the squire would be much in evidence. A revel, I think, has no modern equivalent, being a mixture of fête, gymkhana, Royal Tournament and Olympic Games; in another chapter I have described the revel on White Horse Hill as Thomas Hughes saw it and there is no point in reiterating here; all I need say is that a revel was no "Sunday School outing," for the participants were tough and rude men who called a spade a spade and made no bones about it.

Appleton had a feast on the first Sunday after St. Peter's Day, and Basildon held a revel with backswording and wrestling towards the end of July, presumably just prior to the harvest. Binfield held one annually at the Stag and Hounds inn; at Bourton, on the Wiltshire border, there was an annual fair known locally as the "rout," which was a very genteel affair for that part of the County—games and dancing in the open, if fine, and in a nearby barn when wet, greasy poles and the rest. Alfred Williams describes how the "cunning ones" waited until the uninitiated had removed most of the grease from the pole and, having rolled in the dust and dirt, shinned up the pole with the greatest of ease. Williams also quotes the local rhyme :

"Shrivenham Revels and Bourton Rout,
    The Watchfield pot boils, and the fire is out."

Brightwell celebrated the feast of St. Agaths, Buckland has an annual feast when members of the village club parade the streets headed by a band; Bucklebury and Bradfield shared a revel at Charter Alley. Challow held one on Trinity Sunday, and it is said that people from the outlying villages came to walk the streets during the evening in their "Sunday best," returning the next day to enjoy the games on the village green, and to see the boys diving into the canal after ducks;

on the following Saturday the booths and tents appeared again
for what was called "pinning up." Charlton held its feast on
Whitsunday and Chilton held one about the same time or a
little earlier; Coleshill waited until after harvest, and on the
second Sunday in October held St. Faith's Fair; East Hendred
was ambitious and held a feast on the Sunday following
Ascension Day and a Revel at the end of May. Faringdon
held its fairs in the flat ground near Wadley Hall, and being
well supplied with gypsies and riff-raff from Wantage, these
fairs were pretty rough—stocks were set up and kept fed
with fighters, drunkards and pick-pockets, while women who
caused offence were ducked in the fish-pond! Farnborough
had a feast in June, and Hagbourne held a feast in a barn at
Manor Farm on the second Tuesday after Whitsun, where a
curious custom was the decoration of the president's chair
with bunches of guelder rose. That the Hanneys held their
village games we know from a deposition in the court in
September, 1553, when it was put on record that William
Rychards, Nicholas Kyngeston and others played "ad globes"
in the cornfields and were fined 6s. 8d. ! At Hungerford the
Hock-Tide court and the tuttimen attracted people from miles
around on the Tuesday following Easter week; Kingston
Lisle held a cherry feast on the first Sunday after the sixth of
July, when cherries from the orchards of the "Vale" were
sold in the streets; Lambourn held a sheep fair on St.
Clement's Day, and Mortimer, or Stratfield Mortimer as we
should call it, held two fairs, in April and November and at
Whitsuntide there was a revel. Newbury was blessed with
innumerable fairs, including one of the oldest in England, that
of St. Bartholomew, held on September 4th—the fair was
originally granted by King John in 1215; other fairs held on
the Thursday after Trinity Sunday and on June 24th; in the
time of Elizabeth, there were four fairs held annually on
March 25th, June 24th, August 24th and October 28th, and
additionally, a Michaelmas Hiring fair was held. Reading
held four fairs, Candlemas, May-day, St. James, and the
Michaelmas cheese fair. The first three were chiefly cattle
fairs, though, no doubt, on May-day there were the usual
celebrations; St. James's fair was originally held in Friar

Street and Broad Street, but in 1840 so great was the quantity of beasts that it was found necessary to hold it in the Forbury; the Michaelmas fair was partly concerned with the hiring of servants, who stood in rows while the farmers inspected them, and, no doubt, prodded them with their sticks, felt their calves and looked at their teeth as they would have done with any other animal! But the Michaelmas Fair in Reading was not only for hiring servants but for the sale of cheeses which came up from all the counties of the west by waggon and by barge. In 1795, 1,200 tons of cheese came to the Forbury! The Forbury was crowded not only with cheeses, but with stalls, booths, swings and roundabouts, and for many years Wombwell's menagerie visited Reading for the occasion. This menagerie was famous throughout the country, and when in 1857 it went to the revels of White Horse Hill, it took all the horses in Uffington and Woolstone to drag the animals up to the top, and so heavy was the caravan that it stuck fast four or five times with twenty horses pulling! Sandhurst held an annual feast, for which all the local schools were closed so that children and parents alike could enjoy the day. At Stanford in the Vale there was a fair at the end of July and there was a feast in October on the Monday after St. Deny's Day. In Sutton Courtney the annual fair was held on the feast of Corpus Christi and at Shrivenham there was a revel to which many of the famous backswordsmen from the "Vale" went to meet the Wiltshire men and crack their heads for them. The people of Shrivenham used also to attend the Bourton "Rout" which I have referred to earlier. Uffington, where the revels on White Horse Hill, following the "Scouring of the White Horse," held annually the feast of the Assumption on the first Sunday a fortnight after August 15th. A curious custom in Uffington and Woolstone was perpetuated on St. Thomas's Day, when widows went out "mumping"; "mumping" consists of calling at various cottages, not giving or catching mumps as one might think, but begging, pure and simple. Waltham St. Lawrence held an annual cattle and pleasure fair on August 10th, when goose quills were sold and, so it is said, twenty fat geese were roasted at the Bell Inn to feed the visitors.

Wokingham markets and fairs were famous for bull-baiting and cock-fighting, in fact for drunken brawling of all kinds; Wokingham seems to have been a den of thieves, for ruffians of all descriptions gathered there, fighting for prizes of beer and on the way home murdering, robbing and poaching. The cock-pits drew crowds and so did the unfortunate bull tied to a ring in the market-place—I have read horrible stories of Wokingham bulls tossing small dogs high up over the church steeple, to land a horrible mess upon the spiked railings below or, perhaps, to be caught in the arms of their owners. But the greatest draw of all was to see women fighting in the cock-pits, stripped to the waist and clutching a coin in each hand to prevent hair-pulling! Yes, indeed, a veritable sink of iniquity! Yattendon has celebrated a fair on the "Virgil, Feast and Morrow" of St. Peter and St. Paul, the patron saints of the church, since 1318, the date having been altered to Whit-Monday.

So the County was really pretty gay after all, and in the villages the people looked forward to their annual celebrations far more than they do now to their weekly visits to the cinemas. And there were other forms of celebration too, the mummers, for instance, who toured the villages at Christmas-time, playing in the inn yards or in some local barn. Major Lowsley has published careful details of the mummers' play as acted in mid-Berkshire, the characters being Molly, who was always played by a man, King George, a French officer called Beau Slasher, a doctor, Jack Vinny a jester, Happy Jack a pauper and Old Beelzebub dressed up like Father Christmas. The story is that Beau Slasher fights and wounds King George who is quickly cured (at a cost of £10 from Molly) by the doctor who announces that he can cure "the itch, the palsy and the gout, and any awld 'ooman dead seven year" with his wonderful pill. King George is cured and in turn wounds the French officer who falls; the doctor can do nothing here and it is left to Jack Vinny to try out his special medicine made from "one pennoth o'pigeons milk, mixed with the blood of a grasshopper, and one drop of the blood of a dying donkey" after a tooth has been extracted with a pair of pliers! Beau Slasher rises up and dances. Happy Jack and

Beelzebub enter, there is much singing and dancing and Molly whips the hat around the audience. The chorus to Molly's introductory song is :

> "With hey dum dum,
> With hey dum dum de derry
> Vor we be come this Christmas time
> A purpose to be merry."

I have seen records of the mummers' plays from various parts of the County, and though they vary in small details, the theme is much the same. In Drayton, the mummers replaced Molly and the introductory song by a white-bearded old man, presumably Beelzebub, who does not appear at the end as in Lowsley's version. The knight from France was a "Knight from furring parts"; a stranger and Merrian replaced Jack Vinny and Happy Jack. Compton mummers replaced Beau Slasher with a Turkish knight, but as Lowsley's French officer admitted to coming from Turkish land, this is a reasonable alteration. The Steventon mummers replace King George by an "Africky King" and at Brightwalton Molly becomes Queen Mary. I expect most of the larger towns had their mummers though I have records from only a few; Buckland had its own mummers, and Burghfield, who performed at the Three Firs Inn on the Common on Boxing Day, drew considerable revenue from the crowds which went there to see the hounds meet. Chievely had its mummers, so did Abingdon and Sunningwell.

Then there were the celebrations which came on May-day, for most, if not all of the villages had a Maypole on the green. Various of the songs they sung have been put on record and here are one or two :

THE ABINGDON MAY-DAY SONG

> "We've been a-rambling all the night,
> And some time of this day,
> And now we are returning back again,
> We bring a garland gay.
>
> A garland gay we bring you here,
> And at your door we stand,
> It is a sprout well budded out,
> The work of the Lord's hand."

King Alfred, at Wantage

Chorus:
Why don't you do as we have done,
On this first day of May?
And from our parents we have come
And would no longer stay."

The Abingdon Morris Dances used to tour the neighbouring villages on May-day, taking with them their own Maypole, which had a pair of ox-horns at the top; at the end of the dance they produced a wooden bowl which the villagers filled with beer to cool them from their exertions. The last remaining Maypole in the Vale is said to have been at Longcot and the story of its end is this. Being the last of its kind it was much envied, and one night thirty lads from Ashbury went to Longcot and took down the pole, carrying it back to Ashbury on hand spikes; the pole was seized by men from Uffington, who somehow got it back to their village. Lambourn bloods, not to be out-done, went for it, and in a fight with their Uffington opponents resorted to boiling water as a weapon. The result of this was unfortunate for both the Maypole and the villages, for the parson, fearing further bloodshed, ordered it to be cut up and given to the poor for Christmas firewood.

In Drayton the children sang:

"Good-morning, ladies and gentlemen,
I wish you a happy day,
I come to show my garland
Upon the first of May.
Hail, all hail, the merry month of May!
The spring is coming in,
The cuckoo's voice is heard;
Come out into the fields
To hear my favourite bird.
Cuckoo, Cuckoo, he warbles in the tree,
Cuckoo, Cuckoo, how sweet his voice to me."

At Fyfield, according to Matthew Arnold:

"Maidens who from distant Hamlets came
To dance around the Fyfield Elm, in May."

On November 5th there would be bonfires all over the County and effigies burned; later, fireworks came on the

Round Barrows near Lambourn

scene, much to the horror of timid mothers. The boys sang
a long song as they went round the cottages collecting wood
for the bonfire; one of the verses of this song is :

> "Our Quane's a valiant zawljer,
> Car's her blunderbus on her right shawlder,
> Cocks her pistol, drays her rapier,
> Praay gie us zummit vor her zaayke yer."

and the chorus goes :

> "Holler bwoys, holler bwoys, maayke yer bells ring,
> Holler bwoys, holler bwoys, God zaayve the Quane."

Another November 5th song goes :

> "Guy Vawkes, Guy—'twas his intent
> To blow up the Houses o' Parliament;
> By God's mercy he got catched,
> Wi' his dark lantern an' lighted match.
> Guy Vawkes, Guy—zet up high,
> A pound o' chaze to chawke un,
> A pint o' beer to wash ut down,
> And a jolly vire to ro-ast un.
> Up wi' the pitcher an' down wi' the prong,
> Gie us a penny an' we'll be gone."

Harvest home had its own songs too, one of which was sung
as the last load went off to the farm :

> "Well ploughed, well zawed,
> Well ripped, well mawed,
> Narra lo-ad, awverdrawed,
> Whoop, Whoop, Whoop, Whoop, harvest whoam."

After supper in a barn a long song started thus :

> "Yer's a health unto our Me-uster,
> The Vounder of our Veast,"

and the chorus :

> "Zo drink up, bwoys, drink,
> An' zee as 'e do not spill,
> Vor if 'e do 'e shall drink two,
> Vor that be Me-uster's will."

Harvesting was thirsty work and this little song describes the
quantities and kinds of beer that would be needed in the field :

> "Vorty gallons o' Never Vear,
> Vorty gallons o' Taayble beer,
> Vorty gallons o' Wus nor that,
> Vorty gallon o' Rattletap."

While the reaping was going on one might have heard the good old song,

> "To plough an' to mow,
> An' to rip an' to zaw,
> An' to be a vermer's bwoy-oy-oy."

On Valentine's Day children used to go round the villages singing :

> "Knock the kittle agin the pan,
> Gie us a penny if 'e can;
> We be ragged and you be vine,
> Plaze to gie us a Valentine.
> Up wie the kittle an' down wie the spout,
> Gie us a penny an' we'll gie out."

On Good Friday the children used to sing the usual "one-a-penny, two-a-penny hot cross buns" song, and an old Berkshire saying is : "Blessed is the woman who bakes on Good Friday and five Fridays afterwards, but cursed is the woman who washes on Good Friday or five Fridays afterwards." On Shrove Tuesday Chaddleworth children used to tour the farms singing :

> "Knick-knock, the pan is hot,
> We be come to shroving.
> Barley's dear and wheat's dear,
> That's what makes we come to shroving here."

Another version of this comes from Drayton, where the children sang :

> "Snick, snack, the pan's hot,
> We're come a-shroving.
> Strike while the iron's hot,
> Something's better than nothing.
> Flour's cheap and lard's dear,
> And that's why we come shroving here."

Yet another version is :

> "Snick-snock, the pan's hot,
> We be come a-shrovin',

> Plaze to gie us zummat,
> Zummat's better'n nothun',
> A bit o' bread, a bit o' chaze,
> A bit o' apple dumplin', plaze."

From Sunningwell comes quite a different song :

> "Beef and bacon's out of season,
> I want a pan to parch my peas on."

After dark the children went round throwing stones at people's doors, a practice which, no doubt, made them a trifle unpopular! At Wantage a bell called the "Pan Bell" was rung at eleven o'clock to call people to confession. An old Berkshire saying is "Wash on Ash Wednesday and you wash someone out of the family." The "washing," I take it, refers to the family "smalls" and not to their bodies. On Rogation Day at both Inkpen and Winterbourne, the very ancient custom of blessing the fields was, and I believe still is, carried out, the parson, choir and congregation processing from the church to the fields singing hymns to the accompaniment of the village band. On Maundy Thursday, the children of East Hendred would run round the houses with a clapper or rattle shouting "Money, flour, bacon or eggs," but I can find no suggestion of their offering to wash poor men's feet! Lammas Day is apparently not celebrated with pomp and circumstance, but there are, or were, Lammas lands in North-croft at Newbury, and at Northcourt, outside Abingdon, there is a Lammas Close; Lammas Day was August 1st, and from the night before until Lady Day, March 23rd, certain people, *i.e.*, the inhabitants of Newbury and Northcourt, had the right of pasturage upon these lands; Lammas Day is said to have got its name from the offering of lambs on the Festival of St. Peter in Chains as a thanksgiving for the first fruits of the harvest; in later years a loaf of bread was offered to represent the first fruits. Oak-apple Day, May 29th, was celebrated in memory of Charles II's escape at Boscobel; it was first celebrated in 1660, the year in which he was restored to the throne. On this day it was customary to wear a sprig of oak in the button-hole till noon, after which the oak was discarded and ash leaves worn until sunset. If you see any-body doing this nowadays in Berkshire ask him why! For some reason or other it was called Shick-Shack Day, and Lowsley gives the little couplet :

"The twenty-ninth of Maay,
Shick-shack Daay."

Just why "shick-shack" I do not know, unless it was the old name for the oak-apple. Neither Lowsley nor Humphreys, quoting him in his delightful *Berkshire Book of Song, Rhyme and Steeplechime*, attempts to explain the origin of "shick-shack," nor do they give any explanation for the midday change from oak to ash. Nor can I find an explanation any-where else, and it is not wholly impossible that Oak-apple Day is something very much older than Boscobel. The Wiltshire Oak-apple Day celebration has nothing whatever to do with Charles II,, but relates to an older tradition by which the people of certain villages near Salisbury succeeded in retain-ing a right to gather firewood from a certain wood. It is, therefore, possible that both customs relate to something much more ancient than we credit. Both the oak and the ash are prominent in mythology, the ash particularly so in Scan-dinavia. Both trees in fact have great strength, and in mytho-logy have mystic powers for relieving sickness. In some parts of England hedgers refuse to cut back oak and ash, these being considered sacred trees. Of all trees, the oak is the most important in mythology, and there is an old Druidical belief that whatever grew upon an oak was sent from Heaven and was a sign that the tree had been chosen by God him-self. In addition, the thing which grew upon the oak, but was not part of it, was supposed to be blessed with invulnerability, a quality which would be imparted to anyone who should gather it and wear it, hence, perhaps, the gilding of the "apples" in certain parts of the country. So many of our "ancient" customs derive from something so much more ancient than we expect and the derivation which we commonly ascribe to them relates merely to the revival of some custom whose origin had even then been long forgotten. It is all very interesting, and perhaps a careful search of Fraser's *Golden Bough* might solve the problem, though I can never open that heavenly book without shooting off at tangents in all directions and getting thoroughly immersed in something other than the object of my search. But just what the connection is between Charles II and the ash sprig I still don't know. Spencer wrote : ". . . The warlike beech, the ash for nothing ill. . . ."

In some Berkshire villages there are quaint customs relating to the fair distribution of land. At Aldermaston a certain piece of land called Church Acre is let by "Candle Auction"; a candle is set alight and a pin pushed into it about an inch below the top; those men interested in the Church Acre immediately start bidding a rent for it; the candle burns down and the pin falls out, at which point the bidding ceases and he who has made the highest bid has Church Acre for the next three years. Tilehurst at one time decided who should farm certain strips of land by drawing marked apples from a tub. Near the Lammas Lands of Newbury, a field named Lot Mead probably referred to the Anglo-Saxon custom of dividing lands and distributing them "by lot" to individuals according to their rank and dignity. This sounds a bit crafty, I agree, and, no doubt, those with rank and dignity came off pretty well.

Finally, we come to the end of our tour of the festivities by Beating the Bounds in one or two places. The principle, of course, was for the old men of a parish to walk the youngsters round the bounds, beating their posteriors with rods every now and again to give them good cause to remember the boundary marks. The Ordnance Survey has largely removed the need for continuing this business but for all that it is still carried out here and there. Appleton went out to beat its bounds, or to "Goe the Perambulation" as it was called, on Ascension Day. At Bucklebury the ceremony was carried out during Rogation Week when there were processions with banners and crosses, prayers were said and crosses scratched on the ground. The steward of the manor led the procession, followed by all the important men of the parish all repeating the 104th Psalm when they came to certain places. The small boys were not beaten with rods in this case, but were bumped against walls and posts or dropped upon the ground, one poor chap having his arm broken on one occasion. At a mill-stream through which the boundary ran, most of the water was run off and the boys persuaded with oranges and apples to wade across, the "big shots" crossing by some drier route ! It took several days to complete the job. Cumnor beat the bounds in Rogation time, going across the river by boat to touch the Oxfordshire bank; the Eynsham ferryman had to bring six shillings and eight pence, the Swinford tythe, in a basin of water which the officiating vicar sprinkled over the onlookers, very reasonably having taken care to remove the money first. Hungerford chose Whit Monday, ducking and bumping at the traditional points, but Inkpen used the rod, though paying the boys one penny each for the inconvenience of breakfasting off the mantelpiece. Kennington has beaten its boundary quite recently, for the parish was not created until 1936, when it was synthesised from little bits of Radley, Sunningwell and South Kinksey, and the new bounds were beaten the following May. Rogation-tide would see Newbury's boys being bumped and listening to the 104th Psalm, but at certain prescribed places enjoying refreshments and winding up the day with a good dinner in one of the popular taverns. Before the Restoration, the religious side of the ceremony was strictly adhered to throughout the County, but later this was dropped and only the essential "perambulation" retained.

3. WEATHER FORECAST

Many of the old saws are universal and have nothing particular to do with Berkshire, unless it be the pronunciation. Quite a lot of these sayings refer to the weather and especially to the approaching weather; and not so wrong either, though they refer to a locality too small to replace the weather forecasts from the Air Ministry. Here are some, and if you want to try them out you must go to the place from which they come.

Bray says :

> "When Ashley Hill begins to smoke,
> Then Shottesbrook begins to soak."

Milton says :

"When the leaf of a mulberry tree is as big as a mouse's ear, no fear of frost till next autumn."

Padworth says :

"Wherever the wind is on Candlemas Day
There it will stay till the end of May."

Uffington, Woolstone and Kingston Lisle say :

"Now, chaps, the owl' white-oss is a-blowin' 'is bacca off this mornin'. We shall ae't wet foore night";

and say that

"the owl' white-oss is wearing his cap"

when the top is lost in the clouds.

Other parts of the Downs refer to hills having their caps on, when rain-cloud obscures their higher parts, and so do other parts of England, though I do not think it is said anywhere else in Berkshire, though, perhaps, one might expect it from Combe or Inkpen. Woods are said to be "smoking" or "smoking their pipes" when clouds hang low over them. Generally distributed across the County, the following sayings may be heard :

"A dark Michaelmas and a light Christmas."

"Raain avoor zeven, vine avoor 'leven."

"Red sky in the morning is the shepherd's warning

"Red sky at night is the shepherd's delight."

"No weather is ill
If the wind be still,
But rough wind and storm
Works plenty of harm."

"If it rains on Easter Day,
Plenty of grass but not much hay."

"A wet Good Friday and Easter Day,
A lot of grass and a little good hay."

"When the mist goes up the hill,
Then the rain runs down the drill."

"What be good vor the Hay be bad vor the Turmuts."

"Maayres taails an' mackerel sky,
Not long wet nor not long dry."

Rain is betokened by swallows flying low, cows eating greedily across a field at speed, flies coming into the house in numbers and there are other weather indications too universal to do more than mention, such as oak before ash and its alternative, hard winters and profusion of berries in the hedges, etc.

4. ORNITHOLOGICAL THEORIES

Magpies come in for a good deal of chatter :

"One sorrow,
Two joy,
Three a wedding,
Four a boy."

"One sorrow,
Two mirth,
Three a wedding,
Four a birth."

"One sorrow,
Two mirth,
Three a wedding,
Four a birth,
Five heaven,
Six hell,
Seven the devil's ain sel."

"One sorrow,
Two joy,
Three a wedding,
Four a boy,
Five a sickening,
Six a christening,
Seven a dance,
Eight a lady goes to France."

Tradition makes the blue tit the king of the birds, because in a "high altitude" competition, a tit hid under an eagle's wing until the eagle thought he had won, at which stage out popped the tit and flying upward a few yards easily defeated all the other avian competitors !

Another legend records a magpie attempting to teach a wood-pigeon how to build a nest. The magpie failed in the attempt and the wood-pigeon's nest for ever after consisted of lesson one only and is constructed of but a few twigs, laid across each other.

"A monkey, a magpie and a wife
Is the true emblem of strife."

"Cock Robin is dead in his grave, is dead . . ."

sang the children of Wickham, and were answered by the people from Ashbury, who sang:

"As black as a rook,
As black as a raven,
As black as the devil,
And so is Lord Craven."

In many parts of the County it is believed that bad luck will follow the shooting of a dove. At harvest-time turtle doves do a lot of damage to shocked corn and they taste well, too!

"When 'the pie' was opened
The birds began to sing,
Wasn't that a dainty dish
To set before the King."

The "pie" here refers to Henry James Pye, who lived at Faringdon and who was proclaimed Poet Laureate in 1790.

5. SOME VILLAGE SAYINGS

"Sing before breakfast, cry before night."

"Never go home without stick or stone."

"New bread, new beer, and green wood
Will bring ruin to any man's house."

"Where there's stones there's corn."

"As hard as a ground toad."

"Tadley God help us."

(Tadley is a village just over the Hampshire border reputed, not incorrectly, to be populated by villains and felons.)

"A whistlin' 'ooman an' a crawin' hen
Be-ant good vor God nor it vor men."

" 'E be as proud as a hen wi' one chick."

" 'E needs 'ut as much as a two-ad wants a zide-pockut."

"Two'ast yer bread
An' rasher yer vlitch,
An' as long as 'e lives
Thee 'ooll never be rich."

"Out nettle,
In dock,
Dock shall hev
A new smock;
Nettle shan't
Ha' narrun."

"Stop dancing like a Harry-long-legs round a candle."

"O Lard, make us able
To aat all on the table."

"Elder Staayke an' blackthorn ether
Maaykes a hedge vor years together."

6. SAYINGS ABOUT SOME VILLAGES

Aldermaston :

"When clubs are trumps, Aldermaston House shakes."
V. S. LEAN, *Collectanea*, 1902.

Bisham :

"O Bisham Banks are fresh and fair,
And Quary woods are green;
And pure and sparkling is the air,
Enchanting is the scene."
ASHLY-STERRY, *The Lazy Minstrel*, 1886.

Bray :

"And this is law I will maintain
Until my dying day, Sir,
That whatsoever King shall reign,
I'll be the Vicar of Bray, Sir."
"The Vicar of Bray" (traditional).

Brightwell :

"There's Brightwell and Spotwell
And Merry Mackney,
But lousy old Cholsey is worse
Than all three."
Local verse in HUMPHREY'S *Berkshire Book of
Song, Rhyme and Steeple Chime.*

Cumnor :

"The dews of summer night did fall,
The moon, sweet regent of the sky,
Silver'd the walls of Cumnor Hall
And many an oak that grew thereby."
W. J. MICKLE, 1735-88.

And again :

> "Full many a traveller had sigh'd
> And pensive wept the Countess' fall,
> As wandering onward they espied
> The haunted towers of Cumnor Hall."
>
> > SCOTT, *Kenilworth.*

And also :

> "For most, I know thou lov'st retired ground !
> Thee at the ferry Oxford rides blithe,
> Returning home on summer nights, have wet
> Crossing the stripling Thames at Bab-lock-hythe,
> Trailing in the cool stream thy fingers wet,
> As the punt's rope chops round ;
> And leaning backward in a pensive dream ;
> And fostering in thy lap a heap of flowers
> Pluck'd in shy fields and distant wychwood bowers,
> And thine eyes resting on the moonlit stream."
>
> > MATTHEW ARNOLD, *The Scholar Gipsy*, 1866.

Enborne :

> "Here I am
> Riding upon a black ram,
> Like a whore as I am
> And for my crincum crancum
> Have lost my Bincum Bancum ;
> And for my tail's game
> Have done this worldly shame ;
> Therefore I pray you, Mr. Steward,
> Let me have my land again."
>
> > Traditional, referring to naughty Enborne
> > widows in HUMPHREY'S *Berkshire
> > Book of Song, Rhyme and Steeple
> > Chime.*

Faringdon :

> "Here lofty mountains lift their azure heads,
> There its green lap the grassy meadows spread ;
> Enclosures here the sylvan scene divide,
> There plains extended spread their harvests wide."
>
> > HENRY JAMES PYE, *Faringdon Hill*, 1774.

Hinksey :

> "How changed is here each spot man makes or fills !
> In the two Hinkseys nothing keeps the same ;
> The village street its haunted mansion lacks,
> And from the sign is gone Sibylla's name,
> And from the roofs the twisted chimney stacks."
>
> > MATTHEW ARNOLD.

Hungerford :

> "Hungerford cray-fish, match me if you can,
> There's no such crawlers in the o-ce-an."

East Ilsley :

> "Sleepy Ilsley, drunken people,
> Got a church without a steeple;
> And what is more, to their disgrace,
> They've got a clock without a face!"

> "Ilsley, remote amidst the Berkshire downs,
> Claims these distinctions o'er her sister towns;
> Far famed for sheep and wool, though not for spinners,
> For sportsmen, doctors, publicans and sinners!"
>> Traditional in HUMPHREY'S *Berkshire Book of
>> Song, Rhyme and Steeple Chime.*

Lambourn :

> "And once atop of Lambourn Down, towards the hill of Clere,
> I saw the host of Heaven in rank, and Michael with his spear."
>> H. BELLOC in HUMPHREY'S *Berkshire Book of
>> Song, Rhyme and Steeple Chime.*

Maidenhead :

> "When Taplow Woods are russet-red,
> When half the poplar leaves are shed,
> When silence reigns at Maidenhead."
>> ASHLY-STERRY, *The Lazy Minstrel*, 1886.

Newbury :

> "The famous inn at Speenhamland,
> That stands below the hill,
> May well be called the Pelican,
> From its enormous bill."
>> Traditional.

> "At Newbury, that fatal place,
> Where many a man was mustered,
> And lost his life oh! there it was
> A youth was slain with custard."
>> BALLARD-SHUFF of Newbury.

Pangbourne :

> "O Pangbourne is pleasant in sweet summertime,
> And Streatley and Goring are worthy of rhyme;
> The Sunshine is hot and the breezes are still,
> The River runs swift under Basildon Hill."
>> ASHLY-STERRY, *The Lazy Minstrel*, 1886.

Reading :

> "Both Gods and men now clearly prove
> That Reading is the Court of Love."
>
> Ballad in J. A. BRAIN, Berkshire Ballads
and Other Papers, 1904.

> "In Reading town we ne'er went to bed,
> Every soul there mounted his horse,
> Hoping next day to fill them with dread ;
> Yet I swear by St. Patrick's Cross,
> We most shamefully was routed."
>
> Ballad of the Reading skirmish, sung
to the tune of "Lillibullero."

Streatley :

> "But from the hill I understand
> You gaze across rich pasture-land,
> And fancy you see Oxford and
> P'raps Wallingford and Wheatley;
> And, though the view's beyond all praize,
> I'd rather much sit here and laze
> Than scale the hill at Streatley."
>
> ASHLY-STERRY, The Lazy Minstrel, 1886.

Sunningwell :

> "All the Maids in Sunningwell
> You may put in an Eggshell."
>
> Proverbial saying in HEAME'S DIARY, 1813.

Three mile Cross :

> "A cross lane, a rope-walk shaded with limes and oaks and a cool clear pond overhung with elms."
>
> MARY MITFORD.

Uffington :

> "Before the Gods that made the Gods
> Had seen their sunrise pass,
> The White Horse of the White Horse Vale
> Was cut out of the grass."
>
> G. K. CHESTERTON, Ballad of the White
Horse, 1911.

Windsor :

> "Hail, Windsor! crowned with lofty towers,
> Where Nature wantons at her will,
> Decks every vale with fruit and flowers,
> With waving trees adornes each hill."
>
> Old poem, quoted by LYSONS, 1806.

Wokingham :

> "Oh, nephew, your grief is but folly,
> In town you may find better prog;
> Half a crown there will get you a Molly,
> A Molly much better than Mog."

Ballad of Molly Mog, or the Fair Maid of
the Rose Inn, Wokingham, attributed to
JOHN GAY.

7. "CRAZY AS A COOT"

In 1925 Mr. Humphreys published a fascinating little paper dealing entirely with the eccentric characters of the County. Naturally, the characters are long since dead, in fact they were dead when Mr. Humphreys wrote of them. One can scarcely write of living persons under this heading, and although I know a few that I would feel obliged to classify as eccentric, it behoves me to leave well alone. I therefore admit that I have no first-hand knowledge of the few eccentrics I propose to mention, relying entirely upon such tales as have already been told.

Let us first of all consider misers, and John Elwes is the classic example. Elwes was a wealthy man, having inherited much from his uncle Sir Hervey Elwes, and he came from a stock of misers who had also accumulated wealth. Appointed Member of Parliament for Berkshire, John Elwes made the necessary journeys to London by horse, with nothing more to eat than one hard-boiled egg! In London he "put up" in one of the many semi-derelict houses which he had inherited there. He had no fire and cared not a jot for broken windows and leaking roofs and he went to bed at dusk to save a candle. Yet he was said to be "gentle and engaging," and as an M.P. he was incorruptible and industrious. The night he died he went to bed in his worn-out shoes, a filthy old hat upon his head and with his walking-stick in his hand. He lived much of his life at Marcham, but he owned considerable property in the County and for a while he lived at a house called Hatt Castle near Chieveley.

Another miser lived at Blewbury—in fact, he was curate there for more than forty years. He lived entirely alone, without even a dog to keep him company; it seems that there was little need for him to purchase his rations for he was eternally visiting his "flock," always carefully arriving at mealtime and usually staying on till nightfall. The story says that Morgan Jones, for that was his name, wore the same hat and the same coat during the whole of his forty-two years at Blewbury. This is slightly contradicted by another tale which tells of him swapping his own dilapidated hat for that of a scare-crow—a hodmedod as he would probably have called it if he had picked up the local dialect. We don't know why he died, though we might guess, and he left £18,000 behind him.

A rather different kind of man was Thomas Day, who lived near Wargrave. He spent his life, or nearly all of it, searching for a suitable wife. Unable to locate such a lady by the ordinary methods, Day selected a blonde and a brunette from a Foundling Hospital and set about training them in the ways he would wish of his wife. But this failed, too, and it is not surprising, for one of his tests was to drop melting sealing wax upon the girls' bare arms and to fire pistols at their petticoats! Day then resumed the usual matrimonial channels for a while with no success until at long last a thoughtful friend produced Esther Milnes. Esther must have been as cracked as Thomas, for she married him and, uncomplaining, submitted to his tests of walking barefoot through the snow and of living a life of complete and utter self-denial without any of the comforts a woman might desire. Except for his ideas of domestic bliss, Day was not really a miser, for he must have spent a considerable sum of money wife-hunting, which, I may say, included taking his blonde and brunette pupils to be schooled at Avignon in France. But, alas! he was literally cracked, for a horse threw him on his head and he was dead in a quarter of an hour—his final escapade was to discover if he could break the will of an animal to the same degree as he had done with Esther Milnes! Thomas Day is not known to history for his crazy ideas but for a book he wrote—*Sandford and Merton.*

Another man who failed to find a wife by methods accepted in the better circles was Sir John Dinely. Sir John was one of the Poor Knights of Windsor, and he was a bit frugal if not

Wayland's smithy, Uffington

quite a miser. His daily shopping consisted of a faggot, a candle, a small loaf and perhaps a herring, but meat, butter, tea and sugar he did without. He trudged around in an old cloak and carried an old umbrella, looking for all the world like some tramp. But when in the presence of likely ladies Sir John would whip off the old cloak, revealing an embroidered coat, a silk-flowered waistcoat, breeches of faded velvet, dirty silk stockings and, finally and incongruously, a pair of clogs; his head lived in a powdered wig beneath a fine cocked hat! And what did he do when some fair lady chanced to gaze upon him? Why, he handed her a slip of paper upon which was explained his pedigree, his wealth, and his one and only ambition. Humphreys quotes one of Sir John's advertisements published in a number of the *Reading Mercury* of 1862 and another in the *Ipswich Journal* of the same year. But no matter how lavishly he described himself and his ancestral home, the ladies refused to play, and, poor chap, he died a batchelor in 1808.

A gentleman who obviously had more money than brains was Richard, seventh Lord Barrymore. Richard was mad on practical jokes and spent his time organising and carrying out such acts as are, or used to be, condoned in an undergraduate in his University town, but which were definitely not encouraged elsewhere. He had brothers and sisters as mad as himself, and one sister, Humphreys explains, was nicknamed "Billingsgate" on account of the extreme vigour of her language. Young Lord Barrymore, instead of turning his enormous energy to following hounds over impossible fences, preferred to drive his friends around at breakneck speed in locked carriages, frightening the life out of those not so daft as himself. The streets of Wargrave, where he lived, rang to the catcalls of his rowdy friends, and all the County knew his carriages and liveried servants. He and his friends lived by night and he made a rule that no guest of his should retire before five in the morning. He littered the County with crazy clubs, he gave incredible dinners and he died accidentally from his own sporting-gun. Surtees would have loved him and Lucy Glitters would have fallen for him, but Wargrave must have looked askance and wondered what would happen next.

A downland view from Letcombe Bassett

8. WHIPPING-POST, STOCKS AND PILLORY

So that one should not get the impression that "the good old days" consisted entirely of festivity and happiness, I record here a few tales which give a rather different picture. It appears that in the year 1676 the sum of 3s. 5d. was paid in Hungerford to the Widow Tanner for "iron geare for the whipping-post." Before this new "geare" was ordered, in 1658 to be exact, John Savage, the Hungerford "Town Beadle or Assistant Bailiff," was paid 2d. for whipping one Dorothy Miller; later in the same year he was paid another 2d. for whipping a man. In 1676, the new "iron geare" installed, the cost of whipping was increased, and 1s. was paid for whipping a certain Thomas Pound, while a further 2s. 6d. was paid for attendance and expenses. Two years later a "poore man," after being whipped, was given 4d. and sent "from Tythinge to Tythinge." During this year, 1678, John Savage, still "Town Beadle," was paid 5s. for his "extraordinary paines this year and whippinge of several persons." When Savage retired from the post, he was succeeded by Robert Coxhead, who in 1689 received 4d. for whipping a man and a woman, and later in the year Coxhead received 1s. for whipping "Jasper Yorke's boy and Trust-ley's." In 1690 Coxhead received 4d. for whipping a "vaga-bond" who, upon the completion of the sentence, was given threepennyworth of bread and beer, and at the expense of 6d. a pass was obtained to preclude the necessity of his being whipped again. Finally, in 1694 Coxhead whipped a blind woman who was afterwards given a 1s. pass to Stony Strat-ford, with a present of 2d., and a man who led her into Charn-ham Street was paid 2d. also. In Reading thieves and beggars were whipped in the Market Place or were flogged at the cart's tail from the prison to their homes—and sometimes back to the prison again.

It has been suggested that Newbury was the last place in England to use its parish stocks, for in 1872 "one Mark Turk," described as an "incorrigible bacchanalian," was sentenced to four hours in the stocks for being drunk and thereby causing a disturbance at the Parish Church! The stocks were brought out for the occasion from the Town Hall cellars, and as it was raining Mark was kindly seated under cover and unlike his predecessors in shame he was guarded by a constable from the time-honoured attentions of the crowd. Not so far away, in the Lambourn valley, the stocks were out in the open by the village church, and the offender had to sit on the wet ground unless some sympathetic passerby gave him a bit of sack to sit upon.

In 1633 Lodowick Bowyer was put in the pillory in Reading Market Place. Apart from having his head and hands clamped down, his ears were nailed to the boards, and he was forced, by the painful influence of stones and rotten eggs, to read aloud a confession to the effect that he had, in Reading some months previous, spoken ill of Archbishop Laud. Poor Bowyer was fined £3,000. His punishment was to stand nailed to the pillory three times, twice in London and once in Reading, he was to be whipped in public and branded on the face, and if he survived this ordeal, he was to be imprisoned for life. Thus saith the Star Chamber. In 1664 the Hungerford pillory was repaired and a new " cheek and brace" made for the sum of 2s. 6d. A new one was required by 1686, and cost 10s. in labour and £1 5s. 6d. for timber. In 1721 yet another was built; this time it cost £2 10s. and a Mr. Kimber was paid 5s. for painting it.

9. THE OLDER BERKSHIRE FONTS

About A.D. 634 Bishop Birinus baptised King Cynegils of Wessex by immersing him in the Thames at Dorchester; it is said that most of the men of Wessex followed their king's example. The great ball that was Christianity had started to roll. Baptism was not without its troubles, for there were people who believed in total immersion, there were those who believed in sprinkling water upon the head, there were those who believed in infant baptism and those who didn't. The total immersion of an adult raised a problem of its own when it became desirable to baptise in a church instead of on a river bank. Baptisteries, where the segregated sexes might be immersed, answered this problem on the continent, but in England fonts came into being large enough for the immersion of infants but totally inadequate for adults, who were of necessity "sprinkled." By the thirteenth century "sprinkling" was the generally accepted method for an adult, but up to the time of Elizabeth infants were normally immersed.

A solid, sturdy thing like a font is not easily destroyed and some of the fonts in our parish churches are therefore likely to be of great age. Cromwell, of course, did his best, particularly with the lead fonts, for lead was easily melted down into ammunition for Roundhead weapons, but in spite of Cromwell we have in Berkshire some remarkably interesting fonts which well repay inspection. My friend Dr. Sidney Gilford has made a study of Berkshire fonts and on behalf of the County Architectural Records Committee has amassed a collection of photographs of cottages, churches and fonts which surely must be unequalled throughout the County; and this has been done despite war-time difficulties of travelling and of obtaining photographic material—not to mention the demands made upon a doctor by a town so overpopulated as was Reading. It is only natural that I should turn to Dr. Gilford when I think of fonts, and in answer to my request for some information he has very nobly risen to the occasion and sent me an article on our Berkshire fonts up to and including the thirteenth century. I can do no better than quote him.

"Notwithstanding these difficulties I have been able to visit practically every village and town in Berkshire and the neighbouring portions of adjoining counties and to build up a modest record of their architectural features. At first I was chiefly interested in the cottages, especially in Blewbury, East Hendred, Harwell, Upton, East Hagbourne and other villages on the road to Wantage. Later, I found North Moreton, Sutton Courtenay, Long Wittenham and Wykeham in the north and the villages around Uffington in the west. In the second year the churches were the chief object of my visits, but here I found I could not spare the time to explore them properly and I was handicapped by my indifferent knowledge of architecture, and for these reasons I have found it better to concentrate upon certain details, at present on fonts, but later, perhaps, on doorways if I have the opportunity.

"In most churches we find that additions and restorations have taken place, sometimes in a manner alien to the original building, so that one's mind is confused with the different periods and designs that one sees, and a definite pattern can be obtained only after a prolonged study by an architectural expert. Occasionally the only portion of the original church is the font, as at Radley; very seldom does one find a Norman font in a church which is pure Norman—such a church, for instance, as that at Avington near Hungerford; it has a Tudor porch covering a Norman carved doorway, and a thirteenth-century arch to the vestry, otherwise it is unchanged for 700 or 800 years. This font is one of the most remarkable in England, it is weather-worn and has been neglected; it stands just inside the door with a modern radiator behind, and when I first saw it it had fruit and vegetables lying around it. It has a much-worn cable ornament around the bowl beneath which are eleven arcades, in each of these is a figure standing or sitting; these figures are much chipped. In two of the arcades we find two figures, one pair apparently kissing. Two of the figures represent archbishops and one an abbot or bishop, and they are fully clothed. It is probable that it is at least 800 years old, and is contemporary with the main fabric of the church. In the History of Berkshire (*Victoria History of the Counties of England*) we find the holders of Avington Manor from 1086 to the present day; at this date it was held by Richard Puingiant, passing in 1166 to Richard de Camville who died at the siege of Acre in 1191. The Camvilles held it until 1226 when the son of the Earl of Salisbury took possession until succeeded by the Earl of Lincoln. After this we find the names of successors, Embold, Le Strange, Wm. Coventre, Choke, Dowse, Jones and in recent times Sir Francis Burdett. These names represent several families who followed in the ownership, and it is probable that most of them came to the church and many were baptised in the font, but they can represent only a small proportion of the children of the neighbourhood such as farmers, labourers, craftsmen and others who were brought to the church. The font occupied an important place in the life of the village, and saw great changes taking place. Fortunately, changes were gentler than in the towns so that we find the old fonts chiefly in the villages and very few in the towns. Hungerford is only one and a half miles away, and it has a nineteenth-century church with a fifteenth-century font. In Reading we find two fonts of the fifteenth century, but we must go to Purley to find a beautiful Norman font and to Tidmarsh for a traditional Norman one. Newbury has a modern font and we must travel to Enbourne or along the Lambourn valley and into the hills for the older ones. Faringdon, Abingdon, Wantage and Lambourn have lost their old fonts, which have been replaced by those of later date. This may be due to political or industrial or religious conflicts, or perhaps to a greater desire for progress, which may tend to make us despise the simpler work of the older days. In comparatively recent years the old fonts have been displaced by new ones. In the *Ecclesiastical and Architectural Topography,* published in 1849, we read of Woolhampton—"The font is Norman, round, with circular arches and figures formed of lead, the font itself is of stone"; this font disappeared when the church was rebuilt and very probably was built into the new foundations. At that date too, Sandhurst had a Norman font with a square bowl and cylindrical stem, and Brimpton had a plain round font which was probably Transitional. Lambourn's round font is said to have been cast out and sold as a flower-pot. Fortunately, the Norman font at Englefield, which at one time had been cast out, has since been restored to the church, and is now in the vestry, whilst a modern one is standing in the church. At Wickham, which has been much restored but still has its old tower with long and short work of the Saxon period, there is a modern ornate font as well as an ancient one which was dug up in the grounds outside. Although so many ancient fonts have been replaced, Berkshire is still rich in Norman examples. There are probably about 50 which have stood for 700 years or more, 11 for 600 years, 11 for 500 years, 11 for 400 years, and the rest have been in use only from the sixteenth century or later.

"Of the Norman fonts we find about fifteen which are tub shaped and plain. These occur in all parts of Berkshire, at Aldworth and Compton on the Berkshire Downs, at Kingston Lisle and Longcot in the neighbourhood of Uffington, at Shaw, Chaddleworth and East Shefford, from Newbury into the Lambourn valley, at South Moreton and Appleton towards the north and Binfield in the east. More elaborate examples are found, of which Avington is the most notable. Interesting types are seen at West Hanney, Finchampstead, Enbourne, West Shefford, Purley, Sutton Courtenay (Transitional) and other places. Berkshire contains also three lead fonts—there are about thirty-eight of these old lead fonts in England—two of these are probably of the early thirteenth-century, Long Wittenham and Childrey, and one of the fourteenth at Woolstone. That at Long Wittenham has a large circular bowl and is perhaps the only one in England to stand on its original plinth. On the lower part of the bowl there are thirty figures of archbishops under pointed arches, on the upper part a design similar to that found on one of the lead fonts in Oxfordshire at Warborough just across the boundary. At Childrey we have twelve church dignitaries with crook and book."

10. BULL-RING

Some of us can remember the days of meat, when wives and housekeepers could stand before the butcher's wooden slab and examine a dozen pieces before selecting one, perhaps on occasions placing no order at all yet always being bowed away by the smiling occupant of the striped apron. Tender? Fresh? Yes, but who can remember the question—well baited?

One hundred years ago bull-baiting became illegal, and well-baited meat, in theory at any rate, was no longer available. So bull-baiting had a use, did it? Use or excuse? I'm not sure about this, but it is on record that in 1661 a Newbury butcher, named Edward Caton, was fined 3s. 4d. by a Court Leet for killing bulls without "baiting of them according to custom"! Other butchers were similarly fined and a warning from the Court was sent out to the effect that "if any butcher shall henceforth kill any bull without baiting, he shall forfeit and pay for every bull so killed a similar fine." I very much doubt that any excuse was needed in 1661, when bears and badgers, cocks and rats and dogs everywhere added to life's enjoyments. Why, even men were baited, in the stocks, in the pillory, at the whipping-post, at the cart's tail. No, an excuse was much more necessary for the "softies" of Bourton who danced prettily upon the village green while their neighbours from Shrivenham and Watchfield were washing the blood out of their hair at the "Revels."

Necessary for the quality of meat or not, bull-baiting was a remarkably popular pastime and most Berkshire towns observed the custom; Wokingham was the greatest stronghold of this sport in the County, and was, as I have pointed out elsewhere, a hot-bed of cock-fighting, dog-fighting and human fighting. It happened that in the same 1661 a certain George Staverton, an ardent follower of bull-baiting, bequeathed a house, the annual rent from which, £6, was to provide one bull annually to be baited in the market place. Rents apparently increased, or the cost of bulls went down, for it was not long before the "Staverton bequest" was providing not one, but two or more bulls each year. The Great Day for baiting in Wokingham was St. Thomas' Day, when the Staverton bulls were used, though it is fairly certain that there were "smaller" days throughout the year and market days were also used for baiting.

In a collection of articles edited in 1896 by that energetic writer the Rev. P. H. Ditchfield, Canon Sturges contributes the story of a "bait" in Wokingham Market Place in 1815, and from this and other sources we may presume that the streets were choc-a-bloc with people, with horses and with carriages, every house surrounding the market place had its windows crammed with male and female faces, while men sat on the roofs and clutched the chimneys; the more adventurous thronged the arena and small boys climbed into the branches of the single tree which stood there. The ceremony opens upon the arrival of the alderman and burgesses complete with "ale-tasters," sergeants of the mace and mace-

bearers, all of whom proceed to the Red Lion where the alderman takes up his position in the big window. (The present
Lady Mayor must be thankful that this is not one of her
obligations!) At once the first bull, as often as not his nose
filled with pepper to make him cross, is led in, a dozen strong
men grasping the rope which is attached to his horns; with a
fifteen-foot chain he is fixed to the ring and the twelve strong
men disappear into the crowd. The first dog is now let loose
at the far end of an alleyway of human legs down which he
proceeds, jumping through hoops held at varying heights.
Once out into the open the dog studies his bull, for he has
been trained to know that his part of the performance is to
"pin" the wet nose before him, at the same time avoiding the
horns. The bull, who is presumably not unaccustomed to barking dogs, stands watching for the attack, when he will try to
get a horn beneath the dog's belly. Many a dog is ripped open
or sent screaming up into the air to be caught in the arms of
his owner, or less fortunately, by the spikes on the Town
Hall. The crowd screams, the pickpockets pick, the bull
bellows and the dog on the spikes shrieks in mortal agony;
and so on until the bull tires and a dog "pins." Out come the
twelve strong men, to break the dog from its "pin," and if
the bull is good for more, out comes another dog. Occasionally a bull, not appreciating the improvement to his flesh
and very sensibly resenting his torn and bleeding nose, gives
one gigantic heave and away comes the staple holding the all-
important ring! For a moment there is pandemonium, the
crowd dashing hither and thither, until the twelve strong
men once again assert their authority; once a recaptured bull
was tied to the tree and shook small boys from out of the
branches on top of himself! Finally, Mr. George Staverton's
first bull is dragged away to the slaughter-house to provide
Christmas meat for Wokingham's poor, the sale of the offal
to find them in shoes.

I have attended bullfights which were very interesting, but
never having been present at a "baiting" I cannot say
definitely that it was not; perhaps if one knew the people,
studied the "form" and all that sort of thing, there was something in it. At any rate it was a popular "sport" and attracted

large crowds. But it sounds altogether a shoddy business with none of the pageantry of the Spanish *plaza de toros*—the Wokingham mace, the alderman's chain, the ceremonial batons of the "ale-tasters" in no way equalling the plumes of the *alquaciles,* the embroidered costumes of the *cuadrilla,* the *coleta* and *montero* of the matador; nor could the antics of the dog, cunning and deliberate as they may have been, equal the gracefulness of the *veronica,* the *media veronica,* the *pase ayudado* and the *pase de pecho*; nor could the bull show himself to advantage chained as he was to an iron ring, though at best he was but a great clumsy brute on his way to the slaughter-house and so unlike the lithesome Spanish fighting bull that a matador would throw a fit if confronted with him! Like the Wokingham "fan" who remains unmoved when a dog is ripped in half, the Spanish *aficionado* pays no attention to a horse's entrails which, after all, are no more part of the programme than the English lady being sick beside him. But there is something fascinating about the *corrida* which one simply cannot imagine in the crowded market place in Wokingham. The great arena with its yellow sand, the blue sky, the seats in the sun and the seats in the shade, perhaps a mantilla, tortoise-shell combs and fan, lottery tickets, water-bottles, cushions, black-capped, blue-chinned men—one forgets that the shining black bull with the wide-spread horns is being done to death, that the coloured *banderillas* have got barbed steel points and that red patch on his shoulders is livid flesh where the six-inch blades of the *picos* have wounded him.

Perhaps I must forgive the Wokingham "baiters" after all; perhaps like the Spanish crowd they bear the bull no malice, unless he proves to be a *manso,* a coward who will not fight, and who refuses to give the matador an opportunity to show his artistry and maybe his blood. Perhaps Wokingham would boo and hiss a cowardly dog or one which was badly trained, in the same spirit that Spaniards will hurl abuse (and hats, water-bottles, cushions and stones) at a matador who does not satisfy their expectation; certainly we know that Wokingham dog owners fought and sometimes killed each other when the "bait" was over—a *bronca,* the Englishman's "rough-house," makes a disgraced matador's heart beat faster

than any bull ever did. I say "perhaps" to these possibilities
for I cannot see them as realities : few Romans could have
sat fascinated either by a Christian's ability to avoid the lions,
or by the lion's skill in catching the Christians—it was the
horrible crunching and the screams which drew the crowd;
and similarly in Wokingham it was not the skill of the dog or
the bull, it was the blood and noise that people wanted and it
didn't matter much which of the participants produced it. And
this is where bull-baiting differs so essentially from bull-fight-
ing. No *aficionado* goes to see a bull "killed," he can slip
round to the slaughter-house for that; he goes to the *corrida*
to see a performance in which a bull is "killed"; there is
nothing whatever sadistic about it and he shouts his disap-
proval if the bull is hurt unnecessarily and in an ungentle-
manly manner.

What of the dogs which went rushing through the Wokingham hoops? Bulldogs of course, great neckless fellows who
wore collars only to show their medals. With the greyhound
the British bulldog shares the honour of being the oldest
known breed. According to Canon Struges, most Wokingham
cottages owned a "baiting" dog which was trained by night .
on some unfortunate farmer's oxen ! We all know what is
said about a bulldog's locking bite, and Canon Sturges records
a fearful story of a man, a Wokingham man I fear, though
this is not specifically stated, who won a bet by cutting off each
of his dog's legs in succession without his letting go of the
bull's nose ! Bull-baiting was finally forbidden by law in 1835
after an abortive attempt to stamp it out in 1802. An order
of the Privy Council in 1591, on the other hand, forbade the
acting of plays on Thursdays because that day was the
popularly accepted day for baiting ! And modern Wokingham would rather not go to a play any day of the week than
have to watch a bull baited on one of them.

PART V

Open Road

CHAPTER XVIII

A GUIDE FOR THE DILIGENT
MOTORIST

My object in the journeys which I shall describe is not so much to cover every road and visit every village, but by starting from a number of centres, to provide an introduction to each district, to the "Vale and Downs," to the river valleys and the heathlands. Occasionally, I have taken you to a church but for the most part I have left you to describe this for yourself. You will need a map, or maps I should say, for Berkshire is not content with one, and from these you will see a thousand possibilities not suggested here; and that is my purpose, to whet your appetite and to leave you to deviate up lovely lanes and to stray through majestic woods—if you get lost or arrested for poaching, it's your fault then, not mine. But one word of warning; not all the places covered with purple heather and silver birch are commons, and remember also, please, the blackened ground, red hot and smoking, the heather and bracken gone, the birch and pine twisted and distorted; not only is a beautiful place ruined, but many a man has to make a living from the trees.

In the ensuing pages I will take you over a thousand miles of Berkshire and I hope both your petrol and your patience will stay the course, for it will be well worth it.

1. READING CENTRE
JOURNEY ONE

The Thames valley up to Streatley and the base of the Downs up to Aldworth and back by the wooded valley of the Pang.

The Oxford road runs away from Reading as fast as it decently can, for this surely is the largest of the various large roads leading from the town. Past the greyhound stadium where on Saturdays half of Reading seems to hang about, on past the roundabout and into the country, with the decrepid walls of Purley Park and the pretty lane leading down to a terrible bungalow-town and a riverside disdainful of such eyesores, sweeping with averted eyes to the lovely pools and weir at Mapledurham.

Pangbourne. The Oxford road twists and turns through Pangbourne, where Kenneth Grahame lived and died. Up above in the trees is Bere Court, one-time country house of the abbots of Reading, and not far off stands the much more modern Nautical College, founded by Sir Thomas Devitt in 1917. Lying down below the road, almost in the Thames, the Swan Hotel is worthy of a visit, if only to watch the water rushing over the weir; there is an excuse to go inside the Swan, however, for there on the wall are marked the levels to which the river has flooded the bar and there are photographs to convince you of the truth. A lovely stretch of river runs beneath Shooters Hill, not marred by the dreadful houses locally known as the "Seven deadly sins," for there is always something to watch on the river here and our backs are turned upon them.

Basildon. Up over the railway at Skew Bridge and the road hugs the wall of Basildon Park, whose great mansion stands cold and empty, staring through the trees to Hart's Lock Woods in Oxfordshire. A little farthur on a lane turns down over the railway to the church, where Jethro Tull, inventor of the famous seed-drill, is said to be buried. It is fitting that where this pioneer of scientific agriculture lies, everything that is modern in dairy architecture should now stand, as spotless as ever a farmyard can be, and the bloom on the friesians is the envy of all. In Church Field, Roman tessellated pavements were discovered and largely destroyed by men preparing for the railway line in 1839. Our road runs on past Lady Fane's "Grotto," constructed for her ladyship in 1746; these grottos, built of shells, are a horror of the past, thank goodness, and just a few here or there throughout the country remain to be gaped at by stupefied "charabangers."

Streatley. Our road emerges from beneath tall trees and rooks' nests into Streatley, which is just a little T-piece of roads, tied to Goring by the river-bridge. Ancient roads from the east crossed the Thames here and went up over the Downs. However much the "Lazy Minstrel" preferred to

Faringdon, from the church

linger at the bottom of Streatley Hill, the view from the top is well worth the effort of the climb, and on the return the pint of beer among the shining guns and pistols of the Bull is a fair reward.

Aldworth. Up the hill behind the Bull the road to Aldworth goes, and up it you will go too, if your car can do it, and believe me, many a car has come down in reverse, its engine unable to pull its body upwards any farther, its driver stiff-necked from the awkward descent. In Aldworth the church should be inspected, for here are the "giants," the nine effigies of the De la Beche family who lived in the now departed castle. The mighty yew in the churchyard will attract your attention—it is 30 feet round its trunk and is said to be 600 years old.

Compton. Turning right-handed at Aldworth's Four Points Inn, where the bar must be the smallest in the County and has room for little more than one fat man, we run along towards the open Downs and Compton, where ancient tracks run off to Perborough Castle while others climb to Roden Down and Lowbury Hill. Here in Compton, where sheep were at one time more important than human beings, the Agricultural Research Council has an experimental farm where animals live like royalty, and know it. But we must turn our backs upon the lovely Berkshire Downs and drop down into the forest lands which crown the valleys of the little Pang.

Hampstead Norris. The ancient road which ran from Newbury by the Hampshire border, to Dorchester over into Oxfordshire, takes us past Perborough into Hampstead Norris, lying in its hollow, the home of the great Norreys family. The Norman font from the church is perhaps the oldest in the country, but it is no use looking for it here where it belongs, for somehow it has got to a village called Stone in Buckinghamshire!

Yattendon. Following the Pang for part of the way the road runs to Yattendon, home of the "Snail Watchers" and a "hymnal"; formerly a market town, this place now shows never a sign of hurry and bustle, peacefully looking across the trees of Frilsham. The Court stands high in its wooded

Village pump at Buscot

grounds, and here before the terrace was found the famous "Yattendon Hoard" of bronze implements.

Frilsham. The narrow road opposite the church will take us by commonland and Hawkridge Wood, past a tiny pub where the beer is good and the cakes are better. A bit behind us is the only mediæval church in England dedicated to the lady, Saint Frideswide, a Saxon princess credited with many miracles.

Bucklebury. From Frilsham the road clings lovingly to the narrow weed-covered Pang, until eventually it passes through it; motorists beware, for even when the river-bed is dry this is a nasty place to cross. Into Bucklebury we go, much the same as Jack of Newbury saw it; Queen Elizabeth, Gray, Pope and Swift saw it and loved it, and all visitors will do the same. The church may be visited if only for a curious purpose, for on a window is a fly, its body and legs painted on one side of the glass, its wings upon the other—whatever for? The church is interesting also for its "old world" box pews and its Norman carving. Up at Chapel Row is the Bladebone Inn and the scene of the "old time 'revels.'" After a refresher here—and the draught cider used to be excellent in flavour if somewhat dangerous in effect—back the way we came to the dangerous turn off to Stanford Dingley. The road carries us by Bushnell's Green and over a brook that feeds the Pang. In Stanford Dingley there are two quaint inns, with an alternative to darts in "ringing the bull," a game at which the locals shine and visitors look fools! From here we cross the Pang, having previously gazed into the waters of the "Blue Pool" and surveyed the cress beds, and turning right, sweep along to Bradfield, beneath Greathouse wood.

Bradfield. Crossing the Pang once more and rising the hill we are at once upon Bradfield College, founded by Thomas Stevens in 1850. There is little of village here, the school buildings monopolising even the light of day. The Greek Theatre in its chalk pit should be seen, modelled upon that at Epidaurus. Straight on our road goes, past Modern Side House and down to the Bourne that bounds Englefield Park. The old Deer Park touches our road for a brief moment and further along we get a glimpse of the mansion where Queen

Elizabeth visited Walsingham, to whom she had given the manor; its rightful owner, Sir Francis Englefield, had fled the country, taking his religious tendencies with him to Spain, where he plotted the restoration of papal authority in England. For many generations this great mansion and its estates have belonged to the Benyon family.

Tidmarsh. We must follow the park wall round past the main entrance, past the little lanes that run down to Theale and its cathedral-like church, over the Pang again and between the thick coppices where nightingales sing, till we come to the tiny church of Tidmarsh, nestling against the walls of the Grange. There is much of interest in this church with its decorated Norman doorway and font. We lose sight of the river as we drive on towards Pangbourne under such a canopy of elms that on a windy night no man will venture on this stretch of road unless he must, and then in a flash the water is there beside the road, and the new pumping-station plays at being a miniature Taj Mahal. And so back along the Oxford Road into Reading, unless we prefer to take the lane by Purley Hall into Sulham with its village stocks and up through lovely woods into the Tilehurst outskirts of Reading.

JOURNEY TWO

Up the Kennet Valley to Newbury, through the heather and pine-trees to Burghfield Common; across to Mortimer and down to Swallowfield and the Loddon Valley.

The Bath Road wastes no time in putting Reading behind it and in a very few miles of large houses, for the most part given over now to evacuated Ministries, we are in open country at Calcot, with its golf course upon our right and several tempting lanes running uphill towards Tilehurst and Sulham. Calcot was at one time part of the Manor of Tilehurst, owned by Sir Francis Englefield who broke it off from its parent and sold it in 1604.

Theale. Through some excellent agricultural land runs our road, over the anti-tank ditch which may well stump archæologists of the future, past a sand- and gravel-pit which is a veritable haven for bees and wasps and beetles, past

places where remains from British, Roman and Saxon times
have been unearthed. Towering over Theale is the gigantic
nineteenth-century church, a present from Sophia Sheppard,
who died in 1848 and who lies beneath a fifteenth-century
shrine brought from Oxford. Between Theale and Aldermaston are many delightful roads running northward to the
woods along the Pang and southward over the railway to the
Kennet and the canal to Burghfield, Sulhamstead, Ufton
Nervet and Padworth, the first one passing a little aerodrome
and creeping round hair-pin bends, the last one passing the
ugly petrol pumping-station, its round barrows certainly not
hiding cinerary urns and bones, but thousands of tons of
concrete and petrol pumped from the coast.

Aldermaston is one of the most delightful villages of the
Kennet valley, the park gates gazing down the peaceful street
to the Hind's Head Inn, as though trying to tell the time from
the clock whose hands never move. I have known Aldermaston Street and those gates all my life from a picture in
my father's house, though I did not know then that I should
ever live there, on land that had been a part of the old estate
of the Forsters, whom Henry VIII and Queen Elizabeth
visited, and before that, was owned by Sir Robert Archard,
a Norman soldier of the twelfth century. Once upon a time
there was a regular market in this dreamy village, and once
in 1770 the village schoolmaster made himself famous by
producing the "William" pear; I regret that the original
name, the "Aldermaston" pear has gone by the board. The
church owns three Norman doorways, though only one is
used, the other two being blocked in. From the village we run
back to the Mill House, formerly a flour-mill and now a
guest house, and turning left beside it soon cross the waters
and the railway and we are back on to the main road.

Woolhampton and Midgham are so entwined that it is
difficult to know where one begins and the other ends; Upper
Woolhampton lies above Midgham Green, Woolhampton
House and Midgham House are on a level, Midgham village
is nearly two miles west of Woolhampton and Midgham
station is immediately below Woolhampton shops. Some line,
no doubt, divides them, but what does it matter, for both are

lovely, especially the Woolhampton, or is it Midgham, below the level-crossing where narrow bridges span the water-ways and old men sit on benches outside two little inns. If biting flies have anything to do with place-names, I know quite well which village this belongs to. On the hill above Woolhampton stands Douai Abbey with a wonderful view across the valley to the ridge which is the Hampshire Downs.

Thatcham. With the chimneys of Calthrop paper-mills at last out of sight behind us, Thatcham takes on a new appearance, though there is little new about its cottages and square. Flint implements and a Mesolithic settlement pronounce its age, and its church's Norman doorway is relatively modern compared with these. Some say that Thatcham, with its flint industry by the Kennet-side, is the oldest village in the County. It is best for me not to say anything about the New-bury side of Thatcham—if you are not driving close your eyes.

Newbury. To make a circular tour to Reading we must pass through Newbury either by the main street, on our way bridging the Lambourn and passing the two delightful inns which say farewell to this pretty stream as it runs towards the Kennet halfway back to Thatcham; or, alternatively, by turning off as to the race-course and skirting back-streets until reaching the Basingstoke road. I shall say nothing of New-bury here as we shall visit it with more time to spare in the course of another journey.

Greenham. The lovely commons of Greenham and Crook-ham along the Hampshire border have been sadly disfigured during the war when aeroplanes and gliders and fantastic numbers of Americans were camped there and the lovely road pointing deceptively straight at Silchester was torn to shreds. Greenham was fully occupied in the woollen days and here it was that Mr. Coxeter made the famous coat at Greenham Mills, and long before this the Knights Hospitallers had a Preceptory here.

Brimpton. A bend or two of the road and we find our-selves close to the Hampshire border and close to the Emborne where it runs to meet the Kennet at Aldermaston Mill. Knights Templars and Hospitallers once lived here and their chapel stands to-day, in use as a farm building. Turning right-handed over the brow and down to the bridge over the Emborne, then up to Heathend and the Borson barrows and we reach the heatherland that runs along the Hampshire border to Silchester. Nightjars live here in summer evenings and fallow deer wander through the softwood enclosures. Our road passes through the aerodrome and beside the landing-ground, past what was Aldermaston Park, now largely aerodrome, past concrete sheds and runways, past the spot where the lovely Park Farm stood when I first lived in Aldermaston, past the "Soke" road and the Welshman's road, past "A" clump to the Round Oak Inn.

Padworth. Here is the road that soldiers marched after the Battle of Newbury, the victorious Essex at their head. The church is almost pure Norman and is said to be one of the best examples in England. From Padworth one can run down through Burghfield into Reading, dropping from the ridge to the Kennet and the Holy Brook, but a better way is to turn to Mortimer.

Mortimer. Old Mortimer down by the Foudry Brook is lovely, but, architecturally, new Mortimer above it does not bear mentioning though it serves its purpose I know well.

Swallowfield. Down through Beech Hill and its one-time priory, past the meadows where the Loddon Lily grows and we come to Swallowfield astride the Reading-Basingstoke road. This is the heart of what has been called the "Mary Mitford Land," and here in Swallowfield Church she lies buried. The glimpses of the Loddon here are lovely and the dark water of its sister stream, the Blackwater, swirls through the park. And so the road runs to Reading, through Spencers Wood to Three Mile Cross, where Mary Mitford's cottage waits to be inspected, then out into the flat of the streams and dykes and the sewage farm where rare birds used to nest, till finally up Whitley Hill to the Pump and ahead lies Reading down below us.

JOURNEY THREE

Wokingham, Bracknell and Ascot to Virginia Water; a

short trespass into Surrey; Sandhurst and the sandy places of Crowthorne and Finchampstead.

Wokingham. The road to Wokingham has little to recommend it save a happy glimpse of the river at Loddon Bridge, where in summer boating parties take advantage of this river at its best, and where in winter the cries of wild duck echo from the flooded fields. In Wokingham we find a town as thronged and busy as Reading except that a greater proportion of the people walk down the middle of the streets. Here the silk industry first lifted its lepidopterous head, feeding on the mulberry trees provided for it; here the "Wokingham Blacks" played merry hell with law and order, and streets rang to the cries of men and women watching the bull-baiting, badger-baiting and cock-fighting; here the great bell-foundry stood, and here Molly Mog, who sounds less spotty when given her other title "The fair maid of the Rose Inn," was a celebrated beauty; so beautiful was Molly and so artful, that it is not with surprise we learn that she died in 1766 a spinster, hiding her failure under the name of Mrs. Mary Mogg—we have all of us met girls like Molly! You may, perhaps, hear Wokingham called "Lousetown" and you will wonder why; the reason for this strange and not very beautiful name is that once a group of respectable Wokingham gentlemen sat round a table endeavouring to elect a new mayor, apparently without being able to reach a decision; so a louse was sent for and placed in the centre of the table; after a somewhat erratic journey around the table the louse selected one gentleman and bore down upon him with gathering speed, thus electing him as Wokingham's mayor! So well known was the nickname that at one time you could with safety address a letter to "Lousetown" and I am told that you could book a railway ticket to "Lousetown" without causing a breach of the peace!

I have written elsewhere about bull-baiting in Wokingham's Market Place and you will find nothing there to remind you of this "sport" save the Red Lion Inn, which is probably very much as it was in those days when the alderman took up his position there to view the proceedings. The cockpits, too, have gone, and it is believed that the modern British Restaurant stands upon the site; certainly the alley which leads to it beside the Red Lion is to this day called Cockpits Lane.

Bracknell. One of the best stretches of road in the County takes us to Bracknell, and unless it is market day, we would be best to push on through to Ascot. There is little of beauty to be seen, but those who wish may deviate to Easthampstead where Shelley lived and where Catherine of Aragon lived during divorce proceedings. Another pleasant road runs through sweet chestnut trees to Bagshot, crossing the Roman road from Silchester to Staines on the edge of the park. From recent newspaper reports it seems likely that Bracknell's scanty virtues are to be decreased by the building of a new town to house many thousands.

Ascot. The wide road and the buildings tell what this place is, and during race-week everything is gay with colour— it has rightly been described as a festival rather than a race-meeting, but I find the horses much more attractive than their backers. It is a great place for hornets, and has recently been in the news for another yellow-striped insect, the Colorado Beetle, which somehow intruded itself upon the peaceful agriculture which thrives beneath the great trees of the Windsor area. From Ascot, with its lovely drives and walks through Windsor Park, we follow the road to Virginia Water. The lakes here are artificial and during the recent war were emptied—more interesting to me is the wealth of edible toadstools to be found in the surrounding woods.

Sunningdale. Turning right at Virginia Water, we soon run over the level-crossing into Sunningdale, that home of golf and expensive houses. Everything seems to be new in Sunningdale, the houses, the cars, even the people. Like a flash we are out of it, running along in Surrey heading for Bagshot where we can regain our own territory, for once over the railway bridge just before the famous Cricketers' Inn, we soon get back into Berkshire on the edge of Bagshot Park; the Roman road from Silchester to Staines crosses here and traces of a Roman wayside station have been found. We soon turn on to Nine Mile Ride, near Cæsar's Camp and Wickham Bushes, but we must turn off down to Crowthorne and Sandhurst.

Crowthorne and Sandhurst.   Pine-trees and heather and their true companions, silver birch and bracken and acres of willow herb or Fireweed as it is often called, then Wellington College, with its lovely deodars and rhododendrons and Californian big trees, *Sequoia gigantea, Wellingtonia*, call them what you will, and Sandhurst which has housed the Royal Military College since 1812. It is an area oozing with education and knowledge, and standing aloof, sharing nothing of this, Broadmoor, a tragic place of things gone wrong.

Finchampstead.   The nicest route from Sandhurst takes us back to the Crowthorne road, then through the stately avenue of Sequoias to the Ridges, with views out over the Blackwater valley, over miles of Surrey and Hampshire, till the distant haze seems only to hide the Channel and the continent. The church, supremely aloof, is largely Norman, and stands upon the Devil's Highway, the Roman road, as though it meant to tread it underfoot.

Arborfield.   The road back to Reading goes by Arborfield Cross and the inn called the Bramshill Hunt; Aberleigh of Mary Mitford's *Our Village* was Arborfield which she knew and loved. The old church is now a ruin but a beautiful one, and has given a window of Aaron to its modern successor. Between Arborfield and Shinfield we cross the Loddon, shaded beneath dark trees and from here we are soon upon the Reading road.

Shinfield.   The church, with its seventeenth-century tower, knows the sound of goats and cows and mighty bulls, for the National Institute for Research in Dairying, N.I.R.D., as it is known for short, surrounds it. Here milk and cheese and butter are not things to eat and drink, but things to work with, things to investigate. Pigs, too, and bulls, the biggest bulls you'll ever see, and the Artificial Insemination Centre, with its lovely pens and houses designed by Mr. Cumming, a well-known Reading architect. And so into Reading past the University Horticultural Station, the University itself and the Royal Berkshire Hospital.

JOURNEY FOUR

To Sonning, Wargrave, Henley and Remenham, Hurley, Bisham and Cookham, Maidenhead, Bray and Windsor, and return to Reading through some little villages of the Thames valley.

Sonning. A few short miles past Sutton's trial grounds on the London road and down a lane towards the river and we are in Sonning, one of the happiest and most attractive of Thames-side places. Innumerable flint axe-heads from the river-bed and from the neighbourhood show that even ancient man appreciated this spot. Holme Park, lying right against the river, is the site of a bishop's palace, now marked only by a mound. The present house has recently been acquired for the Reading Blue-coat school, formerly established west of Reading on the Bath Road. The streets are lined with Georgian houses, flowering trees and shrubs their pride. When summer nights are warm, Reading dines at Sonning, and whiles away the evening on the lawns of the hotels which cater both for gourmand and gourmet. A simple walk across the narrow old bridge and one is in another county, with its own hotel, its port and cigar-smoke and night-scented stock. Yes, Sonning is a place in which to linger, a place to remember.

Wargrave. Back to the main road by any of these lesser roads which turn our backs on Sonning, over the Loddon now nearing its end, for it empties into the Thames immediately above Wargrave, sharply off to the left just over the railway and in a mile or so we are in Wargrave with its narrow streets and lovely George and Dragon Hotel. Wargrave has seen some interesting people, including Thomas Day, the crank and miser who wrote *Sandford and Merton*, the crazy Richard, Lord Barrymore, and his equally crazy friends who lived by night like owls and blinked and were embarrassed if they saw the light of day. The church, which was partly destroyed by fire in 1914, has a Norman doorway and a Norman font, the latter standing disconsolate by the gate, its place usurped by a more ornate and fancy thing of the fifteenth century. Wargrave's street is too narrow to linger in, unless we use the car park of the George and Dragon, so let us on our way beside the river to Henley bridge, which we must not cross, for Henley is in Oxfordshire, although its tentacles spread over the river into Berkshire, and in Henley Week, when famous crews have rowed the beautiful reach of

river, blind to all except the stroking oar, the huge crowd
which is Henley's sweeps across to Berkshire for the fireworks and the fair.

Remenham. A narrow road of hair-pin bends takes us to
the hamlet of Remenham with its most attractive little church,
the graveyard across the lane, clinging to the side of towering
Remenham Hill. A mile or two more, past water meadows
running to the Thames and we are in Aston, and the genial
company of the Flower Pot Inn. Here talk is all of guns and
dogs and fishing-lines, and sordid words of politics rarely foul
the air; sometimes this unassuming little inn becomes a veritable arsenal, for it is the headquarters of a clay-pigeon club
and men come miles to test their skill and make the bar a
bedlam of conversation afterwards.

Hurley. From Aston, we pass beneath an ornate foot-
bridge, spanning the valley that is our road and thence up on
to the Maidenhead road, soon to reach Hurley where a Benedictine monastery once stood, and where once Lady Place,
built by Sir Richard Lovelace with money acquired abroad
with Sir Francis Drake, proudly ruled the countryside. The
Norman church has been much altered and repaired, and the
Bell Inn, recently damaged by fire, is considered by some,
though I do not think correctly, to be the oldest inn we have in
Berkshire.

Bisham. Our road runs on to Bisham, where the abbey,
once priory, founded by Sir William Montecute, stands amid
its gardens reaching to the riverside. The priory church saw
the burial of many famous people, few of whom died natural
deaths and several of whom died before the headsman's axe,
and here in 1471 Warwick the Kingmaker was buried; but
this old church has gone and with it the Salisburys, Warwicks
and Nevilles who were buried there. After the dissolution of
the monasteries, the Hoby family held the abbey, for this
priory became an abbey just before the dissolution, eventually
passing to the Vansittarts. Here it was that Lady Hoby
whipped her little son to death and her unhappy ghost was
forced to wander. The people of Bisham once made thimbles
and lace and still make paper.

Cookham Dean, Cookham and Boulters Lock. There

would be little to say for Cookham, once the seat of boot and shoe manufacturing, if it were not for the river bearing down on Maidenhead and Windsor beneath the mighty Cliveden woods. There is a sarsen "tarry stone" in the main street, which is said to mark the bounds of the Abbot of Cirencester, and the old "pound" is still to be seen. The straw boaters and tall starched collars and the equally unsuitable garb of the ladies will no more be seen at Boulter's Lock; the daring girls who showed their ankles would have a fit to-day at the shorts and skirtless bathing-costumes, while the much moustached young men would screw in their monocles and glare at the cads in their open shirts. Times change and monocles are few and far between.

Maidenhead. The road is right against the river into Maidenhead, where night-clubs, day-clubs, rowing-clubs, motorboat-clubs, tennis-clubs, bridge-clubs and every conceivable kind of club can be found for the searching. The river here is nice, if somewhat bogus, but the town is drab to a degree. The old Greyhound Inn, where Charles Stuart was brought from his Caversham House prison to talk with his children, is gone, and a bank sedately covers the ground.

Bray. A brief drive and we are in Bray, where Jesus Hospital, founded in 1609 by William Goddard, is a pleasant reminder of the days before Maidenhead and Bray competed for the greater number of clubs. The vicar, whose name was Simon Aleyn, is buried in his own churchyard, and Ockwells, the "perfect manor house," was built by John Norreys early in the fifteenth century; our road runs past Clewer and St. Leonard's Hill which is supposed to be a Roman beacon, for here in the early eighteenth century a Roman lamp of bronze was discovered and has been perpetuated in the badge of the Society of Antiquaries to whom it was presented.

Windsor. We are now approaching the end of our Thames, which nowhere looks more sedate than flowing smoothly round the town and through the meadows of Runnymede to Staines. I cannot give details of the castle here; volumes have been written, guide-books are available. The view of the castle from the edge of the park is too good to be true, no theatre backcloth could ever reach its stateliness, no castle in the air approach its majesty. Don't miss the Round Tower, Henry the Eighth's Gateway, St. George's Chapel, the Curfew Tower and the Deanery and, of course, the terraces. The park is as delightful as well-kept parks always are, its great elms and oaks shading the herds of resting deer, its lakes a paradise for water-birds; there is a serenity, a calmness which one finds only beneath great trees, the age-long buzz of flies and bees ; Gray's *Elegy* is said to have been inspired here at Windsor by the curfew toll, and what more lovely lines have ever described the peace of the country evening, the peace which was lost but which we now strive to regain.

Binfield. From Windsor Great Park, twisting country lanes take us through Woodside with its popular "Crispin" inn, where mine host and his wife have all the charm that comes from the islands in the Channel, through Winkfield, where the church is largely built of Windsor oaks, through Warfield, where the bees work the limes, filling the summer afternoons with their humming, to Binfield where Pope spent his boyhood in the house his draper father had bought for his retirement. Nearby, Billingbear Park, once owned by the great Neville family, no longer has its stately mansion, and its worldly remains, the original kitchen, has been built into a farm-house. And so the road winds here and there past Hurst to Sandford Mill where the Loddon overflows its banks each winter and the wild duck flight at dusk and dawn. At Woodley, above the Loddon, is an aerodrome where thousands of men build aeroplanes and make Biro fountain-pens.

Waltham St. Lawrence. An alternative route from Windsor would take us through Waltham St. Lawrence, where long years ago the trees of the Great Windsor Forest came right up to the village, and pigs in their thousands snuffled among the oak-leaf bottom. There is little to attract now but those who like yews should go to the churchyard.

Shottesbrooke has the grave of Jacobite Francis Cherry, the hard-riding squire of Shottesbrooke who kept open house for his "non-juring friends to the extent of seventy beds"; he is reputed to have attempted to kill King William III by leading him over a dangerous jump in the hunting-field, but William was a better horseman than squire Cherry imagined !

Near here is *White Waltham*, now the scene of much aerial activity, but once, like the other Waltham, a mere hamlet lying in a forest clearing. *Ruscombe,* part of which is still called Ruscombe Lake, knew William Penn the Quaker, who came here to die in this quiet Berkshire village away from the tumult of his earlier days. *Twyford*, once a bustling village on the Bath Road, with all the clatter and shouting of horses and ostlers, has now turned into a rather uninteresting village with a railway station; the Bath Road now by-passes it through the "Floral Mile"; a nursery and show-ground a joy to behold. Twyford Mill once used the Loddon waters to make silk, and here in the water-meadows the Loddon lilies grow and disappear into gypsy baskets to be sold in the streets of Reading.

JOURNEY FIVE

A tour through the streets of Reading. We might as well start our tour of Reading from the railway station, or stations I should say, because the Great Western and Southern Railways both come to Reading; the former arrived first, in 1840, and it is strange to think that thousands of people flocked into Reading to see the first train draw in. It is said that the fastest journey of that memorable day (March 30th) from London to Reading was exactly one hour and five minutes, a fact which comes to my mind each time I find it necessary to return from London on one of the stopping trains of more than one hundred years later! Before leaving the vicinity of the stations, with its roundabout and bus queues, we should notice the statue of King Edward VII presented to Reading in 1902 by Mr. Martin S. Sutton; it is a bronze figure of the king in field-marshal's uniform, and it was unveiled by H.R.H. Prince Christian of Schleswig Holstein.

From the stations we turn east to the next roundabout where we pass over the spot where the abbey's river gate once stood; parking the car discreetly opposite the Magistrates' Court, in a moment we are at the entrance to the Forbury Gardens, passing the memorial to Reading men who fell in the 1914-18 war; facing us is a gigantic lion, said to be the largest of its kind in the world, standing in memory of other Reading men who fell in the battle of Maiwand in 1880; yet another memorial there is in the Forbury Gardens, to Henry I, by whose inspiration Reading's abbey was constructed. Now is an excellent opportunity to examine the abbey ruins, for details of which I must direct you to another chapter of this book. St. James Roman Catholic Church which stands in the abbey grounds is well worth a visit—it was built in 1840 at the expense of James Wheble of Bulmershe Court, and its font is made from a square block of carved stone which was discovered buried in the ground nearby and which was obviously some part of the old abbey; in the presbytery you can see an original seal which belonged to one of the abbots. Close to the church stands the prison which housed Oscar Wilde and where he wrote his *Ballad of Reading Gaol*; across the Forbury Road is Huntley and Palmer's biscuit factory, fully occupying the twenty-five acre site to which it moved from its less capacious London Street premises in 1846.

Passing over the King's Road traffic lights and avoiding a thousand and one bicycles if it should happen to be midday, we proceed up Watling Street, pausing for a moment to glance at the social welfare centre at Watlington House which Samuel Watlington built in 1688; when Samuel decided to build himself a nice country house he was, no doubt, well aware of the flints and stones of the demolished abbey, readily available to a member of the Town Corporation such as himself, and certainly he did himself proud; Watlington House was subsequently let, in 1794, to a Captain Purvis and then to a Mrs. Littleworth as an establishment for young ladies; between 1877 and 1927 it was the home of the Kendrick Girls' School, now moved to more spacious quarters facing Kendrick Road.

The Royal Berkshire Hospital, which will be almost facing us when we arrive at the top of Watlington Street, was built in 1839 at the expense of a Mr. Oliver, who, sad to relate, was one of the first patients to die in it. On our left, when we have turned west into London Road, is the main entrance to the university, and within its walls is the old house of the Palmers, now given over to the administration of academic matters and to rooms where the university staff can eat and read. Reading School, and Leighton Park School for boys and the Abbey School and the Kendrick School for girls, all lie within a few minutes' drive from the university.

If we now proceed along London Road to the first traffic lights and turn down London Street towards the heart of Reading we shall pass, almost unnoticed, a building at the entrance to Fountain Court where in 1940 was discovered a fresco containing the monogram I.H.S.—Iesus Hominum Salvator; an examination of the house, now a mass of chemical, physical and biological instruments in the making, coupled with an investigation of ancient documents, has led to the belief that this building was licensed in the middle of the fifteenth century as an oratory.

Continuing down London Street we pass over High Bridge, constructed in 1787 to replace the former wooden bridge spanning the Kennet at this point. In a moment we are beside the Upper and the Lower Ship and the George Hotels, famous inns of the coaching days, while across the road ahead of us is the market place where once stood the pillory, stocks and whipping-post; on our left is the old Corn Exchange built in 1854 and damaged by bombs in 1943, which since its repair is used for sales of antique and other kinds of furniture; on our right we will find the usual exquisite window display of the firm of Suttons. Ahead of us is St. Lawrence's Church, carrying us back to the days of the mighty abbey, reminding us that Archbishop Laud was once a Reading boy, and since 1943 reminding us of that afternoon in February when German raiders paid a lightning visit to Reading. The original building of St. Lawrence's dates back to the early twelfth century and a part of the nave of this period still remains, though most of the church is of sixteenth-century work. Of the adjacent municipal buildings the museum should on no account be missed, as among other interesting things there is the Silchester collection and the very lovely needle-work copy of the Bayeux Tapestry which has toured the British Isles and parts of our far-flung Empire.

Passing now westward along Friar Street we come to Grey Friars' Church, first built in 1285 by Franciscan monks and

Tithe Barn at Great Coxwell

destroyed in 1539 by agents of "Good King Hal," after which it was used as a Town Hall, then as a Poor House and later as a prison, becoming once again a place of worship in 1863. In St. Mary's Butts we can inspect the Minster church of St. Mary the Virgin, standing where once a wooden Saxon chapel stood; it contains much of the timber and roofing from the abbey. Ahead of us, in Bridge Street and occupying acres of ground on both sides of the road, stands the vast brewery of Simonds where the Kennet River, curling between the wharves and lapping against ancient piles on its way to the Thames, provides upholders of other breweries with ample material for their jokes!

Up Southampton Street, which is a link between Bridge Street and the Basingstoke Road, stands St. Giles' Church, known from an ancient document to have been in existence since the year 1190; this church was considerably damaged during the Civil War, when it is believed that the steeple was knocked down by cannon-balls; reconstruction work in 1872 did much to obliterate the Norman and fourteenth-century features and draped it in a robe of flint and stone.

Reversing our tracks down Southampton Street, Bridge Street and the Butts and passing Grey Friars' Church, we reach Caversham Road leading us under the railway arch towards the Thames; Caversham, though geographically in Oxfordshire, has been absorbed into the County Borough of Reading; the bridge over which we must cross the Thames was constructed in 1926 to replace an older one which was no longer suited to increasing road traffic. This crossing of the Thames has been important for many hundreds of years, in fact it is fairly certain that before the days of bridges there was a ford here, though it is doubtful if such a ford was usable in winter when the road from Reading to Caversham was flooded; it was not until 1724 that much was done to stop this nuisance by building up to a higher level. In 1560 the bridge was partly of wood and partly of stone, and in 1642 King Charles I gave orders for it to be strengthened (over-night) so that his troops might pass safely into Reading; we also know that at this time it was a drawbridge. Like most ancient bridges it had its tiny chapel, but whether this was

The Thames at Abingdon

mid-way across the bridge or upon the Caversham bank is not
certain, but it was ransacked by Thomas Cromwell in 1536,
and a silver image of "Our Ladye" was put "in a cheste fast
lockyed and naylyd uppe" and sent off to London on the next
barge; when in 1714 Hearne, armed with Leland's *Itinerary*,
searched for this chapel he was told that a house stood upon
the site where, even at that time, the chapel was only believed
to have stood. Wherever it may have stood, we know that the
chapel was dedicated to St. Ann and belonged to Notley
Abbey in Buckinghamshire; so did Caversham Court which
was a rectory of the Augustinian Canons; of this place nothing
remains but the gardens, now belonging to the County
Borough of Reading, which are open to the public.

Above the gardens stands St. Peter's Church amid its
ancient graveyard; little Norman architecture remains in this
church and its steeple is gone, said to have been knocked down
during the battle for Caversham bridge in 1643, at which
time there was a canon mounted upon it. St. Ann's Well, at
the top of Priest Hill, was "discovered" in 1905 when land
was being prepared for building purposes; according to J.
Loveday, who was rector of Caversham in 1727, religious
people used to go from St. Ann's Chapel, on Caversham
Bridge, to a Holy Well, then standing in the hedge between a
field called the "Mount" and a lane called "Priest Lane,"
the latter getting its name from the priests passing along it to
the well; it is now embraced by a garden wall, wears a domed
iron cage on its open top and I very much doubt if many
people stop to look at it.

Out towards Emmer Green lies the great estate of Caversham Park, known at different times as Caversham Castle,
Manor House and Lodge; as a castle, in 1219, it was owned
by William Marshal, Earl of Pembroke; during Elizabethan
times it was owned by the Knollys family and during the reign
of Charles I by Lord Craven; in 1723 Lord Cadogan erected
a stately mansion in the grounds which was burned down in
1850; it was restored and later, in 1922, it became the home
of the Oratory School, and during the war, and since, it has
housed a section of the B.B.C.

2. NEWBURY CENTRE
JOURNEY ONE

East through the northern edge of the Kennet valley towards Bucklebury, then round with the Pang to Marlston, past Grimsbury Camp and Fence Wood to Hermitage and Oare, then back to Newbury by Shaw.

Cold Ash. Newbury I have described in some detail elsewhere in this book, so we will proceed by any of the lanes we care to take just before Thatcham, for they all will take us up out of the Kennet valley to Cold Ash with its beautiful gorse-clad common; the Bagshot sand and gravel ridge here rises higher than anywhere else in the County, and there are some lovely views up and down and across the valley. From Cold Ash there is a lovely shady lane running by Holly Farm, where the patches of sunlight beneath the great trees shine like gold upon the leafy ground; there are other lovely lanes running across Upper Common past Miles Green and Winchcombe Farm, and there are other places, now hideous, beneath concrete roadways and countless thousands of army vehicles awaiting waterproofing, gas-proofing, fire-proofing and all the other proofings peculiar to service vehicles.

Marlston. Outside Bucklebury, where the Frilsham road forks through the dusty bed of the summer Pang, our road drives on to Marlston House, the home of Sir William Alexander. The little church has a Norman doorway but beyond the church and the house and park there is little to keep us from going on to Grimsbury Castle. On the way we pass Wellhouse, which takes its name from a never-failing spring, and there is a place nearby called Boar's Hole, I know not why, but can hazard a guess. Heather so tall that it soon takes the life out of your legs and bracken so tall that nothing less than a giraffe could see over it—Fence Wood would keep me amused for days on end. The car, incidentally, is hardly any use at all, and though I don't suggest it, the horn might be switched on before driving into the bracken—or some boy might be coerced into tooting on it once an hour—you'll see my point when you get there.

Hermitage and Oare. The railway line which follows the ancient road from Newbury to Hampstead Norris and Compton on its way to Oxford does not improve Hermitage. No one seems to know how this place got its name, but presumably some bearded recluse once lived here in the wood. Oare derives its name from ora, a bank or ridge between Oare and *Hermitage*; Roebuck Wood is suggestive but I have seen no roe there, nor met anyone who has; the wood was named long ago and it and Fence Wood are likely enough places; certainly there are Fallow deer in Fence Wood. The road back to Newbury is straight and simple; one might, perhaps, deviate to see the little village of Curridge whose name means Cusa's ridge; for some reason King John visited this place in 1207, no doubt out hunting.

Shaw. Shaw-cum-Donnington are the only two villages in Berkshire linked in Latin. See here the famous house of the Dolmans, built from the flourishing wool trade; like neighbouring Donnington Castle, the Elizabethan Shaw House has seen bloody fighting upon its lawns and some of the cannons captured from Cromwell's forces are in the park. Charles I came here before the battle and was nearly accounted for by a cannon-ball which came through a window in the library. The old church had much Norman about it but it was too dark and too small to be popular, so down it came.

JOURNEY TWO

To the Downs, the Ilsleys and Farnborough and down the Wantage road to Bussock Wood and Snelsmore Common; Newbury town.

Donnington. Standing as it does among tall trees, a good view of the ancient and battered remains of the castle is not easily obtained—a stop is definitely indicated. Two round towers and the gateway remain, a symbol of days gone by, when civil war rent England in twain. In 1644 Sir John Boys, gallantly held the castle for the king, facing terrible odds; the castle was attacked, the castle was sieged—it would not give in; three of its mighty towers were knocked down, much of the castle reduced to a shambles, but still the defenders held out; the attacking force was reinforced, the siege was redoubled but the castle remained invincible—Cromwell's men withdrew leaving it a wreck, almost hidden beneath their cannon-balls. There was once a priory of the Trinitarians here, founded by Sir Richard Abberbury in 1360, but it was burnt down at the time of the second Battle of Newbury (1644); the almshouses and most of the village were burned with it.

Chieveley.   As we go towards Chieveley we can see the mighty Bussock Wood over on the left, but at this stage the temptation must be resisted for we shall return later, on the very edge of the wood. Chieveley's name has been said to mean "field of chives"! The church should be inspected, for it has one of England's three remaining Lenten Veil Screens. The main road takes us straight on past the corner of Langley Wood, where it crosses "Old Street," and for about a mile we can actually drive upon this ancient road, in the direction of *Peasemore*, possibly once a pre-Roman city, now delightfully hidden under elms; the road to Stanmore crossed "Old Street," here a mere track, and close here is a bowl barrow where there are said to be fairies and the remains of a man named Burrow buried in a gold or silver coffin. It is not worth spending time searching—it has been done before now! From Stanmore the road, called Ball Pit Road on maps, runs down into East Ilsley. Beedon, out towards the main road, stands lonely and secretive, like so many of these little downland villages, knowing all yet telling nothing.

The Ilsleys are interesting for their associations rather than for anything that is there to-day. Once a centre of sheep farming and selling, there is little left now to remind one— except the pubs—of the great animal fair in August. Now it is racehorses that make for conversation. The road to Farnborough through West Ilsley is one of the most lovely downland drives imaginable, sweeping up and down, the verges glorious with knapweed and scabious, the rolling cornfields sometimes yellow with charlock and often bloodshot with poppies. West Ilsley is a really sleepy little place, hot in the hollow below the Downs.

Farnborough.   Between West Ilsley and Farnborough our

road once again crosses "Old Street," at a place called Land's
End; the Ridgeway is not far beyond us now, and from Farnborough a track past Moonlight Barn runs up to Yew Down,
across the main road on to Lattin Down where it eventually
joins the Ridgeway. Another ancient track runs back from
Farnborough to "Old Street" at Kiln Barn Woods, and the
old pack-horse trail from Hungerford used to pass through
Farnborough on its way to Oxford. Farnborough church
tower is supposed to have been built of stones taken from
Poughley Monastery, suppressed in 1524. And now you must
choose to run straight down to Newbury on the main road,
or to wander in a labyrinth of lanes through Brightwalton,
Southend, Nodmoor and Leckhampstead. Whichever you
choose, the scenes are lovely and bring you down to the Blue
Boar Inn, where Cromwell slept before attacking Shaw and
Donnington; Bussock Camp is right against the road as it
skirts the wood of that name, and a little farther on is Snelsmore Common, a marshy, boggy place despite its silverbirch
and bracken; the curious little insectivorous plant, the sundew,
can be found here, along the edges of damp places among the
bed of heather roots. One could deviate from here to Winterbourne and Honey Bottom, down to the old ford at Bagnor,
crossing both Winterbourne and Lambourn and so into Speen
and Newbury. From the days of Spinæ, which was somewhere
hereabouts, to the noisy times of Cromwell, this bit of land
north of Newbury has seen marchings and battles, heard the
clash of swords and the roar of cannons. Now it is as happy
and beautiful a piece of English countryside as one could wish
for.

Newbury town. Newbury is one of the unfortunate places
which has an extremely interesting historical background but
has relatively little left to show for it. Despite this, however,
no one can visit Newbury and not realise that there is what
one might call an old-world atmosphere about the place.

So many of the things and places we should like to see in
Newbury are gone; for instance, the Norman castle, which
stood guardian of the river-crossing, has left not a trace;
erected in the early part of the thirteenth century by the Earl
of Perche, it passed through all the ups and downs of castles,

and eventually in 1627 it passed into the hands of the River Kennet Navigation Company, who pulled it down or removed its ruins, as the case may be, in order to make room for the canal wharf which they were proposing to build.

Newbury's arms—a castle with three domed towers—suggest what it looked like at some stage in its life. Likewise the old Guildhall, which, having been in constant use since 1611, was razed to the ground in 1828 because, apart from being pretty dilapidated, it constituted a nuisance to carriages driving through the town. With it has gone the market cross which stood at the south end of the Guildhall, and so have the stocks, whipping-post and pillory, though the first mentioned were brought out for their final use in 1892 for the benefit of one Mark Tuck who had been naughty in church; they may now be seen in the museum. Another building which we should like to visit is Jack of Newbury's house in North-brook Street, where he entertained King Henry VIII and his then Queen, Catherine; alas! the house that had always been open to royalty and other important persons (for Jack was a go-getter) is no more, and if we wish to stand upon the site we must enter Marks and Spencer's emporium.

The little humped-back bridge over the Kennet was built in 1769 to replace a wooden one and remains as delightful as an old bridge can, though it lacks the little shops and houses upon it which one understands were a feature of the wooden bridge; an even earlier wooden bridge which had spanned the Kennet for centuries collapsed suddenly and fell into the river in 1623, much to the "consternation and inconvenience of the inhabitants" it has been said—particularly to those upon it at the time, one would suppose! Yet another building which has gone is the old theatre in Speenhamland which did such good service in the coaching days; the need for this building with its pillared entrance being over, it seems to have been used successively as workshop, auction room and cow-shed—how are the mighty fallen! And during the war years something went which meant much more to Newbury people than the disappearance of a few ancient houses and a castle—I refer to the Newbury Racecourse, which, since its inception in 1904, has given pleasure, not to mention trade, to men and women from far and wide; to the relief of all this has now been set right.

Well, what is there in Newbury that we can still go and see? you may be asking by this time. First of all, there is the lovely Jacobean Cloth Hall standing beside the market place and dating back to the days when Newbury was at the peak of the cloth and wool trade; this attractive building with its beams and overhanging upper storey is now Newbury's museum, a very fitting end for such a building. Then there is St. Bartholomew's Hospital, almshouses boasting a charter granted by King John, and the little Litten Chapel which ministered unto the occupants of the almshouses, and where Jack of Newbury married his late boss's widow. You must certainly inspect the battlemented church of St. Nicholas, which was erected at the expense of Jack of Newbury and his son in the early sixteenth century; death-watch beetles have ruined the original roof and the stained-glass windows are modern, but despite this they are beautiful—there are said to be about five hundred figures involved in the forty windows, and no one who has wandered round this church would doubt that for a moment!

Two battlefields can be visited with ease—the first on Wash Common, where in 1643 the first Battle of Newbury took place; it is commemorated on the site by the Falkland Memorial, a memorial which was intended by the donor of the land to honour the memory of the Royalists and Parliamentarians alike who fell in the battle, on purely historical grounds; the Earl of Caernarvon and other members of the committee set up to erect this memorial were not particularly interested in history, and styling themselves in the inscription as "those to whom the majesty of the crown and the liberties of their country are dear" they unveiled on September 9th, 1878, a memorial of those "who, on the 20th September, 1643, fell fighting in the army of King Charles I, on the field of Newbury, and especially of LUCIUS CARY, VISCOUNT FALKLAND, who died here in the 34th year of his age." I make no further comment except that other inscriptions on this memorial are from Thucydides (in Greek), from Livy (in Latin) and from Burke (in English)—I often wonder just how many people who look at this memorial are interested in what Thucydides, Livy and Burke have to say! The second Battle of Newbury was fought around Shaw and Donnington on the north of the Bath road; the remaining towers of Donnington castle provide ample tribute to the memory of those involved in this drawn-out and indecisive battle of 1644.

JOURNEY THREE

Up the valley to Lambourn and back by the Roman road through Shefford Woodlands and Wickham.

The lovely Lambourn valley road running close beside the river, sometimes on this side, sometimes on that, is a perfect scene of rural England. The Lambourn is a strange stream which, somewhat inaccurately, is said to flood in summer and go dry in winter, unlike its neighbour the Winterbourne, which runs to a more normal routine.

Boxford, a pretty riverside place with a mill, and brooks and streams everywhere. From the common, ancient flint implements have been collected and at Borough Hill an Iron Age Hill-Top Camp stands guardian, and beyond, at Wydfield Farm, a Roman villa has been found.

Welford. With the river washing its walls, and two bridges from which trout can be seen, Welford is perhaps the prettiest village in the valley. The abbots of Abingdon knew it well for they spent their summers there. The church's round Norman tower has been rebuilt, fortunately in its original form, and the Norman font is still there.

The Sheffords. From Welford the road, river and railway run side by side, the road following the tracks of the river, the railway straightly oblivious of all. In East Shefford our road crosses the Hungerford-Wantage road.

East Garston. Between Great Shefford and East Garston the valley road is at its best, king-cups and kingfishers decorating the banks, the railway a discreet distance away. East Garston, with its Scandinavian derivation, has more than once been filmed as a typical English village. It certainly is lovely, and the thatched cottages with the stream swirling past, the dusty road and the little bridges undoubtedly do spell

England. Beyond thatched *Eastbury,* a road and several tracks run up the Downs towards Letcombe Basset and the Ridgeway, where hares wander about like the sheep that have gone, and coveys stand in the stubbles like something carved in sandstone.

Lambourn. Like the Ilsleys, Lambourn was famous for sheep once upon a time, but now for race-horses and absurdly large horse-boxes. The village cross is interesting, for it was erected when Henry VI allowed two fairs and a weekly market to be held there. There is a good walk via Upper Lambourn to Wayland Smith's Cave, passing Lynch Wood where the Lambourn rises and the Strip Lynchets where the road swings round towards Ashdown, and the Hangman's Stone is up on the right towards Croker's hole. At Knighton Bushes the tracks fork alarmingly and you will probably take the wrong one. My only advice is to take the one which leads past the smaller of two spinneys away in the distance. It is a good walk even if you do miss Wayland's cave. Back in Lambourn we take the westward road to Ermine Street near Membury Camp; straight as an arrow the road runs, past all the lovely little copses, the belts, the roundels, past Fieldridge copse and the road to the Country Life Farm at Goodings, past Poughley and its ruined monastery, on to the great crossroads at Shefford Woodlands, straight to Wickham, where the modern road swings round the park, leaving the Roman road to cross it and head for Sole Common. It is a lovely piece of scenery from Wickham down to Speen, through forest more than wood, down into the valley where the Kennet marshes lure the wild fowl and bitterns used to boom.

JOURNEY FOUR

Kennet valley to Hungerford, Inkpen, Combe and Hampshire called Berkshire, through the oaks of Woodhay and the County boundary to Newtown, by Sandleford into Newbury.

If you look at your map you will see that there are two roads from Newbury to Hungerford, a northern one running straight, but none the less pleasant for that, while a lower road twists about through Enborne on the fringe of Newbury's battle in 1643, by Enborne Street, through which thousands of sheep once passed along the "drove" to Ilsley fairs, past the great park of Hampstead Marshall where a mighty house stood until fire took it; in the church are Jacobean box-pews where one could sleep without being seen by any but the Almighty! From here one can cross the Kennet to Marsh Benham and think of beavers and the origin of peat, but we must turn back and follow the wandering lane to Kintbury, where Jane Austen used to stay and where the local chalk was made into whiting. But Kintbury, now a pleasant village, was once a much more important place than it is to-day, witness its name, "Kennet-Borough" and the Hundred which takes its name.

It is worth a detour across the river to see Avington Church, perhaps the least altered Norman church in the County, and where the arch looks as if the strain of supporting the roof is proving too much for it. The Kennet here is at its best and fat trout hang in the shadows, no doubt thinking about John of Gaunt, who granted the town of Hungerford the right of free fishing in the Kennet from Leverton nearly to Marsh Benham, missing only certain private reaches.

Hungerford. One should arrange to reach Hungerford soon after Easter to see the Hocktide tutti-men claim kisses from pretty girls, see the horn which John of Gaunt presented as a seal to certain fishing negotiations, and to hear the Lucas horn, Hungerford's second famous horn, calling men to the court. The poles adorned with flowers which each tutti-man carries represent the ancient sighting staff, the fore-runner of our modern surveyor's outfit. A constable is elected, a toast "the immortal memory of John of Gaunt" is drunk in "ancient Plantagenet punch" and the newly elected constable and his twelve burgesses sit down to a hearty meal. But without its picturesque customs, Hungerford would be rather dull, its main street spoiled by an unpleasant railway bridge. The Bear Inn has been used by several kings and queens who visited Hungerford in the past, but it is now more famous for its parrot! Anne of Cleves came in 1540, Catherine Howard in 1541, Elizabeth several times, William, Prince of Orange in 1687 and then in 1689 William III, Queen Anne in 1690 and again in 1691; so you must agree, the Bear was popular.

While you are in Hungerford you might care to cross the Kennet into Eddington, a mile or so beyond which, at the Denford-Leverton crossing a foul deed was committed one dark night not so very long ago; poachers returning from a nocturnal excursion found it necessary to murder two policemen; one of the poachers was foolish enough to leave his cap lying about in the road and this led to his capture at his job in a Hungerford blacksmith's shop. You will have no difficulty finding the spot where this brutality took place, and if you search very carefully you may even find a hollow in the road surface where one policeman's head is said to have rested— the reason why you may find this hollow is because generations of road-menders have preserved the traditional spot by omitting to fill it in!

Inkpen. From Hungerford one drifts rather like a balloon towards Inkpen, air currents sweeping one up to the clouds and pulling one down into the valleys. The gallows and long barrow should be visited, and in a tearing gale it is a lovely walk between the singing wire fences to stand buffeted against the post of the gallows and to drop down out of the wind for a moment behind the scraggy wizened thorn bushes to light a pipe. The view across the Kennet valley is supreme, and behind, the great ramparts of Walbury remind one that the countryside, now peacefully bending and swaying before the wind, once knew times more brutal, when men bashed out their enemies' brains with stones or pierced their innermost recesses with hand-made spears—nowadays we slaughter our women and children by more up-to-date methods; umbels and scabious grow, to bow before the wind, evading the advances of fritillaries, brown winged and silver-marked beneath.

Walbury should undoubtedly be climbed, not only for the liver, for from the top the views across Hampshire are terrific; the forest of oaks, the hills of chalk, the valley that is the Test and the blue—or is it green?—smudge of the horizon must surely be the fairyland of Grimm and Andersen. And right through the camp the ancient "Old Way" goes, joining Kent with the west, its grass bearing silent witness to the

Neolithic men, the flint vendors, the pedlars, pilgrims and merchants, the shepherds and their flocks who walked this way when the valleys were full of hidden dangers and combes were places to avoid.

From Walbury our balloon drops down into Combe, lost between great hills, more like a place in Wales than Berkshire, its little church and once important manor clinging to the hillside, foundations mingling with the roots of countless trees. And here among the trees, where the soughing of the hill-wind does little more than rustle the crowns of the valley oaks, tiny *Tortrix* caterpillars feeding in their thousands drop their excrement in a never ceasing downpour, so that one looks for rain but sees nothing but the tits, the natural decimators of such pests, upside down below the branches, darting among the reddened leaves of spring. And now for the trespass into Hampshire, the rightful owner of this forest land, and the drive beneath the canopy to Faccombe, turning back to East and West Woodhay (pronounced Woodey) where the golden gorse in spring attracts a myriad of little bees and where in full summer an avenue of limes, three hundred years old, makes honey better than the dusty September heather. This land of woods, deep lanes and golden sun is so much a part of Hampshire, the pull towards Winchester so strong that if at some future date Berkshire loses this to Hampshire we must not complain, we should be thankful that it has been ours, like some silver cup we won, rendered none the less beautiful because it is no longer ours.

And so by Gore End, across the Emborne Stream, we find ourselves upon the battlefield of Wash Common and then beneath the stately trees of Sandleford, where long ago a thriving priory stood, later to be reconstituted by the famous Mrs. Montagu, as a house of beauty, a place where she could entertain Burke, Cowper, Goldsmith and Reynolds. Newbury is now but a stone's throw down the hill and straight ahead are the hangars, the wire and general mess of gliders and American boxes that is an emblem of peace and power in the twentieth century.

3. WANTAGE CENTRE

JOURNEY ONE

To Ardington, Lockinge, the Ginges and the Hendreds; back to Wantage along the Portway or by Scutchamer Knob and the Ridgeway.

This is a short journey and starts on the old Port Way going east to Ardington where in the churchyard lies the famous Lord Wantage, who in his life did so much for this district. A strange man and another benefactor is associated with Ardington—I refer to the artist Robert Vernon who lived at the "House" and was buried in the church in 1849. Vernon started life in 1774 without any money but a flair for horse-dealing which later brought him a fortune; at the same time he was an artist, a sculptor and an art dealer, on his death bequeathing a large number of pictures to the Tate and National Galleries, while the village of Ardington benefited financially. It was Vernon the horse-dealer who put Nelson on to his column in Trafalgar Square, and it was Vernon the artist who mounted our cavalry up to the time of Waterloo— a strange man indeed.

Lockinge. From Ardington little dusty roads take us round Lockinge House, and by the little stream which rushes past the church. One sees the Ridgeway up beyond, crossing Ardington Down and Charlton Fields on its way to White Horse Hill. All around one sees the fields and pastures of the famous Lockinge Estate—farming as it can be done—and on Charlton Field strip Lynchets by Arn Hill remind one of earlier days.

Ginge, West and East. From Lockinge House the road, or avenue I should call it here, passes Betterton House, and crossing ancient trackways coming down from the Ridgeway, takes us to West Ginge and the little Ginge Brook itself. Up above we can see Scutchamer Knob with its mysteries often hidden in the clouds and mists while behind us, little Round-about Hill looks lost in the neat and tidy farm-land. The road, which gets smaller after crossing the Brook, goes on by little East Ginge and then turns away from the foot of the

Downs and rushes straight over Goldbery Hill to West Hendred, taking in its stride the branch of the Icknield Way coming from Hagbourne Hill.

Hendred, West and East. West Hendred is a fascinating spread-out sort of place with Ginge Brook running through it and its mill. Down on the Port Way is the Hare Inn, a not very beautiful addition to the downland scenery but a welcome one, for the roads round here are always dusty. After the pub, the main road crosses the Ginge, running quietly on its way to Steventon, and turning off towards the Downs we are at once in the little street and alley-ways of East Hendred. Mr. A. Humphreys has so ably explored every nook and cranny of this pretty place and filled a book so huge that I hesitate to do more than remind my readers that here in East Hendred was the home of the famous Eyston family, who, when times were difficult, went scuttling over the Downs and along "Old Street" to their hiding-place at Catmore. The church, in addition to all its interesting associations and relics, has a clock made in 1525! John Seymour, clock-maker of Wantage, made it, and as well as telling the time, it strikes the hour, the quarter and the half, and plays a hymn! A wonderful achievement for 1525 and it is one of England's oldest clocks still in use.

When we have finished exploring, we can go back by the orchards to the main road and the ugly notice warning us to beware of troops, and drive along the Port Way back to Wantage; or if we have the energy and the time, we can climb the Golden Mile to Scutchamer Knob and look down on the Hendreds and the Ginges, once a hive of woollen industry, now a peaceful land of orchards lined with military precision and of farm-land like a drawing in a picture-book. For those who want to walk even further, I suggest the Ridgeway over Wether Down, the name, of course, a relic of the days of sheep-farming, to the Newbury road and down Chain Hill into Wantage.

Wantage. If there is time, I suggest you explore the cobbled places of Wantage; the great square with King Alfred, guardian of it, for here he was born, our first English king. The church is full of interesting things, including a silver plate supposed to be one of three owned by Peter the Great. And when in the quietness of the church, one can hardly credit that not so long ago Wantage was the headquarters of all the ruffians and thieves in the south of England, fighting, stealing and murdering after dark, baiting bulls and badgers and shouting drunkenly in the cockpits. The Camel Inn was the favourite of those "types," as modern post-war parlance would call them, and it is said that if the London authorities were looking for some undesirable character, the first place to be searched was Wantage (the next port of call would have been Wokingham). The stocks and pillory must have been in great demand, and eventually the Camel lost its licence and was closed down. And it is even more difficult to imagine, in this drowsy county town, that recently, yes, very recently, a mighty fight broke out in the market place, I shall be discreet and not say who between, during which many shop windows were broken and an officer of the Law kicked into unconsciousness; the next night all the inns were closed for fear of further trouble; but this did not occur because one of the belligerent forces had been confined to base.

JOURNEY TWO

North to Grove, the Hanneys, Lyford and Charney Bassett, Garford, Frilford; westward to Kingston Bagpuize and the County boundary at Newbridge; to Pusey and the River Ock at Stanford in the Vale; Goosey, Denchworth and the Challows.

We leave Wantage, passing down the narrow street by the Letcombe Brook and the old disused canal and the roadside tramway line going to the railway at Wantage Road. In 1876 the first steam tram ran along the lines and Wantage became the first town in England to run such a convenience. Previously, since 1863, a horse-tram service had been in operation. Just before the bridge over the railway, the little agricultural village of Grove lies off the road, with a mill on the Letcombe Brook. Once upon a time a curious Lady Wilmot lived at Grove, who arranged for her skull, with

Abbey gateway, Abingdon
The Thames at Sutton Courtenay

certain ditties of her own concoction inscribed upon it to be kept in a box in Wantage Church !

Hanney, East and West. Right on the Oxford road lies East Hanney, and about a mile to the left by the mill and over the brook is West Hanney, where the church has a Norman doorway, and a fine collection of brasses. East Hanney was at one time held by the Abbey of Abingdon. In 684 Walter Gifford gave a manor in Hanney to a Benedictine priory which he had founded in Normandy. It has often been suggested that the present Priors' Court stands on the site of the old manor, but I do not think that convincing proof of this has so far been forthcoming.

Lyford. A mile or two from West Hanney is the tiny village of Lyford with its manor and grange separated by the river Ock. It was here that Father Campion was captured in 1581 and taken to be interrogated by the great Elizabeth; accused of attempting to overthrow Protestantism, he was racked until he could no longer move and was then hanged at Tyburn. Lyford looks so quiet and peaceful now that it is hard to recall those days of religious fervour when many a country village became involved with one side or the other.

Charney Bassett. From Lyford it is only a step to meet the Ock again on the outskirts of Charney Bassett, with a Norman doorway and other Norman parts easily discernible in the church. This is indeed a typical village of the Vale, set among cornfields and meadows yellow with buttercups, while to the north there is the ridge of higher ground running from Faringdon to Oxford, and to the south rise the rounded summits of the Berkshire Downs.

Garford. A tiny chapelry beside the River Ock, it has little of interest to show except its lovely setting, between the river and the Childrey Brook and the Nor Brook which runs into the Ock near Marcham Mill. South of the village is Garford Field, where there is a tree-covered barrow and where aerial photography has shown rings not visible from the ground.

Frilford. Like Garford, Frilford is a little country village, made modern by a golf-course on its Heath. On Frilford

The old village cross at East Hagbourne
Sinodun Hill, Long Wittenham

Field a Romano-British cemetery once existed and a small villa with tiles and pottery was ˜excavated in 1884.

Kingston Bagpuize. From Frilford. we turn away from Oxford and drive along the open road by Ælfrith Ditch into Kingston Bagpuize. The remarkable name of Bagpuize is, of course, of Norman origin, Kingston being this village's original name. Here are the kennels of the old Berkshire Fox-hounds or the "Old Berks" as this hunt is more commonly known. About three miles ahead is one of the oldest bridges over the Thames, called Newbridge, which it may have been some 600 years ago, and many's the battle which has taken place here to gain possession of the river-crossing where the Windrush joins the Thames.

Longworth. Back from Newbridge, with its beautifully situated hotel, once the "Old Rose" and now the "Rose Revived," on the Oxfordshire bank, we turn by Drayton Moor to Longworth, with its track running over Harrow-down Hill to the Thames where at one time the village owned a wharf. In Longworth lived the famous Dr. Fell about whom were written the lines :

> "I do not like thee, Dr. Fell,
> The reason why I cannot tell ;
> But this I know, and know full well,
> I do not like thee, Dr. Fell."

Those who prefer more serious reading will be interested to know that the author of *Lorna Doone*, Richard Blackmore, was born in 1835 in the rectory where his father was "curate in charge."

The great family of Fettiplace owned the manor during the reign of Henry VIII; later it belonged to the Martens, one member of which, Sir Harry or the Ungodly Harry to give him his more usual title, was M.P. for Berkshire in the first half of the seventeenth century—he ended up in gaol for having signed the death warrant of King Charles.

Hinton Waldrist. A stone's throw from Longworth is Hinton Waldrist where there is a small rectangular Roman earthwork known as Achester or Hadchester; it has been suggested that this camp was used for the horses from Cher-bury Camp across the Faringdon-Oxford road. The manor has passed through the hands of many people well known in history, and in more modern times, too, including many generations of the Loder and Loder Symonds families, who were masters of the "Old Berks" hounds in those days when men lived only to hunt and to talk of horses and hounds and prodigious leaps to the tune of innumerable bottles of port.

Pusey. From Hinton manor we run down over the Oxford road to historic Pusey, where the legend of the famous Pusey Horn is still told. This legend tells how William Pewse discovered a plot against King Canute and was rewarded by a gift of lands at Pusey, the title-deed being the Horn. But the Horn is mounted in silver gilt, engraved :

> "King Knowde geve Wyllyan Pewse
> This horne to holde by they lende,"

and the workmanship is fifteenth century ! The Horn, of course, may be older than its ornamentation, but the story does not ring quite true. Behind Pusey House a track which runs to ancient Cherbury Camp which, though said by archæo-logists to be a true hill-top camp, is in fact down in the bottom of a valley. A flint axe-head and early Iron Age relics indicate that the site had been a popular one long before the Romans came around.

Stanford in the Vale. From Pusey it is a lovely few miles to Stanford, looking all the time at the great ridge of the Downs, with White Horse Hill, though not the Horse itself, standing out conspicuously. The countryside round Stanford is cut by little streams, the Holywell Brook, Stutfield Brook, Land Brook and others all draining into the Ock which runs beside the village; close to the road which runs to Blackacres Farm are three humps, at one time supposed to be barrows, but now disqualified from such dignity.

Goosey. Straight across from the three bogus barrows is the little village of Goosey, but we must go round by the road to cross Stutfield Brook at the appointed place. Goosey is tremendously old, for it was given to the abbey of Abingdon by Offa, King of Mercia, in the year 785 in exchange for Andersey Island close to the abbey. Goosey was also an island once for, its name means "goose island." The Abingdon

monks established a cell in Goosey, the site of which is now
occupied by Abbey Farm. In the little churchyard there is the
base of the village preaching-cross.

Denchworth. A few miles along a narrow lane which has
a shocking double bend where it crosses the Land Brook, and
we are in picturesque Denchworth. In past days, according to
the brass portraits in the church, one family at least in Denchworth was most prolific, for Oliver Hyde of 1516 had ten
children, and William of 1557 had twelve sons and eight
daughters ! From this old church, England's only copy of the
Golden Legend, printed by Caxton in 1483, has gone to the
Bodleian in Oxford. The old moated manor still remains
though considerably altered since the fifteenth century, when
it became the home of the Hydes. It is said that poor Amy
Robsart used to come to the manor from Cumnor during the
last years of her fateful life.

Challow, East and West. From Denchworth a long
narrow lane takes us over the railway line and down to the
Faringdon road, and we find East and West Challow on
either side of us, a mile outside Wantage. West Challow
Church is famous for having the earliest English bell with the
founder's name inscribed upon it; the date is 1283 and Paul
the Potter made it—I have written about this bell elsewhere
in this book. According to Domesday Book, East Challow had
five mills but none of these remain, though Mill Lane and
Windmill Hill and Mill Farm are, no doubt, relics of those
days. A brick kiln and latterly a brewing-trade, followed by
an iron-foundry, coupled with the old Wilts and Berks canal
made Challow a busy place; here the first threshing-machines
in England were made, and the famous Berkshire Plough was
turned out by the energetic Mr. Hart.

JOURNEY THREE

To Letcombe, past Childrey Field and Hackpen Hill, over
Faringdon Road Down into Lambourn, down the valley to
Great Shefford, among the Downs to Fawley and on into
Wantage.

Letcombe Regis and Letcombe Bassett. A twisting narrow

road beside a little Lett Stream runs into and through the two minutely picturesque Letcombe villages, almost hidden beneath the Downs which tower above them; so un-English is the picture that it has been called "Little Switzerland." The Court Rolls of Letcombe Regis are believed to be the oldest in the country. King Alfred is said to have held the manor and King John to have kept a hunting-box where Moat House now stands. A trackway runs up to the Ridgeway and Segsbury camp, but both are more accessible from the Red House on our return route. In Letcombe Basset the road curves round by the watercress beds, constructed over a hundred years ago, and joins the Lambourn road by Childrey Fields. Up to the Ridgeway it goes with beautiful views behind of the Icknield Way and to the left a confusion of hills and valleys, Hackpen Hill, the Devil's Punchbowl, Crowhole bottom and others which hold the Ridgeway up into the sky.

Lambourn. The run down into Lambourn is marvellous, by Faringdon Road Down, with its clumps and belts of trees, and Crow Down, both with their gallops, for we are in the heart of downland's racing-stables. A short turn off by Wether Down would take us to the famous seven barrows but the hour is not yet come to pay this call, so on down into Lambourn, beneath the Sheepdrove. Lambourn is a place where time appears to stand still, where, on a hot afternoon, dogs sleep on the pavement at cottage doors, sparrows sit in rows on fences not bothering to chase the occasional butterfly, even the spotted fly-catcher in the churchyard stays motionless on a tombstone, for the flies themselves are lurking among the grass-stems; the village cross itself sleeps, with no ambition save to remain where it is in this hollow of the Downs. For it can be really hot in Lambourn when a summer sun fills the hollow and no breath of air moves the leaves. Then in a flash some long-nosed car comes round a corner leaving a cloud of dust too lazy to settle, preferring to hang scintillating in the sunlight, and the clock, resting in the church-tower, moves its hand like some sleeper itched by a fly, gives up the struggle and dozes once more. But Lambourn is not always in "siesta" for the racehorse business, with its stream-lined horse-boxes, keeps everyone awake at times, and, as in Ilsley, the race of gnomes is forever fidgeting with its jodhpurs and waiting for newspapers.

From Lambourn we take the valley road towards Newbury, following the stream with its kingcups and trout, over the level-crossing below Eastbury Fields, through Eastbury with its thatch, the stream running between the road and the cottages, so that little bridges are required, on to the bend where the stream forsakes the road and clings to the railway after which it curls beneath the bridges of East Gaston. This section of the road I have described in a journey from Newbury, so we will pass swiftly to Great Shefford, where we turn left-handed off the Newbury road and run for several miles along the most perfect valley, set here and there with copses like pieces of a child's plaything. From the point where the road to Farnborough forks off, a track turns over the Downs by Kite Hill and on past Oakhedge Copse to Wither's Barn, over Stancombe Down, where remains from almost all the prehistoric periods have been found, and then diagonally over Crow Down to meet the main road about half a mile short of the Ridgeway. In all probability the track turned north here to join the Ridgeway where a barrow stands as marker. But we must continue our journey on towards Wantage, turning off towards the Fawleys by Whatcombe where the manor house and the church have long since disappeared.

Fawley and South Fawley. Between the two, in 1883, four skeletons were found and beside them a cup of Castor ware, some small flat studs and a small bottle of New Forest ware. These were Roman bones if they belonged to the pottery, and the bank, which runs from South Fawley northward along a ridge of the Downs to the Ridgeway near Segsbury Camp, has the appearance, to say the least, of having been Romanised. These two little villages have been described as the most isolated villages of the Downs, standing as they do at the base of Woolley Down, midway in the ten-mile stretch between Wantage and Great Shefford. If one wishes to see the granite monument to one who fell in the 1914-1918 war, it stands at the side of the main road between the lanes to the Fawleys. As we approach the Ridgeway, the Downs to left and right are scored with ancient tracks, many of them leading towards the rampart that is Segsbury Camp. And as we cross the Ridgeway at the Red House we cannot but stop and look along it as men before us must have done, wondering how much further on it was to Avebury. From the Ridgeway our road drops steeply down to Wantage, past Furzewick Down and the little lane to Letcombe Regis and Windmill Hill, past Wantage Field and the little streams that once, perhaps, served the woollen industry.

JOURNEY FOUR

Along the Icknield Way through Childrey to Kingston Lisle; up a narrow lane by Fawler into Uffington, and on towards the "White Horse"; by Woolstone and Compton Beauchamp to Ashbury and by Ashdown Park to Lambourn; up into the Downs by Seven Barrows, over the Ridgeway and down Blowing Stone Hill into Kingston Lisle and back into Wantage.

This is, perhaps, the best drive there is through the Vale and the Downs, and many of the things to be seen here have been described elsewhere in this book; I trust that the index will avoid the necessity of repeating myself. Once the correct way out of Wantage has been discovered, we are quickly past Alfred's Well and the road which leads south to the moated manor which is "Antwicks"; past Windmill Hill we go and over West Challow Field to Childrey, which, with Sparsholt, lies just off the road.

Childrey and Sparsholt. Childrey was at one time the home of the Fettiplaces, a great Berkshire family said to have owned property in fifteen counties. The church of Childrey is one to be visited because it contains a rarity in its font of lead; the manor, considerably adjusted, has still a room where Charles Stuart is alleged to have hidden. Then along the Icknield Way towards Kingston Lisle, with the Downs running away to the left and ahead of us, the wooded parkland at the base of Blowing Stone Hill, the gateway to the open Downs which build up White Horse Hill. The Blowing Stone can be inspected now, for it stands in a cottage garden hard by the cross-roads, but we shall come to it again later as we retrace

our way to Wantage. I suggest it be inspected later, for by
then it will have more meaning, will be a last glimpse of the
legends and traditions of the great White Horse, ere we turn
our backs upon this ancient folded countryside.

The road from the Blowing Stone to White Horse Hill is
a delight, the Ridgeway towering above us and combes, gulleys
and ravines rushing headlong towards us, sometimes like
waves flattening out into the ploughed fields that is their
shore, sometimes gathering speed and sweeping beneath the
road; and ahead one keeps trying to pick out the Hill, for no
white horse can be seen from this side. The blues, mauves
and purples of thistles and scabious on the roadside mingle
with the yellows of tiny bedstraws, vulgar mass-produced ragwort and towering umbel, dotted here and there with red of
poppy; many butterfly "Blues" come down to this road, fritillaries flash their jewelry and dowdy meadow-browns gaze
with jealous eyes, criticising the flashy ones, discussing the
latest fashions. Peewits tumble in their play over the ploughed-
up flints, a kestrel, steady on occasionally flicking wings, and
below the road in the bushes, a butcher bird goes about his
grizzly business. Yes, it is a lovely piece of road, I sometimes
think there is none better in the Downs, and then I remember
Letcombe Regis and the Wantage Road below Chaddleworth
and the Fawleys, and I am not sure. There is another way to
approach White Horse Hill, turning by the Blowing Stone to
Kingston Lisle and Uffington through the hamlet of Fawler.
At Kingston Lisle there is a partly Norman church worth visiting for its fourteenth-century door and mediæval murals.

Uffington. At Uffington there is a church which lost its
spire in a gale early in the eighteenth century and which contains a bronze head of Tom Hughes, who was born in the
village in 1822, and who has immortalised this land beneath
the Downs in his books. Outside the church, carved in panels,
are eleven consecrational crosses, said to be the most complete
set of any parish church in England. While in the village we
might well take a glass of ale in one or more of the tiny white
inns which must have known the revels, heard the rough talk
of the sturdy gamesters and, perhaps, repaired many a broken
head; and, perhaps, the winning gamester, crowned with

laurel leaves, would drink his ale side by side with the vanquished, blood trickling down his neck while the kind ladies from Kingston Lisle fuss around him with lily leaves soaked in brandy!—not likely, I think, for blood meant nothing to these men, brandy was meant for drinking not anointing, and the lily leaves could go back to the fops and milksops where they belonged. I have described Dragon Hill, the White Horse, Uffington Castle and Weyland's smithy elsewhere so I will leave you to look them up and visit them on your own. You should also visit the church at *Little Woolstone* and see the thirteenth-century lead font standing upon its Norman base.

Compton Beauchamp. A mile along the road from Woolstone, with its tiny stream, is Compton Beauchamp, once called Compton Regis, for it belonged to Edward the Confessor; it changed its name in the thirteenth century when it was held by William Beauchamp. The manor is moated and so is Hardwell Farm; Hardwell Camp, where at one time Æthelred was supposed to have lain before the battle of Ashdown, is across the road and up the slope of the Downs towards Weyland's smithy. Both Kingston and Compton Beauchamp are shadows of their former selves, as are Odstone and Idstone along the road towards the Wiltshire border.

Ashbury. Our road runs deep beneath the Ridgeway, and looking up we see the wooded gulleys that are Kingstone Combes. In Ashbury, cottages and church seem to cling to the Downs, pulling up their legs from out of the swampy land below, where little streams, once busy turning mill wheels, ferret their way towards the old canal and the river Cole. Without question, Ashbury is one of the most fascinating of our hillside villages. Those who want to see Alfred's Castle should go on into Idstone and follow the track up over the Ridgeway; this Iron Age hill-top camp, sheltered behind the woods of Ashdown Park, has produced quantities of ancient pottery; it is a lovely spot, no less lovely than when Lord Craven first saw it in 1665, escaping, it is said, from the plague in London. He saw but a farmhouse where he built his mansion and that this story is hardly true matters little, for the great mansion standing among its trees was built in

1625, though the manor had belonged to the Cravens since 1544.

During the last century, coursing was the great attraction here, though a hundred years before this, Ann Richards of Compton Beauchamp coursed hares here, and in the inscription for her tomb, which she herself wrote, she makes reference to Ashdown Park. Ann was a wild girl who thought of nothing but the chase, and she would have delighted in Lord Craven's parties down below Tower Hill in Compton Bottom; she would likewise have loved to see the strings of racehorses of to-day, training on the gallops over Kingston Warren Down.

As we pass the big Upper Wood, south of the park, we may see the earthwork which encloses it, where rabbits have given us many fragments of Romano-British pottery; and south of this, by Botley Copse, coins of Valentinian, Claudius II, Constantine I, Constans, Aurelius and Domitian have been found. In Upper Lambourn you can see a tiny agricultural village struggling to keep alive, some racing-stables acting as an injection to keep the heart still beating; up a lane one gets to the sarsen, called by legend the "Hangman's Stone," for here a sheep once hanged its sleeping abductor.

Seven Barrows.   And so we pass through Lambourn, taking the Wantage road and forking to the left below Faringdon Road Down, till we reach the place known as Seven Barrows. I have written of these under "Barrows," but I cannot take you past the place without commenting upon it, for it is a most lovely spot despite its funereal significance. The great Eastmanton Down and Sparsholt Down rise above the ploughed-up ground from which many of the barrows rise, while grandfather to all others is the single Long barrow, quite recently discovered. It seems incredible that a thing this size should have remained undiscovered for so many years, particularly when one thinks of all the archæologists and photographers who must have gazed upon it, but there you are, a bit of ploughing, a cart track, some trees and the disguise is perfect. Our road now gets into open country, the Downs no longer rising sheer above the road for we are riding across an elevated plateau of agricultural land, where part-

ridges dust in the stubbles and buntings sit on the wire fences.
We rise a bit and we are across the Ridgeway which curves
away on the left to White Horse Hill. Immediately we drop
three hundred feet and there beside us is King Alfred's Bugle,
the Blowing Stone, and before us, the Icknield Way to lead us
back to Wantage.

4. FARINGDON CENTRE

JOURNEY ONE

Faringdon and east to Littleworth and Buckland, across
the Thames at Tadpole into Oxfordshire, round by Bampton
and Clanfield to famous Radcot Bridge, by the edge of the
Park and back into Faringdon.

Faringdon. Towns, which are served by a mere dead-end
branch-line of the railway, seem to retain their old-world dust
much longer than others. This point was noticed by J. E.
Vincent nearly fifty years ago when he wrote his *Highways
and Byways in Berkshire*; you will find it true to-day if you
think of Faringdon, Lambourn, Wantage, Abingdon and
Wallingford. Little branch-line or not, there is certainly an
old-world air about Faringdon, and there should be, for here
was a palace of Wessex kings, and here in 925 Edward the
Elder died, perhaps in the same place where King Alfred
died before him. Later, there was a castle built by Robert of
Gloucester which was captured after four days of siege and
ultimately destroyed, when in the twelfth century Stephen
came to the conclusion that the barons were getting out of
hand. The great Faringdon House was bought from the
Unton family of Wadley Hall by Sir Robert Pye; both houses
were involved in the Civil Wars, when Faringdon Church lost
its steeple. You will have noticed that, I expect, for the
stumpy tower gives the impression of something missing;
unlike Uffington, which lost its steeple in a gale, it was hit
by cannon-balls, and if you wish to see what it looked like
before this, you must visit the National Gallery, where there
is a picture, which I personally have not seen, showing some
episodes in the life of a Sir Henry Unton; one of these depicts
his funeral procession before Faringdon Church complete

with its tower. Another picture, though I cannot direct you to this one, shows "The Folly" as it was in 1630, its tall trees casting doubt on the legend that these trees were planted, one each day, by the Pye family, who came to Wadley only in 1621! But the "Folly," which you cannot fail to notice on the eastern outskirts of the town, is always ascribed to the Pyes, possibly because their relative, Henry James Pye, Poet Laureate, in 1790, was a trifle odd! You will like this "Folly" with its fir trees and greensand which can be seen from Uffingdon Castle on a clear day. You will like also the little market hall standing upon legs as if to avoid the rubbish and filth which, no doubt, littered the market place of long ago. You will, too, like the inns which stare at each other across the market place, and after visiting each, perhaps you will seek Bull's-eye Castle, where King Alfred is reputed to have done a variety of improbable things. We must now leave Faringdon on the Oxford and Abingdon road, past the "Folly" and Wadley House, turning off for a peep at the "micro-village" of Littleworth, which lies astride a long and straight lane heading for the marshes and the Thames.

Buckland. And so we reach Buckland village, passing Barcote or Burcote Manor where one William Holcot lived; this Holcot is famous for having done a slight "Vicar of Bray" turn during the reigns of Edward VI, Mary and Elizabeth; it saved his life and his heart now resides in a casket in Buckland Church! The manor of Buckland was granted to one Hugo in 1227 and later held by a man called Thomas Chaucer, quite probably the son of our Geoffrey Chaucer who in one way and another has been associated with Berkshire; a Thomas Chaucer, said to have been Geoffrey's son, was appointed Constable of Wallingford and High Sheriff of Oxford and Berkshire by Henry IV, and in 1414 he took over the castle and manor of Donnington; an influential man, he was Speaker in the House of Commons in 1414 and was four times Member of Parliament for Wallingford. By 1690 the manor was held by the Throckmorton family, who in 1757 built the gigantic house which now stands in its lovely park and which is now owned by Lady Fitzgerald, famous breeder of Kerry Cattle. It was for one of the Throckmortons, Sir

John, that Mr. Coxeter of Greenham mills made the famous coat between sunrise and sunset.

Our road now runs north, past Carswell Marsh and Buckland Marsh, where redshank flash their white wing feathers and snipe and peewits tustle for mastery of the upper air. Then over Tadpole Bridge, where a Roman bracelet, bronze with coiled ends, was retrieved from the Thames, and we are in the Oxfordshire marshes which run back from the river to Bampton. We trespass for some miles here round by Clanfield, crossing back into Berkshire and Faringdon over Radcot Bridge. This bridge was much more important in other days, when to hold the crossings of the Thames was all-important. With Newbridge, it holds the honour of being the oldest of the Thames bridges, having been constructed in the reign of Henry III (1216-1272). Several times in history battles have been fought for possession of the bridge; the first we know of was between Richard II's forces and his nobles, when in 1381 the King's men, 51,000 strong, captained by Robert de Vere, Earl of Oxford, were met and defeated by an army of nobles under Henry of Derby, later to be Henry IV. Here it was that Robert de Vere jumped his horse over the side of the bridge and swam the Thames to safety. Radcot Bridge was again to the fore when, in the Civil War, Faringdon was held by Sir Marmeduke Rawdon against Roundhead forces who knocked down the church spire and the Colonels Littleton and Vaugham were captured; both Faringdon House and Wadley Hall were held for the King and were alternately attacked and defended by Roundhead and Royalist.

Journey Two

Westward to Eaton Hastings and Buscot and down a long narrow lane to Coleshill, or if preferred, a double trespass to Lechlade in Gloucestershire and Highmorton in Wiltshire, crossing the river Cole, which is the County Boundary outside Coleshill, by Badbury Camp to Great Coxwell and down to Watchfield, Shrivenham and Bourton and back to Faringdon by Longcot and Fernham.

Eaton Hastings and Buscot. We leave Faringdon on the

Cirencester road to which town the Roman Ermine Street
runs straight as an arrow from Newbury, and after a mile or
so turn up a narrow lane to Eaton Hastings where, in a micro-
scopic church, the first Lord Faringdon is buried. There is
little of a village to be found, but the views of the Thames,
ours for only a few miles more, fully justified the visit. Buscot
the same, though here we find a village street, a pleasant lock
and weir, and by the lake of Buscot House, a mighty heronry.
The church standing by the river is as peaceful as the water
running past it, and for those who like, here is a Burne-Jones
window. At Buscot we must decide if we shall trespass in
Gloucestershire to look at Lechlade and run down through a
corner of Wiltshire to Highworth, turning east to cross the
river Cole outside Coleshill; but if we are scared to trespass,
there is a lovely road, narrow it is true, running south through
flat farming land to Coleshill, thus saving us some petrol.

Coleshill. No matter which road we have chosen, it will
lead us to the church and the headless village cross standing
below the great trees of Coleshill House, the work of Inigo
Jones, and designed like a French *château*; Coleshill House
has been put forward as one of the best examples of his
work. In a couple of miles we pass Badbury Camp, a true hill-
top camp, but now lost beneath trees.

Great Coxwell. We turn away from Faringdon and come
to the Great Tithe-barn, known all over England by the
frequent appearance of its photograph. The manor was given
to the Cistercian monks of Beaulieu in the thirteenth century,
and so far as is known the barn has been in use since the day
it was erected; it is over fifty yards long, is seventeen yards
wide and has a gigantic arched door and mighty buttresses
supporting its stalwart walls. There are very few of these
giants left in the country, so it is well worth having a look at
this one.

Watchfield and Shrivenham. Both hang to the edge of
Beckett Park, where long ago, in the fourteenth century, the
Becketts held the manor from the king, their rent, two white
capons, to be handed over whenever His Majesty should pass.
The present house is modern, a copy of Tudor style. Much of
modern Shrivenham is due to the Barrington family, holders

of Beckett Park, whose famous ancestor, Admiral Beckett, was buried in the church in 1880. From Shrivenham the road goes over the old canal, not looking quite so "old" here, and after a twiddle round the railway station we run into Bourton.

Bourton. This little village in the extreme westerly corner of the County is so far from the civilisation of Reading, that many do not know of its existence. It is a curious place, perched upon a little hill and surrounded by trees, the stone cottages compassing a green where the village "rout" took place annually; this "rout" was not at all what it sounds, but was much more akin to a fête. By following the road round towards Ashbury, and turning sharply back over the level-crossing, we get back to Beckett Park which we skirt to the south and run over an arm of the old canal into Longcot.

Longcot. The earliest inhabitant we know of from this village lies now in the Ashmolean Museum in Oxford, an early Saxon complete with necklace of beads. Longcot's main claim to fame, however, is unfortunately also concerned with death, for here in the village church is a memorial to Lilian, daughter of Thomas Hughes, who with her vicar husband, Ernest Carter, went down in the *Titanic*; Ernest Carter was a popular vicar in Whitechapel where the memorial originally went, and Lilian's uncle was John Hughes, vicar of Longcot —hence the connection. At Fernham, which is scarcely a village and which looks out over Uffington to the Downs, we turn towards Faringdon once more.

Little Coxwell. Beside the road from Fernham, where an arm of Lower Greensand pushes northward over Kimmeridge and corallian, we pass the remains of an Iron Age hill-top camp, while just outside the village of Little Coxwell, which lies on the base of a triangle of road pointing at Faringdon, the remains of a rectangular Roman villa or camp have been found; as if to confirm this, a small flat ring of Romano-British origin was found in a nearby village garden. On the hillside above Galley Hill are Cole's Pits, which some consider to be ancient diggings into the ironstone bands or the sponge gravel of the lower greensand, while others believe them to be ancient pit-dwellings; a few subscribe to a theory which give these pits to "Old King Cole" and Coleshill on the Wiltshire

border, too. You can take your choice. From little Coxwell
we reach Faringdon, and the ridge which runs to Abingdon
and Oxford.

5. ABINGDON CENTRE

JOURNEY ONE

Abingdon; a justifiable trespass to Culham and Clifton
Hampden in order to approach the Wittenhams, round to
Appleford and close to the river at Sutton Courtenay; by
Milton to the main road at Milton Hill; back to Abingdon by
Steventon and Drayton.

Abingdon. There is something so pleasant about Abingdon, something which is difficult to define; perhaps you will
feel the same as I do, that here, where the Ock runs into the
Thames, and reflections are as pretty as the originals, there
is something of the past still living, something, not reminiscent
of the very ancient days before the abbey was constructed,
but of later days when Abingdon was a prospering centre of
brewing and the woollen industry, when market days brought
men from far and wide, when the narrow streets knew the
Berkshire dialect, and barges from afar carried produce down
the Thames to London.

Long ago, in Neolithic times, there was a settlement near
here, between Abingdon and Radley, where Wexcombe
pottery, flint knives and arrow-heads, and the skeleton of a
girl were found. Relics of Bronze and Iron Age have been
found in small quantities, but it is from Roman times that
most has been discovered. It is said that there were two camps
here, one to the north-east, on Serpen Hill, the other to the
west, though its exact position is not clear. Innumerable
foundations, vases and fragments of pottery have turned up
and a wealth of coins has been gathered from the abbey fish-
ponds, and from various other places. The coins are so varied
that Harold Peake in his *Archæology of Berkshire* has hinted
at the presence of Roman collectors. The abbey of Abingdon,
founded by Cissa in 675, was the most important of the Saxon
religious places; it was furthered by Ceadwalla, and by the
end of the ninth century held lands scattered across the

The Thames at Wallingford

County, at Streatley, Basildon, Bradfield, Appleton, Culham now in Oxfordshire, Lyford, East Hendred, Bray and others. Then it was plundered by the Danes and many of its estates taken by the king in payment for services rendered. The abbey was resurrected, then died again. Again it rose, this time under the Benedictine Ethelwold from Glastonbury; it acquired lands in Welford, in the Hinkseys, at Wickham and at Winkfield, at Lewknor in Buckinghamshire, and at many places between Dorchester and Oxford. Saxon rule ended and the Norman Athelhelm became Abbot, followed by Rainald who did great work to restore the church and to enlarge it. Other abbots followed and eventually Henry VIII dissolved this abbey which had been great for nearly 900 years.

There is little left of the abbey now but the grand old gate-house, which saw the market place at its feet so long before it became a car park and saw the Town Hall rising slowly upon its arches, standing on the place where once a beautiful market cross stood until Waller and his Puritans hacked it down in 1644. You should see the timbered Long Gallery of the Abbey Guesthouse, the pristine Long Alley, Brick Alley and Twitty almshouses by St. Helen's Church. Nor can you leave without seeing the church of St. Nicholas, by the abbey gate, and without wandering down some of the narrow lanes. Modern things happen in Abingdon, but they are best left alone, for their newness spoils the atmosphere of a place so old.

Now we must leave Abingdon, crossing the Thames by a bridge that was built in 1416, due to the energy and generosity of Berkshire men. Our road passes through Andersey Island which, as you will recall, was exchanged by the monks for land at Goosey in the Vale, but the king kept his hawks and hounds on the island and the noise proved too much for the silence of the abbey. We pass from the island, whose southern "coast" is lapped by a backwater of the Thames, shoot by the road down to Culham, past Culham College, past the aerodrome where planes we do not often see inland belong to the Fleet Air Arm, and so to Clifton Hampden where we must pay a toll to escape from foreign territory back into Berk-

Harwell's atomic centre

shire. The bridge is modern and is singularly attractive, its arches reflecting perfectly in the Thames below.

Long Wittenham. It is worth the toll to cross this bridge and run beside the river towards Long Wittenham, with the Sinodun Hills standing up like guardians, as they were in ancient days. Long Wittenham has heard the lapping Thames for many a century. Stone Age hand axes, flint picks, axe-heads and arrow-heads, Bronze Age axe-heads and palstaves, a Romano-British village and pottery fragments, urns and whetstone, a long-necked vase and a graveyard of the same period. Saxon personal ornaments have been found, and there is a mighty cemetery in which nearly 200 graves have been examined. Yes, definitely an old and interesting place. It has a lovely village cross and an ancient church standing on the site of two earlier churches; the "site" was once a barrow, and the last church was erected in 1120; its most precious possession is a lead font from the late twelfth century—it is said that this font was hidden from Cromwell's soldiers beneath a wooden covering, which was not removed until 1839, and thus we now have a lovely font instead of Cromwell having had a few more bullets.

Little Wittenham. A narrow lane through dykes and stubbles takes us to Little Wittenham at the base of Sinodun Hills and Wittenham Wood. With its sister, this riverside village shares in the long prehistoric evolution, though many of the objects found are of a more military nature, spear-heads, shields, swords, scabbards and the like, suggesting that battles for Sinodun camp had been fought here. Possibly, many of the bodies in Long Wittenham cemetery came from here; and don't forget that Dorchester lies just across the Thames and must have exerted a considerable influence on places quite so close. After you have looked at the little church on the river-bank by Day's Lock, you can climb upon Sinodun, and revel in the view, but I have escorted you up already in another chapter so I shall stay below and smoke a pipe.

Appleford. From Little Wittenham our route passes below Sinodun, turns right on the Wallingford road just outside Bridghtwell and runs back towards the railway where Appleford tries to keep as far away as possible from the "line." The church has a few bits of Norman left about it. Prehistoric remains are not so common here as round the Wittenhams, though circles and square enclosures have been recorded from a field south of the church, and from between the railway line and the village of Sutton Courtenay skeletons and pottery of Roman age have been discovered; there was some much more recent fighting here too, for the combined inhabitants of these two villages routed a force of Royalist cavalry under Prince Rupert, and recent finds of skeletons just beneath the surface have been described as belonging to this time.

Sutton Courtenay. Reynold de Courtenay added his name to this village of Sutton in the fifteenth century. Long before this, Sutton had been given to the abbey of Abingdon, and earlier still it had been a Saxon village. The manor house, which was built in the fifteenth century for the Abingdon monks, stands by the river and looks across the road at the fourteenth-century abbey buildings. At the "Wharfe," Mr. Asquith, Earl of Oxford and Asquith, died in 1928, and you can be shown the pew he used in the church; of more interest, however, is the Norman font with its old pointed wooden cover.

Milton. Continuing south from Sutton Courtenay we swing round into Milton where there seems to have been a Roman jeweller's shop, for at places nearby have been found two jewelled brooches each consisting of a silver disc below a bronze disc adorned with ivory bosses, gold, garnets and rose-pattern filigree work; also a shield boss, a silver brooch and a saucer brooch.

Steventon. There is little to keep us in Milton so we pass on over the railway to the orchards of Milton Hill, where we turn back towards Abingdon. Down the steep hill we run into Steventon, a village cut in two by the railway. It is a village, interesting mainly for its huge green with the main road running beside, beneath an avenue of chestnuts and for the raised roadway to the church built by the occupants of the one-time monastery who wished to avoid paddling through the often overflowing brook.

Drayton. I am sorry that this should be the last village

before we get back to Abingdon, because it is swiftly losing
its good looks and rather spoils a tour of pleasant Thames-
side places. Its bell-ringers are famous throughout the
country, as I have mentioned elsewhere, though it has been
said that over-enthusiastic ringers can get the bells a bad
name! A Bronze Age beaker, some Romano-British pottery
and a Roman skeleton with an urn, a ring and some fibulæ are
all that prehistory has so far offered. The Manor House at
one time belonged to the Eyston Family of East Hendred,
and it had its little chapel like their other houses. And so we
leave Drayton behind us, travelling by little Sutton Wick,
where there is a round barrow, down to the long bridge over
the Ock at the western end of Abingdon.

JOURNEY TWO

To Radley and up between the river and Bagley wood to
Matthew Arnold's Hinkseys, to Botley and up a little lane
beside the Seacourt Stream to Wytham; down to Cumnor and
then to Eaton, Bessels Leigh and Appleton; to Fyfield, Frilford and Marcham and then north to Dry Sandford and up
Boar's Hill into Bagley Wood and straight down into Abingdon.

Radley. There is no need to dawdle in Abingdon this time,
and closing our eyes to the railway station which Abingdon
once refused to have and now has got for ever, we run a short
way up the Oxford road, turning off righthanded where the
sign-board is labelled Radley, and passing Barrow Hills we
cruise through open farmland, over the railway and we are in
Radley village, looking across the lovely Thames to the great
woods at Nuneham Courtenay. The church is worth a visit
for its massive beams and pillars, and the font, which is
Norman, stands upon pillar-like legs, each differing in
sculpture. But it is not the village down by the river which is
the chief interest in Radley, but the great public school, St.
Peter's College, standing on the edge of the park.

The history of the manor is interesting, for at one time it
belonged to the abbey of Abingdon and was a hunting-lodge

for the monks—somehow one does not think of monks hunting, particularly not those of Abingdon who could not stand the row from the king's mews and kennels on Andersley Island! With the dissolution of the abbey, the manor passed to Admiral Lord Seymour before he lost his head on Tower Hill in 1548. With what response we do not know, the admiral had courted Princess Elizabeth, then a girl under the age of consent! And this just after his wife had died in childbirth; this wife was Catherine Parr, so the admiral floated in high society! The manor went to the Catholic Bloody Mary, then a princess, who is said to have spent a considerable time there. In 1575 the manor passed to the Stonehouse family and in 1792 to Captain, later Admiral, Sir George Bowyer, who, putting his bank balance into the red by a fruitless search for coal beneath his estate, was obliged to let the place to a Nonconformist school. In 1847, after the Nonconformist school had failed and the mansion had lain empty for years, a Dr. Sewell started what is now known in the public school world as "Radley."

Kennington. From Radley our road runs alongside Radley Large Wood and the very much larger Bagley Wood, better known, perhaps, to those who live in Oxford than to the majority of Berkshiremen. Here in the wood, way back in the seventh century, a hermit built a chapel, and in 670 Heane, nephew of King Cissa of Wessex, founded a monastery, and here, somewhere, is Blake's Oak, where rumour says a man called Blake was hanged for betraying three kings. Kennington itself is a straggling village between the wood and the river, though the railway line, by unfortunate but unavoidable circumstances, has taken up the same position, and almost touches what was once the main Oxford-Abingdon road.

North and South Hinksey. Just past Bagley Wood we find these two villages, immortalised by Matthew Arnold, with Hinksey Hill looking out over Oxford's spires. The two Hinkseys you will not find quite as Arnold saw them, though at one of them the church cannot fail to delight with its stepped roofs and its headless cross standing upon high steps. There must be literally hundreds of paintings and sketches of

this church in existence, some good, some bad, not the least
of which is one by Ruskin.

Botley. Kennington, the Hinkseys and Botley, I always
feel belong to Oxford, by the right of penetration if by
nothing else, for, despite the fact that they are in our County,
Oxford has monopolised them as her suburbs. The church is
not especially interesting—it has some Norman features still
remaining, and it has its old stone cross, headless like North
Hinksey's, standing outside. But the best thing about Botley
is its view of Wytham Woods.

Wytham is reached by a long narrow lane from Botley,
crossing now and again little fingers of water running to the
Seacourt Stream beside the road. Wytham is an attractive
little place set "right against the forest fence," as the old
carol goes, and with a pretty bridge crossing the stream. Over
the stream, close to the County Boundary is the twelfth-
century Godstow nunnery, with some of its ancient walls
standing to this day. Both the abbey and the church contain
bits from Cumnor Hall and from Rycote manor. The abbey
once belonged to the Norris family, and one of them, Francis,
a difficult boy, found life more than he could cope with and
committed suicide with a crossbow!

Cumnor. It is a mere stone's throw to Cumnor, though
the only road there is takes us back through Botley, but no
harm is done, however, for Wytham Woods will keep us
company; Cumnor Place, where Amy Robsart met her fate
in the sixteenth century, has gone, save perhaps for a few
stones here and there; much of it went to Wytham to repair
both the house and the church. The stone porch and doorway
of this church are supposed to be pure Cumnor, as is the east
window, which is said to have been taken from Amy's bedroom; Scott and Arnold have both written of Cumnor and I
have quoted them elsewhere, and likewise I have told the
tale of Amy Robsart. In the church is a nearly life-size statue
of Queen Elizabeth, said to have been made upon Dudley's
instructions for the garden of Cumnor Place, and here in the
church lies Rowland de Penthecost, the last abbot of Abingdon, who surrendered the abbey to Henry in 1539, and who,
according to the scandalmongers, had acquired sufficient

money to purchase Cumnor for himself by means and measures unbecoming to any man, let alone an abbot!

From Cumnor we must see the Thames at Bablock Hythe, and as we have a car, instead of walking by Longleys and the Physic Well, we must drive by Eaton which is tied eternally to Appleton, and reach the river by what is called Eaton Common. The "stripling Thames" looks very lovely here, but I must not eulogise, since it has been done before.

Appleton. As we drive through Eaton we may hear the bells of Appleton ringing for all they are worth, a benefit performance for the ancient woods of Appleton, Tubney and Bessels Leigh, for here we are in a district famous for its ringing. The church, in addition to its famous bells, has a Norman font to which a Jacobean carved cover has been added. One of Appleton's vicars produced in 1624 a son, Edmond Dickinson by name, who became chemistry instructor to King Charles II, performing his investigations in a laboratory, made especially for him beneath the Royal bedchamber! The moated manor house was one of the houses of the Fettiplaces and has two Norman doors, said to be the oldest of their kind in the County.

From Appleton we can see the park of Bessels Leigh manor, where in the reign of Edward I a great tournament took place before the king and his queen, and it was Sir Peter Besils (or Bessels) who provided the stone of which Abingdon bridge was built early in the fifteenth century. The manor later passed to the Lenthall family, one of whom was Speaker in the Long Parliament and who entertained Cromwell in the old manor house, of which little more than the gate-posts now remain. Another Lenthall became Governor of Windsor and a considerable time later another one built the present manor house.

Fyfield. Our road now runs through Tubney Wood, well known to Oxford's budding biologists. The manor house was built in the fourteenth century by Sir John Golafre who also built the church; both have seen the ravages of time and are now considerably altered, especially the church, which was very much damaged by fire in 1893. Here, in this little church, was buried in 1625 a man who had made a name for himself in the world of science, for George Dale was well known for his studies in anatomy. Somewhere in the church is the burial place of "The White Rose of Scotland," Lady Catherine Gordon, wife for a time (she married four times) of Perkin Warbeck. Those who want to see Matthew Arnold's "Fyfield Elm" need not waste their time in Fyfield, but must proceed towards the place where the road forks to Oxford and Abingdon, for here they can see the charred remains; like many an elm it has been struck by lightning, but grows again from its roots and it is known locally as the "Tubney" elm—even in Fyfield, for there is little to be jealous about.

Marcham. Turning south by the golf course, it is a matter of minutes before we have passed Frilford Heath where Romans once buried their dead, and turning to the left we approach Marcham; like Drayton to the south, Marcham is fast losing its old-world beauty; once it belonged to Abingdon Abbey, then it became free, and now it has reverted once more to Abingdon, but not to the abbey this time. The church, besides owning a thirteenth-century porch, is curiously designed and exhibits a copy of the charter given to Abingdon Abbey in 835 by King Egbert and confirmed by King Edgar a hundred years later; by this charter a "man of god" could be tried for naughtiness before the abbot alone, even a ruling king being unable (lawfully) to do so, on penalty of a curse prescribed and placed in readiness by Egbert.

Wooton and Boars Hill. From Marcham we turn towards Oxford, passing the park and Sheepstead House and then leaving the trees of Tubney away to the left we pass the hamlets of Cothill and Dry Sandford and crossing the main road, where the bungalows of modern Abingdon have risen like weeds among the old stone cottages, we start up Foxcombe Hill. With Boars Hill the highest point in the ridge since Faringdon, it would be surprising if Roman remains had not been discovered, and a kiln, some pottery and numerous coins all go to show that not only poets and Oxford's professors have inhabited this select neighbourhood. Jarn Mound is an artificial hill built at the direction of Sir Arthur Evans so that he could see a bit further—the odd name is that of the field upon which the mound stands. Archæologists of the future may well wonder what on earth has happened here and produce some excellent theory as to why two and a half thousand tons of soil should be out of place.

Once again I feel we are in Oxfordshire, and at one time, even the language here was different, though fortunately that dreadful accent (I was at Cambridge mark you, and may be slightly biased) has disappeared. Wooton, down below, has a pleasant cross outside its church, and Sunningwell once was the home of Samuel Fell, father of Tom Brown's odious Dr. Fell. Aspersions are cast at the young ladies of this village in the saying—"All the maids of Sunningwell, you may put in an eggshell"—their chastity being remarkable by its absence !

Perhaps more deserving of notice than this, however, is the undisputed fact that somewhere here, near Wooton, Boars Hill or Sunningwell, the seedling that was to become an abbey developed; Bagley Wood seems to be the general favourite and through this wood our road runs, until it reaches the trees of Radley Park and the Abingdon suburb of Northcourt which in 1326 was "beaten up" and fired by the Mayor of Oxford, assisted by a mob of undergraduates, for presuming to attack the abbey !

6. WALLINGFORD CENTRE

Wallingford to Sotwell and Brightwell beneath the Sinodun Hills, to North and South Moreton and to Aston Upthorpe and Aston Tirrold by Blewburton Hill; the Hagbourne village discreetly avoiding Didcot and then to the cherry orchards and atom piles of Harwell; across by Chilton to Upton and down to Blewbury and then to Cholsey and back to Wallingford.

Wallingford. Once Wallingford could boast fourteen churches and once it was an infinitely more important place than Reading. Once prehistoric men lived here, leaving their flints, their bronze daggers and axe-heads and palstaves, their spindle-whorls and needles; the Romans left so much money and so many other things here that it was at one time believed to be the site of Calleva (Silchester)—they even left us a Roman eagle as though to confirm the fact. Saxons and Danes

left their mark here, Normans strengthened the fortifications;
the great castle was important through much of history, only
losing its power to Windsor in the sixteenth century, and after
a period as a prison, was demolished in the middle of the
seventeenth century.

Why all this importance? The Thames of course, for the
Wallingford crossing was the most important of all until well
into the fifteenth century. The town itself remained important much longer, for a long while being "the" agricultural
market of the County. But there is little enough of all this
might left for you to see. The castle now is nothing more than
a few ramparts, and as Cooper-King points out, nowhere
could Cromwell's soldiers have done their job of destruction
more thoroughly, for not a tower, not a battlement, not a
buttress remains of the fortress where kings have lived and
fought, and where the Fair Maid of Kent, wife of the Black
Prince, died. And like the castle, the monastery has gone and
many of its churches too. The monastery began life as a Benedictine priory built by Robert d'Oyley in the eleventh century;
by the middle of the twelfth century it was rich in lands,
collecting tithes from many of the neighbouring villages; in
1525 it was surrendered to Wolsey.

You will surely find much to interest in the only remaining
tower of St. Michaels, in St. Leonards, Wallingford's oldest
church, in St. Mary's and St. Peter's, both of which have been
almost completely rebuilt; the town hall built in the seventeenth century, when the market place was accustomed to
livelier scenes than the modern stalls of cheap and flashy
clothes, the reels of coloured ribands and the man who sells
some new kind of tin-opener or fountain-pen to a fascinated
and mesmerised audience. The narrow streets, the point duty
policeman at the cross-roads (who, I believe, has to be below
standard size so that he doesn't smash his knuckles on the
surrounding walls in the execution of his duty) and the several
excellent hostelries will all interest, but of all Wallingford, I
like the bridge best, its arches reflected in the broad and graceful Thames, its story going back at least seven hundred years,
tradition even saying nearly double that, to A.D. 600 in fact;
naturally, the present bridge is not the original, which must

have been made of wood, for unlike Radcot bridge and New-bridge its importance has increased with the years, and in any case it was destroyed by Fairfax in 1646 during the Civil War.

Brightwell and Sotwell. Out under the Sinodun Hills lie two little villages, linked together by the Roman road which runs up from Silchester and passes between them. Roman remains are scattered throughout this district and many will surely turn up which so far have remained undiscovered; many were the trackways which ran from the Icknield Way towards the river and the fords, and what annoyance and loss of time all the little streams running into Mill Brook must have caused. These two villages, with their moats tell of more recent times of strife; Brightwell's manor stands where once a moated castle stood until it was destroyed in 1153.

North and South Moreton. You have already climbed the Sinodun Hills to the Wittenham clump and Castle Hill so we will not dawdle here unless to visit Brightwell barrow on its hill, but it is scarcely worth the trouble. So we turn south towards the Moretons at one of England's many Little Londons and now we look fairly towards the ridge of downland beyond Blewburton and Lollington Hills, trying not to notice the railway which seems so incongruous in this picture of rural England.

Both Moretons have pleasant churches and one (South) has a supposedly Saxon doorway; if this is really so, then it is one of our oldest, and in any case it is worth inspecting. In North Moreton there is a story of "Ould Gunter," who was watching a football match in 1598, when he saw the two brothers Gregory set about his own sons, pulling them by the ears! So enraged was the father that he rushed out, drawing his dagger as he ran and he killed the two Gregories. "Ould Gunter," his daughter and the Gregories figure in a witchcraft story which I have told elsewhere. Definitely an unreliable family, though nothing against the sons has so far been discovered.

Aston Upthorpe and Aston Tirrold. In South Moreton we cross the Mill Brook and take the road which leads towards Blewburton Hill, though this is not the road which gives the best views of that hill, for the land which rises up to it is ploughed and the terraces are out of sight round the corner. (The best view, I think, is obtained from the road which runs from Blewbury to East Hagbourne, and a sunny evening should be chosen.) Aston Tirrold, with Stanford Dingley in the valley of the Pang, I give top marks for fascinating place-names, and both are fascinating villages. Racehorses look out from spotless stables, rambling cottages and pleasant houses flank the narrow lanes which wend their way between them. And in a lovely garden here, with the scent of flowers hanging in the dusk of a sweltering August evening I once had the pleasure to sit beneath reddening apples and watched Shakespeare performed as Shakespeare should be, by a company better known in London than in this quaint village below the Downs. Both churches have Norman fonts, and in Aston Tirrold—I refuse to omit the Aston as some do and ruin the charm that can lie in a name—there is another Saxon doorway.

East Hagbourne. The road from Aston Upthorpe takes us across a mass of little streams running to the Mill Brook until we cross the Hagbourne at a spot marked on the map as Tadley. This is a pretty place and I assure you it would not own its namesake on the Hampshire border. The village cross on its five steps is delightful, and here is a church whose tower was once stacked with faggots to send a beacon's warning that the Spanish ships had broken our fleet and had landed an army in our country. But both Hagbournes suffer from their proximity to Didcot as you shall discover for yourselves.

West Hagbourne. We pass a broken cross, at Coscote, intermediate between the two villages, and there is yet another called Broken Cross before we reach West Hagbourne. On Hagbourne Hill, which stands above, was a Roman burial ground beside a branch of the Icknield Way, while out in the distance are the Downs and the Ridgeway. Like the district round Faringdon, there seems to have been here a need for moats, and the manor house still retains three sides of one; an earlier house on this site belonged to the Abbot of Cirencester.

Harwell. From West Hagbourne we run up the main

Wantage road past cherry orchards, that in spring add a much needed air of rural beauty to a district swiftly losing everything that could once be said in favour of it. Harwell was mentioned in Domesday Book, and has, no doubt, been mentioned in books about cherries; the war put it into Air Force books and now it is the seat of nuclear physics—atom research. Poor Harwell, that once lived content to know nothing about atoms, with one branch of the Icknield Way passing through it and another branch drifting along the base of the Downs beside it. Neither atoms nor aeroplanes mattered in those days of flints and bronze and iron, though the sound of Roundhead cannons may well have echoed over the Downs and set the village dogs barking as Cromwell moved in after the Battle of Newbury.

In Harwell village down below the main road there are still pretty houses and in the church there is a window in memorial to Piers Gaveston, friend of the Black Prince, placed there by Lady Margaret Clare, Gaveston's wife (and niece of King Edward III) who lived at the manor.

From Harwell we proceed to Rowstock cross-roads, where there is a useful but quite unexpected garage and we turn towards the Downs. We must pass what was the aerodrome and what now is the Atomic Research Station without me telling you about it—for it is only partly built yet and I know not the secrets. But I do remember this place on what we called D Day, a day we will not easily forget. All the men in the world and all the little tents in the world were gathered here, waiting for their turn to board the gliders behind the twin-tailed planes. It was a truly wonderful sight, which must have made the ancient Downs wonder what was come to pass.

Chilton. We turn off the Newbury road by an inn with a horsey name and run into horsey Chilton, whose name has caused some trouble in the place-name world, meaning, though obviously incorrectly, "Children's Town." It is a wonderfully bleak little place, and so it must have been in the days when men were men and Cromwell's toughs were smashing down the church-tower. The railway, always a hateful thing among the Downs, runs so close to the village that its inhabitants probably bless the scarcity of rolling-stock as much as others curse it. The manor house, to which the Lattons came at the end of the fifteenth century, has been much rebuilt, and the church has been fitted with a new steeple.

Upton. Half way between Chilton and West Hagbourne the Icknield Way crossed our road and we can drive on it to the bridges over the railway at Upton. There is a pleasant inn beside the main road, after which it is best to walk down the lanes which descend into the village, for one sees nothing of it from the road. Once again we find a church worth seeing, for there is another suspected Saxon doorway, and certainly a great deal of Norman architecture; in fact the church is almost entirely Norman and the font, which stands upon a modern base, dates back to about 1100, when Henry I was reviving Anglo-Saxon laws and trying to fend off civil war.

Blewbury. A short run down past Upton Lodge brings us into the long dusty street which to many appears to be all there is of the village. But they are mistaken, for there are narrow lanes which take us between rows of white cottages, a pub or two, some excellent watercress beds and several attractive houses. Saxon walls of wattle and daub, thatched above and alive with insects enjoying themselves when the sun strikes hot; a Norman church a good deal altered by subsequent architectural fashions. The Tudor house, Hall Barn, is said to have been one of Henry VIII's hunting-lodges and later it was evidently involved in the Civil War, for it is on record that both Royalists and Roundheads dined here within half an hour of each other, after the Battle of Newbury. If that is so, the owner of the house, John Fuller, must have had an awkward half hour, for in a land full of Royalists, his heart was evidently with Cromwell, and some ten years ago, hidden behind a beam in the house, a document with Cromwell's seal was found. It was Fuller's membership card! It was dated 1650, so he was not actually a member when the Royalists ate his bread, but still . . .

Cholsey. From Blewbury we run straight on past Blewburton Hill, over the ancient track which comes from Newbury, down into the valley where a dozen ancient tracks run towards the river, past Lollington Hill that looks like a second Blewburton but without its terraces, and up to Kingstanding

Hill where the Fairmile rides along a crest to Lowbury, the open Downs and the Ridgeway. Here we turn off and follow the larger road of the two down to the railway line and Cholsey. Here is a place which was once important, for Ethelred built an abbey and the monks of Reading built a fine church, both to be destroyed by Danes. Much of Norman remains in the present church, and in its tower is one of Berkshire's most venerable bells. Much that is really old has been found near Cholsey—flints, axe-heads and Roman pottery— while up towards South Moreton, there are traces of an Iron Age camp. Down below us on the river's edge is Moulsford, more famous now for its most sophisticated "unvillage-like" hotel, the Beetle and Wedge, and for its even more erudite institution, just outside the village on the road into Wallingford, than for any of its associations with the dim and dusty past when the old road from Silchester to Dorchester ran through it.

BIBLIOGRAPHY FOR BEGINNERS

Bartlett, A. E.: *An Historical and Descriptive Account of Cumnor Place, Berks.* (J. H. Parker, 1850.)
Brain, J.: *Berkshire Ballads.* (J. Thorp, Reading, 1904.)
Childs, W. M.: *The Story of the Town of Reading.* (W. Clay, Reading, 1905.)
Clark, Grahame: *Prehistoric England.* (Batsford, 1940.)
Clinton, W. O.: *A Record of the Parish of Padworth and its Inhabitants.* (Bradley, Reading, 1911.)
Coates, C.: *The History and Antiquities of Reading.* (Nichols, London, 1802.)
Cole, L. G.: *Reading—Official Town Guide.* (Berks Printing Co., 1947.)
Cooper, J. J.: *Some Worthies of Reading.* (Swarthmore Press, 1923.)
Cox, R. Hippisley: *The Green Roads of England.* (Methuen, 1914.)
Deloney, J.: *Thomas of Reading or the Six Worthie Yeomen of the West.* (Robert Bird, London, 1632.)
Ditchfield, P. H.: *Bygone Berkshire.* (Andrews, 1896.)
Domesday Book. (1863 Fascimile, O.S. Office.)
Dormer, E. W.: *Watlington House, Reading.* (Poynder, Reading, 1929.)
Fletcher, W.: *Reading, Past and Present.* (John Snare, Reading, 1839.)
Gibbons, A., and Davey, E. C.: *Wantage, Past and Present.* (William Walter, 1901.)
Godsal, P. T.: *The Storming of London and the Thames Valley Campaign.* (Harrison, 1908.)
Gray, E. W.: *The History and Antiquities of Newbury and its Environs, including 28 Parishes, with a Catalogue of Plants found in the Neighbourhood.* (Hall and Marsh, 1839.)
Grinsell, L. V.: *The Ancient Burial Mounds of England.* (Methuen, 1936.)
Hawkes, J. and C.: *Prehistoric Britain.* (Penguin Books, 1943.)
Hayden, E. G.: *Travels Round our Village.* (Constable, 1901.)
Hayden, E. G.: *Islands of the Vale.* (Smith, Elder, 1908.)
Hewett, W.: *The History and Antiquities of the Hundred of Compton, Berks.* (John Snare, Reading, 1844.)
Hillier, G.: *Stranger's Guide to Reading.* (2nd Ed., Poynder, 1882.)
Hockin, J. R. A.: *On Foot in Berkshire.* (Alex. Maclehose, 1934.)
Howe-Nurse, W.: *Berkshire Vale.* (Blackwell, 1927.)
Hughes, T.: *The Scouring of the White Horse.* (Macmillan, 1889.)
Humphreys, A. L.: *East Hendred.* (Hatchards, 1923.)

Humphreys, A. L.: *The Berkshire Book of Song, Rhyme and Steeple Chime.* (Methuen, 1935.)

Hurry, J. B.: *Reading Abbey.* (Elliot Stock, 1901.)

Hurry, J. B.: *The Rise and Fall of Reading Abbey.* (Elliot Stock, 1906.)

Irving, A.: *Notes on the Natural History of Sandhurst and the Neighbourhood.* (Wellington College, 1880.)

King, Cooper: *A History of Berkshire.* (Elliot Stock, 1887.)

Lamborn, E. A. G.: *Oxford County Histories—Berkshire.* (Clarendon Press, 1909.)

Lawson, J. P.: *The Life and Times of William Laud, D.D.* (Rivington, 1829.)

Lowsley, W. B.: *A Glossary of Berkshire Words and Phrases.* (Trübner, 1888.)

Lyon, W.: *Chronicles of Finchampstead.* (Longmans, Green, 1895.)

Lysons, D.: *Magna Britannia—Berkshire.* (Strahan and Preston, 1806.)

Macfarlane, C.: *A Legend of Reading Abbey.* (Constable, 1898.)

Man, J.: *History and Antiquities, Ancient and Modern, of the Borough of Reading.* (Snare and Man, Reading, 1816.)

Massingham, H. J.: *English Downland.* (Batsford, 1936.)

Mavor, W.: *Agriculture of Berkshire.* (Sherwood, Heely and Jones, 1813.)

Mee, A.: *Berkshire.* (Hodder and Stoughton, 1939.)

Mitford, M.: *Our Village.* (Macmillan, 1893.)

Monckton, H. W.: *Cambridge County Geographies—Berkshire.* (Cambridge University Press, 1911.)

Money, W.: *The First and Second Battles of Newbury and the Siege of Donnington Castle.* (Simpkins, Marshall, 1884.)

Money, W.: *A Popular History of Newbury.* (Simpkins, Marshall, Hamilton and Kent, 1905.)

Noble, P.: *Park Place, Berkshire.* (Turner, 1905.)

Peake, H.: *The Archæology of Berkshire.* (Methuen, 1931.)

Pizer, N. H.: *A Survey of the Soils of Berkshire.* (Bradley, Reading, 1931.)

Ritchie, L.: *Windsor Castle and its Environs.* (Longman, Orme, Brown, Green and Longmans, 1840.)

Roberts, C.: *And so to Bath.* (Hodder and Stoughton, 1940.)

Robertson, J. G.: *The Environs of Reading.* (John Snare, Reading, 1843.)

S(almon), L.: *Untravelled Berkshire.* (Sampson Low, 1909.)

Skeat, W. W.: *The Place Names of Berkshire.* (Clarendon Press, 1911.)

Stenton, F. M.: *The Place Names of Berkshire.* (University College, Reading, 1911.)

Stenton, F. M.: *The Early History of Abingdon Abbey.* (University College, Reading, 1913.)

Stoughton, J.: *Notices of Windsor in the olden time.* (David Bogue, 1844.)

Summers, W. H.: *The Story of Hungerford.* (Whitefriars Press, 1926.)

Taunt, H. W.: *Goring, Streatley and the Neighbourhood.* (Taunt, 1894.)

Topham, E.: *The Life of the late John Elwes Esquire.* (Ridgeway, 1790.)

Vincent, J. E.: *Highways and Byways in Berkshire.* (Macmillan, 1931.)

Walker, J. J. (Editor): *The Natural History of the Oxford District.* (Oxford University Press, 1926.)

Walker, J. W.: *A History of Maidenhead.* (Hunter and Longhurst, 1909.)

Watkins, A.: *The Old Straight Track.* (Methuen, 1925.)

Williams, A.: *Villages of the White Horse.* (Duckworth, 1913.)

Winbolt, S. E.: *Britain, B.C.* (Penguin Books, 1943.)

Wyfold, Lord: *The Upper Thames Valley.* (Allen and Unwin, 1923.)

Finally, there is the voluminous *Victoria County History* (the nearest approach to "everything about everything"), the *Berkshire Archæological Journal*, the *Berks, Bucks and Oxon Archæological Journal*, the "Local Collection" of books, pamphlets and articles in the Public Library in Reading, far too numerous to mention here, and last, but by no means least, the historical notes and queries which have been a feature of the local press for many years.

INDEX

Abberbury, Sir John, 300
Abbey School, Reading, 300
Abingdon, 25, 26, 28, 59, 73, 74, 76, 274, 327, 332
Abingdon Abbey, 59, 62, 68, 333
Abingdon Bridge, 66, 333
Abingdon Lane Down, 33, 44
Abingdon May-day song, 252
Abingdon mummers, 252
Achester, 318
Adders, 155
Ælla, 57
Æscesdun, battle of, 57, 58
Æscwin, 57
Agricultural implements, 215
Agricultural Research Council, 18, 285
Agriculture, development of, 24, 25
Aldermaston, 67, 74, 149, 288
Aldermaston candle auction, 258
Aldermaston ghost, 235
Aldermaston Park, 39
Aldermaston pear, 288
Aldermaston Soke, 38, 39
Aldermaston witch, 239
Aldworth, 18, 32, 57, 58, 275, 284
Aldworth giants, 285
Aldworth yew, 285
Alfred, King, 34, 58, 59, 315, 316, 327
Alfred's Castle, 35, 325
Alfred's Well, 323
Alluvium, 20
Ancalites, 55
Ancient coins, 28, 326, 332
Ancient roads, 25, 28, 29, 30, 41
Andersey Island, 333, 337
Andover, 52
Anne, Queen, 311
Antonine Itineraries, 37
Antoninus Pius, 40
Antredigus, 28
Ants, 113
Antwicks Manor, 323
Appleford, 28, 172, 334
Appleford ghost, 235
Appleton, 275, 333, 339
Appleton feast, 248
Arborfield, 28, 172, 293
Arcadius, 41
Ardington, 36, 314
Ardington Down, 314

Arn Hill, 314
Arnold, Matthew, 337
Artificial Insemination Centre, 79, 293
Ascot, 77, 79, 292
Ashampstead, 57
Ashbrook House, 58
Ashbury, 36, 56, 325, 331
Ashdown, 58, 310
Ashdown, battle of, 325
Ashdown Park, 35
Ashendon, 58
Askew, Thomas, 70
Asser, 58
Aston, 58, 295
Aston Tirrold, 26, 36, 344
Aston Upthorpe, 37, 51, 172, 344
Athelhelm, 333
Atomic Research Station, 79, 345
Atrebates, 28, 55
Aucherius, 86
Augmentations, Court of, 93
Aurelius, 326
Aurignacian man, 23
Austen, Jane, 311
Avebury, 24, 25, 31, 34, 35
Avington, 273, 275, 311

Bablock Hythe, 339
Bacon, 72
Badbury Camp, 330
Badbury Hill, 15
Badger tongs, 124
Badgers, 123, 155
Bagley, Henry, 175
Bagley Wood, 337, 341
Bagley Wood ghost, 236
Bagnor, 26, 306
Bagshot Park, 38, 292
Barcote Manor, 328
Barrow Hills, 336
Barrows, 42–52, 232 et seq.
Barrows, Long, 25, 26
Barrymore, Lord Richard, 269, 294
Barton Beds, 21
Basildon, 32, 38, 175, 216, 284, 333
Basildon ghosts, 236
Basildon, Lower, 38
Basildon revel, 248
Basing House, 73, 74
Bath, 39

351

23*

Thames, River, 16, 22, 25, 31, 36, 37,
38, 39, 51, 55, 75
Thames side walk, 82
Thames Valley, 22, 37
Thatcham, 23, 26, 28, 39, 40, 56, 65,
70, 101, 289
Theale, 26, 28, 38, 55, 74, 287
Thetford, 31
Thimbles, 212
Thorne, John, I, 91
Thorne, John, II, 92
Three Mile Cross, 266, 290
Throckmorton Coat, 78, 209
Throckmorton, Sir John, 328
Thurle Down, 32
Tidmarsh, 38, 151, 173, 274, 287
Tilehurst, 175
Tilehurst ghost, 235
Tiles, 205
Tincommius, 28
Toadstools and toadstool eating,
148–153
Tower Hill, 326
Tree rats, 130
Trees, 194
Trent, River, 22
Tring, 39
Tubney, 339
Tubney Elm, 340
Tull, Jethro, 215
Tuttimen, 249
Twine, 211
Twitty almshouses, 333
Twyford, 26, 298

Uffington, 51, 105, 266, 324
Uffington Castle, 34, 42, 50
Ufton Nervet, 38, 288
Unhill Bottom, 32
Unhill Wood, 32
University College, Reading, 79
Unton, Sir Henry, 327
Upton, 36, 346

Vachell, Thomas, 92
Vale of the White Horse, 16, 19, 27,
28, 36
Valentinian, 326
Valley gravel, 20, 21
Vercingetorix, 28
Verica, 28
Vernon, Robert, 314
Vespasian, 40
Viæ agrariæ, deviæ, militares, vici-
nales, 41
Village sayings, 262
Virginia Water, 38, 77, 292

Wadley House, 327, 328, 329
Walbury, 312
Walbury Camp, 50, 52
Wallingford, 36, 37, 57, 59, 60, 61, 64,
67, 73, 75, 76, 327, 328, 341
Wallingford Bridge, 342
Wallingford Castle, 62, 64, 73
Wallingford Priory, 68
Waltham St. Lawrence, 26, 28, 297
Waltham St. Lawrence cattle fair,
247
Wantage, 36, 126, 274, 315, 322, 327
Wantage Field, 323
Wantage, Lord, 33, 314
Wantage tramway, 316
Warbeck, Perkin, 67
Warborough, 275
Warfield, 173
Wargrave, 268, 269, 294
Warwick, the Kingmaker, 67
Wash, the, 22, 31
Wash Common, 47, 308, 313
Wash Common ghost, 235
Wasing Park, 39
Watchfield, 330
Watercress, 214, 321
Watlington House, 299
Wayland's or Weyland's Smithy, 25,
26, 35, 42, 229, 310, 325
Weather lore, 259
Welford, 309, 333
Wellington College, 121, 293
Wells, William, 174
Welshman's Road, 19
Wessex, 57
West Challow Field, 323
West Court, 37
West Ginge Down, 33
Wether Down, 315, 321
Whatcombe, 322
Whipping posts, 270
Whistley, 57
White family of Appleton, 176
White, John, 173
White Horse, 29, 42, 50, 58
White Horse Hill, 33, 34, 47, 314,
319, 323, 327
White Horse legends, 229
White Rose of Scotland, 67, 340
White Waltham, 298
Whiteknights Park, 79
Whitewater, River, 37
Whiting, 204, 311
Whitley, 290
Whitley Hill, 73
Wickham, 28, 39, 40, 56, 274, 310, 333
Wickham Bushes, 38, 56, 292
Wigod, 60
Wilde, Oscar, 299